Revolu

VILLA JULIE COLLEGE LIBRARY
STEVENSON, MD 21153

Revolution Deferred

The Painful Birth of Post-Apartheid South Africa

◆

MARTIN J. MURRAY

VERSO

London · New York

DT
1970
.M87
1994

First published by Verso 1994
© Martin J. Murray 1994
All rights reserved

Verso
UK: 6 Meard Street, London WIV 3HR
USA: 29 West 35th Street, New York, NY 10001-2291
Verso is the imprint of New Left Books

British Library Cataloguing in Publication Data
A catalogue record for this book is available from the British Library

Library of Congress Cataloging-in-Publication Data
A catalogue record for this book is available from the Library of Congress

ISBN 0 86091 577 8 (pbk)
ISBN 0 86091 365 1

Typeset in Monotype Bembo by Lucy Morton, London SE12
Printed and bound in Great Britain by Biddles Ltd

Contents

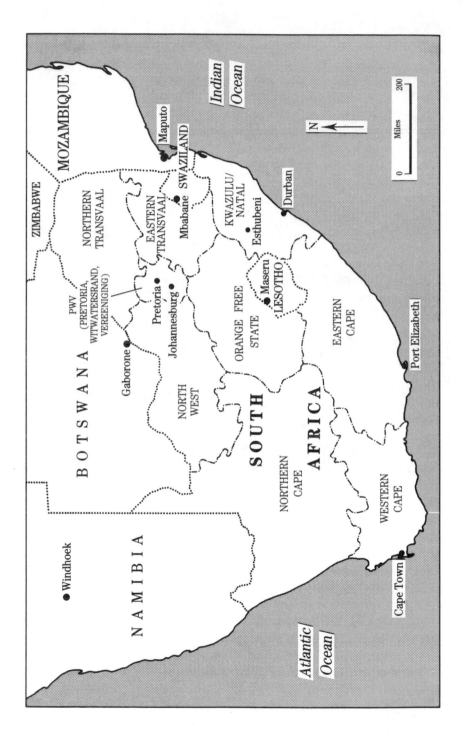

Preface

This book is a study of contemporary politics in South Africa. Its main purpose is to offer a conjunctural analysis of contending social forces set against the background of long-term economic stagnation and political deadlock. In particular, it aims to provide a coherent understanding of the much-anticipated collapse of white minority rule (along with the apartheid system that sustained it for nearly half a century), and to make sense of the origins and development of new forms of political representation and legitimation that approximate nonracial parliamentary democracy. The book also permits some partial answers to the fundamental question of whether the present situation constitutes a genuine 'new beginning' for South Africa that will in time yield greater economic equality, racial justice and social harmony.

The point of departure for this analysis is the decisive turn of events of February 1990, including the unbanning of outlawed political organizations; the release of political prisoners; the dramatic return to public life of Nelson Mandela, after serving twenty-seven years, six months and one week of a life sentence for sabotage and conspiracy to overthrow the white minority Government; and the tentative start of informal negotiations over the terms of a new nonracial constitution. These watershed occurences put into motion a complex and multilayered process of political conflict and accommodation that led to the demise of apartheid as a formal system of legalized segregation, and culminated in South Africa's first nonracial elections on 26–28 April 1994. Taken together, this interconnected cluster of events, compressed into a single frame of reference circumscribed by the temporal coordinates of February 1990 and April 1994, forms a distinctive period of South African political history, a singular historical 'moment' that can reasonably be said to possess a peculiar coherence, wholeness, and significance of its own.

The approach developed here is not particularly original, and it owes its existence to the writing and thinking of South African activist-intellectuals whose immediate concerns with shaping the future necessarily blend carefully researched scholarship and politically committed partisanship in a much more convincing way than is realistically possible for a foreign observer like myself. What I have tried to do is to piece together a coherent, logically consistent argument out of a puzzling *mélange* of newspaper accounts, journalistic commentaries, informal interviews, and scholarly research that has produced a rather large and generous body of accumulated empirical knowledge not readily available to the general reader of South African affairs. The immediacy of the events in question automatically ensures that this study is necessarily located in that clouded, indeterminate field somewhere between an academic work of historical reconstruction and a political intervention of a decidedly partisan kind.

The text is organized primarily as an analytic narrative where 'theory' and 'history' coexist indiscriminately. On the whole, I have tried to maintain a delicate balance between a chronologically consistent account of events and their repercussions on the one side, and a critical assessment of key ideas and themes on the other. I have tried to maintain, as circumstances warrant, an ongoing dialogue with the conclusions and hypotheses contained in the abundant available literature, but this was not always possible. Certainly, theoretical ideas infuse the text, but I have made no concerted or systematic effort to contribute to a 'theory-building' exercise, or to test the validity of general theoretical propositions. In reality, this is a work of social navigation, a political exploration into the uncharted waters of the present conjuncture, where the whirlwind of current events, unfortunately, provides few stable landmarks with which to fix one's bearings.

The overarching objective of the book is to explain the nature and character of the current political transition in South Africa and, as such, to establish the inner connections between the rise of post-apartheid parliamentary democracy and the 'dead weight' of embedded structural continuities left over from the past. As such, the analysis is guided by three logically distinct but overlapping antinomies: continuity and change; organization and spontaneity; and surface appearances and structural underpinnings. These sets of oppositional, dialectical pairs operate as the central organizing principles for the text and, as such, provide a broad interpretive framework through which to make sense of all that has, and has not, happened in the recent past. Each of these antinomies contains an in-built creative tension that pulls the analysis in opposite directions. These points of reference are essentially heuristic devices that provide a convenient means, via the methodological technique of paired comparisons, for approaching key problems and questions. The first – continuity and change – underscores the basic tension between emphasizing the commonalities between the old political order and the emerging one, in contrast to laying stress on the decisive ruptures and qualitative breaks with the past. This distinction between continuity and change constructs a context for understanding the extent to which what has happened in South Africa over the past several years either forms part of an ongoing, uninterrupted, evolutionary transformation from authoritarianism to democracy (what mainstream political scientists would celebrate as 'political modernization'), or constitutes an original situation that has fundamentally and uniquely altered the trajectory of South African political history.

The second antinomy – organization and sponteneity – is concerned primarily with questions of political strategy and mobilization. It provides a framework for distinguishing the degree to which political organizations (for example, political parties, civic associations, trade unions, and youth and student groups) are able intentionally to harness and direct the energies of their imagined constituencies toward particular goals. This paired opposition offers a context within which to assess critically the extent to which political actions and outcomes are the consequence of self-conscious intervention, or are the result of spontaneous eruptions of popular will. It also encourages greater sensitivity to the understanding of politics as an autonomous sphere of action, thereby allowing us to avoid – as Craig Charney makes clear – the kind of functionalist reductionism that treats political organizations as simply receptacles for social groups ('community', 'youth', 'women', 'workers') which in turn express themselves through them.

Finally, the third antinomy – surface appearances and structural underpinnings – places emphasis on the shifting vantage point from which to view South Africa's ongoing political transition. This antinomy, which in crucial ways resembles Braudel's distinction between *l'histoire évenémentielle* and conjunctural history, and parallels Marx's effort to distinguish outward appearance and hidden realities, provides a logical mechanism for differentiating between the ephemeral and the durable, between shadow and substance, or between physiognomy and morphology. It allows us to depart occasionally from those seemingly profound events that are the most conspicuous in order to accentuate conflicts that are more prosaic but often more decisive in the long run. In addition, this point of reference permits us to draw a line between visible shifts in the field of events, without lasting meaning or historical significance, and deeper, invisible modifications in the embedded structural foundations which carry enduring social weight.

One underlying aim of this study is to lay bare the circumstances that shaped the social identities of organizations, associations and individuals distributed across the class spectrum, and that influenced their political behaviour, attitudes and aspirations. To this end, I focus primarily on the complex patterns of interaction, involving a fluid mixture of conflict and accommodation, or competition and cooperation, among a vast array of social categories, including organized and unorganized workers, employers and business associations, the unemployed and marginalized, parties and organizations, township residents and hostel dwellers, farmers and farmworkers, youth and elders, 'warlords' and *comstotsis*, and the like. If there is a common denominator that runs through the assorted and disparate topics, it is the stress on the limits and possibilities for political action within the context of a shifting balance of class forces.

Socio-historical studies are inescapably artefacts of their particular times and places, and this book is no exception to that general rule. The analysis is invariably grounded in a specific set of political circumstances and reflects the political mood of the period in which it is written. It takes, perhaps without sufficient reflection or forethought, certain frames of reference as a priori truths, and only the passage of time will provide the necessary historical distance required to judge their appropriateness. All too often, as the collective memory of past events fades with the passage of time, mythologies constructed in conformity with current political agendas and contemporary fashion replace critical evaluation and judgement. I think that a usable past, something helpful as a guide for future political action, requires an accurate record of what actually happened and why. Yet to link a detailed description of historical events with an analysis of an ever-changing, evolving situation requires considerable talent, and I only hope that I have at least partially succeeded.

My knowledge of South Africa was virtually non-existent before 1977, at which time I was fortunate enough to have been offered an all-too-brief visiting lectureship at the University of Cape Town. Over the subsequent years, I have benefited immeasurably from the hospitality, support and criticism of so many South Africa friends and acquaintances that it would be impossible to acknowledge them all. In undertaking a project of this magnitude, I have accumulated particular intellectual debts to numerous people. In June–August 1993, I went to South Africa under the sponsorship of a Fulbright Research Fellowship. Out of habit born of political necessity, I hestitate to mention everyone who helped me to understand the emerging realities of the new South Africa. Yet many deserve special mention. In Cape Town, Ginny Volbrecht, Meshack Mochele, Mike Koyana, Neville Alexander and David Kaplan were extremely hospitable and gracious in so many ways. In conversations with

Fred Hendricks, Elaine Salo, Robert Davies, Patrick Harries, Wilmot James, Bill Nasson, Morris Szeftel, Sonya and Brian Bunting, Marcus Solomon, Judy Head, Frank and Pearl Molteno, Mercia Andrews, Brian Ashley, Jamey Klassen and Hamid Mahate, I gained particularly valuable insights into the labyrinthine layers of contemporary politics. In his own indomitable way, Patrick DeGoede forcefully drove home the difference between the Russian and the French revolutions. David Lincoln and Mary Simons were generous with their time and friendship. Helen Bradford, among other things, renewed my interest in hiking. In Durban, Rob Morrell, Mike Morris and the staff at the Centre for Social and Development Studies were particularly generous. Bill Freund, Geoff Schreiner, Christine Lucia and Bill Cottam assisted in a variety of ways. In Johannesburg, I thoroughly enjoyed the lively and entertaining companionship of Patrick Bond, Mzwaneli Mayekiso, Langa Zita, Dale McKinnley and Heidi Kriz. I learned a great deal from conversations with Craig Charney, Richard Levin, Daniel Weiner, Nthutang Carter Seleka and Salim Vally. Siyonbonga Ndabezitha and Matthew Richard are valuable friends. On the academic side, Eddie Webster, Charles Van Onselen and Judy Maller offered helpful insights on a range of issues.

It goes without saying that no work of social analysis is infallible, and this book undoubtedly contains its share of questionable interpretations, stylistic deficiences and inadvertent factual errors. A large number of those people to whom I am indebted would surely not wish to be associated with many of the ideas and perhaps ill-formed opinions expressed here. They, of course, are not responsible for my handling of the material. The compelling purpose of a project of this sort is to describe to a wider audience what has happened in South Africa's recent past and explain why. I only hope that the inevitable errors of fact and judgement are not so glaringly egregious that the whole project is somehow compromised.

I would like to express my appreciation to Colin Robinson, Managing Director at Verso, for making the original suggestion that I write a second edition of *South Africa: Time of Agony, Time of Destiny* (London 1987). I would also like to thank Gopal Balakrishnan for raising the daunting prospect that I undertake an entirely new book. In excellent written comments on the whole manuscript, Jane Barrett, a long-time trade-union activist and former general secretary for the COSATU-affiliated Transport and General Workers Union, exposed numerous shortcomings in the original manuscript. I only hope that I was able successfully to incorporate most of her valuable insights in the final version. Phyllis Kuhlman and Nancy Hall covered my tracks by doing much of the work I should have done. Rhonda Levine urged me to get it finished, despite long delays brought about by my single-minded obsession with reading everything I could get my hands on. Without her help, this book would not have been completed. My eldest son, Jeremy Robert, would have preferred that I write a 'mystery book' for second-graders. My other son, Andrew Dana, instinctively knew he could always find me at the computer. He really enjoyed punching away at the keyboard.

I would also like to acknowledge my gratitude and respect for David Webster, who was tragically struck down by a cowardly assassin's bullet on 1 May 1989. In just the short time I spent with him in late 1983, he taught me to appreciate the distinctiveness of South Africa's music, and how to wheel around the Witwatersrand townships without a map. I cannot forget his genuine zest for life and his confidence in a better future. Finally, I dedicate this book to my mother, Margaret Louise Claeys Murray, and the memory of my father, Robert Vincent Murray. They gave me the encouragement and the space to act on my own beliefs and to chart my own path, wherever it might lead.

Martin Julius Murray
Binghamton, New York, June 1994

Glossary of Acronyms

ACO	Alexandra Civic Organization
AEU	Amalgamated Engineering Union
(A)FCWU	(African) Food and Canning Workers' Union
AHI	Afrikaanse Handelsinstituut
ANC	African National Congress
APLA	Azanian People's Liberation Army
AUBTW	Amalgamated Union of Building Trade Workers
AVF	Afrikaner Volksfront
AVU	Afrikaner Volksunie
AVW	Afrikaner Volkswag
AWB	Afrikaner Weerstandsbeweging (Afrikaner Resistance Movement)
AZACTU	Azanian Confederation of Trade Unions
AZANLA	Azanian National Liberation Army
AZANYU	Azanian National Youth Unity
AZAPO	Azanian People's Organization
BAMCWU	Black Allied Mining and Construction Workers' Union
BCAWU	Building Construction and Allied Workers' Union
BCM(A)	Black Consciousnenss Movement of Azania
BLAs	Black Local Authorities
BOSS	Bureau of State Security
BPC	Black People's Convention
BWB	Boereweerstandsbeweging
CAHAC	Cape Housing Action Committee
CAST	Civic Associations of the Southern Transvaal
CAWU	Construction and Allied Workers' Union
CAYO	Cape Youth Congress
CBM	Consultative Business Movement
CCB	Civil Cooperation Bureau (or *Burgerlike Samewerkingsburo*)

CCAWUSA	Commercial, Catering and Allied Workers' Union of South Africa
CDF	Conference for a Democratic Future
CMBU	Confederation of Metal and Building Unions
CNETU	Council of Non-European Trade Unions
CODESA	Conference for a Democratic South Africa
COSAG	Concerned South Africans Group
COSATU	Congress of South African Trade Unions
CP	Conservative Party
CUSA	Council of Unions of South Africa
CWIU	Chemical Workers Industrial Union
DBSA	Development Bank of Southern Africa
DCC	Directorate of Covert Collection
DMI	Directorate of Military Intelligence
DPSC	Detainees' Parents Support Committee
ECCO	Eastern Cape Civics Organization
ETB	Eastern Transvaal Boerekommando
FA	Freedom Alliance
FAWU	Food and Allied Workers' Union
FCWU	Food and Canning Workers' Union
FCI	Federated Chambers of Industry
FEDSAL	Federation of Salaried Staff
FHA	Federal Housing Authority
FITU	Federation of Independent Trade Unions
FNLA	Frente Nacional para a Libertação de Angola
FOSATU	Federation of South African Trade Unions
GDP	Gross Domestic Product
GAWU	General and Allied Workers' Union
GWU	General Workers' Union
HNP	Herstigte Nasionale Party ('Purified National' Party)
HRC	Human Rights Commission
HWU	Health Workers' Union
IBIIR	Independent Board of Inquiry into Informal Repression
IFP	Inkatha Freedom Party
IMA	Interim Measures (and Local Government) Act
IMF	International Monetary Fund
IRRC	Investor Responsibility Research Center (US)
ISCOR	Iron and Steel Corporation
JMCs	Joint Management Centres
JSE	Johannesburg Stock Exchange
KZP	KwaZulu Police
KZT	KwaZulu Transport Company

LGNF	Local Government Negotiating Forum
LRAA	Labour Relations Amendment Act
MCA	Mamelodi Civic Association
MDM	Mass Democratic Movement
MEWUSA	Metal and Electrical Workers' Union of South Africa
MK	Umkhonto weSizwe
MP	Member of Parliament
MWU	Mynwerkersunie (Mineworkers' Union)
NACTU	National Council of Trade Unions
NAFCOC	National African Federated Chambers of Commerce and Industry
NEC	National Executive Committee (of the ANC)
NEF	National Economic Forum
NEHAWU	National Education, Health and Allied Workers' Union
NIC	Natal Indian Congress
NMC	National Manpower Commission
NP	National Party
NPKF	National Peacekeeping Force
NSMS	National Security Management System
NTB	National Training Board
NUM	National Union of Mineworkers
NUMSA	National Union of Metalworkers of South Africa
NUSAS	National Union of South African Students
OAU	Organization of African Unity
PAC	Pan Africanist Congress
PAM	Pan Africanist Movement
PASO	Pan Africanist Students' Organization
PBKG	Pretoria Boerekommandogroep
PEBCO	Port Elizabeth Black Civic Organization
PFP	Progressive Federal Party
PPWAWU	Paper, Printing, Wood and Allied Workers' Union
POPCRU	Police and Prison Civil Rights Union
POTWA	Posts and Telecommunications Workers' Association
PWV	Pretoria/Witwatersrand/Vereeniging
RDP	Reconstruction and Development Programme
RENAMO	Resistência Nacional Moçambicana
RSCs	Regional Services Councils
SAAWU	South African Allied Workers' Union
SABS	South African Boilermakers' Society
SABTA	South African Black Taxi Association
SACCAWU	South African Commercial, Catering and Allied Workers' Union

SACCOLA	South African Consultative Committee on Labour Affairs
SACOB	South African Chamber of Business
SACOL	South African Confederation of Labour
SACP	South African Communist Party
SACTU	South African Congress of Trade Unions
SACTWU	South African Clothing and Textile Workers Union
SACWU	South African Chemical Workers' Union
SADCC	Southern African Development Coordination Conference
SADF	South African Defence Forces
SAEWA	South African Electrical Workers' Association
SAIC	South African Indian Council
SAMWU	South African Municipal Workers' Union
SANCO	South African National Civic Organization
SANLAM	South African National Life Assurance Company
SAP	South African Police
SARB	South African Reserve Bank
SARHWU	South African Railways and Harbours Workers' Union
SAS	Special Air Services
SASO	South African Students' Organization
SATLC	South African Trades and Labour Council
SATU	South African Typographical Union
SBDC	Small Business Development Corporation
SDU	Self-Defence Unit
SEIFSA	Steel and Engineering Industries Federation of South Africa
SFAWU	Sweet, Food and Allied Workers' Union
SSC	State Security Council
SWAPO	South West Africa People's Organization
TDF	Township Defence Force
TEC	Transitional Executive Council
TGNU	Transitional Government of National Unity
TGWU	Transport and General Workers' Union
TPA	Transvaal Provincial Administration
TUCSA	Trade Union Council of South Africa
UDA	Unilateral Declaration of Autonomy
UDF	United Democratic Front
UNITA	União Nacional para a Independência Total de Angola
UWUSA	United Workers' Union of South Africa (Inkatha-affiliated)
VAT	Value Added Tax
WCCA	Western Cape Civic Association
WHAM	'Winning hearts and minds'
WOSA	Workers' Organization for Socialist Action

Introduction

> If it is true that a people's wealth is its children, then South Africa is bitterly, tragically poor. If it is true that a nation's future is its children, we have no future, and deserve none ... [we] are a nation at war with its future.... For we have turned our children into a generation of fighters, battle-hardened soldiers who will never know the carefree joy of childhood. What we are witnessing is the growth of a generation which has the courage to reject the cowardice of its parents.... There is a dark, terrible beauty in that courage. It is also a source of great pride − pride that we, who have lived under *apartheid*, can produce children who refuse to do so. But it is also a source of great shame ... that [this] is our heritage to our children: the knowledge of how to die, and how to kill.[1]

The political changes that have taken place in South Africa over the past several years are unquestionably irreversible, despite whatever ill-advised efforts might be mounted to resist them.[2] The unbanning of political organizations, the release of political prisoners, the return of exiles, the wholesale repeal of legislation sustaining the apartheid system, the opening of political dialogue on how to incorporate the disenfranchised majority into the mainstream political process, and the successful completion of the country's first nonracial general elections in April 1994, signalled a fundamental shift in the trajectory of South African political history. There were unmistakable signs across the length and breadth of South Africa that the old, established political order was dying, and at a pace that just a few years ago would have been unimaginable. What caused some surprise was that the sudden denouement of the once seemingly invincible apartheid system was not accompanied by the kind of violent civil war pitting black revolutionaries against an entrenched white establishment that some political analysts, extrapolating from prior southern African experiences in Rhodesia/Zimbabwe, Mozambique, and South West Africa/Namibia, had so gloomily forecast as the seemingly inevitable outcome of enduring political polarization and conflict.

Shadow and Substance

What is unmistakable in South Africa today is that the long nightmare of absolute white domination of the political sphere has come haltingly and painfully to a close. A great deal of what has happened over the past several years signifies a genuine victory for the liberation movement and a definite setback for the beleaguered defenders of the status quo. Yet it is not always easy to distinguish between the disintegration of an older established order with deep historical roots, and the birth of a new and decidedly more fragile one. What is clear is that South Africa has entered a protracted period of turbulent political transition and painful economic restructuring where the outcomes of these intertwined processes are far from certain. The dominant classes will use every means at their disposal to cling to what they have, and the nonpropertied social strata who have been heretofore excluded from the world of wealth, power and privilege will demand a more equitable distribution of available resources. Yet the peculiarity of South Africa's racially inscribed capitalism underscores the need for considerable caution in critically evaluating a situation that is as fluid and confusing in its immediate particularity as it is difficult to locate within a wider comparative-historical framework. The future of South Africa has repeatedly proven difficult if not impossible to predict, and for this reason alone it is just too early to tell what the lasting historical significance of the events of the past several years might be. Nevertheless, at the risk of oversimplifying what are indeed overwhelmingly complex issues, it is possible to advance some provisional and tentative observations that can perhaps assist in distinguishing real and enduring changes from illusory and groundless ones, and as a consequence, provide some helpful clues about where South Africa might be heading.

At this historical juncture, unstable and complex as it is, it would be premature to portray the striking changes that have taken place in South Africa as the first, tentative steps of a historic 'forward march' leading inexorably toward a *grand finale* where the country's long-standing problems of racial discrimination, poverty and deprivation can and will be adequately addressed. After all, the extreme disparities in property ownership and the accompanying gap between rich and poor in South Africa are structural in nature, and these inequalities rest on a solid bedrock of crystallized class power and privilege. South Africa's political economy is characterized by a peculiar mixture of ingredients: the legacies of labour coercion and economic concentration, undue dependence upon overseas investment, skilled labour shortages amidst layers of 'casualized' work and widespread unemployment, and weak internal markets. These essential continuities with the past constrain the present and foretell the future. Any efforts genuinely to confront South Africa's glaring class and racial divisions requires uprooting and immobilizing entrenched power centres.[3]

Speaking metaphorically, much of what has happened in South Africa since de Klerk's rise to political power has resembled a surrealistic journey 'back to the future', where the way forward required a return to the past. The National Party leadership, the self-professed and 'born again' champions of equal rights and nonracialism, charted a political course that included carrying out a belated democratic revolution and bringing about national reunification 'from above'. Without making apologies for apartheid, de Klerk wanted to pretend that it never happened. By undertaking a great historical leap backward to the pre-1948 political watershed (if not to the 1910 Act of Union), the National Party hoped to retrace its steps, and in the process recast its historically tarnished image, in order to embark on the alternative historical route not taken.

But the National Party cannot turn back the clock. The situation might be similar, but the circumstances are entirely different. Dismantling the scaffolding that sustained apartheid rule for nearly half a century stripped away the odious mythology of 'separate but equal'; but simply eliminating the legal armature of white supremacy could not by itself even begin to erase the grim bounty of enforced segregation. The failure to initiate a thoroughgoing overhaul and restructuring of the state machinery, including the destruction of the old apartheid apparatuses in the civil service, judiciary and security forces, ensures that the new post-apartheid political arrangement will look startlingly like what it replaced and will leave real economic power in the hands of the propertied white oligarchy.

The terminal crisis of white minority rule and the apartheid system has not been not matched by the emergence of a clear-cut historical alternative that breaks cleanly with the past. The grotesque legacy of white supremacy lingers on, leaving an unequivocal, suffocating imprint on the post-apartheid future. No one truly believes South Africa is moving toward an era of tolerant pluralism, where the incorporation of the black majority into a common race-blind political framework will by itself resolve the social fragmentation and dislocation associated with deeply embedded structural inequalities. At this historical conjuncture, the balance of political forces resembles a type of fiercely contested stalemate, or what Nicos Poulantzas termed the 'unstable equilibrium of compromise'.[4] What is taking place in South Africa is not a simple linear progression from the rigid, constricted apartheid social system characterized by legally sanctioned racial discrimination to a race-blind post-apartheid meritocracy, but rather a complex and multifaceted transitional process involving an almost imperceptible realignment in the structural underpinnings that sustain capital accumulation and intertwined with a sea-change in surface appearances on the terrain of politics. These overlapping changes interact and affect each other, yet they conform to dynamics all their own.

The Riddle of Continuity and Change

In a period of profound disorder and turbulence, it is often continuity and stability, Charles Maier reminds us in another context, that require careful attention and explanation.[5] The social hierarchies that define and sustain the day-to-day realities of South Africa have proved to be remarkably resilient and tenacious, despite the social turmoil and upheaval that swirls around them. Conflict and violence are today inextricably interwoven into the social fabric of everyday life in South Africa, but their corrosive and damaging effects are skewed unequally across the social landscape. With all that has happened, the real nerve centres of entrenched power and inherited privilege – the corporate boardrooms and the upper echelons of the state bureaucracy – have shown themselves remarkably durable and resistant to change.

The bargain that the white oligarchy has struck is to trade exclusive political power for continued economic advantage. The survival and adaption of political and economic elites goes hand-in-hand with the containment of the aspirations of the working class and the poor. The watershed events of February 1990 unleashed a riptide of unrealistic expectations about the speed and direction of political changes. 'Mandela has been released', a woman from the sprawling squatter settlement named Khayelitsha outside Cape Town wrote to a local newspaper in March 1990, 'now where is my house?'[6] Millenarian sentiments of this sort, which express the accumulated hopes of ordinary people for the immediate redress of long-standing socio-economic grievances, have been put on hold, lingering in a state of suspended animation, awaiting political action on the part of state managers willing to tackle South Africa's seemingly intractable problems of unemployment and underemployment, township decay and neglect, inadequate schooling and health care, along with a host of other social ills associated with underdevelopment and stagnation. The initial optimism that greeted the unbanning of political organizations and the release of political prisoners soon faded away, and the prevailing mood in the townships, squatter camps and impoverished rural settlements became one of mounting confusion, fear and despair. The hopes for a smooth transition to nonracial parliamentary democracy were marred by what was no less than an epidemic of politically related violence that divides communities, exacerbates existing socio-economic and socio-cultural cleavages, and terrorizes ordinary people.

The striking paradox that casts its long shadow over the slow and painful birth of post-apartheid South Africa is that, for all that has happened, not much has changed. Perhaps it was the sobering recognition of this situation that prompted world-renowned poet Dennis Brutus purportedly to say in reaction to returning to South Africa after decades in exile: 'Is this what people have sacrificed their lives for? If we are supposed to have won, how is it that those who are supposed to have lost seem not to have lost anything?.'[7] It is this basic paradox, fleetingly captured in this poignant, heart-wrenching observation, that is the key to understanding the current political conjuncture. Of course, posing the question in this way is not to imply, with a dispassionate cynicism born of social distance, that the eclipse of apartheid rule and the inauguration of nonracial parliamentary democracy are merely superficial window-dressing without substance and significance. But it is to suggest that the emotional appeal of 'that great day when freedom arrives' is a misguided metaphor quite inappropriate in assisting us to situate the present conjuncture in a wider historical framework.

At present, South Africa is torn between two worlds so cruelly different that it is indeed difficult to imagine how they might be logically or even temporally connected. Yet they are, and it is their apparent separateness that lends a tragic dimension to this transitional period. Only with the benefit of hindsight will it be possible to produce a holistic, coherent understanding of these turbulent times. On the one side, the theme of continuity is unable, by itself, to yield a convincing portrait of a historical moment that, in the virtually unanimous assessment of all political analysts, has been both momentous and colossal in its social and political implications. Yet on the other side, to characterize the transition from authoritarian rule to parliamentary democracy as a veritable 'political revolution', as many mainstream commentators have done, is to overstate the extent to which 'free and fair' elections by themselves mark a decisive rupture with existing institutionalized sources of political power. By operating on the implicit assumption that 'free and fair' elections are the defining criterion for democracy, this Panglossian view largely restricts its focus to formal political processes and coalitions, downplays the Gordian knot of enforced 'power-sharing' and the inertia of entrenched state bureaucracies, and obscures the infrastructure of power embedded in the relations linking private production and consumption. The Manichaean portrayal of a sharp divide between white minority rule and post-apartheid parliamentary democracy exaggerates the peculiar nature of South Africa's political *rapprochement*, where a heterodox coalition of urban and intellectual 'mod-ernizers' were able to reach agreement on a brokered deal laying down the rules of the game for political contestation. What enforced 'power-sharing' accomplished, according to one commentator, was to secure 'some five to ten years of benevolent autocracy, rather than a functioning de-mocracy'.[8]

The political developments that have taken place in South Africa in the recent past evolved from a complex series of conflicts and compro-mises among diverse social groups and organizations, where the results, however fixed they might appear at the moment, are subject to challenge and revision. Having acquired full-fledged citizenship in an undivided South Africa, formerly disenfranchised people are no longer 'pariahs in the land of their birth' – as Solomon Plaatje so eloquently put it in 1913. But, taken by themselves, the formal rights of citizenship do not ensure economic well-being and social advancement, political tolerance and stability, racial equality, and greater opportunity for collective escape from a social world filled with hopelessness and despair. These real-life problems are inextricably linked with class issues, and it is these class issues that have proven to be quite intractable and resistant to fundamental modification.

1

Shifting Political Alignments in the Twilight of Apartheid Rule

In a landmark address marking the opening of parliament on 2 February 1990, President F.W. de Klerk ended months of speculation about the willingness of the National Party leadership to steer a reformist course by announcing sweeping changes in the political landscape of South Africa. In a single stroke that went far beyond what virtually all his critics had expected, de Klerk proclaimed the repeal of restrictive regulations, in place for nearly thirty years, outlawing the ANC, the SACP, and the PAC; pledged the imminent, unconditional release of Nelson Mandela, along with scores of other people imprisoned for political offences; relaxed legal restrictions on thirty other political organizations, including the UDF and COSATU; and lifted the 'banning' orders on 374 anti-apartheid opponents, including some who had not been free to speak publicly or to organize since 1952. The immediate objective of de Klerk's announcement was to break the political impasse that had developed after months of semi-secret discussions with the ANC by removing the remaining stumbling blocks to nascent negotiations over a proposed new constitution.

This striking volte-face in the political direction of the ruling National Party surprised friend and foe alike. Millions of people around the world greeted with a degree of enthusiasm bordering on euphoria the opening of political dialogue on how to include the disenfranchised majority into the mainstream political process. The concessions that de Klerk and the National Party Cabinet pieced together, as a prelude to the opening in December 1991 of formal negotiations on a new nonracial constitution that would extend equal political rights to all South Africans, bore eloquent testimony to the failure on the part of a succession of National Party regimes and their predecessors to extinguish an enduring spirit of popular resistance. By expressing a willingness to negotiate a peaceful way around what threatened to be an inevitable bloody showdown with its sworn enemies, a ruling party – for the first time in South African history – openly acknowledged that it was no longer possible to deny the black majority a significant role in shaping the country's destiny. There is no doubt that the unbanning of political organizations fuelled an enormous self-confidence amongst the forces of resistance. These events, compressed into a short space of time and appearing almost larger than life, marked an unprecedented watershed in South African political history and indeed heralded the onset of a bold new era in South African history. In the heat of the moment, normally cautious political observers hailed the National Party as a benign catalyst for genuine change, and even Mandela succumbed to the temptation, praising de Klerk as a 'man of integrity'.[1]

At the time of their unfolding, these events seemed to suggest for many people that a relatively swift and largely peaceful transfer of political power from the hands of the white minority to the majority was poised to take place. Yet in a short span of time, the initial optimism born in the exhilarating moment of triumph gave way to a sobering pessimism about what it was historically possible to accomplish under the difficult and trying circumstances of a deeply entrenched white power structure and ongoing political violence. Seen in retrospect, how can these striking changes, and particularly the dizzying pace at which they came about, be properly understood? Do the remarkable events of South Africa's recent past carry sufficient social weight to have truly altered the course of South African history? Or are they mere fleeting images, to paraphrase Fernand Braudel, 'with their deceptive vapors, fill[ing] the consciousness of contemporaries', without lasting historical significance? Can de Klerk's actions be understood as a magnanimous gesture, symbolizing, like Paul on the road to Damascus, a genuine 'change of heart', or were they merely cynical ploys designed to 'buy time' for the propertied white oligarchy? What were the stark realities that led the both NP under F.W. de Klerk and the ANC leadership to reach the conclusion that the negotiated settlement was not only possible but also historically necessary? What were the new fault lines of social conflict that emerged as a direct result of political realignments? Is apartheid really dead, or will it continue to survive, tragically metamorphosed in a ghastly new guise? Has the turbulent transition to nonracial democracy energized the forces of change, or has it effectively channelled the popular movement into corporatist cooptation and a parliamentary cul-de-sac? Answers to these and other questions are the key to understanding the possibilities for fundamental transformation of the political and economic structures of South Africa.

'Playing for Time': The Scramble for Power in the 'New' South Africa

A recurrent theme in political analyses of the South African situation has long been the claim that the National Party regime and the apartheid system were on the brink of imminent collapse. The common refrain 'How long will South Africa survive?' underscored the gloomy, dooms-day forecasts of a seemingly inescapable violent showdown between the white minority regime and the liberation movement. Despite repeated predictions of such cataclysmic breakdown by 'five-minutes-to-midnight' prophets at key moments in South African history, the dominant class bloc continued to survive and, at times, even gain new strength in spite of its manifest weaknesses.[2]

In February 1989, F.W. de Klerk was elected by party caucus to re-place the ailing P.W. Botha as head of the National Party, and, following a bitter power struggle, he was named acting president in August.[3] The consequent reshuffling of prominent figures in both the leadership of the National Party and the upper echelons of the civil administration marked a decisive turning point in the approach of the embattled white minority regime to the enduring problems of political instability and social dis-order. Botha and his colleagues had promised reform, but, in the end, their piecemeal efforts to give apartheid a cosmetic 'facelift' ran aground with the 1984–86 insurrection. The brutal suppression of the rebellion, relying as it did upon heavy-handed use of policing tactics, the military occupation of the restive townships, and blanket restrictions on civil liberties, triggered a worldwide backlash of unexpected proportions cul-minating in the international disinvestment and sanctions campaigns. Wilful political intervention of this sort provided some leverage on Pretoria to accelerate its half-hearted 'deracialization' project. But in truth, these efforts by well-meaning outsiders to bring the ruling white oligarchy 'to its senses' paled in comparison with the deleterious effects of the global market reaction to South Africa's unsteady business climate. The combi-nation of capital flight and the drying up of international loans starved local enterprises of investment funds and put unprecedented pressure on political elites to arrive at a workable solution to the long-standing politi-cal crisis of legitimacy, representation and rule.

The dramatic way in which de Klerk chose to break the political logjam caught nearly everyone off guard at the time.[4] His sincere pledge to dismantle the apartheid edifice that sustained legalized racial discrimi-nation and to enter formal negotiations over a new nonracial constitution signalled a decisive turning point in South Africa's tumultuous political history. Seen in retrospect, however, the actions themselves do not seem

nearly so surprising once they are situated within the broader socio-
historical context. When de Klerk and his reform-minded advisors
assumed the reins of government, they inherited an economic recession
with no end in sight and a fragile political stalemate held in check only
by the real threat of military intervention. What seemed clear was that
this combustible mixture was ready to explode at a moment's notice. The
verligte power-brokers were desperately seeking a solution to long-term
economic malaise and recurrent political instability. In a real sense, the
National Party leadership was clearly reacting to what had already
happened on the ground, rather than charting a fundamentally different
political course of its own accord. In dispensing with the basic premises
of classical Verwoerdian apartheid, de Klerk abandoned an outmoded
bureaucratic *mélange* of overlapping and sometimes contradictory regulations that had become not only ideologically indefensible but also
virtually unenforceable. Jettisoning this entire repertoire of discriminatory
legislation was a daunting task indeed: the legal armature sustaining apartheid consisted of more than fifteen thousand regulations and two hundred
separate laws.[5]

The trickle that began in 1986 of unauthorized *treks* of prominent
businessmen and well-known politicians to confer with the exiled ANC
leadership in Lusaka soon turned into a flood, despite the official quaran-
tine prohibiting 'talking with the enemy'. For the status-conscious, hob-
nobbing with ANC notables in a frontline venue became a treasured
badge of distinction, and these high-profile 'media events' ironically overshadowed considerably more serious meetings between the exiled ANC
and the internal United Democratic Front (UDF)/Mass Democratic
Movement (MDM) leadership along with key COSATU figures. These
consultations that brought the 'old guard' leadership in touch with a truly
heterogeneous range of organizations and individuals inside South Africa
were crucial in shaping the ANC's analysis of the internal balance of
internal forces, and they signalled the beginning of a gradual yet inexorable
process by which the Congress movement effectively 'unbanned' itself.
By lifting legal restrictions on political organizations that had grown in
stature and reputation during their long years of underground existence,
de Klerk tacitly acknowledged that state-sponsored repression was an
ineffectual instrument for restoring political stability.[6]

De Klerk and his inner circle were only the last of a long line of
powerful Afrikaners who, in the name of preserving the privileged position
of the 'white race', ruled with an iron fist for close on half a century.
These National Party notables were fully aware of the latent dangers
inherent in the rapidly changing circumstances. For them, timing was
everything. These men scrambled to stay ahead of the game, because they

intuitively understood, as Alexis de Tocqueville observed over two hundred years earlier, that the ruling classes are most vulnerable to being overthrown from below when they lose their grip over the pace and direction of political reforms initiated from above. For them, the main question facing the National Party was how to create and institutionalize a new political system which would ensure it a continuing role in governing the country and, equally important, protect the property and personal freedoms of the increasingly diverse white communities of South Africa.[7]

What made de Klerk's manoeuvres so stunning was not so much that he was able to carry them out without a massive reaction amongst the white electorate, but that the timing was brilliant. A few years earlier, it would have been unthinkable for National Party leaders to contemplate the unconditional release of prisoners, return of exiles, and the wholesale dismantling of apartheid. But while the situation remained the same, the circumstances were different. If Mandela had died in prison, he would have been instantaneously transformed into a martyr. But a freed Mandela was capable of making mistakes, and the failure of 'unbanned' organizations to deliver on promises of change would certainly 'demystify' the liberation movement. Put in broad historical perspective, the ruling National Party found itself in a gradually deteriorating economic and political situation where officially sanctioned repression of popular aspirations offered at best a temporary respite from what appeared to be the inexorable disintegration of white minority rule. Despite its limited room for manoeuvre, the National Party was still able to act decisively within its inherited parameters. By taking steps before they were truly forced to do so by unbearable pressures not of their own making, the National Party leaders were able to steal the march on their political opponents to both the left and the right. This modest *coup de maître* enabled the National Party leadership, at the early stages of hesitant dialogue, largely to determine the pace of reform and greatly to influence its direction. Getting the negotiations process off the ground permitted National Party leaders to portray themselves as visionary trailblazers, or the modernizing elite of Afrikaanerdom.

In thus starting the process, de Klerk and the National Party pursued a two-pronged strategy. On the one hand, his team of reformist advisors used the drawn-out negotiations to play for time, calculating that by bringing together all shades of political opinion, and by swamping the process with large numbers of players, they could effectively squeeze such concessions out of their opponents that they could dilute a radical outcome. On the other hand, by coaxing their adversaries into compromises, they hoped to use negotiations to divide their rivals by driving a wedge between moderates and hardliners. One of the main lessons the National Party learned from its experience in brokering an end to the SWAPO-led armed struggle in Namibia was that a protracted process of negotiations 'allows the public, local and international, to appreciate some of the less appealing characteristics' of the other side.[8]

The conventional wisdom in the world of *Realpolitik* is that rival political parties cannot hope to achieve at the conference table what is denied them on the battlefield. This truism applied equally to South Africa. The ruling National Party under de Klerk's leadership declared a willingness to negotiate the terms of a truce, not a wholesale surrender of political power. While the venue and the tactics changed, the underlying objective of the white oligarchy, to maintain economic and political power, remained the same.[9] 'Before transferring power, the Nationalist Party wants to emasculate it', Allister Sparks argued. 'It is trying to negotiate a kind of swap where it will give up the right to run the country its way in exchange for the right to stop the blacks from running it their own way.'[10] By shifting the terrain of political action from confrontation to dialogue, South Africa's ruling elite effectively abandoned the ground that had sustained over forty years of trench warfare under apartheid rule. Once crystal-clear, the dividing line between progress and reaction, between qualitative change and the status quo, and between victory and defeat, became blurred as it was viewed through the distorting lens of the negotiations process.

Wholesale Political Realignment

The broad gulf separating the two main rivals in the high-stakes negotiating contest could be traced to entirely different political philosophies. The essential difference between the constitutional proposals of the ANC and those of the National Party was that the former advocated the concentration of state political power, and the latter its fragmentation. Specifically, the ANC wished to maintain and even strengthen the existing centralized state apparatuses; the National Party, in contrast, proposed a decentralized federal system where the countervailing powers of regional governing bodies offset whatever tendencies there were to concentrate political power in the state. The National Party wanted regions and municipalities to possess original powers that the central parliament could not take away, while the ANC insisted that all power for these bodies be derived from, and hence subject to, parliament.[11]

Despite these apparent differences and the accompanying posturing, the ANC and the National Party agreed on the broad outlines of what the new constitution should include. They concurred that it should contain a Bill of Rights, even though they disagreed on what such a Bill might enshrine. Both parties accepted that South Africa should continue to exist as a unitary state, and that the homelands should be formally re-incorporated into the country. Both accepted that there should be a degree of devolution of power to local authorities and that there should be a mixed economy, though the National Party favoured greater privatization of state-owned assets, while the ANC wanted powerful state agencies to assume a greater stake in macro-economic planning.[12]

These broad areas of agreement underscored the extent to which a fundamental political realignment had taken place in South Africa. For decades the main battle lines were racially drawn between white people defending minority domination and black people demanding equality. Seemingly overnight, political alliances were recast, dividing those pledged to negotiating a way out of the political impasse and those who feared that a negotiated settlement would lead to compromise on basic princi-ples. At one end of the political spectrum, far-right political organizations refused to participate in 'all-party' talks about South Africa's future, charg-ing that the National Party had 'sold out' the 'white race' and did not have a legitimate mandate to negotiate with 'terrorists' and 'communists'. The National Party was unable to bridge its schism with its largest rival on the right, the Conservative Party, whose Afrikaner nationalist leaders repeatedly called for 'self-determination' embodied in a *Boerstaat* (white homeland). The Inkatha Freedom Party (IFP) echoed this theme of regional autonomy in a federal state, and its flirtations with far-right parties and its 'on-again, off-again' relations with multi-party negotiations were the most visible signs of its fissiparous relations with the political main-stream.

At the other end of the spectrum, the Congress-aligned political organizations clustered around the ANC remained estranged from their smaller yet less accommodating Africanist, Black Consciousness and socialist rivals in the liberation movement. These organizations were stead-fastly committed in principle to a popularly elected constituent assembly as the sole mechanism for carrying out the transfer of political power from the white minority to the majority, and they strongly objected to the participation in constitutional negotiations of 'puppet bodies' such as the homelands administrations. The erstwhile effort to cobble together a tactical alliance of 'pro-constituent assembly' organizations, called the Patriotic Front, showed promise but faltered before it got off the ground, amid charges of 'bad faith' and backroom dealings.[13]

The National Party that orchestrated the demise of apartheid bore only the slightest resemblance to the organization that originally brought this formal system of racial discrimination into being. The metamorphosis began slowly, but gathered a full head of steam under the guidance of Botha and de Klerk. Botha presided over the transformation of the party from a democratic, federally based patronage-dispensing organization to a highly centralized executive body with inordinate power vested in its 'higher circles'. Once the self-styled saviour of the Afrikaner 'little man', the Nationalists with de Klerk at the helm became 'the organising and structuring political mechanism for capital'.[14] Despite a series of embarrassing setbacks that greatly tarnished its reputation, the party generally managed to stay ahead in the political game. In moves which would have been unthinkable a few years earlier, the Nationalists actively courted the favour of black business and 'community leaders', sought tactical alliances with moderate black political organizations, appointed 'non-white' Cabinet ministers, and opened its membership to people of all races. In the dying days of the moribund tricameral parliament, the National Party took virtual control over both the (Coloured) House of Representatives and the (Indian) House of Delegates after MPs in minuscule 'racially designated' parties switched their allegiance to the 'new Nats'.[15]

Yet the National Party encountered huge difficulties in its efforts to recast itself in a nonracial mould and to carve out the middle ground of the political spectrum. But it was an uncanny survivalist instinct that drove party reformers to seek a wider role in South African political life, one that involved more than representing increasingly fragmented white constituencies and trying to safeguard their sectoral interests. By restructuring its political message to appeal to a broader constituency, the National Party was intent on laying claim to the centre-right of the political spectrum. In this sense, it approximated a sort of nascent Christian-democratic party of the 'new' South Africa.

At the same time, the ANC transformed itself from an underground movement espousing guerrilla warfare and popular insurrection to a legal political party resembling a European-style social democracy on the centre-left of the political spectrum. This metamorphosis was not easy. Below the surface unity there was restiveness and disappointment. Young militants who had been the backbone of popular resistance to apartheid rule were confused and angry about the decision of the leadership not only to enter into negotiations with their former sworn adversaries but also to give away so much without tangible evidence of reciprocity. There were tensions between returning exiles and those who had remained in the country building the trade unions and the MDM. It was the older exiles who seemed to obtain the coveted posts in the movement, and it was this perception of undeserved preferential treatment that contributed to resentment. Yet despite its organizational weaknesses and internal grievances, the ANC exhibited a remarkable record of unity that held firm under the increased strain. The ANC gradually developed a more collective style of leadership, and the unchallenged authority (but not stature) of its president, Nelson Mandela, slowly faded.[16] The ascension of a sophisticated, younger leadership gave the organization a new dynamism that was initially lacking in the months following its unbanning. After Cyril Ramaphosa, former head of the National Union of Mineworkers (NUM), assumed the post of secretary-general, the ANC quickly developed a more efficient administrative machinery capable of responding much more promptly to the demands placed upon it.[17]

The broadly based, ideologically diverse anti-apartheid movement entered the post-1990 period of openness with an inherited imagery of political and social conflict derived from nearly thirty years of quasi-legal and sometimes underground existence. Whatever its tactical differences, the protean 'liberation movement' had historically coalesced around a common strategic outlook: the eradication of the odious apartheid system and, by forcible means or otherwise, the full-scale transfer of political power from the white minority into the hands of the black majority. The battle lines were sharply drawn between the white minority regime presided over by the National Party and buttressed by a motley array of collaborating hangers-on, on the one side, and the 'liberation movement' divided between the main Congress-oriented current and its smaller Africanist, Black Consciousness and socialist tributaries, on the other. After February 1990, the familiar signposts of 'liberation politics', particularly the clarion call for armed struggle and popular insurrection, lost much of their previous meaning and inspiration. In an era of multilateral negotiations and high-level compromise, pragmatic realism slowly gained the upper hand, and the radical ideas that accompanied 'the politics of confrontation' during the 1980s seemed strangely out of place.

The Limits of the Possible

By championing as much market competition as possible and promoting as little state intervention as necessary, the National Party leadership adopted a programme of explicitly capitalist reform. How ironic it was that this Afrikaner elite, who trumpeted the virtues of business freedom and personal liberties as a bulwark against state-managed programmes of socio-economic upliftment, owed its very class existence to massive state intervention and to the denial of political rights for the majority. The de Klerk administration wished to address the ongoing economic malaise and resolve the political crisis of legitimacy at a single stroke by incorporating the ANC and its allies into a governing partnership at the top with as little change at the bottom as possible. By engineering a consensus on an elaborate system of checks and balances embodied in the new constitution, the National Party also hoped effectively to ensnare the ANC in the 'give-and-take' *Realpolitik* of pluralist party politics, thereby hampering its capacity for unilateral action.[18]

In the post-1990 period, the two main allies of the powerful business class and the ruling National Party were the changing international balance of forces and the power of capital, both global and local. The collapse of the Soviet-style economic planning models in Eastern Europe and the Soviet Union raised serious doubts about blueprints for socialism that began with nationalization of the commanding heights of the economy, centralized planning, and single-party rule. One by one, the political regimes in the frontline states gradually abandoned their previous commitments to socialist economic transformation and the rhetoric of Marxism–Leninism as the guiding principles for political renewal. The socialist left in South Africa was confronted with two burning questions: What is socialism? and How would it work in South Africa?

In the same vein, the charmed centres of established socio-economic power in South Africa accepted as an article of faith that property rights and market freedoms were morally and functionally equivalent to political rights guaranteed in a democratic 'civil society'. By enshrining existing property relations in a Bill of Rights, the propertied and privileged classes wished to protect their immediate self-interests. Business leaders and their political allies spoke the language of 'equity through growth and stability', and piously agreed that the redress of deep-seated socio-economic inequalities ought to be a priority for whatever post-apartheid Government emerged. In the short run, they hoped that a 'new realism', born of the collapse of the Soviet-style command economies, would have a sobering effect on ANC thinking, thereby dampening the previous enthusiasm for state intervention as a means of alleviating mass misery. The aim of large-scale corporate interest groups was to define South Africa's prevailing inequalities as welfare problem that could be addressed through redistribution of social surplus rather than as a problem linked with the logic of capitalist production itself. Business leaders insisted that only a market-propelled growth strategy was capable of generating sufficient wealth to spill over to those most in need of socio-economic upliftment.[19]

On the other side, the ANC/SACP bloc reasoned that a new constitution guaranteeing equal rights and universal franchise would establish a political platform from which to launch a wider assault on the centres of entrenched political power and social wealth. The eventual outcome of these rival visions depended, on the one hand, upon the ability of the dominant bloc of class forces to engineer a coherent and purposeful reform programme that could effectively divide its opposition, and, on the other, the ability of the mass movement to sustain a level of mobilization effective enough to push the reformist project well beyond what the de Klerk administration had originally intended.[20]

Peddling Prosperity: Scenario Planning for the 'New' South Africa

Because of its closer ties to large-scale industry and big finance than its predecessors, the de Klerk administration introduced more coherence into economic policy-making. South Africa's Reserve Bank, the driving force behind the National Party's economic-recovery strategy, adopted a strict monetarist policy advocating cutting inflation by tightening the money supply, rejuvenating a feeble investment climate by means of deregulation and liberalization, and encouraging the expansion of manufacturing through export-led growth. After forty years of selective state intervention geared primarily to shifting economic power from the English-speaking propertied classes to an emergent Afrikaner elite, the ruling National Party jumped on the *laissez faire* bandwagon in vogue throughout the capitalist world, pledging to withdraw the state administration from economic management and to carry out a 'privatization' campaign by dismantling the state monopolies and selling off their assets. During the long reign of apartheid, the state sector absorbed the steel, oil-from-coal production, transport, telecommunications, and the defence industries. At its peak in the 1970s, the state administration employed one-third of all economically active white wage earners. Even after the privatization of the giant Iron and Steel Corporation (ISCOR), the state sector still owned more than 50 per cent of the country's fixed assets.[21]

The National Party echoed the refrain of large-scale business conglomerates, championing the neo-liberal virtues of market liberalization and deregulation as historically sound solutions for reversing economic decline. According to this confident scenario, a negotiated settlement would end the political stalemate, and, in turn, would bring about much-needed stability resulting in a rapid influx of overseas investment. In short, the absolving power of the free market, coupled with minimal doses of state intervention, would 'kick-start' the powerful yet stalled engine of economic growth. This recovery strategy, commonly known as 'redistribution through growth', suggested that the spillover from a revived business climate would eventually trickle down to benefit the disadvantaged by means of an expanding jobs base and increased social spending.[22] This approach, described by critics as neo-liberal export-oriented growth, stressed the restructuring of the economy, and the manufacturing sector in particular, mainly through market adjustments aiming at 'getting the prices of goods, money, and factors of production right'.[23] In this model, productive and capital-intensive modern industry would operate as the underlying dynamo energizing economic growth in an internationally competitive environment. The 'redistribution through growth' approach was normally accompanied by an 'almost dogmatic plea for an unbridled free-market economy' and veiled threats by South African corporations to pull up stakes and invest elsewhere if the first post-apartheid government began to tinker with compensatory redistributive policies.[24]

Critics of this growth model labelled it the '50 per cent solution' because, in their estimation, it would exacerbate the polarizing tendencies already taking place in the occupational division of labour and drive a wedge between the 'haves' and the 'have-nots'. The political objective of this 'redistribution through growth' approach involved appealing to the material interests of black propertied classes, along with the professional and managerial middle class, small traders, and the new skilled, clerical and supervisory working class, while leaving the unskilled black working class, along with the marginalized sectors living on the periphery of the 'mass consumption economy', to fend for themselves.[25]

Economic Thinking and the Congress Alliance

In exile and in opposition, the Congress movement had held its own diverse constituencies in check by emphasizing a litany of grievances which it promised, without order of preference, to address once it gained access to political power. Its purposefully vague anti-capitalist rhetoric gave the ANC leadership considerable ideological leeway successfully to stitch together a loosely defined coalition of interest groups that included workers and aspirant entrepreneurs, Christians and Communists, and the unemployed and the middle class, around a shared political objective of dismantling apartheid rule. This almost single-minded attachment to a common goal enabled the Congress movement to defer difficult, and potentially divisive, decisions about principles of economic management to a time after the achievement of nonracial political democracy.

At the time of its unbanning, the ANC had produced little along the lines of a comprehensive, operational blueprint for the post-apartheid economic order. On balance, the ANC had long embraced a kind of anti-monopoly populism that dovetailed with socialist-inclined, progressive social movements around the world. Over the years, Congress proclamations on economic matters were generally relegated to brief commentaries sandwiched in the midst of key political documents, or else cloaked in populist slogans suggesting a commandist role for the post-apartheid state and calling for the redistribution of social wealth in order to bring parity between privileged whites and the oppressed black masses. Whatever economic platform that could be pieced together from ANC policy statements consisted largely of a judicious mixture of state intervention plus social-democratic reform; or, to put it more specifically, 'nationalization' of the 'commanding heights of the economy' along with conventional welfare-state formulas that included, notably, massive state spending on health care, education, housing, and so forth. The precise manner in which the ANC proposed to carry out the redistribution of socio-economic resources, once it assumed political power, was never clearly spelled out, apart from a cluster of salient propositions contained in the 1955 *Freedom Charter*. In the absence of a precisely formulated economic doctrine, the ANC leadership – when pressed by outsiders – more often than not invoked these basic principles, including the transfer of the mines, banks, and monopoly industries 'to the ownership of the people as a whole', and wholesale land reform.[26] In January 1990, Mandela reaffirmed these Charterist tenets when he proclaimed that 'the nationalisation of the mines, banks, and monopoly industry is the policy of the ANC and a change or modification of our views in this regard is inconceivable'.[27]

After its unbanning, the most important and substantial pronouncement on ANC economic thinking was contained in the 1990 *Discussion Document on Economic Policy*. This document was the end product of a year-long process of deliberation between radical economists and policy analysts sympathetic to the ANC and COSATU.[28] One main purpose behind this policy statement was to provide, in bold strokes, a preliminary explanation for South Africa's economic stagnation and to offer a tentative framework for economic recovery. Working together in loosely linked 'think-tanks', the largest of which was the Macroeconomic Research Group, ANC-aligned economists produced a series of semi-official reports that pointed to the weak growth record of South Africa's sheltered manufacturing industries, along with the limited size of the internal market, as the two principal causes for lingering economic stagnation.[29] In order to revive the sluggish manufacturing sector and to bolster local consumption, these radical economists advocated a comprehensive programme linking the expansion of labour-intensive, basic consumer-goods industries geared for the domestic market to improvements in living standards 'of the poorest, most oppressed and disadvantaged people in South Africa' and the creation of much-needed jobs.[30] This ambitious plan for economic recovery pivoted on the premiss that economic choices could not be divorced from political ones, and its success depended upon an activist state administration making use of direct taxation and other fiscal inducements both to compel and to encourage large-scale industry and mining to make specific financial contributions to the redistributive process.[31]

The 1990 *Discussion Document*, along with subsequent ANC policy statements, contained approving references to a 'mixed economy' and an intrusive role for state managers in economic matters, but included little of the rhetorical populism that characterized earlier, albeit vague, pronouncements on economic matters. The views included in this document were consistent with the ANC's long-standing 'aversion to the abuse of market power by monopolies' and its faith in a benevolent state to provide economic outcomes superior to market-oriented alternatives.[32] The *primum mobile* that anchored this alternative economic strategy was termed 'growth through redistribution', where 'redistribution acts a spur to growth and in which the fruits of growth are redistributed to satisfy basic needs'.[33] In the ensuing discussion, three slightly different variants of this 'growth through redistribution' formula emerged: demand redistribution to stimulate employment; 'commandist'-style state interventionism, or what was called 'macro-economic populism', grounded in selective nationalization and the dismantling of the huge conglomerates; and so-called 'inward industrialization' to act as the prime stimulus triggering sustained economic growth.[34]

From the outset, establishment economists and mainstream policymakers subjected this alternative economic strategy to blistering criticism. In a stylized format that resembled Albert Hirschman's tripartite classification describing the rhetoric of reaction, detractors suggested that the untested formulas upon which the ANC's reformist initiatives rested would invariably be counterproductive, ineffectual and too expensive to sustain.[35] Business executives stood firm against any redistributive strategies which were even vaguely confiscatory because of their 'anti-market' bias. The National Party cautioned its adversaries against seeking quasi-socialist, state-managed panaceas to South Africa's economic ills, warning against politically motivated promises of 'quick-fix' solutions to overhaul the economic system overnight.[36]

Economic Snake Oil: 'Faith, Hope and Foreign Bankers'

South Africa's highly concentrated corporate business sector loomed large as the main obstacle blocking the path of state-managed economic recovery programmes. The four top companies listed on the Johannesburg Stock Exchange (JSE) – DeBeers Consolidated, Anglo-America Corporation, Gencor, Barlow Rand – control around 80 per cent of total stock equities and maintain a virtual stranglehold on large-scale business investment and financing in the country. While ANC policy-makers hinted broadly that they might subject these octopus-like conglomerates to strict antitrust legislation in the future, these corporate giants wasted no time in mobilizing the enormous financial and intellectual resources at their disposal to combat whatever impetuous efforts might be mounted to meddle in what they considered to be their private affairs.[37] In manoeuvres both designed to pre-empt radical restructuring of big corporations through anti-trust legislation and to avoid compulsory affirmative-action programmes meant to increase employment and training opportunities for black employees, several conglomerates moved fast to bring black people into management and to appoint them to corporate boards of directors, to transfer some assets to black-owned or -managed consortia, and to 'unbundle' huge holding companies.[38]

The task of fiercely guarding the interests of the propertied classes fell largely to the corporate associations of capital. In anticipation of an expected elite-managed transition to parliamentary democracy, South Africa's giant conglomerates commissioned a host of business advisory groups, university-linked 'think-tanks', and private consultancy firms, to fashion futuristic forecasts about where the 'new' South Africa might be heading. Almost overnight, 'scenario planning' became a veritable cottage industry. The once-bland normative projections underwent a subtle transformation from open-ended efforts to map future possibilities to increasingly 'stylized, cliché-ridden efforts' to shape a corporatist bargain between big capital, organized labour and the state administration. 'Scenario planning' gradually evolved, as one astute political analyst observed, from 'corporate survival strategy to social-contract parable'.[39]

These teams of experts took the lead in formulating market-driven growth strategies that specifically excluded various types of state intervention, including 'nationalization', as useful mechanisms for carrying out the redistribution of material resources on a non-market basis. Johannesburg Consolidated Investments economist Ronnie Bethlehem, for example, put forward a scenario that was called – in the sort of effortless humour that only those safely entrenched in power can muster – 'Faith, Hope and Foreign Bankers'. This proposal suggested a corporatist-style accord between business and labour where 'the haves need not be hurt at all' and the state would create 'the incentives for the private sector to deliver the wherewithal of improving the disposition of the deprived masses'.[40] Scores of 'policy entrepreneurs' peddled economic miracle cures, scurrying around and telling establishment politicians what they wanted to hear.

The ANC leadership came under relentless pressure from the International Monetary Fund (IMF), the World Bank, the Development Bank of Southern Africa (DBSA), and the Consultative Business Movement (CBM) – home of South Africa's enlightened capitalists – to abandon its proposed inward industrialization programme in favour of a more 'realistic' investment-led, export-oriented growth strategy. In order to loosen the ideological grip of macro-economic populism on ANC thinking, business consultancy firms issued dire warnings about the dangerous inefficiencies of nationalization, the cost-ineffectiveness of excessive social spending, the fiscal burdens of a bloated state bureaucracy, and the need for a friendly business climate to stimulate investment and hence create jobs.[41]

The ANC and the 'Great Economic Debate'

What came to be called the 'Great Economic Debate' in South Africa was underpinned by two stylized facts: first, the wider global context where neo-liberal, market-oriented strategies for economic growth and development were dominant, and, conversely, state-centred socialist models were widely discredited; and second, the sobering realization that 'the old power in South Africa [was not] genuinely on the point of collapse or disappearance'.[42] For decades before the ANC was unbanned, South Africa's free-enterprise lobby expressed considerable fear that the Congress movement was unswerving in its commitment to widespread nationalization and was bent on a commandist-style role for the state administration. Yet as the ANC gradually unveiled its concrete policy proposals for the post-apartheid economic order, these anxieties proved to be largely unfounded. Within the ANC, the 1990 *Discussion Document*, along with subsequent policy statements, triggered a far-reaching political debate, which included its COSATU/SACP alliance partners, on perplexing questions such as nationalization, compromise and cooperation with capital, the future of South Africa's large-scale monopolies, and the extent of active state intervention to control the economy. The once-confident fondness within the radical wing of the ANC for *dirigiste* solutions to socio-economic problems was dealt a crippling blow by the sudden collapse of the commandist-style centralized planning in the Soviet Union and Eastern Europe.

The relentless pressure of South Africa's free-enterprise lobby paid handsome dividends for the proponents of *laissez faire* state policies. The 'strengthened hand of the free market lobby in our own national economic debate', as one SACP economist acknowledged, forced the ANC to rethink its prior endorsement of state-managed solutions to long-standing structural inequalities.[43] As one commentator suggested, with a tone of obvious delight, 'any lengthy discussion with senior ANC economic policy officials indicates that their policy thinking has become far more flexible and innovative and far less doctrinaire over the past four years.'[44] The terrain of discourse gradually shifted away from even half-hearted advocacy of an overarching commandist role for the state administration. ANC policy-makers accepted the idea of a 'mixed economy' as an article of faith, stressing selective intervention whereby key state agencies would target specific sectors for particular assistance, and emphasizing that nationalization, if it took place at all, would only be undertaken if a convincing case could be made that the benefits in each instance outweighed the costs.[45]

The search for political stability rested on complex trade-offs, and these compromises preponderantly rewarded moderate and centrist forces and softened the anti-capitalist current within the ANC. As the formal multiparty negotiations process moved inexorably toward a historic compromise, the ANC adjusted to the anticipated burdens and opportunities of political office by jettisoning some of the radical posturing that had characterized its years of exile. 'By its very nature,' Bundy argued, 'negotiation involves concessions, the pursuit of agreement tends to move partners towards centrist, compromise positions.'[46] What caused particular ideological soul-searching for ANC-aligned economists was the perceived need to formulate socio-economic policies within the constraints of crisis management and under conditions where business enterprises, large and small, remained firmly in private hands. Unable to project an all-embracing programme for socio-economic restructuring independent of the existing worldwide capitalist consensus, the ANC leadership was forced to fall into line, complying with the rules and protocols of market-driven orthodoxy. Where it had once seemed to hint at the historical possibility of a radical restructuring of the prevailing economic system, the ANC moved unsteadily toward seeking solutions within prevailing institutional frameworks that involved harnessing the power of market forces to spur a more balanced distribution of economic growth.

Within the leadership circles of the tripartite alliance, there was a noticeable paradigm shift in socio-economic discourse and policy discussions which distinguished a more accommodating set of assumptions, experiences and propositions from that of earlier more uncompromising ones. While the Congress movement was composed of a mixed bag of political tendencies, its 'economic brain trust was filled with market-inclined economists and businessmen', as one commentator put it, with some exaggeration. 'Its orientation is strongly toward the small but influential black middle class.'[47] Ironically, the radical-sounding slogan 'from resistance to reconstruction' provided the controlling metaphor for moderating voices seeking a *modus vivendi* with the established white oligarchy. At a time when neither capital nor labour were sufficiently powerful to secure the realization of their own interests, 'reconstruction' entailed some form of class cooperation in order to implement a programme of economic recovery. For some ANC radicals and trade-union militants, the direction of ANC economic thinking seemed to suggest that the leadership had reneged on its prior commitments to nationalization, reversed its policy positions on employing powerful state agencies pro-actively to redress long-standing structural inequities in the allocation of land and basic services, and made notable concessions to neo-liberal monetarist prescriptions. Many grassroots political activists believed that the ideological discourse that accompanied the multi-party negotiations shifted the national debate on political and economic matters, along with the expectations of the progressive movement, in a rightward direction.

Blending Economic Recovery with Political Stability

There were visible signs that the ANC leadership had reached some sort of accommodation with the capitalist goals of rejuvenating profitability, maintaining labour peace, and improving productivity in order to ensure the global competitiveness of South African industries. Both at home and abroad, Mandela made a series of significant gestures toward big business that strongly indicated that the ANC leadership had embraced the market-governed logic of the free-enterprise system. The twin objectives of restoring business confidence and attracting foreign investment seemed to swamp all other considerations. In what one Johannesburg observer humorously called the 'Nelson and Derek Road Show', Mandela and finance minister Derek Keys travelled in September and October 1993 with a team of senior delegates from various political and business groups to Europe and North America to press their case for foreign investment. They argued with one voice that if the transition to a post-apartheid political and economic system was to succeed, it must have the enthusiastic support of overseas investors.[48]

Speaking at the United Nations on 24 September, Mandela came full circle from previous ANC policy, inviting well-wishers to turn the sanctions campaign into a platform to market South Africa as an investment destination for foreign capital, 'to lay the basis for halting the slide into socio-economic disaster in South Africa'.[49] After he made this call for an end to economic sanctions, Mandela 'expressed clear pro-business views'.[50] On 1 October, he gave the keynote address at a landmark conference in Washington on the subject of 'Institutional Investment in Post-Apartheid South Africa', where he urged the states and cities in the USA that still had laws in force forbidding them to invest in South Africa, or to deal with companies that invested in South Africa, to rescind these restrictive codes immediately.

Less than two weeks later, Mandela 'whetted the appetite of potential foreign investors' at the Confederation of British Industry with investment incentives such as the lifting of exchange controls, the promulgation of antitrust laws, the introduction of capital-protection measures, and a policy of guaranteed repatriation of profits. He unequivocally confirmed that the ANC was committed to a generally free-market economy, and he pledged that an ANC-led government would take decisive steps to 'guarantee the security of all investment against expropriation'. Mandela also sought to reassure nervous foreign investors that the ANC stood for an 'investor-friendly' policy of guaranteeing unimpeded repatriation of 'after-tax profits and the proceeds accruing to them as a result of the sale of their business activities in South Africa'. He invited investors to pay particular attention to the potential development of black-controlled businesses in South Africa.[51] In an address to South African businessmen the following month, Mandela declared that the ANC had found it necessary to abandon its long-held ideological commitment to 'nationalization' of the mines and banks, or risk losing overseas investment.[52]

According to the US-based Investor Responsibility Research Center (IRRC), the number of US companies opening offices or establishing subsidiaries in South Africa has grown steadily since mid 1991, when then President George Bush lifted the 1986 ban on new US investment there. The increased willingness of US companies to return to South Africa reflected a more relaxed political climate in the USA regarding the prospects for a healthy business environment after elections. Since Mandela's United Nations speech, the US Congress cleared the way for South Africa to begin receiving IMF loans, lifted most remaining federal restrictions on doing business in South Africa, and urged the quick removal of state and local sanctions. Within months, 121 state and local governments lifted sanctions, leaving at the time of the 26–28 April elections only 58 jurisdictions where restrictions had not yet been repealed. The Commonwealth, the OAU and the United Nations announced the lifting of trade and investment sanctions, leaving the arms embargo as the only real sanction against South Africa that remained in place.[53]

For the optimists, South Africa seemed poised on the threshold of shedding its odious pariah status and triumphantly re-entering the 'community of nations'. With more than six hundred listed stocks, the Johannesburg Stock Exchange boasted a market capitalization of $215 billion. The JSE was the largest emerging market in the world, bigger than those in Mexico, Malaysia, Taiwan, South Korea, China, and all of Eastern Europe.[54] Yet there was a decided down side to this Panglossian outlook. Despite plaintive pleas by Mandela, the hoped-for huge influx of overseas capital was not immediately forthcoming. While companies were enthusiastic about re-establishing their presence in South Africa, they were much more cautious about making equity commitments. Many multinational firms that entered the South African market decided not to invest capital directly, but instead to follow the less risky route of forming non-equity links with South African companies, such as licensing arrangements or distribution agreements. In pronounced contrast to leading companies like Eastman Kodak, Honeywell, Procter & Gamble, and Sara Lee Corporation, which were re-entering the South African market after disinvesting in the 1980s, the IRRC found that not one of the top one hundred US commercial banks reported making new loans to South Africa. In the main, overseas investors maintained a hesitant, 'wait-and-see' attitude because of deep concerns about political stability and the business climate.[55] Inside South Africa, there was a strong residual antipathy toward the IMF and the World Bank among ANC officials and supporters, 'together with general caution about new borrowing on the global marketplace'.[56] Numerous political analysts reacted with growing concern to the ANC's warm embrace of the IMF and the World Bank, issuing dire warnings that the stringent terms of international loans from these sources could tie a Gordian knot around progessive social policies.[57]

2

The Fateful Bounty
of Apartheid

South Africa's business community is either foolish, or possessed of great faith. Whichever the explanation, it is difficult to find a senior business executive who is not optimistic about the future. Considering the seismic changes occurring in the country, this is an amazing state of affairs.[1]

South Africa is currently in the midst of a deep economic and social crisis whose eventual outcome is still beyond the horizon. This perilous economic situation is the result of both the long-term structural deceleration in economic growth and a conjunctural paralysis triggered in large measure by massive capital flight, a belt-tightening debt-rescheduling programme, and the worldwide sanctions campaign.[2] Most analysts believe that the anticipated political transition toward parliamentary democracy and equality before the law will not truly succeed unless the current economic downturn can be reversed. No transition from political, military or racial dictatorship has triumphed in recent times in such rapidly deteriorating economic conditions as those South Africa faces at the present conjuncture. Independent business consultants estimate that the South African economy requires a real growth rate of at least 5 per cent per annum to sustain the political metamorphosis over the next five years. Yet according to the bleak scenario prepared by the South African Reserve Bank (SARB), the country can expect a real growth rate varying from zero to 3 per cent per annum for the same period. Realistically speaking, poor economic performance and social breakdown pose at least as great a threat to future stability as the already complicated process of negotiating a new constitutional framework.[3]

By any standards, South Africa faces an ongoing socio-economic crisis of frightening proportions. Economists generally agree that double-digit inflation, a bloated state sector, high taxes, protectionist trade barriers, a poorly educated labour force and corporate mismanagement have contributed to the overall feeble health of the economy. The visible signs of economic stagnation are everywhere. While reliable statistics are difficult to come by, it has been estimated that at least 5.5 million people, or somewhere between 40 and 46 per cent of the economically active population, are currently unemployed.[4] Seen in comparative terms, this rate is roughly equivalent to that of the Great Depression in the United States in 1929. Leading experts in the field forecast that by 1995 an estimated 7.8 million will be gainfully employed, while 7.2 million will be out of work. One striking sign of the investment crisis is the fact that, as of 1990, the formal small-business sector contributed 26 per cent towards the gross domestic product (GDP) and generated approximately 75 per cent of new jobs, while it accounted for 38 per cent of all existing employment opportunities. Around 75 per cent of South Africa's 1.4 million to 1.6 million business enterprises were small-scale operations. With just 5 per cent of the population owning 88 per cent of the wealth, South Africa exhibits perhaps the most unequal wealth distribution in the world. The majority of South Africans survive on income levels on or near the official poverty datum line, and for the first time in decades white unemployment is steadily rising. Around 84 per cent of those who live in rural areas barely exist below the so-called 'minimum living level' of R700 (US$250) a month for a family of five. It has been estimated that racial parity in social service spending would cost almost a quarter of the GDP, with education expenditures alone more than doubling current outlays. In short, to bring educational, health and housing provision for so-called African, Indian and Coloured people up to a baseline white standard would require a state investment programme of not less than R20,000 million ($8 billion) a year for ten years.[5]

The Contours of Protracted Economic Malaise

Despite the starry-eyed wishful thinking of South Africa's business class, the prospects for a miraculous reversal of economic fortunes are dim indeed. Even a quick glimpse at long-term economic trends clearly reveals that South Africa's current economic malaise is only symptomatic of a prolonged decline with deep and tangled historical roots. Inflation has exceeded 10 per cent every year since 1973, and climbed to 15 per cent at the end of the 1980s before the upward trend was reversed largely because of the strict monetarist policy of the SARB. During the 1980s, real per-capita growth averaged −1.2 per cent per year, compared with +1 per cent in the 1970s and +3 per cent in the 1960s. Except for mining, the value of the country's capital stock has actually declined. For the past decade, sluggish domestic and foreign investment in manufacturing has severely hampered competitiveness in world markets. The steady decline in fixed investment as a proportion of GDP, which in 1992 reached its lowest level in real terms since 1971, means that at present only seven in every hundred new entrants to the labour market find work in the formal sector, compared to more than seven out of ten in the boom years of 1965–70. From 1980 to 1990, employment in mining, farming and manufacturing showed no growth at all, while the labour force continued to expand at a rate of around 300,000 workers per year. With 300,000 to 400,000 new workers coming onto the job market each year during the 1990s, South Africa will need phenomenal annual economic growth rates of 6 to 7 per cent just to keep pace with the expanding labour force, let alone confront the backlog of years of accumulated unemployment. Yet in the early 1990s, South Africa experienced zero economic growth, along with a per-capita decline in real income of around 5 per cent per year.[6]

During the height of the 1984–86 township rebellion, the refusal of international banks like Chase Manhattan Bank to extend short-term credits to South Africa triggered an avalanche of corporate divestitures as multinational corporations, worried about the high-risk investment climate, rushed to sell their assets, sometimes at bargain-basement prices, to eager South African firms. The international sanctions campaign, which did not begin in earnest until 1986, exacerbated market forces already at work, especially the flight of capital that had actually begun much earlier in the mid 1970s. The impact of sanctions, which consisted of three principal measures (disinvestment, trade restrictions, and restraints on long-term credit) has remained a contentious source of much debate.[7] Nevertheless, from 1984 to 1991, capital outflows totalled almost R30,000 million ($12 billion), including about $1 billion of disinvestment by US firms. On a broader scale, from 1975 to 1989, more than half of net savings went abroad. Existing debt repayment agreements meant that South Africa faced further capital outflows of almost R20,000 million ($8 billion) until 1993. Economic experts forecast that the country would only be able to meet its onerous long-term debt obligations by new borrowing on international capital markets. Yet lending agencies like the IMF and the World Bank expressed reservations about approving loans until a stabilizing 'internal consensus' was reached.[8]

The origins and the causes of the current socio-economic crisis have been explored in greater detail elsewhere and need not detain us here.[9] Suffice it to say that the entire structure of accumulation governing the 'long boom' of economic growth during the 1950s and 1960s gradually unravelled over the subsequent two decades. The first indications of the emergent exhaustion of the 'racial Fordist' growth model appeared in tandem with the worldwide economic downturn that began in the early 1970s.[10] At the time, mainstream economists generally blamed South Africa's slowdown on a concatenation of conjunctural factors, including declining export earnings linked to the falling world price of gold, increased unit labour costs brought about by rising real wages for black workers following the 1973 strike wave, the worldwide 'oil shock', and capital flight in the aftermath of the 1976 Soweto uprising. Despite confident forecasts of a reversal of South Africa's economic fortunes, periodic upswings of growth activity proved to be both temporary and ephemeral. The failure of sustained economic recovery to materialize during the 1980s prompted analysts to reassess their earlier stress on the cyclical nature of the economic downturn and to seek instead structural and systemic explanations for lingering stagnation.[11]

Described in broad terms, the growth model that propelled capitalist expansion and development in the post-World War II period rested on three main pillars: primary extractive industries producing minerals for export; sheltered manufacturing that favoured import substitution over exports; and a racially constructed division of labour that insulated skilled white labour from competition with largely unskilled low-wage black labour. An emergent corporatist-style alliance cobbled together between large-scale business associations and the ruling National Party effectively transformed the South African economy from one largely dependent upon extractive and agricultural pursuits into one where – for the first time – industrialization predominated. Flushed with their victory in the watershed 1948 elections, the architects of apartheid established a statutory framework for racial segregation designed to regulate black labour, erected high tariff walls to protect fledgling local industries from the stiff competition of cheaper imports, and created state-owned companies to provide basic inputs – including iron and steel, energy sources, and public works related to transportation – required for industrial expansion. The rapid pace of industrialization can be indicated by some simple statistics. For example, the contribution of manufacturing to GDP climbed from 14 per cent in 1946 to 23 per cent in 1980. In contrast, the contribution of agriculture declined from 13 per cent in 1946 to 5 per cent in 1983. As a whole, the share of the primary sector in GDP declined from 31.7 per cent in 1950 to 18.4 per cent in 1984, while the share of the secondary sector increased from 14.1 per cent to 25.5 per cent over the same period.[12]

Over the past two decades, the slow yet inexorable disintegration of the 'racial Fordist' growth model produced severe cracks in the socio-economic firmament and coincided with the mounting political challenge to apartheid rule. The effects of long-term stagnation are clearly visible in the gold-mining industry, the manufacturing sector and commercial agriculture. A brief survey of the dismal economic performance in these three arenas sheds valuable light on what indeed is a complex economic crisis.

Historically speaking, the gold-mining industry has been the cornerstone of South Africa's economic well-being. Gold and other minerals have been by far and away the largest single source of foreign exchange. In 1990, minerals contributed 48 per cent of total exports, and gold alone accounted for 31 per cent.[13] Yet in recent years, the industry has experienced 'its greatest crisis since deep-level mines began'.[14] The Chamber of Mines admitted that around 40 per cent of South Africa's gold is produced at a financial loss and that profitability has deteriorated to the lowest levels in real terms since the 1960s. For decades, gold generated half of all foreign exchange in South Africa and contributed at least 20 per cent of all taxes. During the 1970s, this standard formula for economic growth faltered as shortages of skilled whites, cheap migrant labour, energy and ore put upward pressure on the working costs of production. By 1990, the contribution of gold production to export revenues had slipped to around 25 per cent, in contrast to approximately 51 per cent a decade earlier. Because of a lack of training and limited investment in new technology, South Africa's gold mines were far less productive than their counterparts in Australia and North America. Employment in the industry declined from 534,000 in 1986 to around 380,000 in 1993. The painful irony is that the industry was built on cheap labour. In 1994, labour accounted for 50 per cent of total costs, and South Africa's gold mines – which were once recognized as among the lowest-cost producers in the world – became one of the highest.[15] In all other major mining countries of the world where trade unions were active, wages for mineworkers were above those in the manufacturing sector. However, in South Africa, not only did the average wages for mineworkers not reach the level of those paid in manufacturing, but they fell considerably below the poverty datum line, or what has been called a 'modest low-level standard of living'.[16]

The growth of manufacturing provided the key stimulus for economic expansion during the postwar boom. The scale and scope of import-substituting industrialization greatly enlarged productive capacity in selected fields, but especially consumer durables. On balance, the manufacturing sector was relatively capital-intensive and relatively diversified, but it depended to a large extent upon imported intermediary products, capital equipment and semi-automatic technology. A fair share of manufacturing firms developed close ties with multinational corporations in order to secure access to up-to-date technology and, increasingly, new sources of capital. These linkages assumed the form of licensing and patent agreements, in addition to outright joint ventures.[17]

One basic feature of South African corporate relations is the high degree of concentration and centralization of capital. A small number of huge holding companies operate as giant cartels, with tentacles that extend into totally unrelated fields of economic activity. In the 1980s, approximately 45 per cent of the total capitalization of the top one hundred industrial corporations was controlled by ten of them. It was also estimated that seven companies controlled 80 per cent of the value of the R90 billion shares listed on the Johannesburg Stock Exchange (JSE). Each of the four major 'axes of capital' – Anglo American Corporation, South African National Life Assurance Company (SANLAM), Old Mutual, and the Rembrandt Group – maintained a controlling interest in major manufacturing, financial and mining activities.[18]

The rapid rise of manufacturing in the 1960s was matched by its steady decline in the 1980s. Between 1960 and 1965, for example, the average real rate of growth of manufacturing output was 10 per cent. In contrast, this figure dwindled to –1 per cent between 1980 and 1985. For the first half of the 1960s, the average annual growth of manufacturing was 7 per cent compared with –1 per cent between 1980 and 1985. In the 1980s, industrial employment experienced negligible growth overall, but, paradoxically, expanded in peripheral areas, particularly in the Bantustans where huge financial incentives and extremely low wages attracted investment in labour-intensive manufacturing enterprises.[19]

Economic recovery in the manufacturing sector is seriously hampered by a number of structural weaknesses. The particular pattern of import-substitution industrialization substantially reduced the importation of such items as consumer durables, fabricated metal products (except machinery) and food. Nevertheless, this development came at the expense of increased reliance on capital equipment, intermediate goods and advanced technologies from abroad. Another striking feature of South Africa's industrial development is that the manufacturing sector has manifestly been unable to achieve a level of genuine competitiveness on international markets. In comparison with Brazil, South Korea, or Mexico, for example, industrial (that is, non-mineral) exports are negligible, and these are by and large absorbed by captive markets within the southern African region. Finally, South Africa's highly skewed income distribution has tended to limit the development of the domestic market for low-income goods such as food, clothing, basic housing and simple manufactured articles.[20]

At present, commercial agriculture is under greater financial strains than at any time since the 1930s. White farmers, whose numbers have shrunk dramatically to around 65,000 from 130,000 two decades ago, currently face a harsher, more competitive market environment. In 1990, the contribution of agriculture to GDP slipped to an all-time low of 4.6

per cent. Farm debt reached R17 billion ($4.7 billion), a figure which translates into an interest burden equivalent to 36 per cent of net farm income.[21] The debilitating effects of accumulated debt, along with low rates of return on investment and declining terms of trade, betrayed moribund symptoms of a deeper, structural crisis of capital accumulation in agriculture. Ownership and wealth are widely skewed. The steady growth of farm size was accompanied by an even more rapid concentration of production in agriculture.[22] Six per cent of all farmers – the backbone of the industry – own over half of the farming resources in the country. Thirty per cent of all farmers provide 75 per cent of all agricultural products. One per cent of all farmers produce 16 per cent of all farming incomes. This small concentrated group of modern, up-to-date farmers is a far wealthier group than South Africa's top business executives.[23]

Beginning in the 1930s, the state administration lavished generous subsidies on marginal farmers, in part as a way of assisting 'poor whites' to survive in the countryside. Farmers benefited from cheap loans to improve agriculture, grants to conserve soil and water resources, and subsidies to boost production through price support for maize, wheat and dairy products. In the 1970s, the ruling National Party began to reverse this long-standing policy of subsidization after the Marais/DuPlessis Commission had reached the conclusion that state benevolence had actually retarded agricultural productivity by keeping poor, 'unscientific' farmers on the land.[24]

In perhaps no other sector has the 'born-again', neo-liberal attitude of de Klerk and his Cabinet had such a profound and far-reaching impact. As the National Party broke free from its traditional constituency obligations, those state supports which once offered white farmers a privileged niche in the apartheid system virtually disappeared. Key state officials under de Klerk actively pursued a market-oriented approach toward commercial agriculture, reducing state aid and producer subsidies, removing import restrictions, and deregulating state controls in areas like marketing and pricing. The prognosis is that commercial agriculture will remain a comparatively unrewarding area of investment. There is likely to be a continuing decline in the relative contribution of agriculture to the GDP, lower foreign-exchange earnings on foreign exports, a further consolidation of large farming units favouring 'agri-business' operations, and an unstemmed flow of rural work-seekers and their families into urban areas. Given agriculture's important forward and backward linkages, vital export revenue role, and highly labour-intensive character, the changes that have taken place will undoubtedly affect South Africa's overall economic well-being.[25]

Disintegrating Apartheid and the Evolving Labour Market

The great transformation of the capitalist world economy over the past several decades has strongly influenced qualitative changes in the labour market in South Africa. Both the speed and direction of these structural shifts have varied considerably from sector to sector, from industry to industry, and even within each industry. For these reasons alone, generalizations are difficult to make. Yet at the risk of oversimplification, it is possible to identify a number of broad trends which provide some indication of the future social composition of the labour force and have significant implications for working-class politics in the coming years.

Since the 1970s, the rapid pace of economic restructuring in South Africa has resulted in both increased occupational differentiation amongst black wage-earners and a profound 'deracialization' of the labour market. On balance, South Africa has experienced a proportional growth of professional, semi-professional, clerical, technical and non-manual occupations in the non-primary sectors of the economy. While white wage-earners have continued to dominate the professional, managerial and supervisory places in the technical division of labour, black (particularly so-called Coloured and Asian) wage-earners have percolated upwards in the occupational hierarchy in greater numbers than ever before. The old rigid racial division of labour, which depended upon legally codified 'job colour bars' and 'job reservation', became hopelessly blurred as black wage-earners not only mixed with whites in the areas of technical, semi-professional, non-manual, routine white-collar and skilled occupations, but in some job categories even surpassed them. Since jobs in these sectors have grown rapidly both as a share of total employment and in absolute terms, employment for all racial groups has increased within them. Coloured, Asian and African wage-earners have joined rather than displaced whites at these levels. One of the most striking shifts in the labour market has been the movement of African workers into semi-skilled and skilled jobs. With around two million African workers filling these positions by 1990, it appeared that this new skilled/semi-skilled segment has finally superseded the unskilled manual and menial non-manual African proletariat as the numerically dominant stratum of the African working class employed in the formal sector.[26]

Sketched in bold strokes, the labour market in the early 1990s was principally divided into three, virtually autonomous, sub-markets which existed side by side and rarely overlapped. At the bottom, the fast-growing secondary labour market consisted largely of unskilled jobs with high turnover, little security of employment, and poverty-level pay rates. Because it was composed of both an active army of labour and a floating reserve, this segment included perhaps 70 per cent of the entire work-force, particularly unskilled and non-unionized workers, most migrants, rural labourers, those trapped in the informal sector, and the unemployed. Places of employment tended to be small-scale operations characterised by low profits, low wages and low productivity, with severe barriers to unionization. In contrast, the independent primary market consisted of technical, professional and supervisory occupations offering long-term employment with considerable job security, well-defined career paths and relatively high pay. This segment was generally characterized by relatively high wages, high productivity and high profits, but low employment opportunities. Finally, the subordinate primary labour market included chiefly semi-skilled operatives in industrial employment. By and large, what distinguished these workers from the secondary market was that they were virtually all unionized, and therefore benefited from the employment advantages gained in collective bargaining.[27]

At the same time that large numbers of unskilled, semi-employed workers have suffered a steady decline in employment opportunities, workers who have retained their jobs, and especially unionized workers, have often gained substantially from the restructuring of employment. In the formal sector, many wage-earners have experienced an upgrading of skills, have become more secure in their employment, and have earned rising real wages. This combination of growing unemployment for some workers and more stable, skilled and better-paying jobs for others created new lines of division within the working class.[28] With the exception of the new skilled, clerical and supervisory positions, workers in the occu-pational hierarchy from semi-skilled jobs downward – coupled with those without work – suffered from chronic mass misery and socio-economic deprivation. With unemployment over 40 per cent of the active work-force, the cruel irony of the South African situation was that to have secured steady work in the formal sector amounted to a privileged status.[29]

South Africa's continuing economic slump conspired both to under-mine the marketplace bargaining power of those wage-earners with steady employment and to marginalize the working poor, the unemployed and the unemployable. As business enterprises grappled with lower profit margins, unemployment via retrenchments increased dramatically.[30] For many work-seekers, particularly the young and unskilled, the prospect of working in the formal wage sector simply evaporated. The workforce has always been characterized by a large proportion of causal labourers, that is, wage-labourers excluded from normal full-time working relationships and hence locked into precarious, part-time or temporary work, floating back and forth between formal wage employment and alternative ways of eking out daily existence. In the past, this casual labour market was synchronized with the business cycle where upturns in economic activity resulted in expanded hiring and, correlatively, downturns produced lay-offs. However, the situation that developed in the 1990s was different. Economic forecasts projecting future trends suggested that increased investment resulting in economic growth and expansion – if and when it occurs – will not be matched by increased employment opportunities for black workers. As a general rule, large-scale corporate enterprises, particularly those situated in highly competitive, up-to-date manufacturing sectors, began to revamp their business operations in accordance with the so-called 'post-Fordist' growth model, with its emphasis on advanced technology, 'participatory management' techniques, and 'flexible accumulation' strategies. These shifts in outlook went hand in hand with the slow but steady expansion of subcontracting. Put in theoretical terms, the movement toward subcontracting represented an embryonic 'informalization' of existing formal enterprises, whereby large-scale firms sought to reduce their labour costs in the face of a strong labour movement by 'putting out' work to small-scale businesses located at certain township industrial parks or 'hives'.[31] Industrial restructuring along these lines posed a serious challenge to the trade-union movement not only because the mounting numbers of subcontracted, non-permanent workers exposed new divisions within the workforce, but also because the growth of 'outwork' operations threatened the job security of union members.[32]

The whole range of life-chances – from access to housing to medical care, education and pensions – depends on employment. Those millions outside of the formal economy – in the backyards of townships, in the shack settlements ringing the cities, and in desolate huts in the barren countryside – formed the nucleus of a floating but permanent underclass. The popular organizations made little appreciable headway in organizing these marginalized 'outsiders', and the trade unions were unable to develop a workable political programme linking employed and unemployed workers. With the ranks of the unemployed swelling, the state security forces were able to find ready recruits for their clandestine 'unofficial' policing operations. Local 'warlords' pulled together partisan vigilantes from among those seeking the protection of their patronage networks, and puritanical, fundamentalist church cults competed with petty criminals, swindlers and drug peddlers for the souls and pockets of the downtrodden.[33]

The Informal Sector: 'Survival Strategy' or Incubator for Micro-Capitalism?

Finding a solution to unemployment and underemployment represents perhaps the single greatest challenge to the first post-apartheid government. Critics accuse employment pessimists, with their doomsday scenarios and bleak forecasts of continuing economic stagnation, of exaggerating the problem by ignoring the vibrant, fast-growing informal sector that is crucial to any scheme for easing the crisis of joblessness. During the 1980s, when it became abundantly clear that the formal sector was incapable of absorbing the legions of unemployed work-seekers into wage-paid employment, National Party reformers prescribed a market-driven policy of 'controlled deregulation', a bland euphemism for legalizing the informal sector, as a 'quick-fix' panacea for the social ills of poverty, instability and violence. The lifting of legal restrictions, coupled with selective state support for black-owned micro-enterprises, produced tangible results, creating new income-earning opportunities where none existed before and legitimating what had in the past operated as part of an 'informal economy' encompassing all unlicensed, unregulated income-generating activities pursued 'underground', without the official sanction of the authorities. In 1989, the Central Statistical Service estimated that there were some 304,000 full-time black informal-sector operators in South Africa, to which could be added 1.9 million part-time informal-sector entrepreneurs and 350,000 employees, accounting for more than 2.5 million people, or almost a third of the economically active black population. According to a Human Sciences Research Council study released in 1992, an estimated six out of ten unemployed South Africans were involved in informal-sector activities.[34]

Radical free-market theorists hailed the growth of the informal sector, contending that it held out the promise of a virtual economic rebirth, as aspirant entrepreneurs 'enter the game' and new employment opportunities were created for the jobless masses. South Africa's business elite also climbed onto the bandwagon, extolling the virtues of unleashing entre-preneurial instincts and issuing dark warnings against alternative routes like state-assisted jobs programmes.[35] Critics charged that the skyrocketing informal sector reflected a deeper structural crisis of worldwide proportions, and that its multilayered ranks were filled largely with people driven by desperation to gain at least a modest income rather than by some market-triggered impulse to earn profits. They suggested that the informal economy resembled a permanent 'holding tank' where much activity must be classified as 'survival' rather than 'voluntary' petty entrepreneurship, and where many self-employed would prefer instead to have a formal-sector job.[36]

A word of caution is in order here. Not only is the available statistical information notoriously suspect, but the existing conceptual frameworks are incapable of providing an adequate understanding of the complexities of casual work and household survival strategies. The concept 'informal economy' is at best a descriptive one, an inherently slippery term which is useful only if it is carefully linked to other concepts possessing greater precision, clarity and depth. In its everyday usage, the idea of 'informal economy' embraces multiple social relationships that makes concise definition and classification difficult. Its only specificity is its ambiguity, and to endow the term with analytical powers when under the most propitious circumstances it is only a suggestive social category leads invariably to much conceptual confusion.[37]

Properly understood, the informal economy refers not to a static condition with fixed boundaries, but to a dynamic process characterized by unregulated income-generating activities that vary substantially in different geographical contexts and historical circumstances.[38] Equally important, the informal economy does not only encompass the range of survival niches occupied by destitute people desperately seeking much-needed means of household subsistence, but also includes unregulated income-generating activities that result in a standard of living for some individuals that far exceeds opportunities available in wage-paid employment. Conventional dualistic models suggest that the informal sector comprises a 'disguised' second economy distinct from the visible formal sector. Yet this understanding is a gross oversimplification. The formal and informal sectors do not represent disconnected, autonomous universes, but instead are symbiotically linked. They constitute 'poles on a continuum of economic activity', with individuals engaged in both simultaneously or oscillating between the two over the course of a working lifetime as opportunity and need arise'. Many who take part in petty commerce and related activities do so as part of wider household income-pooling strategies that also include more or less regular wage incomes.[39]

Initial research into the informal economy in South Africa emerged largely in response to the recognition of the severity of structural unemployment and an awareness of the failure of influx controls to stem the tide of urban migration. The inability of city-based employers to absorb the legions of work-seekers into formalized wage labour left a void for a huge floating population, often described as marginalized, for whom there was no realistic alternative but to engage in the petty trade of goods and services on their own account as a means of survival. These early studies sought to estimate the size of the informal sector, to describe the characteristics of particular informal occupations, and to catalogue and survey the huge variety of informal-sector enterprises or households at particular geographical locations. This pioneering research provided a great deal of valuable descriptive material, and cross-sectional surveys gave the first approximations of the sheer scale of the urban informal economy in apartheid South Africa.[40]

Recent research has moved beyond relatively static cross-sectional surveys to focus on both longitudinal and 'branch-specific' studies as a means of identifying areas of constraint and opportunity for small-scale informal enterprise. These studies demonstrate that the array of un-regulated income-generating activities is remarkably heterogeneous with respect to type of behaviour, mode of organization, and degree of social acceptability. The informal economy spans the entire spectrum from retail distribution, means of transport, personal services and small-scale produc-tion, to begging, prostitution and petty crime. In organizational terms, the diversity of small-scale activities extends from backyard manufacturing 'sweat-shops', through small-scale family enterprises, workshops, market and street stalls, to proto-socialist types of collectives and cooperatives. 'Small' can be 'beautiful', but it can just as easily be anti-social, cruel and dangerous. If the pursuits of street hawkers, itinerant door-to-door sales-men, or unlicensed taxi drivers infringe upon certain existing concep-tions of legality, their customers typically do not regard such activities as socially unacceptable, illegitimate or life-threatening. In contrast, some income-generating activities, especially those closely linked with the criminal underworld and including drug-dealing, weapons-smuggling and trafficking in stolen goods, often pose serious threats of bodily harm to producers and consumers alike.[41]

All too frequently, popular accounts of South Africa's informal economy take a naively simplistic view, celebrating the initiative, energy and busi-ness acumen of rags-to-riches entrepreneurs, while ignoring the largely invisible contributions of relatives, friends and acquaintances whose dis-parate unpaid labours laid the foundation for this success. Located within this broader framework, it must be acknowledged that the informal economy 'simultaneously encompasses flexibility and exploitation, produc-tivity and abuse, aggressive entrepreneurs and defenceless workers, liber-tarianism and greed'.[42]

There is also a tendency, particularly evident in certain planning circles, to conceive of the informal economy strictly in market terms, that is, as having predominantly to do with money-making and survival in the most basic economic sense.[43] This narrow focus, however, abstracts income-generating activities from their wider cultural context, and hence ignores socio-cultural meanings attached to patterns of personal association and social interaction. In South Africa, such diverse activities as shebeen-keeping, the herbal medicine trade and gangsterism have played such a vibrant role in the formation of a distinctive township culture that to confine them within the narrow conceptual boundaries of the 'informal sector' misses their wider social significance.[44] Historically speaking, informal-sector activities in South Africa have been both a source of opportunity for economic advancement and upward mobility for some income-pooling households and individuals, and a veritable sinkhole of exploitation and degradation for others. This two-edged sword dangles precariously over the heads of all those who participate in the informal economy, with the occasional miraculous success of the 'self-made', Horatio Alger entrepreneur juxtaposed against the typical situations of bare survival, silent desperation, and ceaseless drudgery.[45]

Most activity in South Africa's informal economy is concentrated in the trade and service sectors, particularly retail clothing, footwear, food and other household items, and the provision of personalized services such as hairdressing, repair of mechanical devices, transport and house-hold chores. Unlike the case in most other 'developing' countries, South Africa's informal manufacturing sector is profoundly undeveloped. Few of the goods sold in the informal sector are produced 'informally'. Instead, whole sections of the formal manufacturing sector, especially clothing, have in the main oriented their production for sale to informal hawkers and traders. An extensive network has come into being, penetrating all corners of South Africa and stretching into neighbouring countries. Much of this informal trade takes place in the larger cities, with hawkers often travelling great distances from smaller towns in search of cheap wares. In both Durban and Johannesburg there are night-time marketplaces that cater to itinerant traders from all parts of the country and the region.[46]

The single example of the black taxi industry can enable us to grasp something of the inner logic and contradictory dynamics of the informal economy.[47] The phenomenal growth of the taxi trade, from 'a few hundred 6-seater Valiant sedans in the late 1970s to some 80,000 10- and 16-seater mini-buses in the 1990s', prompted enthusiastic free-market lobbyists to herald the new industry as 'the showcase of black capitalism', a genuine 'success story' epitomizing the enterprising spirit of black entrepreneurs who had a dream and made it into reality. Despite licensing restrictions, entrance control, and geographical limitations on economic freedom, black taximen gradually 'upstaged the moribund, state-sponsored transport sector'.[48] Under pressure from the powerful black taxi association, the government legalized the independent taxi trade in the mid 1980s and issued a 'blizzard of new permits' to meet rising demand. Banks joined informal township savings associations in extending credit to the emer-gent taxi entrepreneurs. By the end of the decade, the industry was hailed by one mainstream economist as the 'flagship of the informal sector'.[49]

But the accolades bestowed on the 'black taxi revolution' must be tempered against the unpleasant backdrop of ballooning accident rates, exorbitant fares and endemic violence, which marred the industry.[50] Over-worked and underpaid taxi operators overload their vehicles, ignore speed limits, skip safety inspections, and yield no ground to their competitors, thereby putting the lives of their passengers at grave risk. Undoubtedly, much of the intense feuding since 1987 can be attributed to hasty de-regulation and unmonitored competition. With the previous barriers to entry eliminated, overcrowding of prime routes and market saturation were inevitable. In the battle for economic survival, brutal 'taxi wars' pitting rival cartels and associations against each other erupted with in-creasing frequency, resulting in widespread destruction of property and claiming the lives of scores of innocent passengers. 'In a suffocating economy,' one journalist noted, 'the taxi business has become a cutthroat industry with its own rules and its own savage culture of enforcement.'[51]

Yet the repetitive cycles of violence which plagued the taxi industry cannot simply be reduced to capitalist competition alone. The increased reliance of rival taxi associations on armed enforcers and urban street gangs to 'guard their markets and protect their assets' acted to 'inculcate a culture of violence by promoting the belief that the economic and politi-cal problems of taximen were best solved by terrorizing their competitors into submission'.[52]

The Chaos of 'Orderly Urbanization'

For decades, the Sisyphean efforts of state functionaries to stem the tide of African urbanization were tantamount to wishing water would run uphill. Since they defined the terms through which access for black South Africans to jobs and housing in the 'white' urban areas was authorized, the pass laws functioned as the linchpin of the entire system of influx control. Yet over the long haul, the entire cumbersome bureaucratic machinery was no match for the harsh economic realities that pushed impoverished and jobless African families out of the rural areas and pulled them toward South Africa's cities and towns.[53] What evolved in South Africa over the course of the apartheid era was a complicated process of urbanization that displaced black people over a wide geographical area, linked to white municipalities and places of employment via long-distance commuting. This process of displaced urbanization came into existence not so much as the direct result of planned state policy, but as the unanticipated consequence of the countless forces pushing and pulling black people in seemingly contradictory directions. On balance, 'displaced urbanization' consisted of three elements: first, the relative concentration of population in the homelands since the 1960s; second, the diversion of state expenditure on housing to the homelands, albeit on a grossly inadequate scale, and coupled with a deliberate freeze on black housing in 'white' urban areas; and third, the widespread commuterization of the black labour force.[54] As Hindson has shown, the primary aim of influx control was simultaneously to enforce temporary migration and promote the stabilization of a permanent urban African proletariat. The central contradiction in this whole system of segregating and regulating the movement of urbanizing Africans arose out of the unattainable objective of trying to secure a suitable supply of labour while minimizing the presence of Africans in the metropolitan areas. The formal operations of influx control were inherently unstable, and state planners were continually inventing new ad hoc contrivances, like efflux control, forced removals, 'black spot' eradication, and slum clearances, to keep the entire edifice from crumbling.[55] What was paradoxical was that this peculiar concoction of apartheid policies regulating the movement and settlement of black people ironically provided the main impetus towards urbanization. In the final analysis, state officials were forced to abandon their efforts to prevent urbanization, and instead tried to define its limits, to keep it from uncontrollably 'swamping' the established 'white' areas, and to guide the inevitable influx of black people towards new, sprawling black townships and squatter settlements on the peripheries of cities.[56]

The repeal of the pass laws in 1986 marked the demise of the formal operation of influx controls and, along with the legalization of freehold tenure for township housing, signalled the beginning of a prefigurative post-apartheid state policy which the technocrats called 'orderly urbanization'. By accepting in principle that African urbanization was both inevitable and economically desirable, state planners shifted emphasis from centrally managed, racially defined statutory means of curbing the influx of black people into the urban areas, to informal mechanisms for regulating the movement and settlement of work-seekers within specific regions.[57] This 'orderly urbanization' policy depended upon recognizing the artificiality of the homeland boundaries and called instead for the development of metropolitan-centred planning regions where private enterprise and the free play of market forces would assume the main roles in shaping the economic geography of South Africa.[58]

With the unveiling of Regional Services Councils (RSCs) in 1987, the National Party hoped to 'deracialize' and, consequently, depoliticize civil administration at the local level. The RSCs represented a flexible alternative to the rigidly demarcated, racially defined system of local government that prevailed under apartheid. By absorbing all local government units – white municipalities together with black townships – in a particular metropolitan region into a single operative body, state officials granted administrative recognition to the de facto reality of distinct regional economies.[59] The most significant feature of these innovations in civil administration was the way in which this bureaucratic reorganization created yet another buffer between central state authority and local initiative. By delegating responsibility for the management of metropolitan areas, state officials in Pretoria effectively immunized themselves from unwanted criticism of local policies and practices. One of the peculiar anomalies that characterized the declining years of apartheid rule was the steady expansion of sprawling squatter settlements nominally located within the jurisdictional boundaries of the homelands but in close proximity to 'white' metropoles and towns.[60] In earlier years, state officials washed their hands of the situation, arguing that these 'dumping grounds' were the sole responsibility of homelands governments. With the advent of administrative reorganization, they reversed earlier policy by redefining geographical boundaries, using the RSCs 'to extend local government outward in preference to black people moving inwards'.[61]

As the central state administration gradually withdrew direct fiscal support for local government, the RSCs became increasingly dependent upon raising their own revenue from the regional tax base. The overarching logic behind the RSC policy was to create intermediate management bodies with primary responsibility for providing essential services to local administrative units. The RSCs acted as conduits for the redistribution of various resources within a wider metropolitan area, 'from the wealthier to the poorer sections, or, to put it more simply, from the white municipalities to the Black Local Authorities [BLAs]'. In this way, the state administration hoped to avoid the disastrous mistakes of the early 1980s, when Pretoria made the impoverished townships solely responsible for their own 'up-grading, and thereby invit[ed] the inevitable popular backlash'.[62] The conjoined policies of 'deregulation' and 'privatization' went hand in hand with the changing face of local government. Deregulation enabled state agencies, and particularly the RSCs, to identify and release more land for black urban development. In the main, this policy meant the allocation of more land to enlarge the spatial boundaries of existing townships, primarily to encourage the development of 'up-scale', elite suburbs catering to middle-income black homeowners, and to regulate the growth of informal shack settlements that mushroomed out of control on the fringes.

Under the terms of new 'privatization' guidelines, state agencies put existing government-owned housing stock up for sale at subsidized rates to those who were renting. By leaving the provision of housing to the private sector, the financial burden of home improvements became the sole responsibility of individual homeowners. The aim of these 'privatization' measures was to relieve state housing authorities of their landlord role and hence depoliticize the housing issue by eliminating the grounds for rent boycotts. By allowing the provision of housing to be determined by market forces alone, 'orderly urbanization' policies exacerbated existing cleavages between the 'haves' and the 'have-nots'. Chronic poverty and joblessness meant that formal home ownership remained an impossible dream for most black people. By one estimate, only one in ten black families earned enough to afford a typical 'matchbox' house costing a minimum of $13,000.[63] Those unable to purchase conventional housing at market rates, or self-built 'starter' houses offered by the South African Housing Trust, or the Urban Foundation's FHA Homes, were literally forced to 'house themselves' on minimally serviced sites on the fringes of the urban areas.[64]

The incorporation of the townships into the RSCs undermined the apartheid-era configuration of urban space that maintained a sharp divide between white municipalities and black townships. The establishment of a metropolitan foundation for urban financing permitted the revitalized black local authorities to tap into external sources of funds in order to pay for much-needed upgrading projects. This transfer of financial resources from white municipal areas to black townships marked a dramatic reversal of apartheid urban policies, which rested on the premiss that the townships ought to operate as financially self-sufficient units. What paralleled this fiscal restructuring was a new emphasis on the privatized provision of services, whereby electricity, water, garbage collection and sewerage disposal were extended to township residents on a individual cost-recovery basis.[65]

The National Party pushed ahead, on a grand scale, with plans to sell the assets of many of the giant state-owned monopolies. On a smaller scale, the Office of Privatization introduced investment opportunities in the provision of local government services, with the aim of stimulating small-scale black entrepreneurship and creating a public culture favouring free enterprise.[66] Likewise, the Small Business Development Corporation (SBDC), a joint state–private sector agency, became increasingly involved in facilitating the upgrading, or 'formalization', of existing backyard manufacturers. This effort gradually expanded from its initial emphasis on the creation of a far-flung series of township 'industrial parks' to include infrastructural assistance and a wide range of support services designed to incubate small-scale enterprises and to catalyse black entrepreneurs.[67]

Prefiguring Post-Apartheid South Africa

The eclipse of apartheid has reshaped South Africa's urban landscape, and nowhere are these unsettling trends more in evidence that in the Pretoria, Witwatersrand and Vereeniging (PWV) region. The PWV stretches from Vereeniging/Vanderbijlpark in the south to Pretoria and Winterveld in the north; from Springs/Brakpan in the east to Randfontein/Krugersdorp in the west. It is estimated that by the year 2000 this densely settled, interconnected mega-metropolis will be home to approximately 12.3 million people, or one quarter the total population of South Africa. According to a 1991 Urban Foundation study, an estimated 2.5 million people in the PWV are sheltered in informal housing (excluding the almost half million languishing in the Winterveldt squatter settlements), at least 25 to 40 per cent of black people are unemployed, and around 70 per cent live without access to electricity or running water. Johannesburg proper lies at the geographical centre of this sprawling conurbation. It is a hub for a far-flung transportation network that spreads throughout southern Africa, and it is the main information-technologies and tele-communications gateway linking South Africa's cartelized business con-glomerates with all points on the compass. Johannesburg has long acted as a magnet for commercial transactions, banking and finance, and special-ized producer services. Transnational corporations seeking to penetrate African markets have located their headquarters there. All in all, Johannes-burg exhibits the ideal-typical features, albeit in truncated and abbreviated form, that characterize what Saskia Sassen calls the 'global city'. While it surely cannot be classified in the same rarefied league as New York, London and Tokyo, it qualifies as a second-tier embodiment of the world's leading financial centres. Over 200,000 people work in the central business district alone; more than a million enter its boundaries every day. Within this complex and heterogeneous urban space, population densities vary considerably, with around 250 people per square hectare in Soweto, over 300 in Alexandra, and between 30 and 60 in the rest of Johannesburg.[68]

While it certainly represents an exaggerated example, Johannesburg epitomizes the torturous metamorphosis of the classical apartheid city. A quick glance at the social geography of the city and its outskirts provides a striking portrait of the disintegration of the familiar patterns of social order, and offers perhaps a prescient foretaste of what is to come in the rest of urban South Africa. The spatial configuration of the greater Johannesburg metropolitan area reflects the collapse of the apartheid-era organization of urban space. Like all other major cities in South Africa, Johannesburg is no longer an insulated and carefully policed 'white oasis', a well-protected fortress of white middle-class privilege surrounded by black working-class 'feeder' townships. What is often overlooked is that it was not just the relentless frontal assault of mobilized mass protest on the citadels of white power that toppled apartheid, but a largely undetected, molecular process of gradual decay that eroded formalized segregation from inside. Because of acute housing shortages in the outlying townships and the inordinate amount of time required to travel back and forth, larger and larger numbers of black people had over the years sought accommodation closer to the city centre. In areas historically reserved for exclusive white ownership and residence, the steady accretion of illicit living arrangements, or 'backyard occupancy', transformed the inner ring of quasi-residential neighbourhoods into so-called 'grey areas'. This process took root and flowered in inner-city neighbourhoods well before formal residential segregation was legally abandoned, and confirmed for all intents and purposes that the police and the courts were unable to enforce existing influx control regulations. Until the abolition of the Group Areas Act, most of these urban residents were not lawful tenants. While the authorities made relatively few arrests, greedy entrepreneurs nevertheless took full advantage of the situation, and overcrowding of available housing units and 'rack-renting' became commonplace.[69]

What paralleled this pattern of illegal occupancy and overcongestion of residential space was the steady increase in the number and density of emerging slum areas. In places like Joubert Park, Dornfontein, Hillbrow, Berea, and the North East Central Business District, economic decline and infrastructural deterioration of the built environment occurred at an alarming pace. Despite vociferous denials, bank 'red-lining' reinforced a pernicious pattern of disinvestment in inner-city neighbourhoods, and the resulting physical decay and social blight accelerated 'white flight' to the relative safety and comfort of the outlying suburbs. The influx of perhaps two million illegal immigrants, especially destitute refugees from war-ravaged Mozambique, work-seekers from drought-torn Zimbabwe, and petty traders from Zaire, Kenya, Swaziland and elsewhere, added a new dimension to the urban mixture. These clandestine newcomers preferred the anonymity of inner-city areas like Hillbrow and Berea to established but distant townships like Soweto, Katlehong and Daveyton. These unskilled itinerants who swelled the ranks of the informal sector formed the cutting edge of a wider African diaspora that included skilled craftsworkers, European-trained professionals, and businessmen seeking financial security at the southern tip of the vast continent.[70]

Always and everywhere, petty theft, house break-ins and muggings are permanent features of those urban landscapes where rich and poor come face to face. But it was the exponential increase in anti-social crimes like armed robbery, car hijackings at gunpoint and murder that transformed pockets of Johannesburg into what were regarded by some as 'no-go' danger zones. At a distance, the city skyline is a truly magnificent sight, rising as it does so abruptly out of the veldt. Because of its peculiar place in world history as 'egoli', or the 'place of gold', Johannesburg can boast a distinguished inventory of architecturally magnificent historic buildings. Despite these visible symbols of past splendour, however, the city centre is no longer the exclusive preserve of 'white Johannesburg'. High-rise office complexes, clustered in the downtown business district, rise majestically above the crowded streets. They stand like hermetically sealed fortresses replete with guarded underground parking garages, and tethered to outlying residential suburbs by ribbons of freeways that offer a convenient arterial escape from the seething urban caldron. The social relations of the built environment coalesce largely around an almost paranoid security consciousness. For the white middle classes, personal safety seems to be a paramount preoccupation, but it must also be understood as the most evident expression of a deeper collective fixation. The cruel irony is that, while legalized apartheid has all but disappeared, the ideology of racial separation lives on in countless conscious and subconscious ways. Lifelong indoctrination ensures that white people are largely inculcated with a value orientation which puts a premium on social isolation along racial lines. This way of thinking reinforces 'racialized' patterns of work, recreation, residence and consumption.[71]

Spatial dispersion has been white South Africa's collective response to 'deracialization'. A vibrant, polyglot street life in bohemian pockets like Yeoville attests to the actual possibility of imagined historical alternatives, but these places are the exception to the rule. The exodus of white residents from the inner-city commercial areas like Hillbrow and Joubert Park is virtually complete. While there are countervailing currents, the silent march of the white professional-managerial strata has also begun in earnest from the outer ring of residential neighbourhoods like Yeoville, Lorenzville and Braamfontein. The great divide is Empire Road and Louis Botha Drive, Johannesburg's modern Rubicon. To cross this northern line means to enter into a different world of wide, tree-lined boulevards, spacious homes surrounded by high fences topped with shards of broken glass or razor wire, policed by vicious dogs and locked seemingly as tight as Fort Knox. Private security guards patrol the quiet, leafy neighbourhoods, on the lookout for suspicious-looking black males without ostensible purpose for being there. Casual conversation in the northern suburbs invariably leads to talk of fears of a possible racially inclined bloodbath. Personal safety, financial security and alleged declining community standards form a trilogy of palpable concern, repeated mantra-like as if these formed the core of a well-rehearsed script. These residential enclaves provide spatial and social insulation from the new South Africa. The proliferation of huge, cocoon-like shopping malls, like the surreal paeans to bourgeois conspicuous consumption in Rosebank and Rivonia, ensure that most suburbanized white 'Joburgers' never have to set foot downtown.

New circuits of capital accumulation and financial speculation have pulled and pushed the centre of economic gravity away from the metropolitan centre. Businesses, large and small, have abandoned the old downtown heartland concentrated around Commissioner and Market streets, and have relocated to outlying satellite towns like Sandton, Kempton Park, and Randburg to the north; Boksburg, Springs and Benoni to the east; Germison and Alberton to the south; and Roodepoort, Randfontein and Krugersdorp to the west. The relocation of corporate headquarters, business services and retail outlets to high-rise office buildings and upscale malls in these 'edge-cities' has irrevocably transformed the spatial configuration of the urban landscape. Ten years ago, the main artery connecting Johannesburg and Pretoria passed through virtually uninhabited grassland. If current trends persist, the entire corridor will shortly resemble a compressed agglomeration of intermixed housing developments, office complexes, warehouses, and retail and service outlets.

3

On the Edge of Extinction: Black South Africa in Town and Country

You always remember your first sight of Alexandra township, it is so striking. Visitors to Johannesburg's nearest black ghetto expect to see many high-rise buildings, after being told that 350,000 people live in this small area of 1.6 square kilometres. Instead, you are immediately surprised as you enter 'Alex', dodging cows, goats, chickens, and mangy dogs that no owner would claim, all roaming the streets, scavenging in litter-pits for food. But you quickly conclude that this is not, by any means, a rural scene, as shack huts of plywood, cardboard and zinc roofing stretch before your eyes like a muddy sea, occasionally punctuated by old 1920s-era brick houses. Alex is unlike any other urban area in the world. No South African township is so well-developed politically nor so densely populated, so devastated by unemployment and economic despair, and socially tense.

Mzwanele Mayekiso, President, Alexandra Civic Organization[1]

Virtually all cities outside the core zones of the world economy are starkly polarized along two dimensions. On the one side, there are the formal urban areas established and regulated in terms of conventional town-planning procedures. On the other, there are the shantytowns that, by and large, grow and develop without official sanction. These areas, commonly known as informal settlements, provide shelter for a growing proportion of the world's expanding urban population.[2] Makeshift housing is an inescapable fact of life, and the observation that unregulated and unauthorized informal settlements 'can no longer be regarded as unfortunate appendages to the real city, [because] in many parts of the world, they *are* the city', attests to their permanent place in the global urban landscape.[3]

What is happening in South Africa is no exception to this general rule. Despite the manifest shortfall of available housing units in the established townships, the steady stream of impoverished work-seekers flooding to the urban areas has continued unabated. This steady influx of newcomers exceeds the carrying capacity of the already overcrowded townships, and the excess spills over into the informal settlements that have sprouted largely on vacant land within the borders of existing townships or in the buffer zones between townships and industrial districts. The Independent Development Trust estimated that one in six South Africans, or about 7.8 million people out of a total population of close to 40 million, live in informal housing – a quaint euphemism for what, upon closer inspection, turns out to conceal a wide variety of different living arrangements.[4]

In general terms, informal housing can be broadly defined as 'shelter constructed outside of the formal housing delivery mechanisms'.[5] The Urban Foundation distinguishes two general categories. First, there is 'spontaneous' informal housing that falls entirely outside the framework of conventional town planning. This category includes 'backyard shacks' and 'outbuildings' erected on existing sites within established townships, along with 'free-standing' informal settlements built on vacant land, such as Crossroads outside Cape Town. Second, there is informal housing constructed within the framework of officially sanctioned 'site-and-service' schemes, such as Orange Farm, Ivory Park, and parts of Khayelitsha. There are an estimated one hundred such schemes in South Africa incorporating a population of approximately one million.[6]

By far and away the largest concentrations of informal settlements are located within the PWV and the Durban Functional Region, where according to an 1991 Urban Foundation report 2.2 million and 1.8 million people, respectively, lived in makeshift accommodation.[7] According to the Human Sciences Research Council, Cape Town is the fastest growing metropolitan region in the country, with about 7,000 new arrivals each week. Most migrants find shelter in informal housing.[8] All in all, more than 250,000 people are crammed into approximately 60,000 shacks scattered in clusters of varying size around the city. If backyard shacks are taken into account, the number living in informal housing easily exceeds 300,000 people. The bulk of the estimated half million residents of Khayelitsha, the prime 'dumping ground' for the floating population of the Cape Town metropolitan region, live in jerry-built housing. New settlers at a rate of about 2,000 per month arrived there virtually penniless and homeless, swelling the ranks of those who had no alternative but to seek shelter by whatever means they could.[9]

With housing construction in the established townships at a virtual standstill and a huge backlog of more than 1.2 million units in urban areas alone, the numbers of people crowding into informal settlements on the urban periphery or constructing their own makeshift shelter on vacant land within local township boundaries grew at an alarming pace.[10] A few examples should suffice. According to official sources, there were 245,000 people living in informal housing at Inanda near Durban, 29,000 at St Wendolins near Pinetown, 104,000 squatters at Mookgophong at Naboomspruit in the Northern Transvaal, 42,000 at Ikageng near Potchefstroom, 55,000 at KwaDela near Davel, 47,500 at Tembisa near Kempton Park, 60,000 at Uitenhage, 69,000 at Reeston/Gompo near East London, and 30,000 at Crossroads near Cape Town.[11] About half the population around Port Elizabeth, some 300,000 people, live in shacks. These settlements ossified into rudimentary towns, like the one called Soweto-by-the-Sea, where an estimated 130,000 people coexist, nearly 300 to an acre. Within this foetid, teeming slum of recycled wood, plastic, and corrugated iron, each communal water tap is shared by at least 600 people.[12] All in all, the proportion of African people living in informal housing on the PWV is fairly typical at 43 per cent. In the Durban metropolitan area, the Western Cape and Port Elizabeth the proportion of the African population living under informal conditions is higher at 69 per cent, 58 per cent, and 55 per cent, respectively.[13]

Counterfeit Urbanism and the Township Wasteland

The townships represent a grotesque expression of counterfeit urbanism. Devoid of all the ostensible benefits normally derived from being part of a metropolitan area, they accumulated all the disadvantages: overcrowding without standard amenities like electricity, running water, sewerage and garbage disposal; densely packed settlement patterns with few paved roads; high crime without proper policing; relative proximity to the cities without adequate transportation. Despite the much-ballyhooed infrastructural upgrading schemes and state subsidies to nourish small business opportunities, the socio-economic situation in the urban townships deteriorated badly during the 1980s. In 1991, only 7 of the 271 townships outside the Homelands were fully supplied with electricity, and these were all located in the Cape. Around 38 per cent of the housing units on the West Rand and 48 per cent on the East Rand were not electrified.[14] It has been estimated that the average four-roomed 'matchbox' house accommodated thirteen people, and in some townships on the East Rand the average occupancy rate per dwelling was as high as twenty-four people. The numbers of homeless people who live in illegal tin shacks and brick outbuildings constructed in the backyards of formal houses within existing townships jumped dramatically to over 2 million. By the 1990s, nearly 60 per cent of the stands in African townships on the Witwatersrand accommodated backyard dwellings, and these housed around 44 per cent of the urban African population. Ironically, these backyard shacks have become a valuable source of income for township homeowners, transforming exploited people into micro-exploiters in their own right, and further exacerbating tensions between the 'haves' and 'have-nots'.[15]

Contrasting images

Alexandra, Johannesburg's most notorious urban slum, nestles cheek-by-jowl with Sandton, a posh satellite city at the northeast corner of the metropolitan fringe. 'Alex', in the popular argot of township residents, furnishes unskilled workers for surrounding factories, and the maids, cooks, cleaners, nannies, gardeners, street sweepers, and thieves for the northern suburbs a stone's throw away. On several occasions, apartheid planners targeted Alexandra for demolition, but each time its residents escaped the angry wrath of the bulldozers. Long a hotbed of radicalism, 'Alex' gained worldwide recognition for a string of highly successful bus boycotts in the 1950s, which preceded the similar actions in Montgomery, Alabama, that catapulted Martin Luther King to international acclaim.

The best place from which to comprehend visually the true meaning of Alexandra is from its eastern rim, along the hilltop overlooking the valley below. This densely packed slum symbolizes the dark underside of urban living: between 250,000 and 350,00 people are packed like sardines into less than 5 square kilometres of stench and squalor. A few main paved arteries crisscross the township, dividing it into distinct zones, but the lasting impression is of a patchwork pattern of dilapidated houses, backyard hovels, one-room shops, and tiny 'spazas' (street-vendor kiosks). Jerry-built shanties perch precariously along the erstwhile banks of the dirty meandering creek which bisects the very heart of the teeming slum. To navigate its narrow streets is a logistical nightmare, as all manner of gasoline-driven vehicles compete for space with ambulatory pedestrians. With the approach of darkness, Alexandra is suddenly transformed into a blended mass of monotonous shapes and muted hues, as the acrid smoke of thousands of coal-fuelled fires creates a noxious blue-grey haze that settles with a darkened pall over stationary and moving objects alike, creating a surreal and haunting atmosphere of doom and foreboding.

The multistorey hostel complexes stand out against the skyline as the most prominent fixtures of the built environment. The feared Madala hostel complex, looming large on the western edge near the crest of the ridge which gives Alexandra its peculiar bowl-like shape, was transformed into a fortified citadel of Inkatha reaction, inhabited by IFP irregulars, gangsters and trained snipers. The area around it, nicknamed 'Beirut', became the centre of ongoing violence. Families living in the immediate vicinity of the hostel complex were driven away; and block after block of houses were razed to the ground to give way to a virtual 'no-man's land'.

The dusty 'mean streets' and siege mentality of Alexandra contrast sharply with the spacious thoroughfares and fancy shopping malls – veritable 'consumer palaces' – that grace the nearby plush northern suburbs just beyond the horizon. Sandton, the Beverly Hills of white South Africa, is an affluent suburb with quiet, tree-lined streets and upscale palatial malls catering to an upper-middle-class white clientele. Yet even in a decaying urban wasteland like Alexandra, it is possible to detect the embryonic signs of class divisions. The thin ribbon of new, garish multi-storey homes, replete with high fences and vicious guard dogs, that sit uncomfortably on its eastern edge overlooking the inhospitable valley below, attest to the presence of a small middle-class crust of *nouveaux riches*.[16]

The Township Miasma

Over the course of the 1984–86 popular rebellion, the entire web of administrative and repressive controls, including town councils and policing mechanisms, in close to half the townships in South Africa was swept away.[17] During the insurrection, militant youths, called 'comrades' or *amaqabane*, had surged to the forefront of the popular struggle, squaring off in violent confrontations against the security forces and assisting civic associations in carrying out political campaigns, like stayaways and consumer boycotts, which they sometimes monitored in particularly autocratic and harsh ways. At discrete times and places, as Mzwanele Mayekiso eloquently demonstrates, popular organizations like the Alexandra Action Committee were able to mobilize, organize and establish proper organs of 'people's power'.[18] Yet it was often the case that a tangled skein of 'unruly elements' became the main 'foot soldiers' in the township war zones. These were the ones 'who carried the twin leitmotifs of ANC strategy at the time': 'people's war' and 'make the townships ungovernable'. In the rush to destroy the local organs of state power, the popular movement 'often turned a blind eye to the excesses of these youthful militants'. Political activists frequently romanticized and idolized well-meaning yet reckless militancy as the work of the 'young lions'.[19] Yet the 'comrades' often lacked the necessary political experience and, as Jochelson contends, were 'relatively uninitiated in principles of political organization and disciplined political behavior. If their conduct was roughshod, it was often aimed at the "right" targets.'[20]

Despite their sacrifices, township activists were unable to fill the political vacuum by replacing the odious government apparatuses with popular organs of 'people's power'. In particular, the political movement did not have the capacity to translate the resulting political stalemate into a new, crystallized balance of forces resembling 'dual power'. In time, state-organized repression took its toll. Partially thrown off balance, the political opposition was forced into what amounted to a tactical retreat, and was only able to regroup in a semi-legal, quasi-clandestine existence after years of painstaking effort.[21]

In the long and painful aftermath of the popular insurrection, townships across the length and breadth of South Africa became trapped in a vicious cycle of irredeemable debt and nearly continuous protest. The unanticipated consequence was often a deteriorating quality of life, increased hardship and misery, and a climate of fear and despair.[22] In the typical scenario, township residents, angered over any number of grievances, collectively refused to pay rents and service charges, draining the treasuries of the black local authorities and plunging them hopelessly into bankruptcy. In the Transvaal alone, rent and service boycotts were under way in fifty-two out of the eighty-two black local authorities in the early 1990s. Neither the enticement of negotiations nor the threat of 'switch-offs' of services effectively worked to bring an end to the protests that seemed to sputter along on their own momentum.[23] Some white municipalities, especially in places where the Conservative Party controlled local government, were particularly intransigent in their refusal to negotiate a *modus vivendi* with township residents. In response, civic associations often launched consumer boycotts of local white-owned businesses in the hope of pressuring local authorities to restore services.[24] In several well-publicized cases, notably Alexandra, the Vaal Triangle, Soweto, Kimberley, Benoni and Atteridgeville, civic associations signed pathbreaking accords with local authorities where they agreed to suspend long-standing rent and 'service charge' boycotts in exchange for the restoration of services and cancellation of huge accumulated debts. However, the resulting political standoff in countless townships across the country meant that normal operations of local government ground to a virtual halt.[25]

Gangsterism and factional violence

In a tragic sense, the popular movement reaped what it had sowed. The bittersweet legacy of years of political upheaval produced what some called a 'lost generation' stranded in a social limbo caused by the social disintegration of black communities.[26] Cut loose from their ideological moorings, some youthful militants drifted toward a precarious existence on the margins of politics. To the extent that the experienced political leadership lost the capacity to instil discipline into the swelled ranks of the 'comrades', the distinction between political activism and indiscriminate thuggery sometimes became blurred. The degeneration of this self-styled political vanguardism into the more mundane pursuit of self-aggrandizement prompted activists on the ground to coin the term *comtsotsis* as a way of describing the unseemly mixture of former 'comrades' who turned to gangsterism and common crime. In scores of strife-torn townships, organized gangs of unemployed youths relied on intimidation and harassment to enforce a political agenda, often waging violent campaigns against their political rivals that transformed whole communities into warring camps. The security forces were undoubtedly quick to exploit these differences by infiltrating *agents provocateurs* into the ranks of rival groups in order to foment factional violence; but political analysts also blamed a growing 'culture of intolerance' for internecine bloodletting between liberation organizations.[27]

The heavy-handed behaviour of the notorious Mandela Football Club, Winnie Mandela's team of personal bodyguards in Soweto, perhaps best epitomized the grave danger that overlooking and even condoning questionable actions in the name of the 'freedom struggle' could easily degenerate into petty gangsterism.[28] In places like Shatale in Lebowa, Komga in the Eastern Cape, and elsewhere, *comtsotsis* terrorized residents and waged a violent war against ANC activists who sought to provide direction and discipline. In Khutsong township near Carletonville, a local gang known as the 'amaZim-Zims' collaborated with the SAP in a bitter 'turf war' against a rival ANC breakaway group called the 'Gadaffis'.[29] In several townships, ANC-aligned 'comrades' fought pitched battles with AZAPO and PAC loyalists. In Umlazi outside Durban, sporadic fighting continued for more than a year between ANC-aligned 'comrades' and members of a local gang known as 'Kaptenaars'. Like the notorious 'Amasinyora' gang which terrorized residents in nearby KwaMashu, the 'Kaptenaars' were originally 'comrades' who belonged to UDF structures, but broke away after rejecting the UDF's code of conduct.[30] In Sebokeng, former Congress-aligned 'comrades' known as the 'Five Star Gang' carried out the worst mass slaying in South African history, coldbloodedly killing at least forty-five people at a funeral vigil for an ANC member in January 1991.[31]

Accompanying this politically motivated factional violence was a dramatic escalation of gangsterism and organized crime pure and simple. Criminal gangs were certainly not recent phenomena in South Africa's townships.[32] For example, even before the outbreak of popular unrest in the mid 1980s, there were around 278 organized gangs operating on the Cape Flats, the sprawling zone of working-class ghettos in Cape Town.[33] Criminal leagues like the Ama-Adderley gang in Guguletu near Cape Town, along with the Gigolos, Corner Boys, and Young Americans on the Cape Flats long worked the underside of private enterprise, dealing in stolen cars and other disposable merchandise, drugs, and liquor.[34]

In the wake of the township rebellion, the destabilization of family life, the decomposition of the education system, declining expectations of finding wage-paying employment, the breakdown of informal networks of control and order, and the compulsion to escape from overcrowded and impoverished homes all fed directly into the growth of 'a violent and criminal youth culture'. The conjoined processes of marginalization and social deprivation went hand in hand with multiplication of youth gangs.[35] The insouciant attitude of the police with respect to crime prevention provided hooligans with wide room for manoeuvre. In Soweto, the notorious 'Jackrollers' cruised the township streets in search of women, whom they abducted in broad daylight and whisked away to places where they were gang-raped. In Maokeng township near Kroonstad, the feared 'Three Million Gang' terrorized local residents for many months before township youths formed self-defence groups to repel their attacks. Repeated clashes between the gangsters and township residents had left scores of innocent people dead.[36]

Lawlessness, crime and the vanishing police

The years of political turmoil, the high rates of permanent unemployment, growing despair and hopelessness, and school closings created fertile ground for a growing anarchic climate in which lawlessness flourished. Common crime skyrocketed, and by the late 1980s had reached all-time record levels. In 1990, serious crime rose by a record 8.5 per cent, the highest annual increase in a decade, and probably the highest single-year increase in South African history. Over fifteen thousand persons were murdered, a per-capita rate that surpassed US figures by an astonishing five times.[37] The Greater Cape Town area was bequeathed the dubious distinction of 'crime capital of the world'.[38] According to estimates of the Human Sciences Research Council, in South Africa in 1990 a serious assault was committed every 4 minutes, a car hijacking every 9; a break-in every 3; a rape every 26, and a murder every 45 minutes.[39] In Soweto alone on a 'normal' weekend, especially at the end of the month, an average of 9 murders, 19 rapes and 43 robberies take place.[40]

The ghastly massacres that attracted international attention were only larger-scale examples of what had become routine occurrences in South Africa. Well-armed gangs raiding homes, or attacking commuters in trains and taxis, transformed the townships into dangerous places, especially at dusk – the 'killing hour'. The grisly spectacle of unrelenting violence was built on a surplus of weapons. In 1990, 1.1 million South Africans had permits for 2.7 million firearms. Criminals were also heavily armed. More than 7,700 firearms were reported stolen from their white owners in

1990 alone, and security officials estimated that there were at least 30,000 unlicensed firearms illegally in the possession of criminals and others.[41] AK-47 semi-automatic rifles were easily procured in the townships, the spillover of guerrilla wars in Mozambique, Angola and elsewhere. Well-organized gunrunners had little difficulty smuggling these weapons into South Africa from neighbouring countries.[42] Criminal syndicates in Mozambique purchased these weapons for R50 (US$15) each and sold them in Natal and the Witwatersrand for between R1,000 ($300) and R2,000 ($600) each.[43] High-powered assault rifles of this sort became the weapon of choice in ordinary robberies. Put in comparative perspective, in virtually any week during 1991 and 1992, the township death toll from violence equalled that of the Los Angeles riots.[44]

The rising tide of political violence and lawlessness created such a disorderly situation that the security forces, disenchanted with reform and accused by uncooperative residents of sponsoring destabilization in the townships anyway, were at a loss as how to respond. The numerical strength of the SAP, of which 60 per cent was black, climbed steadily to around 110,000 members in 1992. Yet the police force, which was stretched so thin that it was unable to cope with the broad upsurge in common crime, limited its large-scale actions to high-profile sweeps of the downtown tourist areas, and military-style 'search-and-seizure' operations in the townships. There was mounting evidence that police officers, frustrated by rising crime and the perceived inability of the court system to convict serious criminals, resorted to summary executions of those suspected of involvement in crime rather than arresting them.[45] The SAP patrolled so infrequently in white communities that frightened residents, who lived with high walls and burglar alarms, turned with increasing frequency to hiring private security firms to guard their homes and businesses. The 'wild west' atmosphere fuelled white anxieties and contributed to a 'siege mentality'. Reactionary, ultra-right paramilitary groups exploited white fears, taking advantage of the deteriorating situation to stage dramatic displays of 'protecting' white residential areas from the alleged *swart gevaar* ('black peril').[46]

Yet black people were the most frequent victims of violent crime.[47] Faced with the apparent craven indifference of the local police in combating gang-related violence, township residents responded in a variety of ways, ranging from organized street patrols to protect their communities, to impromptu 'people's courts' which punished wrongdoers, and, in some cases, in-depth educational campaigns. On occasion, angry residents simply 'took the law into their own hands', resorting to 'witch hunts' for notorious gangsters who were subjected to 'instant justice'. In a lawless environment where normal mechanisms for preventing and punishing crime were absent, the chorus of voices calling for the creation of self-defence militia rang loud and clear.[48]

Inward authoritarianism: local strongmen and their fiefdoms

Informal settlements were intrinsically violent places, where the police, the law and the courts retained only a loose grip over the regulation of social interaction. While substantial numbers of residents of these areas owed their political allegiance to the ANC, real power was wielded by a galaxy of strongmen, or 'squatter lords', who in many instances were locked in bitter rivalries with local civic associations. These 'squatter lords' were pivotal figures who exercised power because they possessed '*de facto* control over resources', like the allocation of land, access to much-needed services, and ultimately the threat of force against dissidents and rivals. They 'collect[ed] rents and levies in exchange for protection', extending the reach of their autocratic rule by a judicious mixture of 'fear and allegiance'. Tyranny was woven into the social fabric of daily life in informal settlements, and the power relations that arose out of the pyramidal structure of clientelist networks appeared almost feudal in nature.[49]

The social origins of this contemporary 'warlordism', in all of its variations and guises, can be traced to a fundamental structural weakness inherent in the turbulent transition from authoritarian rule to parliamentary democracy. The sudden unravelling of the largely repressive mechanisms which held the apartheid system in place proceeded apace with the growing failure of embattled state officials to exercise social control through forceful or persuasive compliance with existing laws and institutions. This 'de-legitimation' of the prevailing 'rules of the game' was accompanied by the virtual collapse of law and order in the townships and informal settlements. The opening of new 'arenas of contestation' brought the state administration, grassroots political organizations, and local power-brokers onto a collision course. In places where *de facto* regimes of social control were not firmly established, local strongmen sought to occupy the social space left vacant in the wake of a retreating apartheid state administration and at a time when a genuine 'civil society' – with a single common jurisdiction under a shared status of citizenship and a legal system that applied equally to all – existed only in the imagination.[50]

Strongmen 'ply their trade in the mean streets of [the informal settlements] and their style of operation typically reflects the precarious nature of the dangerous and sometimes desperate measures necessary for survival in these environments'. They constructed their domains among the socially deprived and marginalized groups, largely the unemployed or casually employed urban underclass, along with those people desperately clinging to a meagre existence in shantytowns and shack settlements – the periphery of the peripheries – after abandoning hope of 'finding a livelihood in the rural areas from which they escaped'. Their *modus operandi* careened wildly back and forth between benign paternalism and despotic arbitrariness, or what Lemarchand has described as the patrimonial and repressive extremes of political clientelism.[51]

Always and everywhere, fierce competition over access to scarce resources was the inevitable outcome of jobless families seeking shelter on the fringes of established townships. Tensions within informal settlements frequently erupted into violence, sometimes leading to terrible carnage. A few examples should suffice. The sprawling shack settlements that mushroomed around Durban, for example, metamorphosed into a complex *mélange* of what one political analyst calls 'powerful fiefdoms whose chief characteristics are a medieval code of power and patronage quite insensible to the reach of the law'.[52] The combustible mixture of criminal gangs, *comtsotsis*, warlords and vigilantes ensured a seemingly endless cycle of violence.[53] In Cape Town, squabbles over the allocation of sites in Macassar, a new 'site-and-service' area for squatters displaced from an older settlement called Green Point, eventually led to violence and murder. Macassar, which had toilets, running water, mast lighting and tarred streets, was located about five kilometres from Khayelitsha towards the sea on the Cape Flats. A self-appointed 'warlord' in Green Point, one of Khayelitsha's most dilapidated and dangerous shack settlements, charged residents about R32 ($14) for bogus 'ANC membership cards' which were only photocopies.[54]

The rise and fall of Johnson Ngxobongwana, the most notorious strongman on the Cape Flats, illustrates the kind of 'essentially opportunistic and self-serving manoeuvring' that was typical of these local powerbrokers. Even before he formed the Western Cape Civic Association (WCCA) and became its first chairman in 1982, Ngxobongwana had acquired a popular reputation as a political activist, a genuine champion of squatter rights, and an indefatigable fighter who opposed every conceivable state-erected obstacle to the influx and settlement of 'his people' at Crossroads. For the next several years, he played the role of 'squatter patriarch' within the leadership of the UDF-affiliated WCCA, and tirelessly orchestrated the resistance to state efforts to remove squatters from the teeming Crossroads 'squatter camp' and transfer them to the new township called Khayelitsha. Nevertheless, Cape Town activists were somewhat sceptical of his true motives, regarding him as an unreliable ally prone to expediency. By 1985, it became evident that Ngxobongwana had switched allegiance from the UDF to the local state authorities, in exchange for carte-blanche power to remain 'the boss on his own turf'.

In the ensuing bitter showdown over control of the sprawling squatter camps, Ngxobongwana mobilized a vigilante army of 'elders' known as *witdoeke*, and they succeeded in driving UDF supporters from Crossroads and from KTC, an adjoining shantytown, in weeks of heavy fighting.[55] In 1987, the legal status of Crossroads was upgraded to that of an official Black Local Authority, and Ngxobongwana became the first duly elected mayor. Following the unbanning of the ANC in 1990, he faced a renewed challenge to his local authority. Jeffrey Nongwe, chairman of the headman committee, an erstwhile ally, and a veteran *witdoeke* commander responsible for the destruction of UDF strongholds barely four years earlier, boosted his own claims to popular legitimacy by 'converting' to the ANC. In the ensuing bloody power struggle, Nongwe emerged victorious, expelling Ngxobongwana and his followers to Driftsands, a provincial nature reserve beyond Khayelitsha, where he allegedly flirted with the PAC.[56] In 1994, the chameleon-like political career of Ngxobongwana took yet another bizarre twist: his name, along with that of Mali Hoza, another former *witdoeke* 'warlord', appeared on the list of National Party candidates for the Western Cape legislature.[57]

Volatility at the margins

Since the 1913 Natives' Land Act, a combination of the 'military', the 'magistrate' and the 'market' served to dispossess black people of land and to control their movements as 'temporary sojourners' seeking work in the cities. The apartheid social engineering schemes merely streamlined existing legislative and administrative policy and, as a consequence, accelerated the complex processes of forced removals, rather than initiating them as most liberal analysts imply. This story is well-known and need not be repeated here. Suffice it to say that the collapse of the apartheid rural/urban regime had less to do with far-sighted reformist initiatives than with its internal contradictions.[58] Following the abolition of influx controls in 1986, the state administration largely abandoned legal or administrative mechanisms and demolition procedures to remove urban squatters forcibly in favour of negotiation and compromise. Even the draconian 1988 amendment that dealt with the prevention of squatting in urban areas was used sparingly, even though forcible removals in the rural areas continued virtually unabated under the guise of 'homeland consolidation'.[59] The relaxation of legalized segregation marked a significant shift in state urbanization policy. Under mounting pressure brought about by both organized and unorganized resistance, state officials moved away from all-encompassing efforts at bureaucratic control and turned instead toward trying to manage the spatial form of urbanization. This modification in official policy corresponded to emerging global trends – namely, liberalization, deregu-lation, and the withdrawal of the state administration from 'civil society'. In the twilight of apartheid, the law consistently favoured those with access to or control over property.[60]

Urban squatters were nothing new in South Africa. In the early 1990s, perhaps as many as ten million people had no formal shelter in South Africa. Informal settlements sprang up on the fringes of virtually every township. Behind these dry statistics cataloguing South Africa's ill-fortune lurked the grim reality of millions of rootless people trying to eke out a marginalized existence in the midst of unending poverty and terribly bleak surroundings. The squatter camps were a labyrinthine maze of passage-ways and makeshift huts constructed of mud, recycled plywood, plastic tenting and sheet metal – the detritus of affluent 'consumer society' – where sewerage or running water were nonexistent. It was not uncommon for political analysts to interpret the routines of daily life in the squatter camps through a stereotyping prism that produced two wildly contrasting images. At one exaggerated extreme, shantytowns were portrayed as veri-table 'dens of iniquity' plagued by anti-social violence and crime, where frightened and cowed residents were subjected to the venal, autocratic rule of powerful 'warlords' flanked by armed auxiliaries who dispensed summary justice and profited from the ill-gotten gains of racketeering and 'protection money'. At the other extreme, these places were loftily described as informal settlements where residents heroically struggled against all odds to bring in a steady income by means of informal-sector activities, to raise stable families, and to inject a modicum of dignity into their otherwise hardscrabble lives by supervising garbage collection, polic-ing their own communities, and organizing crèches, schools and health clinics. Both of these images contain a kernel of truth. By focusing solely on static and fixed categories like employment and housing, it is often easy to overlook the inherent dynamism of the 'squatterizing' process. Millions of people in South Africa have been in what might seem like constant motion, chasing illusive dreams of stability and permanence. The results of these myriad processes defy simple classification.

Emboldened by the prospect of a new government sympathetic to their needs, squatters did not wait for the country's first nonracial elections to map out their own vision of post-apartheid South Africa. In numerous places across the country, homeless people steadily encroached on lands to which they had been previously denied access. By taking matters into their own hands, they tested the resolve of discredited local white authorities to forcibly evict them. The example of how an estimated fifteen thousand homeless settlers invaded a choice piece of urban real estate called Cato Manor in Durban, South Africa's second largest city, illustrates a recurrent pattern of squatter determination in the last days of apartheid. What makes the illicit land occupation at Cato Manor so different was that this tract of '5,000 hilly acres about three miles from City Hall is layered like an archeological dig with the rancours of South African history'. After expelling Zulu-speakers from the region in the last century, the British colonialists subdivided the area into estates for wealthy whites. As Durban boomed, Indian immigrants bought the land, and by the 1920s had built a vibrant centre of shops and affluent homes, mosques and temples. When African people flooded into Durban in search of work, the law prohibited them from owning land in cities. Indian landowners rented out plots for shanty settlements in Cato Manor. African resentment of the landlords exploded in anti-Indian rioting in 1949, and an orgy of looting, burning and killing focused on Cato Manor. In the 1950s, Durban officials declared Cato Manor a white area, and forcibly removed African squatters to townships on the edge of the city. Apartheid planners then turned on Indian residents, expropriating their property and expelling them, paying only nominal compensation in return. Like District Six in Cape Town, the land remained largely vacant for decades, as a combination of legal challenges, bureaucratic gridlock, and official reluctance at 'rubbing salt in festering wounds' for fear of further alienating potential Indian allies, effectively prevented full-scale development of Cato Manor.

Squatters first entered the area in 1990, hidden by thick vegetation and the surrounding hills. However, those who brazenly encroached on land within view of white landowners were quickly expelled. This cat-and-mouse game of steady building followed by demolition continued until mid 1993. As plans put forward by a multiracial commission to use the empty tract for integrated, low-cost housing stalled, city officials acquiesced to the relentless pressure of the homesteaders. According to official estimates, the squatter colony grew more than tenfold in the last six months of 1993, nourished by two compelling factors: the instinct that the de Klerk administration was unwilling to risk a political crisis by trying to evict the squatters forcibly, and the hope that by staking a claim they would be the first in line when South Africa's first elected nonracial government decides to upgrade squatter settlements by replacing makeshift shanties with permanent low-cost housing.

Indeed, the case of Cato Manor was overlaid by the cruel ironies of venal apartheid social engineering that was carried out under the short-sighted guise of maintaining territorial segregation. But this peculiarity should not distract us from understanding the broader significance of this illegal land rush where government officials did little or nothing to block the migration. On a wider scale, the successful resolution of pending land disputes in favour of squatters who claim land by right of occupation effectively sent a message to the 'country's millions of homeless that the way to get a house is to invade the cities and suburbs'.[61]

The Homelands: Creating and Sustaining a Docile Periphery

During the 1980s, the Botha administration embarked on an ambitious scheme to turn the townships into showpieces of reform, pumping money into 'improvement' projects designed to create an entrenched black middle class with 'a stake in the system'. Yet, these programmes were carried out at a human cost which was cruelly borne in the homelands. These impoverished areas, generally far removed from South Africa's main urban centres, have consistently contained around 60 per cent – between 15 and 18 million – of the country's estimated 27 million African people. Although it varied from place to place, unemployment in the homelands was authoritatively estimated at around 50 per cent of the economically active population. About 70 per cent of households fell below the generally accepted poverty datum line, and disease and malnutrition were commonplace.[62]

The principal aim of the policy of industrial decentralization was to provide 'employment and housing in the peripheral parts of South Africa in order to create an environment sufficiently attractive to persuade blacks not to move to the metropolitan areas'.[63] Because sustained economic growth was vital to the success of 'displaced urbanization', Pretoria eagerly offered lavish financial incentives in order to lure investment capital to designated 'growth points' in the nominally 'independent' homelands. Investment consortia from the East Asian newly industrializing countries – particularly Taiwanese corporations, but also entrepreneurs from Hong Kong, the Philippines, and South Korea – jumped at the opportunity for quick profits.[64] In the main, the ruling cliques in the homelands 'created an attractive investment climate for footloose industries' at the expense of the health, wages and working conditions of the captive local workforce.[65] In the absence of minimum-wage legislation, and under circumstances where trade unions were outlawed, European and Asian companies often hired workers at wages of less than US$2.00 per day.[66]

Putting Humpty Dumpty together again

From their inception, the homelands administrations were little more than private fiefdoms where local 'strongmen' ruled with an iron fist and took advantage of their command over the governing apparatus to enrich themselves and their cronies. With the crumbling of apartheid overrule, the

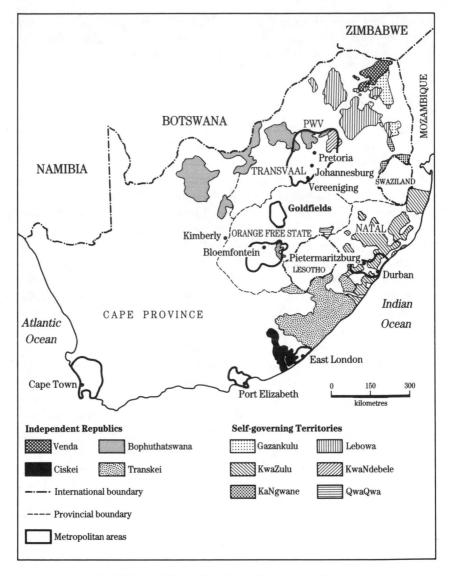

South Africa's Homelands and Metropolitan Areas

Verwoerdian vision of a constellation of independent states circling passively in orbit around Pretoria was swept unceremoniously into the dustbin of history. In large measure, homelands leaders and their satraps were left to fend for themselves, and in the mad rush to avoid the unwelcome fate of being folded back into the parent country without a way of at least cushioning the fall, these surprisingly truculent offspring reacted to the fluid situation by seeking out a veritable crazy-quilt of political alliances as a means of brokering their own futures.[67]

Just as Poland took a leading role in dismantling the Eastern European status quo, Transkei headed the disintegration of the homelands. After ousting the notoriously corrupt Kaiser Matanzima in a bloodless coup in December 1987, Major-General Bantu Holomisa, along with a cohort of young fellow officers of the ruling Military Council, openly called for the reincorporation of Transkei into South Africa proper and sought to strengthen relations with banned organizations, particularly the ANC.[68] The release of Mandela in February 1990 triggered a groundswell of jubilation in the homelands, which quickly ballooned into a torrent of popular anger directed at Pretoria's hand-picked henchmen. In the space of ten days, three of the 'independent' homelands were shaken to their foundations. In Ciskei, Brigadier Oupa Gqozo staged a pre-emptive coup d'état that toppled President-for-Life Lennox Sebe, thereby cutting short the hated dictator's backroom efforts to conclude a deal with Pretoria before he was forced to negotiate with a future ANC-led government. The ensuing street celebrations provided an opening for the embittered crowds to settle accounts with one of Pretoria's most ruthless henchmen. The mood quickly turned ugly as rioters looted and burned in Mdantsane, Ciskei's largest township, and in the industrial park Fort Jackson, targeting symbols associated with the despised Sebe family.[69] In Bophuthatswana, the aging president, Lucas Mangope, suppressed popular demonstrations calling for his resignation by ordering police to shoot to kill, and extended the state of emergency already in place in the Odi-Moretele region northwest of Pretoria to cover the whole 'ministate'.[70] In Venda, a minuscule pocket of land straddling the Limpopo River in the far northeastern Transvaal, widespread protests demanding reincorporation into South Africa led to the ousting of its inept president, Frank Ravele.[71]

The political turmoil that rocked the homelands reflected a deeper crisis of legitimacy. Why relatively well-financed 'strongmen' in the homelands were unable to forge solid and lasting political alliances with the relatively large and powerful local middle classes – the fledging ruling classes – has been a matter of some debate and conjecture. Suffice it to say that, on balance, local entrepreneurs in the many homelands relied largely upon 'the politics of patrimonialism', that is, they manipulated 'vertical ties of clientelism', encouraged 'separatist ethnic ideologies', and made use of violence and vigilantism, in order to compensate for their economic vulnerability.[72]

In the official mind, the homelands, with their supercilious palace intrigue and comic-opera politics, eventually outlived their usefulness as 'tribal' dumping grounds. For years, Pretoria had poured billions of rands into the homelands to keep a coterie of mismanaged administrations afloat and to maintain corrupt and venal autocrats in power. Contrary to conventional wisdom, homelands rulers were not always compliant quislings. These men, in their greedy pursuit of wealth and power, wilfully plundered or squandered their treasuries, leaving the people to endure lives filled with privation and hopelessness. In 1986, the political regimes that ruled Venda, Transkei and Bophuthatswana (often hailed as the most successful of the homelands) all declared bankruptcy. In response, Pretoria imposed stringent conditions for bailing out these insolvent administrations, including the unilateral appointment of white South Africans and other foreign nationals to senior government posts in order to restore a semblance of order over financial affairs. In those homelands where seconded SAP officers or freelance white mercenaries took charge of security matters, black sovereigns became little more than untrustworthy and unreliable figureheads with lavish expense accounts and elaborate means of repression.[73]

This intrusion by Pretoria into homeland affairs was not matched by any appreciable improvements in fiscal responsibility. In fact, most of the 'self-governing homelands' operated for years with seconded South African civil servants, who assumed responsibility for the lion's share of homeland administrative duties. Recurrent charges of inefficiency, corruption and profligacy were a constant source of embarrassment for Pretoria, and a nagging reminder of the failed dream of Verwoerdian 'grand apartheid'. In September 1993, Pretoria unilaterally dispatched a team of experts to assume complete financial control over Lebowa, one of the apartheid-invented 'self-governing' states of South Africa, amid charges from banks that the administration had insufficient funds to meet its payments and revelations of fiscal disarray and impropriety. When chief minister Nelson Ramodike ordered this task force to leave, Pretoria deployed a security force from the SAP's Internal Stability Unit to guard key installations and protect its officials. This drastic action merely underscored the gravity of financial collapse that bedevilled the homelands administrations.[74]

The decision of the National Party under de Klerk to abandon the homelands system was primarily the result of its desire to reassert control over its volatile peripheries rather than a manifestation of its commitment to reform.[75] In the uncertain political climate, homelands ruling cliques manoeuvred for leverage as regional power-brokers. Some leaders, like Holomisa and Enos Mabuza, chief minister of KaNgwane, cast their lot with the ANC. Others, like chief minister Mangosuthu Gatsha Buthelezi of KwaZulu and Hudson Ntsanwisi of Gazankulu, relentlessly waged violent campaigns against their generally pro-ANC opponents.[76]

Before the sudden collapse of the Mangope ruling clique in March 1994, the general consensus among political observers was that Bophuthatswana – popularly, if disparagingly, known as 'Bop' – might prove particularly intransigent in obstructing elections and resisting incorporation. For historical, cultural, geographical and political reasons, this bizarre political entity, composed of six separate chunks of land straddling three provinces of the 'mother country', stood out as South Africa's most petulant 'problem child'. Mangope, who defiantly rejected popular demands to reincorporate the territory into South Africa, vowed that Bophuthatswana would 'be an independent state 100 years from now'. Bophuthatswana officials claimed that it was British imperialists who, in the late nineteenth century, deprived them of the right to become part of the Bechuanaland protectorate, and that this historical injustice was cemented when Botswana achieved independence in the 1960s while apartheid still reigned supreme in South Africa. They also strongly proclaimed their homogeneous ethnic identity – an emphasis which led to heightened tensions on the boundaries of the territory among non-Tswana speakers. In strictly economic terms, what made Bophuthatswana different from the other homelands was that it sat astride an estimated one-third of the world's platinum and chrome deposits and contained large reserves of other scarce minerals, including vanadium.[77] Sun International, owned by the flamboyant Sol Kerzner, placed two of its thirty-odd 'pleasure domes' in the territory. The first one, the lucrative gambling playground called Sun City (or 'Sin City' to most of its patrons), boasted 1.5 million visitors a year, most of whom flocked to see topless shows and other extravaganzas not allowed in South Africa. The newest crown jewel, named the Lost City, was located about one hundred miles north of Johannesburg on eighty arid acres surrounded by bushveld. This US$300-million resort was resplendent with a 338-room Palace Hotel and accompanying casino, a grand fan-shaped pool with 'surfable, six-foot-high waves breaking on an ersatz white beach', five water slides, and a sixty-acre jungle featuring a rain forest, a desert and a swamp, along with 1.4 million imported plants and shrubs. Like the mythical Xanadu brought to life by Samuel Taylor Coleridge, the Lost City 'is a fabulous work of fiction, for nothing in it is real'.[78]

Despite its economic advantages, Bophuthatswana remained heavily dependent upon South Africa. Around 21 per cent of its budget came directly from Pretoria, and around 30 per cent from the Southern African Customs Union. Around half the labour force work as migrants in South Africa. Ever since its nominal independence from South Africa in 1977, the Homeland 'attracted hordes of international con-men', and 'corruption [took] some truly bizarre forms'. The erratic Mangope surrounded himself with right-wing advisors of questionable reputation, including Rowan Cronje, the real power-behind-the-throne in the showcase capital of Mmabatho. A former cabinet minister in white-ruled Rhodesia, Cronje worked in Ciskei before coming to Bophuthatswana where he assumed the posts of minister of defence, minister of state, minister of aviation, and chief negotiator at the World Trade Centre talks. A host of other ex-Rhodesian whites played significant roles in key state ministries and in the business field.[79]

The Agrarian Question

Despite long-standing occupation of the countryside by white farmers, the legitimacy of white land ownership is still not firmly established in many rural areas. White claims to proprietorship over prime agricultural lands were initially achieved through the exercise of brute force, and successive white minority regimes sanctioned these ill-gotten gains through a concatenated *mélange* of oppressive laws and regulations. Two main legislative pillars – the 1913 Natives' Land Act and the Development Trust and Land Act of 1936 – effectively prohibited the purchase of land by Africans outside of the demarcated areas. The 'scheduled areas' where Africans were permitted to buy land comprised only 13 per cent of South Africa's total land mass.[80]

The development of the Bantustans during the heyday of Verwoerdian apartheid and the accompanying state policy of 'forced removals' were merely the logical extensions of the cherished white-supremacist goal of maintaining territorial segregation along racial lines. The time-worn, racialist convictions of many white farmers underpin the asymmetrical power relations and superexploitation on the land. The increasingly vulnerable economic position of an expanding number of white farmers also reinforces durable and recurrent patterns of abusive behaviour against farmworkers and their families. The roots of the violence on the white-owned farms can be found deeply buried in the history of land deprivation and the intense economic exploitation of black farm labour since before the turn of the century. This situation has translated into extremely authoritarian and coercive relationships between farmers and workers. For the farmers, intensive labour exploitation is perceived as a necessary prerequisite for their economic survival.[81] This inheritance is overlaid by superannuated patriarchial ideologies which further license and endorse exploitative codes of behaviour on the part of landowners. The old-fashioned racialist values to which farmers ascribe further entrench their own sense of omnipotence in relation to their black workers and justify their continual ill-treatment. The complicity of the courts and the police in maintaining the seamless web of indifference, brutality, and exploitation on the land serves to condone the status quo.[82]

The possibilities and limits of land reform

The most politically sensitive and volatile problem facing any post-apartheid government of whatever social and political composition will be land reform and food production.[83] The plain fact is that South Africa has been a net exporter of foodstuffs while millions of impoverished, landless black families are undernourished and virtually starving. The enormous disparity of land ownership – 87 per cent was set aside for whites, who comprised about 13 per cent of the population – was an emotion-laden issue, riddled with layers of competing interests that received scant attention at the World Trade Centre negotiating forum.[84]

Experts realized that a successful agrarian reform programme aimed at providing a livelihood for millions of landless black families required substantial land redistribution.[85] Yet, how can, and will, land reform in South Africa be realistically implemented? The ANC, along with other sections of the liberation movement, was vague on this perplexing question.[86] There was a recognizable fear that any outright expropriation of white-owned farmland would ignite a massive backlash by right-wing forces. On the other hand, raising the funds to buy out white commercial farmers seemed a pipe dream. The millions of black families forcibly evicted from the land set aside for exclusive white ownership over the course of the past eighty years have legitimate claims for redress of grievances. Yet because the process of forcible removal and subsequent dislocation was so massive, it remained unclear how practical the endeavour to reconstruct a black small-scale owning class might be.[87]

The advent of the 'new' South Africa unleashed a torrent of accumulated demands for greater access to agricultural, grazing and residential land.[88] Despite the gradual demise of apartheid regulations, the balance of class forces in agriculture remained favourable to white farmers in general, and to core white farmers in particular, or the one-quarter who produce three-quarters of total marketable surpluses. Under the guiding hand of de Klerk's most trusted reformers, the 1991 White Paper on Land Reform paved the way for the repeal of the odious Land Acts, but left agrarian property rights and social relations intact. These mildly ameliorative reform initiatives went hand-in-glove with the neo-liberal proposals of the Development Bank of Southern Africa (DBSA), a financial institution modelled on the World Bank and a significant source of investment capital for rural development. DBSA planners argued that black smallholders should serve as the engine for more equitable economic growth in agriculture. Yet this endorsement of equal 'opportunities for all' in a 'democratic, non-racist and non-sexist' South Africa must be tempered by the planners' doctrinal belief that 'the market mechanism should be the primary instrument facilitating land reform.'[89] To counter neo-liberal 'development' discourse advocating export-oriented growth strategies for agricultural development, the ANC developed policy guidelines calling for a nationwide programme of land reform and redistribution. Adopted in May 1992, this programme earmarked large tracts of land owned by the state as central to land reform, and identified the establishment of a land claims court as a major priority in order to 'address demands and grievances concerning land restoration and land rights including ownership'. This programme advocated a significant restructuring of agriculture with less reliance on large-scale, heavily capitalized plantation-like farms to allow for the diversification of agricultural production systems. It also included a demand for affirmative action 'within a viable and sustainable economic development programme' where the major beneficiaries will be the 'landless, rural poor and women who have been deprived of rights to land through patriarchal systems of land allocation and tenure'.[90]

In their policy pronouncements, the ANC leadership left open the possibility of expropriation of privately owned land – subject, of course, to 'just compensation' in the context of the 'public interest'. Yet an entrenched property clause in the ANC's proposed Bill of Rights ran the risk of making it virtually impossible to implement an all-embracing agrarian reform programme. Without access to massive financing, the state administration would find itself unable to acquire sufficient amounts of arable land to make redistribution plausible and meaningful.[91]

The land 'time bomb' and simmering rural unrest

Debates around private-property rights lie at the very heart of the agrarian question in South Africa.[92] Critics warn that political strategies too closely linked with neo-liberal doctrines of market-generated economic growth often act to cement an alliance around a consensual programme of modest liberal reform from above coupled with cautious self-restraint from below.[93] Yet in countless numbers of instances, the rural poor who suffered the enforced diaspora of apartheid have demonstrated little interest in pious pronouncements urging self-restraint. In areas plagued by poverty and obdurate disputes over property ownership, land hunger has provided a powerful stimulus for independent action. The symptoms of a silent, protracted struggle to regain access to arable land can be observed across the length and breadth of rural South Africa. Sparse grazing for cattle brought about by the worst drought in a century has caused rural people to clash with nature conservationists over the use of land in places like the famous Kruger National Park, the Madikwe Game Reserve near the Botswana border, and elsewhere.[94] Tired of government intransigence, 'double-speak' and broken promises, impatient rural communities seized unoccupied lands from which they had been forcibly removed during the heyday of apartheid, thereby staking a claim to what they regard as their legitimate ancestral lands. In numerous other places, rural people occupied state-owned lands or 'squatted' on the vacant farms of absentee landowners, in anticipation that a future post-apartheid government would view with favour their claims for redress of past injustices.[95]

The simmering tensions in the countryside increasingly boiled over into armed attacks on isolated farms, unexplained arson, pilfering of standing crops, and the wholesale looting of livestock. These disparate actions must be seen in the context of rising rural impoverishment, including the cynical moves of white farmers to reduce their workforces by expelling farm labourers and their dependents. Beginning in 1991, a spate of armed assaults on white-owned farms carried out by the Azanian People's Liberation Army (APLA) in the Eastern Cape along the Transkei border sent shock waves through tightknit white rural communities close to King William's Town, Aliwal North and East London. Between January and June, 1993, there were more than thirty separate attacks on farms in places like Nelspruit and White River in the Eastern Transvaal. While much about these incidents remained clouded in obscurity, farmers were convinced that the motives were largely political, and that these attacks represented part of an orchestrated campaign to drive them off the land.[96] A representative of a district farmers' union in the Northern Transvaal charged, with obvious exaggeration, that perhaps as many as ten thousand farmers were prepared to leave their farms because of the growing threat to their security.[97] Whatever the truth of these claims, what ought to be abundantly clear is that these attacks were only the most visible expression of an enduring struggle, with deep historical roots, over access to landed property.[98]

Whatever the ultimate moral verdict, these armed assaults on white-owned farms boosted the once-languid reputation of APLA, and allowed the PAC to make some political gains, particularly amongst disaffected and militant youth. These attacks also had a cathartic effect on the popular masses that extended beyond Pan Africanist circles. The sometimes celebrated slogan, 'Kill the Boer, Kill the Farmer', popularized by ANC Youth League leader Peter Mokaba, attested to the fact that armed violence had captured the imagination of Congress supporters as well.[99]

The rising tide of rural violence brought the inevitable backlash. As the scale and scope of the armed attacks intensified, white farmers began to mobilize against what many regarded as a brewing race war. The heightened sense of anxiety assumed the character of an old-fashioned moral panic. Farmers' associations called for the deployment of former Koevoet and 32 Battalion soldiers to bolster rural security. Well-trained commando units expanded their night-time patrols of farming areas. Ex-military officers volunteered to give free advice on security preparedness to white people in the rural areas. Experts on 'terrorism' lectured on 'common sense precautions to take which could save lives or prevent injury'.[100] 'An integrated security system is required: [electric] fence, [two-way] radio, burglar bars, lights, and a self-defence system too', the security advisor to the Transvaal Agricultural Union warned. 'Men, women and children should be armed and ready to defend themselves in the case of an attack.'[101]

4

Destabilization and Counter-Revolutionary Warfare

The 1984–86 popular insurrection marked a significant watershed in South Africa's tumultuous political history. Under the watchword 'adapt or die', the white minority regime under the leadership of P.W. Botha had embarked on a cautious reformist course during the early 1980s. This strategy of piecemeal tinkering with the existing modes of political domination backfired. In the end, these belated efforts to provide the apartheid system with a much-needed 'facelift' failed to enlist sufficient political support to sustain the momentum of reform 'from above'. Township residents reacted to these half-hearted, cosmetic political concessions by staging a largely spontaneous uprising that eventually spread across the length and breadth of South Africa. By the time the hydra-headed rebellion was crushed, virtually the entire administrative apparatus that had regulated apartheid over-rule lay in ruins.[1]

The stage-managed, unilateral manner in which the white oligarchy sought to open the political system undoubtedly played a part in determining the severity with which it was subsequently closed down. State-organized repression formed the cornerstone of 'crisis management' policy both during and immediately following the outbreak of open rebellion.[2] The Botha administration managed to break the back of the above-ground popular resistance by the massive display of superior military force, along with an expedient use of the courts and the judicial process. The omnibus emergency regulations, which included blanket restrictions on press freedom, prescriptions on political organizations, prohibitions on public events, along the with drastic curtailment of civil liberties, equipped the SAP and SADF with wide latitude and discretion to suppress efforts at mass mobilization, to silence opposition, and to stifle dissent.[3]

Following the 1986 declaration of the nationwide State of Emergency, the security forces rounded up close to 25,000 persons, many of whom were detained without trial for long periods.[4] A long string of political 'show trials', often held in remote venues and frequently conducted *in camera* with 'mystery' witnesses who had been coerced or tortured into testifying for the prosecution, effectively criminalized above-ground political activities. In the Alexandra Treason Trial, for example – a marathon case in which Moses Mayekiso and others were eventually acquitted in 1989 – the security forces achieved their aim of keeping 'high profile' activists out of circulation for years. The initial clampdown severely restricted the exercise of individual civil liberties and prohibited the staging of public events, including mass meetings, funerals, and other displays of popular resentment, for fear of provoking confrontations that would inevitably lead to bloodshed. In February 1988, the security forces extended the ban on outward political activity to include seventeen political and human-rights organizations. These groups were restricted from undertaking any further political action, although they retained their legal status. The state security apparatus also attempted, albeit with only partial success, to limit the functions of COSATU to those activities relating solely to 'bread and butter' shopfloor issues. By 1989, the list of restricted anti-apartheid organizations had climbed to thirty-three.[5]

These extraordinary powers gave the Botha administration unprecedented leeway to reassert the state monopoly of organized force and violence. With its leadership detained or having fled into hiding, the popular movement appeared to be left rudderless in the immediate aftermath of the country-wide insurrection. The graduated restoration of the semblance of law and order in recognizable 'trouble spots' enabled the Botha administration in large part to regain the political initiative which it had forfeited as a result of its clumsy efforts to impose unilaterally the 1983 constitution, including the tricameral parliament with separate chambers for so-called Coloureds, Indians, and whites, on a sceptical and wary populace. Yet the widespread use of wholesale repression, which was applied more less indiscriminately on openly hostile communities, could ensure nothing more than outward conformity and passive consent.[6]

Counter-Revolution from Below

In the decade after P.W. Botha rose to power in 1978, the security establishment had come to play an increasingly prominent role in policy-making at the highest levels of government, including the setting of national priorities and the promotion of semi-secret campaigns of regional destabilization.[7] Guided by the principles of the 'total strategy' doctrine, which blurred the distinction between foreign and domestic policy matters and security issues, the Botha administration sought to streamline, centralize and coordinate state decision-making procedures in order to counteract the total onslaught directed against 'white South Africa'. The nerve centre facilitating the expanded input and active participation of military-trained technocrats was the revitalized State Security Council (SSC).[8] Under Botha's tutelage, the SSC was transformed from a relatively obscure and inactive advisory board on intelligence matters into a policy-formulating body involved in strategic planning in both domestic and foreign affairs. Virtually overnight, it replaced the Cabinet as the most influential state agency in the government, and eventually became, in the words of one analyst, 'an extremely powerful body with horizontal and vertical tentacles that embrace almost every aspect of public policy-making'.[9]

This 'militarization of the state' crystallized during the 1984–86 popular rebellion, which the Botha administration crushed by means of a combination of military force and draconian security legislation.[10] Because of the widely held perception that the 'stabilizing actions' of the security forces were vital to achieving their political objectives, reformist-minded civilians in the Botha administration allowed leading figures in the South African military, police and intelligence services virtual free rein over the formulation of a comprehensive strategy for reimposing law and order. These 'securocrats' presided over the creation of the National Security Management System (NSMS), as the operational arm of the SSC was known. The NSMS allowed the security establishment to institutionalize and extend its influence in policy-making from the SSC down to local township level. The organizational infrastructure of the NSMS – its life-blood – was the far-flung, labyrinthine network of coordination committees known as Joint Management Centres (JMCs).[11] The essential task of the JMCs was to coordinate the implementation of state security policies on the ground, as well as to supply intelligence on local conditions and grievances. All in all, there were eleven main JMCs spread across the country, and their areas of jurisdiction corresponded to the ten SADF military command boundaries, plus Walvis Bay. The JMCs were chaired by a senior civil servant, usually a senior officer in the SADF or SAP, and consisted of around 60 regional representatives of military, police and civilian agencies in the particular area. Beneath the JMCs, there were approximately 60 sub-JMCs which overlapped with the jurisdictions of the Regional Services Councils, and somewhere between 350 and 448 mini-JMCs placed in local areas such as townships. The operations of the JMCs were regarded as classified information. All participants in the NSMS were required to take an oath of secrecy which made them subject to penalties under the Protection of Information Act.[12]

The NSMS became, as one political observer put it, a 'militarized

bureaucracy' operating in tandem with the regular civil service to promote the coordination of state security.[13] In 1986, state security officials
designated thirty-four townships as 'oilspots', or key target areas declared
to be 'high-risk' security zones.[14] The JMCs that were placed in each of
these townships became launching pads for novel urban pacification and
restabilization efforts that combined repression with socio-economic upgrading schemes.[15] By emphasizing the improvement of material conditions in the townships, state security experts drew from conventional
counterinsurgency theories. These views were premissed on 'low intensity
warfare' doctrine which held that military force alone was incapable of
defeating a revolutionary guerrilla insurgency, and that effective pacification
depended upon a calculated effort at political and economic reform.
According to the 'securocrats' who gained valuable experience in the
painfully bitter war against SWAPO in Namibia, genuine improvements
were required in order to 'cut the ground from under the feet' of 'revolutionaries' who were perceived as 'exploiting' real grievances for their
own advantage.[16]

This emphasis on 'winning hearts and minds' (WHAM) marked a
decisive shift in state security thinking from the moribund 'total strategy'
doctrine in vogue during the early 1980s to the Machiavellian tenets of
'counterrevolutionary' warfare. While the ultimate end of containing the
black opposition remained the same, the new security doctrine over-
hauled the means of achieving these goals. The WHAM programme
reflected a conversion from the almost exclusive reliance upon magisterial
visions of reform orchestrated from above toward recasting the foundations for 'counter-revolution' from below. Repression did not emanate
from a single source, but was decentralized in accordance with local
conditions.[17]

One main objective of the NSMS was to bolster the credibility and
legitimacy of local-government structures. 'By a judicious mix of security
action and socioeconomic upliftment', the NSMS sought to 'raise the
cost of confronting the state whilst simultaneously enhancing the benefits
of cooperating with it'.[18] The task of the JMCs was to isolate and
neutralize popular leaders, identify local grievances into order to defuse
explosive community issues, and eliminate the revolutionary climate in
the townships.[19] This pre-emptive strategy – 'buying off revolution' or
'reform by stealth', as it was called – enabled the security forces to be far
more discerning in the selective repression of the popular movement and
its key leaders.[20] At the same time, local-government bodies could claim
credit for JMC-sponsored infrastructural improvements, such as street lighting, paved roads, refurbished schools and sports facilities. The aim of this
'counterrevolutionary' strategy was to clear the path for the emergence of

an auxiliary class of accommodating black leaders who would exchange their complicity in local government for a modest taste of privilege and power.[21]

As the intensity of the open clashes between the security forces and township residents subsided, the SADF accelerated its active engagement in civic-action programmes with the aim of providing basic infrastructural support for those communities whose 'leaders' proclaimed allegiance to the forces of law and order. The long-term goal, as one prominent National Party official put it, was to 'get a sufficient number of prominent leaders to participate so that eventually those who still lust after revolution will become as irrelevant in South Africa as they are in the US or Britain'.[22]

Fragmented State Apparatuses

In the minds of its apprehensive critics, the NSMS represented a prototype prefiguring the formation of a quasi-police state. By usurping many of the normal functions of administration, the security establishment created what amounted to a permanent 'shadow government' which exercised considerable power behind a virtually impenetrable veil of secrecy. This shift in the mechanics of state power prompted many political analysts to charge that the security forces had managed to stage a 'creeping coup', replacing ineffectual 'dovish' civilians with 'hawkish' top military brass.[23] Yet by laying so much stress on what appeared to be the omnipotent power of the 'securocrats', the 'militarization thesis' failed to grasp the institutional flexibility inherent in the existing state structures. After he assumed the post of state president in 1989, de Klerk acted quickly to reaffirm civilian authority at the commanding heights of the state apparatus and to limit the policy-making functions of the security establishment. It thus became evident that the 'emergency powers', which vested extraordinary powers in the hands of the 'securocrats', were only temporarily expedient measures, and did not signal the onset of a military dictatorship as many anti-apartheid activists had feared.[24]

The secretive rise to prominence of the 'securocrats' must be understood in the socio-historical context of ongoing efforts to rationalize a bloated and inefficient state administration, fractured along the fault lines dictated by the moribund political logic of Verwoerdian apartheid. A central aspect of South Africa's conjunctural crisis was political, that is, the breakdown of outmoded forms of representation, rule and legitimation.[25] The tremendous ad hoc expansion of state branches and departments during the heyday of apartheid, along with the accompanying growth of the state bureaucracy, led to increased fiscal strains, growing inefficiency and bureaucratic incoherence. Contrary to conventional wisdom, the apartheid system never amounted to a monolithic, all-encompassing programme of social engineering, but instead was composed of a tangled skein of overlapping and sometimes contradictory policies that required constant vigilance and tinkering.[26] During the formative years, the ruling National Party deliberately divided the state administration into pieces in order to accommodate the requirements of implementing 'separate development'. Vertical divisions between the central, provincial and municipal levels of government are not particularly unusual, but in South Africa the exigencies of residential and territorial segregation created a bureaucratic nightmare of racially separate jurisdictions radiating outward from the central state apparatuses to administer satellite townships and peripheral homelands. In addition, the battery of laws and regulations designed to maintain the apartheid system divided the state administration horizontally, notably by creating bureaucratic cleavages along racial lines.[27]

Many state functions, especially those involving internal security, transport and communications, simply could not reasonably be divided either along ethnic or territorial lines. Horizontal divisions created a confusing web of overlapping jurisdictions without a clearly demarcated chain of command. The resulting bureaucratic inefficiency was compounded by competitive rivalries between branches of the state apparatus and the carving out of mini-fiefdoms by self-interested functionaries. The much-vaunted rationalization that began in the mid 1970s and continued during the Botha years addressed some problems associated with the fractured state administration by reducing the number of departments and streamlining the decision-making process. But improvements were predominantly confined to the first tier of government, and affected vertical more than horizontal divisions.[28]

The Botha administration used the tricameral constitution, the insurrectionist threat, and the States of Emergency to shift political power away from Parliament and the National Party and to concentrate real decision-making inside the executive branch. Seen in retrospect, what triggered the rapid 'militarization of the state' was the breakdown of administrative apparatuses along the volatile outer perimeter, most notably the town councils and the homelands governments. But this fusion of political power must be understood as more than simply the institutional, reflexive response of the security establishment to perceived insurrectionary impulses from below. It also represented a 'top-down' effort to provide coherence and stability to fragmented state apparatuses at the core of the state administration. 'For as long as apartheid reasoning stayed in place,' Seegers cogently argued, 'the pieces in the administrative jigsaw could not come together – except on the basis of co-ordination induced by the threat of revolution.'[29] By establishing an alternative chain of command and by sanctioning the crossing of jurisdictional boundaries, the NSMS sought to bypass existing state administrative channels. The security establishment used 'legalized terror', including draconian State of Emergency legislation and its greatly enhanced powers of intimidation, to stifle and suffocate 'above ground' dissent. Yet in a strict sense, juridical guarantees were never abolished, and hence the courts and the 'rule of law' retained their formal autonomy. In other words, constitutional 'protections' existed side by side with extra-constitutional 'emergency' powers, establishing in effect parallel and competing lines of authority oscillating between civilian and security apparatuses. Far from providing a means of escaping the deepening political crisis, the proliferation of power centres merely exacerbated the existing administrative stasis and incoherence.[30]

South Africa's 'Dirty War': Manufacturing Violent Stability[31]

The ferocity of the 1984–86 popular rebellion came as a rude shock to the ruling white oligarchy. What distinguished this uprising from earlier episodes in South African history was not only the duration and intensity of open confrontations, pitting mostly unarmed township residents against well-armed and highly mobile police and regular army units, but also the unprecedented degree to which broad layers and sectors of the subordinate classes actively participated – or at least approvingly acquiesced – in pushing the townships, ghettos and squatter settlements beyond the frontiers of governability and rendering 'the system' unworkable. Often with only the vaguest idea of the specific programmes of the organized political movements, angry township residents took the initiative and resolutely stood their ground against the withering fire power of the army and police. The battle lines were constantly in flux, without recognizable fronts or fixed positions. Civic associations, student groups, youth congresses and trade unions – the most elementary organs of popular defence – displayed inordinate degrees of endurance and tactical flexibility in the face of a relentless and formidable enemy. The abrupt awakening of political consciousness in areas of the country, both urban and rural, with little or no previous record of visible protest took both the organized political movements and the security forces by surprise. The cumulative effect of these countless clashes was to undermine thoroughly the semblance of law and order and normalcy that the white minority regime required to maintain administrative control.[32]

As the scope and the scale of street-fighting declined, the war-weary SAP and SADF withdrew from the spotlight, transferring primary responsibility for enforcing law and order in the black townships to auxiliary policing units. Over the course of the popular uprising, scores of black policemen, vilified by township militants as 'collaborators' and targeted for revenge, had been killed or had resigned from office and fled for their lives. In order to fill the vacuum left by their hasty departure, state authorities established a special municipal police force, known colloquially as 'Greenflies', who were often recruited from unemployment fund queues, or from the ranks of local thugs and former bodyguards of town councillors. The SAP cobbled together auxiliary units, some of whom were pushed into the line of duty with so little training and preparation that they were nicknamed *kitskonstabels*, or 'instant police'. These adjunct units, which quickly developed an unsavoury reputation for indiscipline, unleashed an unrestrained reign of terror upon black communities. Their brutish behaviour, ranging from murder to assault and destruction of property, operated as a useful vehicle for officially sanctioned proxy repression under the convenient cloak of the Emergency news blackout.[33]

This expanded use of auxiliary forces dovetailed with the strategy of counterinsurgency where the SADF and SAP faded into the background, yet continued to play a covert coordinating role.[34] Yet no matter how momentarily effective these policing mechanisms were, they could neither resolve the crisis of legitimacy nor restore the status quo ante. The popular rebellion demonstrated beyond a shadow of a doubt that the collaborative networks embedded in the homelands administrations and township councils were the weakest links in the apartheid chain. As these twin bulwarks on the outer perimeter of the central state apparatus began to disintegrate, the entire framework of indirect rule, through which privileged black elites had found a niche within the apartheid system, came unglued. It was at this juncture that legally sanctioned, conventional mechanisms of control blended with extra-legal, informal and surrogate repression.[35]

The spectacular rise of vigilantism, which Charney defined as 'the unlicenced use of private violence to defend an oligarchic clientelist state under popular challenge', can be traced to the desperate efforts of local power-brokers to reassert their authority and to rebuild patronage links that had eroded or collapsed.[36] Although heterogeneous in social composition, homelands despots, town councillors, the propertied township petty bourgeoisie, and shantytown 'warlords' shared a vested interest in the status quo. These local elites, sitting astride clientelist networks arising from their ability to mobilize desperately needed resources and to dispense small favours, recruited petty gangsters, hoodlums and other lumpen-proletarian elements to assist them in restoring their version of 'law and order' amidst the township chaos and anarchy.[37] In the main, vigilante groups were reactive, arising in areas where popular organizations had made headway in mobilizing local residents. They gained easy access to weapons, frequently acted in collusion with security forces, and routinely terrorized residents of black communities to force them into silent passivity.[38]

Viewed through the wide-angle lens of popular insurrection and brutal counterrevolution, it is easy to oversimplify the behaviour and motives of vigilantes. Political observers, sometimes too preoccupied with the strong currents of change and progess, often paid too little attention to the dead weight of inertia and conservativism. Vigilantism cannot be understood as simply the compliant extension of the security forces. While formal and informal linkages between vigilantes and the security forces were incontrovertible, the socio-political foundations for vigilantism must be situated within long-standing cleavages dividing black communities. These conflicts, which lay dormant over the course of the popular insurrection, erupted with particular ferocity in the chaotic aftermath.

The social bases of vigilante activity largely mirrored those of opposition to the apartheid system. If civic associations, youth groups, trade unions and women's organizations spearheaded the resistance to white minority rule, vigilantism drew its sustenance from local elites, like township businessmen, 'tribalist' elders and patrimonially organized men, who derived their power from their ability to reward clients in subordinate and dependent groups. As Charney persuasively argues, vigilantism was 'the *riposte* of the state-linked petite bourgeoisie', along with their dependants and followers, to meet the revolutionary challenge threatening to turn the world upside down. When the conventional avenues facilitating the manipulation of scarce resources disappeared, conservative power-brokers mobilized, and even forcibly conscripted, their male followers along neo-traditional lines in a violent bid to intimidate their opposition and restore stability. Unable to make a drastic break with the past, and mistrusting the sometimes bellicose arrogance and posturing of the youth, working men of middle age often clung all the more tenaciously to anti-quated patrimonial creeds that gave order to things. This deeply embedded cast of mind provided a fertile ground for vigilante recruitment. These 'terror' gangs were not simply the docile instruments of state-sponsored repressive machinery: they were active participants who took it upon themselves to settle old grudges. It was precisely this 'home-grown' character and unpredictability that made vigilantism so effective and dangerous.[39]

Vigilante leaders emerged from the ranks of those social groups who were sidetracked in the insurrectionary upsurge that gripped the black residential communities: policemen who saw their colleagues attacked and killed, their homes burned and destroyed, and their social status annulled; urban gangsters who once operated with a great deal of impunity, and whose power and livelihood were challenged by the young 'comrades' and their street committees; local notables and influentials, many of whom played prominent roles in the town council system, who were pushed aside in the rise of alternative structures of 'people's power'; small business-men allied with town councillors, who experienced the wrath of residents who regarded them as thieves and exploiters; 'traditional' authorities with roots in rural 'tribalist' culture, who were ignored by the popular move-ment and whose bases of organizational control were directly threatened by the spread of legitimacy of political organizations like the UDF; and, finally, erstwhile UDF supporters who lost out to rivals in bitter 'power struggles' inevitably spawned by the chaos and confusion inherent in insurrectionary periods.[40]

Vigilante violence traversed a number of distinct stages from its origins at the height of the township rebellion. These trajectories have been admirably analysed by a number of political commentators, and the details should not detain us here.[41] Suffice it to say that while vigilante activities largely conformed to local dynamics all their own, the sweeping patterns that emerged from widely dispersed areas of the country and over time were remarkably similar. As such, vigilantism constituted much more than a random series of isolated, unconnected incidents. In scale, it resembled the unconventional type of counterinsurgency known elsewhere as 'dirty war'. The terror it unleashed was uncertain, stealthy and unexpected. Vigilante activities enabled the security establishment to disguise covert state-sponsored repression under the convenient but woefully imprecise idiom of 'black on black' violence. The spectre of impoverished gangs of township residents locked in bloody, hand-to-hand combat, as witnessed nightly in all its horror on state-owned television and displayed in grue-some pictures in morning newspapers, provided the ruling white olig-archy with a propitious opportunity to manufacture a modern-day 'moral panic'. By issuing dire warnings about the bleak prospects for the future under an ANC-dominated government, incumbent opinion-makers con-tributed to an entrenched white *laager* mentality. The real human cost of vigilantism cannot reasonably be reduced to mere statistics, but these numbers clearly indicate the sheer scale of the unrelenting violence. The cumulative toll of the ongoing mayhem was staggering: from 1985 to 1992, between six and seven thousand people died as a result of vigilante attacks alone.[42]

'In the heart of the whore': the grim merchants of death[43]

For years, political observers harboured strong suspicions that the security forces, or perhaps renegade freelancers attached to far-right paramilitary groups, operated secret 'hit squads' which were responsible for a whole string of unexplained terrorist acts, including unsolved 'disappearances' and assassinations, mysterious burglaries and break-ins, arson attacks and bombings.[44] This type of hit-and-run warfare escalated dramatically during 1988 and continued, with varying levels of frequency, even after the unbanning of political organizations in 1990. These actions were very seldom successfully investigated, and the culprits were rarely if ever brought to justice.[45] The cold-blooded murder of David Webster, a lecturer at the University of the Witwatersrand who was gunned down in broad daylight by 'unknown assailants' on 1 May 1989, merely underscored the widely held belief that professional killers, whose mission it was to eliminate outspoken critics of the apartheid regime both at home and abroad, operated with official protection, or at least with official connivance.[46]

Political analysts searched for historical analogues through which to situate the meaning of this extra-legal violence. Because of the possible links between right-wing groups and the armed forces, some compared extra-legal violence in South Africa to the Algerian experience, where in the last years of French colonial rule the *pieds noirs*, the French settler minority about to lose its exclusive grip over state power, entered into an 'unholy alliance' with disaffected military men to form the underground *Organisation de l'Armée Secrète* in order to terrorize the indigenous population of Algiers. Others likened the growth of vigilante activities to the Contras in Nicaragua or RENAMO in Mozambique.[47] While these analogies had a certain ring of truth, none adequately captured the peculiar blend of legalized suppression of popular dissent coupled with extra-legal violence. In South African human rights circles, it was the conventional wisdom to refer to this type of violence as 'informal repression, simply because – unlike arrest and detention, the search of homes, house-arrest, and crowd control – there are no laws governing it'. But the concept 'informal repression' was misleading. A great deal of accumulated evidence, at first largely circumstantial but increasingly 'hard', suggested that many operations falling under this generic heading were officially sanctioned within the command structures of the SADF and were brought about with resources only available to those acting in an official capacity.[48]

In November 1989, *Vrye Weekblad*, a progressive Afrikaans-language newspaper, published the shocking 'confessions' of a contrite former captain in the security police, Johannes Dirk Coetzee, who provided detailed information about covert 'death squad' activities carefully cocooned within the security police bureaucracy.[49] 'I was in the heart of the whore,' Coetzee proclaimed. 'I was the commander of the South African police death squad.'[50] These sensational disclosures offered a rare first-hand glimpse into the sinister, Machiavellian underworld of 'counterrevolutionary' warfare. Coetzee pulled back the veil of secrecy to reveal direct security-force links to secret 'counter-insurgency' training camps, to special 'anti-terrorist' units (composed largely of repentant ex-guerrillas, known as *Askaris*, whose primary task was to intercept and capture infiltrating guerrillas), and to a long list of unsolved overseas assassinations.[51]

Bowing to intense external pressure, de Klerk appointed a judicial commission of inquiry headed by Justice Louis Harms with a mandate to investigate these allegations of covert police and military involvement in 'hit squad' activities. From the outset, the Harms Commission ran into sizeable roadblocks. Its efforts were frustrated at every turn by misplaced and missing documents, the falsification of public records, and the deliberately evasive responses of high-ranking police officers. These deliberate delaying tactics fuelled widespread suspicions that the security establishment was engaged in an elaborate 'cover-up' designed to switch the blame for assassinations and 'dirty tricks' onto rogue policemen who were operating without orders from their superiors. Much to the disappointment of human-rights advocates, the Commission dismissed Coetzee's testimony, concluding that he was an unreliable witness with a 'fertile imagination' and 'psychopathic tendencies'. In the end, the Harms Commission reached the much-criticized conclusion that the available evidence was not sufficient to prove the existence of officially sanctioned police 'hit squads'.[52]

During the course of its ongoing probe of official wrongdoing, the Harms Commission inadvertently stumbled upon chilling evidence of a secret military-linked 'special operations' unit, known as the *Burgerlike Samewerkingsburo*, or Civil Cooperation Bureau (CCB), which had a list of two hundred targets, including Nelson Mandela, trade-union leaders, journalists and clergy. Formed in 1985 with the approval of Minister of Defence Magnus Malan, the CCB recruited former police and military personnel into a clandestine group consisting of between 150 to 180 members, and spent R27 million (US$58 million) annually on the covert cells and luxury benefits for secret agents.[53] These sensational disclosures strengthened the hand of those who accused the de Klerk administration of tolerating, if not secretly conniving with, a mercurial 'third force', or 'hidden hand', concealed within the labyrinthine layers of the security establishment, with the aim of sabotaging the peace process, sowing discord between rival political organizations, and destabilizing the country.[54]

Low-Intensity Conflict

The sheer volume of sinister attacks directed against selected opponents of the white minority regime sent a frightening signal that, despite the exposures of South Africa's 'death squads', political activists both at home and abroad remained at risk.[55] Two examples are the murder of ANC lawyer Bheki Mlangeni, killed in his Soweto home in 1991 by a miniature bomb concealed inside the earphones of a booby-trapped cassette player; and the assassination of Chief Mhlabunzima Maphumulo, a leading member of the ANC-affiliated Congress of Traditional Leaders of South Africa. Both bore the distinct signature of professional 'hit squads'.[56] Unexplained assassinations of political activists, including scores of ANC and Inkatha officials involved in local peace-making efforts, heightened tensions and sparked revenge attacks.[57] Despite repeated denials of official wrongdoing, charges of security-force involvement in a recurrent pattern of well-executed ambushes on commuter trains (once peaceful gathering places for political proselytizing), random 'drive-by' shootings on taxi ranks, and vigilante raids on ANC strongholds, along with a host of other acts of indiscriminate violence, had become so frequent that they were taken for granted in the townships.[58] 'We see a strange hand', the progressive *Weekly Mail* editorialized, 'that is turning local conflicts, even family feuds, into massive conflicts between rival political organizations, using professional, highly-trained and well-armed "hit squads".'[59]

Revelations of 'dirty tricks' campaigns sponsored by various branches of the army and police gradually came to light after de Klerk took office in 1989. A steady stream of 'whistle-blowers' from within the security establishment, including Dirk Coetzee (SAP), Felix Ndimene (SADF Special Forces), Major Nico Basson (Military Intelligence), and Colonel Gert Hugo (Military Intelligence), gave further substance to the claim that the National Party government deceitfully pursued a 'two-track' strategy combining negotiations with covert destabilization of the ANC and its allies.[60]

Under mounting public pressure to respond to these charges, de Klerk appointed a special investigative body, called the Commission of Inquiry into Public Violence, under the chairmanship of Justice Richard Goldstone, to look for clear proof of alleged official links with the covert 'third force'. Operating with an open-ended budget from the Ministry of Justice, the Goldstone Commission began in 1991 to assemble a formidable team of lawyers and investigators who were given sweeping powers to raid and search, subpoena witnesses and compel testimony. The Commission, which looked into everything from taxi wars and township massacres to arms smuggling and alleged 'dirty tricks', spent many months sifting through a morass of charges and denials that the security forces played a clandestine role in orchestrating township violence. The accumulated weight of court evidence on the activities of secret state agencies, as well as the sworn testimony of repentant defectors and survivors, revealed a clear pattern of murderous intrigue directed against opponents of the white minority regime. In May 1992, Transkei military ruler General Bantu Holomisa dropped a bombshell when he released to the media a document recording a military signal made in June 1985, ordering the 'permanent removal from society' of Matthew Goniwe along with three other political activists from Cradock in the Eastern Cape. This top-secret document implicated high-ranking military officers with direct links to the SSC. Political activists had long suspected official state involvement in the brutal murders of the Cradock Four at the height of the popular insurrection. Within anti-apartheid circles, the subsequent inquiry re-opened festering wounds, raising questions about the fates of scores of other political activists who had gone missing without a trace and sparking demands for Nuremberg-style trials to punish the killers.[61]

In November 1992, the Goldstone Commission provided irrefutable evidence of a 'third force' sanctioned at the top levels of the Directorate of Military Intelligence (DMI) when it revealed the existence of a top-secret military intelligence unit called the Directorate of Covert Collection (DCC), specializing in 'dirty tricks' against political opponents. The crux of these fresh revelations centred on the approval of senior DMI officers to the hiring of a former military CCB operative and twice-convicted murderer, Ferdi Bernard, to lead a task force whose mission was to smear the reputation of the ANC by linking its armed wing, Umkhonto weSizwe (MK), with criminal acts and crime syndicates involving drug dealers, prostitutes and shebeen owners (illicit liquor dealers). What made this secret plot particularly galling was that it was hatched almost eighteen months after the ANC was unbanned and after the government had declared that clandestine operations of this sort had ceased. The Goldstone Commission also uncovered another secret operation, code-named 'Project Echoes', whose objective was to discredit the ANC by falsely linking MK with the Irish Republican Army and the Palestine Liberation Organization. 'Echoes' had been authorized by high-ranking military officers, including SADF chief, General Georg Meiring, and senior DMI officer Brigadier Ferdi van Wyk, who was responsible for coordinating the South African government's disinformation and de-stabilization propaganda campaign against SWAPO prior to the Namibian elections in 1989/90 – and had originated with the chief of staff of military intelligence, Lieutenant-General Witkop Badenhorst.[62]

De Klerk reacted to the growing public outcry over these embarrassing disclosures by summarily dismissing sixteen senior SADF officers and suspending seven others. For the first time, the state president openly acknowledged the existence of a core group of dissident, right-wing military officers entrenched in the security establishment who had long been involved in illegal or unauthorized activities and malpractices designed to sabotage efforts at political accommodation with the black majority. Yet these purges left many questions unanswered, particularly the extent to which military intelligence operated on its own initiative or with the tacit approval of the National Party Cabinet.[63] Unchallenged reports listing the names of several alleged civilian auxiliaries strengthened suspicions that the former CCB had not really been dissolved as de Klerk had strenuously insisted, but had been allowed to 'survive in spirit, if not in name, within the DCC'. While de Klerk's opponents on the left felt he did too little, too late, to discipline dissident officers, his enemies on the right thought that he did too much, too soon. The Conservatives accused him of disloyalty to the country's soldiers and of sacrificing dedicated officers merely to appease the ANC.[64]

The origins and composition of the 'third force'

There is, certainly, no foolproof means of uncovering the precise background and operational organization of the subversive 'third force'. Yet by piecing together available evidence, it is possible to draw a composite picture of its genesis and to speculate about its social composition. The instigators of this unofficial state-sponsored violence – South Africa's 'dirty war' – could be found in the well-fortified circles of semi-autonomous military operatives who, disagreeing with de Klerk's alleged capitulation to revolutionaries and communists, were determined to obstruct all political initiatives for a phased transition to power-sharing and eventual majority rule. This powerful cabal consisted of a complex network of 'securocrats' who rose to power during President Botha's term of office at a time when secretive state agencies like the SSC, under the guise of the NSMS, enabled high-ranking military officers to assume extensive decision-making authority at the highest levels of government. The web-like clique spanned both the military and the police, but its true power centres were regional and were vested in past and present operatives of the army Special Forces and 'disbanded' covert forces. This secretive trust was astute enough to 'sub-contract' much of the dirty work to assorted 'hired guns', including such *dramatis personae* as the elite police counter-insurgency unit operating in Namibia before independence, called *Koevoet* (Crowbar); Section C–1 of the Security Police, composed of former MK guerrillas operating crack 'hit squads'; and the CCB, the notorious counterinsurgency unit spawned by the DMI.[65] In addition, special units assembled under the command of the SADF Special Forces were believed to be closely linked to the activities of the 'third force', which was blamed for a whole range of senseless killings, including 'train massacres', random shootings and selective assassinations of political activists. The Special Forces consisted of four active Reconnaissance regiments (or Recces), which functioned as the operational arm of the DMI. Other elite counter-insurgency units, such as the 44 Parachute Battalion, along with the 31 and 32 ('Buffalo') Battalions, were also associated with the Special Forces.[66] The fearsome 'Buffalo' Battalion, South Africa's only true 'foreign legion-naires', was composed almost exclusively of Portuguese-speaking merce-naries recruited in Angola from the *Frente Nacional para a Libertação de Angola* (FNLA), and conferred with South African citizenship as a reward for service. This unit, which had been deployed extensively in the town-ships of pre-independence Namibia, was accused of extreme brutality and flagrantly arbitrary behaviour during its patrols of Rand townships.[67]

After Zimbabwe gained independence in 1980, the SADF launched a secret scheme, code-named Operation Winter, which was designed to recruit men who had served with the disbanded Rhodesian Special Forces. Hundreds of Rhodesian Special Air Service (SAS) and Selous Scouts sol-diers, both white and black, fled south to the safety of white-ruled South Africa. The Rhodesians brought with them rogue units operating under the name of *Resistência Nacional Moçambicana* (RENAMO), which had originally been created by Rhodesian intelligence and trained by the Rhodesian SAS. The SADF Special Forces quietly assumed command over RENAMO, and quickly expanded the secret war of destabilization against the Frelimo regime in post-independence Mozambique.[68] Many of the Rhodesian veterans were incorporated into Four Recce, based in Saldanha and which specialized in operations against Angola, and Five Recce, which had operated in support of RENAMO since its inception. These were the only two Recce units that contained black troopers, mostly veterans of the Angolan FNLA, Rhodesian SAS units, or young men abducted from Mozambique and forcibly conscripted. Some Rho-desian veterans, along with former members of the Namibian-based *Koevoet*, were redeployed with South African units, including the KwaZulu Police Force. The Special Forces created a vast network of front organi-zations designed to provide a convenient façade for their covert opera-tions. One such creation was the CCB, a 'death squad' which came under the nominal command of the head of Special Forces but whose staff did what they wanted, operating on the 'need to know' principle. They worked under cover of legitimate civilian businesses, and consequently created a complex network of vested interests.[69]

The full extent of Cabinet-level connivance in these clandestine activities will perhaps never be known. Whatever the origins and specific social organization of the 'third force', its purpose was evident. The scattered, diffuse pattern of extra-legal violence suggested not the existence of a single, all-embracing conspiracy under central coordination, but instead countless mini-conspiracies with regional roots. The principal aim of 'third force' violence was to exacerbate existing cleavages, generally socio-economic and ethnic in nature, in order to divide local communities into warring factions, pitting migrants against squatters, permanent residents against vulnerable newcomers, Zulu-speakers against Xhosa-speakers, Inkatha loyalists against ANC supporters, youth against elders, and so on. In time, many black residential areas became embroiled in a low-level civil war, where the lines of division could not be easily classified into strictly class and/or racial antagonisms.[70] In their haste to emphasize the stark contrasts between the forces of progress and those of reaction, political analysts often gravely oversimplified the jagged fault-lines cutting both horizontally and vertically across South Africa's socio-economic landscape. The cumulative impact of the 'third force' violence – in line with the doctrines of low-intensity conflict and counterinsurgency warfare – was to transform the townships, ghettos and squatter settlements into microcosms of the wider civil war, thereby creating divisions that impeded the implantation of enduring ties of solidarity amongst those social groups which share more or less identical life-chances, and undermining the formation of fixed and stable political organization.[71]

Domestication of Low-intensity Conflict

Despite de Klerk's efforts to bring the military establishment under tighter civilian control and into line with the reform process, 'hardline' senior officers in the SADF, including SADF chief Andreas 'Kat' Liebenberg, balked at accepting de Klerk's stated aim of power-sharing in an elected transitional government. They insisted that the inevitable consequence of the reformist route would be more bloodshed and chaos. These generals closed ranks against the campaign to expose a subversive 'third force' in the military ranks, and demanded amnesty for past abuses. They consistently assured de Klerk that there was no SADF involvement in township killings, in spite of evidence that factions in the SADF, at least up to brigadier level, had worked actively to frustrate a settlement with the ANC.[72] Despite his willingness to sacrifice a few key officials in the SAP and the SADF, de Klerk remained a partially immobilized captive of the 'securocrats' left over from the Botha era. He could not afford to alienate the mainstream security establishment because his entire reformist programme depended upon the loyalty and goodwill of the military and police to ensure internal security during the difficult period of political transition, or as a fall-back in the event that the reformist initiatives failed to produce a negotiated settlement.[73]

Not surprisingly, the existence of dissent in the military mirrored the profound chasm within the white electorate between those who supported the pace and direction of de Klerk's reformist programme and those who bitterly opposed it. On the eve of nationwide elections scheduled for April 1994, the SADF represented a cross section of white political sentiments. Key elements in the 'third force' remained a semi-autonomous and powerful presence inside the vast security establishment, with its complex bureaucratic layers and Byzantine 'backdoor' channels of communication. Although they were unable to operate with impunity, as in the mid 1980s – a time when some leading 'securocrats' advocated the implementation of a wholesale 'Argentinian solution' to stamp out political opposition – they still represented a potent force of reaction. A small but highly trained and motivated officer corps, based in DMI and Special Forces, continued to maintain some operational control over special units. Consequently, they were able to call upon their own supplies of arms and ammunition, which were smuggled into South Africa from Mozambique, captured from ANC arms caches, and diverted into South Africa from former military bases in Namibia. 'Third force' elements were also able to finance their own operations from the proceeds of an overlapping illicit trade in gun running and ivory poaching, along with rake-offs from organized crime. Many of the businesses funded by DMI, using the disbanded CCB project as 'deep cover' and as financing conduits, continued to function as self-sustaining and often highly lucrative undertakings. 'Third force' detachments were also sustained through an illegal fringe of civilian former operatives, South Africa's true 'dogs of war', who had fallen afoul of the official hierarchy in the military or police, but were willing recruits for special missions.[74]

Carrying the moral burden of apartheid

The silence of the highest political authority spoke louder than words. The failure of high-ranking state officials, and especially de Klerk himself, to offer an official apology for apartheid, let alone provide compensation to its victims, reinforced the view that the nearly half-century of social engineering intended to perfect an ideal racial order was merely an ill-advised mistake and a costly error, but not a crime or a moral aberration. If the legalization of banned organizations and the opening of negotiations with former opponents had been accompanied by genuine expressions of guilt and repentance, then the National Party government would have signalled official condemnation and abhorrence of the state-sponsored regional destabilization campaign and the unofficial 'dirty war' at home. Official acknowledgement of wrongdoing is the starting point for healing the wounds of the past. Without a moral break with apartheid, the de Klerk administration allowed the impression to linger that the security forces fought a 'just war' against the opponents of the white minority regime which, under current circumstances and for tactical reasons alone, had come to an end.[75] Under these circumstances, it was not surprising that the well-indoctrinated defenders of 'white civilization' against 'black terrorists' did not come in from the cold. These were the same highly decorated forces that sponsored the brutal destabilization campaigns throughout southern Africa; that were given virtual carte blanche authority secretly to train and support RENAMO in Mozambique and UNITA in Angola; that unleashed 'death squads' both inside and outside South Africa to eliminate opponents of the white minority regime; that prepared Inkatha and the KwaZulu police for similar destructive ends inside South Africa; and that built networks of informers and became expert at 'turning' captured guerrillas against their former comrades.[76]

The low-intensity counterinsurgency warfare launched during the 1984–86 popular uprising, and under conditions that in many respects resembled the first stages of a revolutionary seizure of state power, seemed to acquire a life of its own, carried out under the cloak of secrecy by clandestine operatives long after the official state ideology that originally sanctioned these actions had assumed a considerably more conciliatory tone.[77] In the aroused climate of fear and anxiety even small 'third forces' were able to thrive and trigger major confrontations with little effort. Indiscriminate assaults on train commuters, random shootings of both ANC and Inkatha loyalists, and professional-looking assassinations of selected local leaders fuelled anger and sparked revenge attacks. Once set in motion, the escalating spiral of violence became self-perpetuating. Even though de Klerk promised to 'depoliticize' the police by shifting their primary duties to crime prevention, the SAP was unable to shed its long-standing stigma as a partisan force responsible for the enforcement of apartheid and prone to the excessive use of lethal force. Despite its reputation for efficiency in other matters, the SAP made only half-hearted attempts to bring those responsible for the township violence to justice. For the most part, police recruits were poorly trained and lacked a professional ethos. In countless 'unrest' situations, the SAP was rightly blamed for gross incompetence, routine brutality, and callous disregard for human life. An ingrained 'shoot to kill' mentality contributed significantly to officially sanctioned violence in the townships. The predominantly white

anti-riot arm of the SAP, known as Internal Stability Units, was the main
instrument of law and order in troubled townships. These special detachments were reviled by residents as unwanted occupiers.[78] There was also
widespread documentary proof that police units on the ground continued
avidly to throw their weight behind those who opposed the Congress-
aligned 'comrades' in street clashes.[79] Despite claims that officially sanctioned abuses had been curbed, scores of political prisoners continued to
suffer grievous bodily injuries and to die in detention from police torture, and senior officers and Cabinet ministers seemed indifferent to the
fact. While the SADF and SAP sought to attribute responsibility for excesses to overzealous underlings, the source of the official terror rested
with a hard-core leadership of the security forces who were 'steeped in
the culture of covert operations'.[80]

5

The Roots of Political Violence

Generalizations about the origins and causes of politically motivated violence in South Africa are difficult to make. After all, the hydra-headed conflicts that divided the country have deep roots in the country's tangled past. Every region, locality and community bears its own particular scars of racial hatred and abuse, and the way in which the resulting animosities play themselves out must be understood in terms of their own peculiar dynamics. During the 1990s, the quickening pace of change had an un-settling effect on those at the bottom who feared that they had been sidelined in what many cynically perceived as a narrow 'power struggle' between elites. The deteriorating economic situation rendered the bitter competition over scarce resources even more acute. The loosening of old bonds unleashed a torrent of accumulated anger and frustration that often spilled over into unadulterated violence. As new fissures tore open the social fabric, long dormant disputes surfaced once again and additional sources of conflict were suddenly created out of whole cloth.

As Heribert Adam and Kogila Moodley have suggested, perhaps no other aspect of the current conjuncture 'has elicited more divergent explanations and misinterpretations than the ongoing political violence'.[1] It has been variously attributed to a whole host of factors, including (1) de Klerk's double agenda and the unreformed, unrepentant, and 'trigger-happy' security forces; (2) a shadowy 'third force' of right-wing elements safely hidden inside the security establishment and committed to derailing the government's negotiations agenda; (3) ANC–Inkatha rivalry, fuelled by the personal ambitions of Buthelezi and engineered on the ground by overzealous Inkatha warlords; (4) the ANC's campaign of armed struggle, the strategy of ungovernability, and revolutionary intolerance combined with the ideology that 'political power comes out of the barrel of a gun'; (5) ingrained tribalism, unleashed by the erosion of white repression and the loosening of the rigid social controls that previously held 'black on black' violence in check; (6) the legacy of apartheid in general, including enforced migrancy and the disintegration of family and kinship networks, the creation of homelands and manufactured tribalism, high unemployment among an entire generation of 'lost youth' without education or appreciable skills, and the collapse of routine policing and social control mechanisms in the deteriorating townships.[2]

While such analyses provide useful insights into the current South African situation, they nevertheless often fall prey to the simplifying tendency to reduce the violence to a single cause. As a result, they fail to account for the complexity of the ongoing social strife, and the social forces and structural conditions that energize and sustain it. By focusing too narrowly on the assignment of blame and culpability, monocausal explanations run the risk of diverting attention from a more comprehensive analysis of crosscutting social conflicts rooted in the harsh historical realities of South Africa.[3]

Schlemmer has provided a useful approach to understanding the ongoing violence by distinguishing between general background conditions, predisposing factors, and triggering events.[4] Background conditions include high levels of structural unemployment and a high degree of dependence upon casual wage work; dislocation caused by rapid urbanization; and the collapse of family and kinship networks. Predisposing factors include the social alienation of rural migrants immersed against their will in sociospatial urban environment dominated by a 'disrespectful' youth subculture, intergenerational cleavages, the intensified competition for scarce resources, and limited opportunities for realistic improvement of life chances in a social climate of uncertainty and fear. Once sparked and under way, the violence almost invariably becomes self-perpetuating.[5]

The 'Sweeping Inferno'

Yet, whatever its particular origins and specific causes, the politically motivated violence that surged through the townships, informal settlements and contested rural communities has taken a terrible toll. The 'body count' of dead and seriously maimed continued to mount at any appalling rate. In the first four years after de Klerk lifted the ban on opposition groups and released Mandela, more than 12,000 people died as a result of political violence.[6] From 1990 to the end of 1992, an average of almost 10 persons per day were killed in politically related unrest. During the first few months of 1993, the death toll declined to around 4.5 per day, well below the average for the previous years. Yet after July 1993, when the IFP and the right-wing Conservative Party abruptly withdrew from the World Trade Centre negotiating forum, the situation took an ominous turn for the worse: over the next three months, at least 1,600 people were killed in political violence, an average of around 18 per day.[7] These figures raised fears that political intolerance had reached such dangerously high levels that South Africa was once again on the verge of sliding into 'an abyss of threatened anarchy'.[8]

Whatever their dizzying magnitude, statistics alone cannot convey the chilling reality of daily life in the strife-torn areas. Ordinary people in the hardest-hit townships, as Marais put it, 'spend their nights in fear and their weekends burying the dead'.[9] The violence was so endemic that it became, to use Hannah Arendt's phrase, 'terrifyingly normal'.[10] Its sheer randomness caused a haemorrhaging of political support for the popular organizations. The violence had a way of taking on its own macabre momentum, which once under way was difficult to contain and bring to an end. It fed on itself in an unending spiral of attacks and retaliatory counterattacks; and this cyclical choreography prompted some political analysts to suggest that the South African situation had come to resemble 'the politics of the last atrocity'.[11]

The ANC placed the blame for the ongoing violence squarely with the ruling National Party, insisting that high-ranking state officials had no intention of putting a halt to the constant turmoil in the townships and squatter settlements because it was part of a cynical ploy to keep a grip on the reins of power. Political analysts noted with alarm that the violence 'appears to be switched on and off at strategic moments'. This grim observation seemed to confirm the suspicions of those who detected a conspiratorial hand in the unrest – that powerful, state-linked partisan forces were actively engaged in a campaign of destabilization.[12] For years, anti-apartheid activists claimed that the so-called 'black on black' violence – a terribly imprecise phrase with racialist undertones – was merely a continuation of covert operations linked to the security forces, and they pointed to the dismal failure of the South African police to capture and prosecute more than a handful of the perpetrators as proof of state complicity.[13] Yet the situation was certainly more complex, and to focus solely on secret conspiracies or covert manipulation is to ignore the wider socio-economic framework and historical context within which township violence took place.

Inkatha and the Politics of Destabilization

The roots of the long-standing animosity between the liberation movement and Mangosuthu Gatsha Buthelezi's Inkatha were inextricably inter-twined in the social fabric of apartheid itself. Because Buthelezi worked within the framework of the Bantustan system, his opponents labelled him a puppet of the white minority regime that he had long publicly opposed. His enemies charged, with some justification, that Inkatha operated for years as the cornerstone of the state strategy of divide and conquer, and they invariably cited Buthelezi's strong-handed rule over KwaZulu, supported and financed by Pretoria, as damning evidence of his collusion with the government.[14]

Yet to dismiss Buthelezi cavalierly as a 'stooge' of Pretoria understated the degree of survivalist compliance with Inkatha's particularly compelling form of clientelism on the part of impoverished, mostly rural Zulu-speakers. Inkatha dominated every aspect of economic, political and cultural life in KwaZulu, recruiting for its Youth Brigade in schools where Inkatha's philosophy formed part of the curriculum, enrolling civil servants who risked losing their jobs if they did not join, and operating mainly as a clientelist-patronage network umbilically tied to the KwaZulu state budget.[15] Unlike the ruling cliques of other homelands, Inkatha boasted a large membership, a formidable organization, and a degree of legitimacy both at home and abroad. Because of his staunch opposition to sanctions and his strident advocacy of a free-market economy, Buthelezi became the darling of overseas conservatives.[16] Inkatha's effectiveness as a potential ally in a right-of-centre coalition arose from its popularity with the West and with big business as an independent, conservative critic of apartheid.[17]

However, there was a seamy side to Inkatha's rise to prominence. Buthelezi and a core of loyal lieutenants forged Inkatha into a political party that laid claim to nearly 2 million paid members. Critics disputed the accuracy of this figure, contending that Buthelezi's power-base was largely restricted to the impoverished rural areas of KwaZulu and that support for Inkatha was unlikely to take root in the urban townships of the PWV area where nearly half of South Africa's 7 million Zulu-speakers live.[18] According to estimates in 1992, Inkatha's political support among black people was at most 12 per cent and perhaps as little as 6 per cent. Yet most political observers dismissed even these rather modest figures as too generous.[19] Buthelezi's appeals for democratic pluralism in South Africa never extended to KwaZulu, the homeland that he ruled for over twenty years. He held the key portfolios of chief minister and minister of police and presided over a legislative assembly that tolerated no serious opposition. Inkatha's influence derived precisely from KwaZulu's formal place on the outer perimeter of South Africa's fragmented state apparatuses.[20] The homelands status of KwaZulu enabled Inkatha to make use of draconian security measures, thereby preventing the unhindered existence of political opposition in the areas under its nominal control. The rapid expansion of the functions of the KwaZulu Police (KZP), along with the overall 'para-militarization' of KwaZulu, provided Inkatha with what was in effect its own private army with strong organizational links to Pretoria's security establishment.[21]

War without end: the 'killing fields' of Natal

The origins of the overtly political violence in Natal can be traced to bitter rivalry beginning in August 1985 between Inkatha loyalists and their opponents for control of the dismal townships and overcrowded squatter settlements near Pietermaritzburg and Durban. One of the first indications of the violent confrontations to come was the Inkatha-sponsored vigilante attacks on bus drivers in the Midlands area. These bus drivers were employed by the KwaZulu Transport Company (KZT), but were organized by the COSATU-affiliated TGWU. Inkatha loyalists viewed them as 'traitors' for their refusal to work during 'stayaways'.[22] As the popular rebellion unfolded in Natal, Inkatha sided with the status quo, and took advantage of bloody street rioting that blended tragically with intra-ethnic violence to challenge the growing popularity of the UDF and COSATU. The fighting, which turned youths against their elders, community against community, and eventually became embedded in local and personal feuds as well as in criminal activity, flickered off and on for months.[23]

The fighting erupted once again in earnest during 1987 when UDF affiliates tried to organize support in the Natal Midlands around Pietermaritzburg and were confronted, sometimes violently, by Inkatha 'warlords' who saw their primacy in carefully nurtured local fiefdoms threatened for the first time. With slight variation, the violence tended to follow a common pattern. As Inkatha lost ground in the older, settled townships like Edendale, Imbali and Ashdown, its local leaders turned to the surrounding informal squatter settlements to secure an alternative base of support. Inkatha gained the allegiance of 'shacklords' in these sprawling shantytowns who, with the assistance of fearsome vigilantes called *amabutho*, controlled the profitable extortion and protection rackets which thrived in the troubled atmosphere spawned by massive unemployment and rampant crime.[24] Without legal rights to land, shack-dwellers living on the fringes of most large towns throughout Natal were dependent on local 'power-brokers' with whom they traded obedience and levies, tribute and other payments for residential security. 'Warlords' sought the protection of Inkatha and the KwaZulu authorities to uphold their de facto rights to land and to consolidate their hold over the shack areas.[25] The example of Thomas Shabalala, the self-proclaimed 'mayor' of a sprawling squatter township named Lindelani on the hilly outskirts of Durban, illustrated a common pattern. Shabalala, 'in many ways the quintessential ward boss', ruled his fiefdom with what critics said was a 'mixture of terror and patronage'. In Lindelani, he controlled the allocation of nearly all community services – from establishing health clinics and schools, to the distribution of pensions, to police and fire protection. He also owned and operated the largest fleet of taxis in the area.[26]

In 1988, Inkatha stepped up its campaign to enrol new members in the townships and squatter settlements, resorting in many instances to methods of intimidation just short of outright coercion. In protest, the youthful militants known colloquially as *amaqabane* ('comrades') burned down the homes of municipal councillors who were active in the Inkatha recruitment effort. Older Inkatha loyalists retaliated, thus setting in motion a protracted cycle of revenge and reprisal.[27] What soon became apparent was that the Congress-aligned popular movement did not confront a fragile and compromised expression of the central state apparatus, but came face to face with local government structures backed by a political movement with a social base of support and bolstered by the considerable administrative and repressive machinery of the KwaZulu homeland. By 1989, the violence had metamorphosed into a low-grade, but insidiously brutal, civil war which spread outward from the townships and peri-urban squatter settlements on the fringes of the cities to eventually engulf outlying rural communities, transforming this once-picturesque landscape into a grotesque replica of Cambodia's 'killing fields'.[28] From 1987 to 1990, the number of deaths in the Ntshongwseni valley (the so-called 'Valley of Death') near Pietermaritzburg, the epicentre of the ongoing carnage, was twice the number killed in Beirut during the same period.[29] Burning and looting figured prominently in the fighting that in time assumed the characteristics of an organized 'scorched-earth' campaign. As the battle lines hardened, participants frequently organized themselves into large-scale and quasi-militarized units outfitted with an assortment of instruments of destruction ranging from spears and clubs to petrol bombs, homemade rifles and automatic weapons.[30]

Seen in retrospect, the causes of the Natal violence had as much to do with the competition and despair engendered by acute land shortages, poverty, illiteracy and joblessness on both sides as with manifest ideological differences.[31] The Natal/KwaZulu region has a long-standing reputation as an area plagued by interminable social conflicts unrelated to politics per se, and these chronic tensions often required only a minor catalyst to spark a wider conflagration.[32] Reliable evidence gathered from independent sources indicated the passive collusion, if not outright intervention, of the security forces in violent clashes in which most of the victims were anti-Inkatha youth, suffering at the hands of Inkatha 'warlords' whose activities seemed largely immune from interference or legal action.[33] For example, while political activists had long suspected official connivance, the 1992 conviction of Captain Brian Mitchell on charges of masterminding the Trust Feed massacre in the Pietermaritzburg 'war zone' in 1988, in which eleven Inkatha members were mistakenly killed in a night-time raid, provided the first clear-cut, indisputable proof of security-force complicity with Inkatha 'warlords' and direct involvement in indiscriminate killings.[34] The chronic violence blended political differences with blood feuds which sprang more from personal animosities than from rival ideologies. Combatants on both sides often appeared to be motivated more by the desire to control territory or avenge killings of family and friends than by explicit political goals.[35]

At a February 1990 rally attended by more than a hundred thousand Congress supporters in Durban soon after his release from prison, Mandela called upon his supporters to 'take your guns, your knives, and your pangas [machetes] and throw them into the sea'. But this impassioned appeal for calm fell on deaf ears, and the faint hopes for peace spawned by Mandela's freedom proved ephemeral. The fresh outbreak of organized violence that erupted in the Natal Midlands in late March signalled a new phase of major, calculated escalation of fighting. Amid mounting tensions in the area, Inkatha 'warlords' massed an impromptu army estimated at around twelve thousand 'warriors', divided into separate battalions called *impis* and equipped with shotguns, rifles and spears. These legions, each numbering several thousand fighters apiece and recruited mainly from Inkatha-controlled areas of Sweetwaters, Taylor's Halt and Elandskop, mounted a full-scale assault from KwaZulu territory on ANC strongholds in the embattled Edendale complex located on the western outskirts of Pietermaritzburg. During what became known as the 'Seven Days War' (25–31 March 1990), Inkatha battalions, which were ferried by bus from place to place by the KwaZulu police, fought pitched battles with ANC supporters across an area of 'a couple of hundred square miles'. By the time the blitzkrieg fizzled out, whole communities lay in ruins, dozens of houses had been set ablaze, hundreds killed or seriously injured, and thousands of people had fled for their lives.[36] In strictly military terms, Inkatha scored an impressive victory. In the skirmishing that dragged on for nearly two weeks in the greater Pietermaritzburg area, over 200 people were killed and 20,000 were made into refugees, almost all of them UDF supporters or people not prepared to show allegiance to Inkatha. By one tally, Inkatha loyalists accounted for only 10 per cent of those killed in the one-sided fighting.[37]

Events in Natal had taken an ominous turn. As the bloodletting gained momentum, political activists accused the SAP of cooperating with Inkatha regiments in the lethal 'war zone', and these charges reinforced the long-standing perception that the KwaZulu-based organization was functioning as a cancerous outgrowth of the repressive state system based in Pretoria.[38] The organizational links between the SAP and Inkatha provided substance to these allegations. Beginning in 1987, the head of KwaZulu's police force, who reported directly to Buthelezi, was Brigadier Jacques Buchner, a seasoned 22-year veteran of the security branch of the SAP. One of the foremost experts on counterinsurgency and an accomplished specialist in interrogating and 'turning' former ANC guerrillas, he was long suspected as a stalwart of the 'third force' operating inside the security establishment and an architect of the strategy of using black surrogates to foment so-called 'black on black' violence. Before his untimely retirement in 1992, Buchner almost singlehandedly transformed the KwaZulu Police (KZP) into a formidable pro-Inkatha armed force.[39]

Until early 1990, the political violence in Natal had been largely contained within the Greater Durban area and the Midlands around Pietermaritzburg. However, in the wake of the unbanning of the ANC, the fighting escalated dramatically and spread in ever-widening circles to engulf rural areas that had been previously unaffected by the conflict. The entire region was 'flooded with illegal arms as never before'. This sudden proliferation of modern weaponry brought a new frightening dimension to the conflict. Around 90 per cent of the casualties in the fighting were victims of gunshot wounds. This increase in the firepower of the warring factions also ensured that greater numbers of victims would be killed in single incidents. Various peace efforts from both the UDF/COSATU and Inkatha collapsed due to the inability of leaders to impose discipline at grassroots levels.[40] All in all, the cost of the politically motivated violence in the so-called 'Zulu Wars' in Natal for the four years beginning January 1987 reached an estimated R2.5 billion (US$1.5 billion), as whole areas were laid waste, around 20,000 homes were destroyed, nearly 100,000 people were forced to flee, and close to 6,000 people lost their lives.[41] Yet the worst was yet to come.

The War on the Rand

The first phase: 'dying like flies'[42]

Seen in retrospect, the 'Seven Days War' marked the opening round of a dramatic war of manoeuvre. In the first heady months that followed its legalization, the ANC tried to rally all other political organizations be-hind its banner and to isolate Inkatha. In July, the ANC/COSATU/SACP alliance partners mounted a highly successful nationwide work stoppage, in which three million workers stayed at home and businesses lost nearly $300 million in production, in order to draw attention to the carnage in Natal and to isolate Inkatha. Strike demands included the disbanding of the KwaZulu police, the arrest of Inkatha 'warlords', and the dismissal of SAP officers who assisted Inkatha *impis* in their bloody rampages.[43]

This strategy backfired. In a fateful escalation of the rivalry between the ANC and Inkatha, the vendettas spawned in the Natal 'war zone' were transported like an airborne virus to South Africa's industrial heartland as the power struggle between the two organizations assumed a wider, national political significance. In a calculated manoeuvre designed to meet the challenge of the new political circumstances and to promote a claim to national rather than regional status, Buthelezi sought to remould Inkatha from what was largely regarded as an ethnic-based cultural movement into a self-styled national political organization called the Inkatha Freedom Party (IFP).[44] The proximate cause for the unexpected explosion of violence was the much-publicized IFP recruitment drive targeting the fifty-six single-sex hostels housing close to 175,000 men, mainly Zulu-speaking migrants who had come to the greater Johannesburg area in search of jobs. Inkatha's purpose was crystal-clear: to reclaim its self-professed mandate to speak on behalf of Zulu-speakers, despite the diaspora that left them stranded on the fringes of the Rand townships. But Congress supporters resented what they regarded as this brazen effort on the part of the IFP – which had been largely sidelined as a major player in South Africa's political drama in the wake of the unbanning of the ANC – to establish a permanent beachhead in predominantly ANC strongholds.

During August and September 'the country descended into its bloodiest two months this century', as close to a thousand black people were killed in the townships surrounding Johannesburg.[45] While many observers were quick to label this 'faction fighting' as primarily ethnic in origin, the descriptions of pseudo-political 'tribal warfare' pitting 'Zulus' against 'Xhosas' gloss over the deeper social cleavages created by nearly a half century of enforced racial and ethnic separation and deprivation in the urban townships. The clashes sprang primarily from a power struggle, the battle lines of which – unlike in Natal, with Zulu-speakers on both sides – were drawn between Zulu-speaking hostel dwellers aligned with the Inkatha movement and the primarily Xhosa-speaking residents of nearby squatter camps who supported the ANC.[46]

Strangers in a strange land: hostel-dwellers as social outcasts

Why the hostels? These huge, multistorey housing complexes were occupied mainly by migrant labourers, the bulk of whom were Zulu-

speakers from rural Natal seeking jobs in the cities. By taking control of
the maze-like hostel complexes, sometimes providing shelter for as many
as 20,000 men each, Inkatha hoped to make organizational inroads in the
Rand townships. At the time of the outbreak of violence, there were
around 243,000 migrants in 130 hostels sprinkled throughout the whole
PWV triangle.[47] Hostel dwellers generally harbour a conservative outlook, and many have a long history of conflict with the more urbane,
'worldly' township residents, particularly the politicized youth, who in
turn often look down upon them as illiterate country bumpkins, calling
them *iziqhaza* (stupid people), *makontraka* (contract workers), or other
equally dismissive and contemptuous names.[48]

But one must probe beneath these surface layers of mutually reinforcing
stereotypes to uncover the deeper meaning of these conflicts. Any genuine
understanding of the actions and motives of hostel-dwellers must begin
with the powerful stigma attached to residence in these uniformly overcrowded, dilapidated, barracks-like accommodations. The architects of
apartheid self-consciously conceived of the hostels with the strict enforcement of the rigid migrant labour system in mind. These bounded and
territorially segregated enclaves were located purposefully on the fringes
of settled townships to ensure their social isolation. The hostels were
designed as instruments of social confinement where, as Mkhondo put it,
'inmates were forced to live in squalid conditions without day-to-day
contact with normal family life'. 'Their bungalows were filthy and cold
and greeted everyone with an unbearable stench', he continued. 'Heaps
of garbage littered the floors.' Even after the collapse of influx control,
the hostels remained degraded spaces that were widely recognized as the
'dumping grounds' for impoverished rural migrants. Hostel dwellers have
been typically stereotyped as marginalized men, prone to bouts of heavy
drinking and rumoured to be unrestrained in pursuing the sexual companionship of township women. For their part, recent immigrants to the
urban fringe, condemned by economic necessity to seek shelter in the
hostels, have long been keenly aware of their enforced exile in such a
hostile and oppressive environment. They intuitively knew that their stig-
matized place of residence made them objects of scorn and ridicule, and
they felt the shame and humiliation that comes from the derogatory judge-
ments of outsiders.[49] Not surprisingly, hostel dwellers displayed considerable hostility, resentment and bitterness. The often violent and anti-social
ways in which hostel inmates lashed out against those whom they perceived, rightly or wrongly, as their tormentors must be understood in the
wider context of the socio-spatial environment which branded them as
social outcasts.

Before the outbreak of hostilities, few hostel dwellers were zealous

Inkatha supporters, but most were fiercely opposed to the young 'comrades' who expressed allegiance to the ANC and who 'blatantly defy traditional norms by shrugging off the conservatism of their elders'.[50] During the late 1970s and early 1980s, trade unions affiliated with FOSATU had built a reasonably strong bases in the hostels, with the leadership drawn from the ranks of migrant workers. A key campaign coordinated by FOSATU in 1983 was organized around opposition to new influx control measures. Yet by the late 1980s it became clear that the trade-union movement had neglected hostel workers as a specific constituency, and even though this inattention did not result in mass resignations, it did contribute to the collective sense of isolation.[51]

Inkatha was able skilfully to tap into the huge reservoir of accumulated resentment by trawling the deeper emotional currents of humiliation, isolation and impotence coursing through the foetid, overcrowded hostels. By incessantly hammering away at fears fuelled by the exaggerated belief that the ANC had set its sights on unilateral political domination, the IFP – not in the boardrooms of Natal's sugar barons where Buthelezi was also building support, but on the ground among Zulu-speaking migrants – transformed itself into a touchstone for those who distrusted the motives of the Congress leadership and who suffered at the hands of their intolerant followers.[52]

The violence was contagious, and once under way it quickly developed a dynamic and momentum of its own. Yet the fighting was not random. While the clashes stemmed from the political rivalries between Inkatha and the ANC, the common denominator accompanying the violence was a desperate struggle for land and security. Those in established townships, who were materially better off, felt threatened by the steady influx of recent arrivals desperate for jobs and accommodation. The resulting competition for scarce resources inevitably led to social tensions, and these quickly coalesced around 'tribal' identities, political affiliations and geographical ('home-boy') affinities. The fighting itself involved 'the poorest of South Africa's poor': Zulu-speaking migrants drawn mainly from rural Natal, and impoverished newcomers crowded into makeshift squatter camps, both desperately seeking a permanent place in the cities. Labour-market segmentation created deep fissures between, on the one hand, professionals and skilled workers with a modest stake in the system, and, on the other, unskilled workers and unemployed who competed for temporary, casualized work. These intra-class divisions were reflected in the growing socio-economic stratification in the townships, where there was a clear social hierarchy of which hostel dwellers and inhabitants of the burgeoning squatter camps occupied the lowest rungs.[53]

The anatomy and geography of places like Thokoza, Vosloorus, Kwa-

Thema, Daveyton and Katlehong on the East Rand revealed a grim story of social divisions implanted long before the spasm of violence erupted and overlaid with the newer rivalries of a political struggle for preeminence in South Africa's industrial heartland. Nearly 125,000 migrant workers lived in thirty-one hostels in townships east and south of Johannesburg, where the 'factional' violence was concentrated. More than 90 per cent of the workers in the gold and coal mines were migrants, housed in hostels near their place of work. In Soweto, for example, the five hostels officially accommodated 13,000 residents, though unofficial estimates put the occupancy rate as high as 39,000. As the battle lines were hastily drawn, Inkatha loyalists in the squalid hostels forcibly evicted non-Zulu speakers and those who refused to swear allegiance to the IFP. The hostels became paramilitary staging areas from which vigilantes – called *rooidoeke* because of their distinctive red headbands – planned and executed their forays into the townships. When young 'comrades' mounted counter-attacks, the hostels became fortresses in which to retreat.

The uneasy coexistence between the hostel dwellers and residents of squatter camps broke down in the face of tension and bloodshed, exposing raw ethnic identities. Yet the passions which animated the vicious fighting cannot be simply or primarily ascribed to ancient tribal enmities, despite the plain truth that the labels 'Xhosa' and 'Zulu' provided recognizable insignia for the combatants to rally around. The legacy of different languages, customs and histories has been undeniably real and not a figment of the imagination. In the inevitable conflicts over scarce resources that arose in the day-to-day struggle for survival, ethnic identities certainly played a role in providing convenient lines of demarcation through which embattled communities sorted out differences. But to enthrone 'tribalism', and all the primordial loyalties the term suggests, as the principal explanatory variable in South Africa's ethnic patchwork is wholly inappropriate. What made the outbreak of ethnic animosities even more perplexing was that both Zulu-speakers and Xhosa-speakers have been marginal forces in the vast townships of the East Rand, the heart of South Africa's iron and steel industries. All in all – if it is possible to speak in such typological terms – Zulu-speakers accounted for only about 20 per cent of black South Africans living and working in the Johannesburg and Pretoria areas. Most prosperous local residents tended to be Sotho-speakers, who were largely immune from the carnage.[54]

The interregnum

In late August, the security forces cracked down in a belated effort to stem the slaughter, designating twenty-seven townships 'unrest areas' and providing the SAP with wide powers to arrest and search people without warrant and to seize weapons. A police dragnet of the hostels and shanties produced an awesome armoury of deadly weapons ranging from primitive spears and axes to limpet mines, machine guns and hand grenades.[55] On 15 September, the security forces ordered a massive crackdown, codenamed Operation Iron Fist, involving the large-scale deployment of SADF and police riot units to the war-torn townships, the cordoning off of migrant workers' hostels with razor wire, and the imposition of night-time curfews. These measures, while they helped to extinguish the violence, drew the ire of political activists, who said they resembled in miniature the State of Emergency lifted in three of four provinces earlier in the year.[56] Township residents accused the state authorities of craven indifference to their suffering. They also charged the SAP with favouring Inkatha 'war parties', providing them with armed escorts, and allowing them to brandish what were euphemistically termed 'traditional weapons', such as spears, axes, pangas and clubs known as knobkerries, while teargassing and disarming their opponents. Eyewitnesses claimed to have observed police supplying Inkatha loyalists with firearms. The security forces vehemently denied these charges, yet the claims of impartiality rang hollow.[57]

The Rand violence was accompanied by a string of mysterious attacks, including random 'drive-by' shootings carried out by balaclava-clad assassins who cruised the townships and downtown Johannesburg in minibuses, and a spate of 'taxi rank' bombings. In the most macabre incident, and what proved to the first of a series of similar events, gunmen boarded a Soweto commuter train at Jeppe station and opened fire, killing at least 26 people and seriously injuring over 100.[58] In a deteriorating situation that was rapidly approached anarchy, witnesses reported seeing white men with blackened faces, or wearing hoods, at several battle-grounds mingling with attacking bands, including the well-coordinated Inkatha armed assault on the Phola Park squatter camp on 12 September in which the raiding party set a thousand shacks on fire and virtually flattened the place.[59]

The cool efficiency of these widely dispersed operations fuelled suspicions that a 'hidden hand' was at work stirring up township animosities. Senseless killings of this sort bore a striking resemblance to the style of random terror carried out by RENAMO in Mozambique. Some observers hinted darkly that the security forces were harbouring a renegade 'rogue element' composed of right-wing extremists bent on destabilizing the fragile political situation and sabotaging the fledgling negotiations.[60] Political activists, with their fingers on the pulse of township politics, also blamed a mercurial 'third force' of *agents provocateurs*, with possible links to the security forces, for fanning the flames of 'black on black' violence.

Rumours and conspiracy theories flourished in such a climate of night-marish violence.[61]

Yet the intervention of the security forces alone failed to explain key aspects of the recurrent pattern of the conflict; in particular, why the violence spread so quickly, why it affected some townships and not others, and why the battles raged most often between the more impoverished sections of the township communities, particularly those in squatter camps and the hostel dwellers. The combustible mixture of social isolation from mainstream township life, historically entrenched ethnic bonding, and the fragility of long-term employment prospects created fertile conditions that organized vigilantes, criminal gangs and the extreme right were quick to exploit. The roots of the conflict lay with the legacy of apartheid, whose policies were 'primarily responsible for the desperate poverty and social fragmentation' of the townships, where marginalized groups like hostel dwellers and squatters lacked 'meaningful channels for expressing and resolving grievances'. Bands of young 'comrades', frustrated by the futility of their existence despite the worldwide euphoria anticipating the awaken-ing of the 'new' South Africa, roamed the streets, 'brazenly flaunting pangas, petrol-bombs, and other home-made weapons, answering only to themselves'. While spouting the rhetoric of liberation, these 'comrades' were, in the words of Garson, 'little more than gangsters whose political tactics amount to public violence and battling with the police'. These youths, many of whom lived in squalid squatter camps, contributed to the cycle of violence by defending the township residents against the incursions of Inkatha and other political opponents, and by waging an often indiscriminate war of retribution on the hostel dwellers. Both hostels and squatter camps were situated on the fringes of most townships. Since many hostels, like those in Soweto, were located near railway lines, hostel dwellers rarely needed to enter into the heart of the townships. This fact contributed to their extreme isolation and explained why railway stations were the sites of many bloody battles.[62]

The second phase: turning the violence on and off

In seeking ways to restore calm in the townships, Mandela abandoned an earlier pledge and reluctantly agreed to face-to-face meetings with Buthelezi. This acknowledgement of a role for Buthelezi, whom the Congress had demonized as its adversary and a puppet of the white mi-nority regime, marked a stunning reversal of policy and signalled a politi-cal triumph for Inkatha, which had been sidelined as a major player in South Africa's political drama since the unbanning of the ANC.[63] The political standing Inkatha was unable to achieve through friendly persuasion, it was able to acquire through an orchestrated campaign of social violence. In this sense, Inkatha was able to have its cake and eat it too. By encouraging its militant supporters to engage in provocative acts that would almost certainly result in bloodshed, Inkatha maintained constant pressure on the ANC. While simultaneously doing virtually nothing to curb the carnage carried out in its name, Inkatha ensured itself a place in negotiating stability in the townships.[64]

The solemn talk of peace had little concrete effect on curbing the escalating violence. In Thokoza, Inkatha-aligned hostel dwellers battled with ANC supporters at the nearby Phola Park squatter camp.[65] As if following a well-rehearsed script, the second 'War on the Rand' erupted in March 1991, threatening once again to plunge the townships near Johannesburg into anarchy and chaos. The Inkatha-controlled hostel complexes in Soweto (Meadowlands, Dobsonville and Diepkloof) became flashpoints in the bloody confrontations between *rooidoeke* and township residents. But the brunt of the violence took place in Alexandra township, situated on the northern outskirts of Johannesburg, where the carnage claimed over seventy lives in two weeks of heavy fighting.[66] The vicious battles centred around the Madala (M–1) hostel complex, which Inkatha loyalists had transformed into a fortress from which to launch attacks and to which to retreat when necessary. The entire area around the hostel – called 'Beirut' and 'Iraq' by terrified residents – was laid waste.[67]

Against the backdrop of this unrelenting violence, Buthelezi reiterated his claim that the IFP, the ANC and the National Party were the major political players in South Africa, and he called for a leadership 'troika' consisting of himself, de Klerk and Mandela to guide the country toward a new democratic order.[68] While the ANC demanded the outlawing of 'traditional weapons' at public events, Buthelezi insisted that these were legitimate expressions of 'Zulu tribal identity'. Yet it was modern weapons, such as pistols and AK–47s, that caused the vast majority of deaths in the factional clashes that claimed between 550 and 600 deaths in the first three months of 1991 – the second worst period on record.[69]

The Waning Fortunes of Inkatha

For years, political analysts suspected that a mysterious 'third force' operating under the cover of the security forces had worked hand-in-glove with surrogates to aggravate rivalries between political groups and to incite 'black on black' violence. The aim of these covert efforts, ranging from sponsorship of vigilante activities to selective assassinations, was to destabilize the fragile political situation while simultaneously avoiding 'blatant displays of repression'.[70]

The *Weekly Mail* newspaper spearheaded the drive to expose the covert collusion between the security forces and Inkatha in waging a secret war against the ANC. A former CCB operative, Felix Ndimene, swore that SADF personnel conducted a sophisticated counterinsurgency course for an elite unit of 200 Inkatha fighters at a secret base in the Caprivi Strip before Namibia achieved political independence. Retired army major Nico Basson alleged that the SADF supervised training of Inkatha members in counterinsurgency at a military base near Barberton, supplied AK–47 rifles to key Inkatha members, and provided covert assistance in setting up clandestine cells in townships where the IFP had little influence.[71] What also came to light was that one of South Africa's largest private security firms, Springbok Patrols, supervised paramilitary training for groups of Inkatha members.[72]

The 'Inkathagate' scandal

The shocking disclosures in July 1991 that Cabinet ministers had secretly funnelled funds in order to advance Inkatha's rivalry with the ANC opened a Pandora's Box of allegations of official wrongdoing. Leaked documents revealed that the security police had grown alarmed at the possibility of a *rapprochement* between the ANC and Inkatha, and in August 1989 proposed the idea of promoting Inkatha and Buthelezi as an alternative to the rising popularity of the ANC. The *Weekly Mail* published documentary proof, including confidential police and bank documents, indicating that Buthelezi had met security police on numerous occasions to consider ways of shoring up Inkatha's dwindling support, and that the security police had begun secretly funding Inkatha shortly after Mandela's release from prison in February 1990.[73]

What became known as the 'Inkathagate' scandal produced a cascade of further revelations of high-level collusion between the security forces and Inkatha, including evidence of considerably more secret funding than was initially acknowledged; financial assistance for Inkatha's 'sweetheart' labour front, the United Worker's Union of South Africa (UWUSA), over a six-year period; secret military training for IFP recruits at Mkhuze at a remote base in Northern Zululand; official connivance in Inkatha-led vigilante activities; and sponsorship of criminal gangs like KwaMashu's notorious AmaSinyora gang and Ermelo's Black Cats.[74] These gangs took advantage of the political confusion to 'terrorize communities and kill activists'.[75] These startling revelations damaged the credibility of the ruling National Party, tarnished de Klerk's already fragile personal reputation as a 'neutral' peacemaker and honest referee, and severely compromised Inkatha's dubious claim that it was an independent political player deserving of a prominent place equal to the ANC in South Africa's ongoing constititional negotiations. De Klerk reacted to these embarrassing disclosures by denying any knowledge of secret payments to Inkatha. By demoting Law and Order Minister Adriaan Vlok and and Defence Minister Magnus Malan to minor portfolios in the Cabinet, de Klerk hoped to restore a modicum of confidence and trust in his government and to regain the lost momentum in the negotiations process.[76] These allegations of collusion between the security forces and Inkatha painted the IFP as 'hired guns' for Pretoria. The ties between Buthelezi, whose strenuous denials of any knowledge of these clandestine activities strained all credibility, and the National Party were loosened.[77]

The 'Culture of the Gun'

The unrelenting warfare on the Rand gave substance to the fear that the townships were slipping closer to open civil war, and underscored the growing perception that the ANC were unable to prevent the violence and protect loyalist communities. The ANC came under growing grassroots pressure to deploy its MK guerrillas to protect township residents against the violence. The hesitant response of the ANC prompted prominent civic association figures to accuse the leadership bitterly of abrogating its responsiblity.[78] Vicious clashes between chronically unemployed residents of Mthe Holomisa and Mandela Village squatter settlements on the outskirts of Katlehong on the East Rand, the *rooidoeke* rampages in Diepkloof and Dobsonville in Soweto, Inkatha vigilante attacks on the Chicken Farm squatter camp, and the before-dawn military-style assault (involving over a thousand Inkatha-aligned hostel dwellers escorted by SAP units) on the Swanieville squatter camp near Kagiso on the West Rand were the most visible expressions of near-continuous strife.[79] Township residents accused the security forces of dereliction of duty, inaction in stemming assaults and counterassaults, and open collusion and connivance with vigilantes. Witnesses reported that professional assassins armed with rifles and shotguns were using the hostels as hideouts, and 'somebody [was] supplying guns, and training and sophisticated knowledge and techniques'.[80] The ANC accused Inkatha members of plotting with the security forces to 'fan the flames of violence', while in turn Inkatha emphasized the alliance between the ANC and the SACP as proof of a conspiracy to seize and monopolize power.[81]

'[I]n the townships there is a war already', van Niekierk argued. 'The ANC is paying a bloody price for being projected as the likely winner of a one-[person], one-vote election'.[82] The growing loss of confidence in the ANC's ability to defend the strife-torn townships had the corrosive effect of undermining its base of political support. Township residents had demanded that the ANC supply them with weapons with which to defend themselves after the violence first got under way in mid 1990. These pleas for assistance went largely unanswered. The SACP – with strong ties to MK – initially floated the idea of establishing self-defence units after the ANC suspended its armed struggle in August 1990. Leading MK cadres produced a confidential booklet entitled 'For the Sake of our Lives', describing in detail how self-defence units (SDUs) could be formed and deployed nationwide under the guidance of the ANC's military wing. The plan as it was originally conceived was never fully implemented. In the midst of the dramatic escalation of political violence in 1991, grassroots ANC activists urged township residents to arm themselves, pledging to assist civic associations in establishing armed 'self-defence committees' in the event that the state security forces were able to disarm fighting factions, and promising that returning MK soldiers would assume a 'leading and active role' in training volunteers.[83] MK military commander Ronnie Kasrils declared that these defence units were vital for the ANC's survival because the security forces, in collaboration with Inkatha vigilantes, were waging a full-scale war against the Congress. The motive behind these joint operations was to weaken the ANC and inflate the strength of Buthelezi and Inkatha.[84] The IFP leadership reacted with outrage against police raids – undertaken at the ANC's request – on hostel complexes around Johannesburg aimed at confiscating weapons and disarming hostel dwellers. Inkatha central-committee member Musa Myeni ominously pledged to deploy 100,000 armed Inkatha fighters to Soweto if the ANC failed to halt street clashes there. This threat underscored the growing tendency of all political organizations to grope toward the formation of self-defence units, private militias, and paramilitary squads.[85]

The National Peace Accord signed between the ANC, the National Party government and Inkatha in September 1991 outlined a Code of Conduct designed to temper the kind of random violence which had transformed scores of townships and squatter camps into 'war zones' where innocent bystanders were increasingly victimized. While this agreement was hailed at the time as a breakthrough in dampening down tensions, it assumed that the leaders were genuinely interested in reconciliation and were not actively involved behind the scenes in fanning the flames of discord, and that they were capable of exerting control over their grassroots constituencies. While the Code of Conduct was never strictly adhered to, the National Peace Accord did put in place some administrative mechanisms for local mediation and established a Peace Monitoring Force, which actually proved to be relatively effective at certain times and places. The Peace Secretariat, which evolved out of the Accord, waged an uphill battle to stem the tide of communal violence.

Yet on the ground, rival factions largely ignored these pleas for peace from above, and the township battles ebbed and flowed according to local dynamics all their own.[86] In areas hardest hit by the politically motivated violence, the ANC was unable to maintain a tight grip over its followers. Youthful militants, overlooking the frequent calls for discipline from national leaders and acting on their own initiative, were drawn into the 'culture of the gun', as one commentator graphically put it. Immediately following its unbanning, scores of angry youths, with little genuine political understanding, flocked to the banner of the ANC. What slowly dawned on them was that their current problems – few jobs, gutter education, deteriorating township services, material deprivation – were unlikely to disappear suddenly 'when freedom arrives'. This realization that time was standing still in the townships led to mounting frustration and growing cynicism about what the future might hold. ANC-aligned 'comrades' became 'restless for weapons to defend themselves'. In an atmosphere of factional violence and lawlessness, the ability to handle a gun and fighting prowess 'account for a good deal more than political accountability'. Confusion reigned supreme in many areas where well-armed and ANC-led SDUs slipped beyond the ANC's control. Returning MK exiles were sometimes enlisted to provide training, but the ANC vehemently denied that it supplied weapons. In some instances, rival defence units emerged, transforming what were once genuine grassroots initiatives to curb the violence into vicious and divisive 'power struggles in what were once remarkably united communities'.[87]

ANC leaders, and Chris Hani in particular, admitted that some SDUs operated outside the guidelines laid down by the national leadership, which prohibited violence and intimidation. Many undisciplined 'comrades', proficient in the use of weapons and with the know-how to secure them (whether from MK arms caches or from gunrunners), climbed to power in the controversial defence units, blurring the distinction between legitimate defence measures undertaken by communities and criminal violence. Lacking strong organizational links with the ANC leadership, wayward SDUs sometimes degenerated into 'pockets of gangsterism and warlordism'.[88]

The Grim Legacy of Ungovernability and Lawlessness

The 1984–86 popular rebellion had unleashed a torrent of profound conflict, contradiction, and ambivalence that left an enduring imprint on the political landscape. Deep divisions between the youth and the older generation; the animated hostility between the permanently urbanized township residents and the avalanche of migrants and recent arrivals, the clash between a 'Westernized' urban culture and conservative rural folk-ways; and an invidious 'culture of political intolerance' – all gradually wormed their way into the routines of daily life. The townships under-went a frightful process, sometimes rapid and sometimes gradual, of social disintegration and collapse. In the context of massive unemployment and the deepest recession in South African history, a so-called 'lost generation' of township youth, largely uneducated and politically and socially voice-less and marginalized, were lured, as Nhlanhla Maake put it, into a 'culture of violence and violation'.[89] Within this seamless web born of hopeless-ness and frustration, it was difficult to pinpoint where political violence stopped and petty gangsterism began. Undisciplined youth, lacking clear political motives, coalesced with criminal elements to exploit the insecurity and confusion, thereby contributing to an aura of lawlessness. 'Large areas of the townships', one observer noted, 'are being held to ransom by gangs of *tsotsis*, as the youths are called who are hijacking cars, frequently killing the occupants, robbing delivery trucks and demanding vast amounts of protection money from local businesses'. Soaring crime and a rising tide of calculated assaults on police transformed the sprawling squatter settlements, with their densely packed housing patterns and narrow alley-ways, into 'no-go' areas for the security forces.[90]

In the townships, the hostels stood at the centre of bloody, tit-for-tat warfare between Inkatha and the ANC-aligned township residents.[91] Many of these huge, fortress-like complexes became arms factories, warrior training camps and havens for fugitives, which even the police were un-willing to enter for fear of attack. IFP loyalists expelled 'non-Zulus' and political undesirables in their own version of 'ethnic cleansing'. According to the Independent Board of Inquiry, a human-rights monitoring group in Johannesburg, Inkatha-sponsored 'war parties' launched more than 300 separate attacks on neighbourhoods, commuter trains and taxis from their bases in the hostel complexes, killing more than 1,200 people in the two-year period beginning in mid 1990. The ANC consistently demanded that Inkatha supporters be prevented from brandishing so-called 'cultural weapons' (spears, swords and clubs) during public rallies and marches, and that the authorities cordon off the hostels, conduct regular searches for weapons, and eventually replace these neglected, uninhabitable accommodations with family units. On the other side, Inkatha insisted that the hostels fulfilled a vital function of providing poor rural people with needed housing. By constantly reminding their followers that the ANC wished to phase out the hostels, IFP leaders were able to exploit the fears of the hostel dwellers that the ANC was engaged in a sinister plot to deprive them of the only fragile toehold they had in a hostile urban environment.[92]

Gun battles, ambushes on taxis and crowded places which claimed scores of innocent victims, and random attacks on trade unionists and political activists have 'become a way of life' since 1990.[93] Commuter trains, once peaceful gathering places for political debate, became sites of extreme danger. According to the South African Human Rights Commission, the number of people who died in train attacks in the first three months of 1992 outstripped the combined figure for the whole of 1990 and 1991.[94] Townships like Alexandra were transformed through months of fighting between hostel dwellers and 'comrades' into South Africa's 'own little Beirut'.[95]

The violence, whether politically motivated or criminally intended, was part of a spiral of lawlessness pushing the townships towards further chaos and anarchy. The causes for the 'mini-wars' that tore communities asunder were often difficult to establish: some were skirmishes between rival political factions; others took the form of revenge attacks involving hostel-dwellers and township residents, or ethnic and family disputes which, in conditions of worsening poverty and despair, rapidly escalated into full-scale battles. Violence rapidly became the principal method of settling disputes in a country with no long-standing tradition of political tolerance and a history of severe repression, and where the police and judiciary were widely distrusted and feared.[96]

The Killing Routine in Natal

The visible, explosive 'War on the Rand' that dominated public consciousness during 1990 and 1991 overshadowed the changing tableau of bloody conflict that surged through Natal. Unlike other political contests in South Africa, the struggle for hegemony between the ANC and Inkatha was raw and unmediated. But the process of polarization that pushed the rival organizations toward open war was neither uniform nor inexorable. In searching for answers to this riddle, political commentators often appealed to ideological differences. At the risk of oversimplification, it was possible to distinguish the Inkatha loyalists and ANC supporters, respectively, along an ideological spectrum ranging from traditional, primordial tribalist loyalties at one extreme, to modernist, cosmopolitan outlooks at the other.

But different mind-sets alone cannot account for the resultant depth of social fragmentation or the endurance of the organized violence that tore townships, squatter settlements and rural communities asunder. To explain the historical specificity of the Natal 'civil war' depends upon understanding the peculiar political geography of the region. The rise of Inkatha as a mass movement following its founding in 1975 testified largely to the rapid transformation of a delicate urban–rural balance of political power. First and foremost, Inkatha was incubated under the protective wing of the KwaZulu homeland, and the Zulu nationalist mantle that surrounded it reflected the defensive reaction of Zulu-speaking political elites whose position at the apex of a clientelist hierarchy depended upon at least slowing the erosion of customary power and preserving a tribal identity in the face of the steady breakdown of village communities and the massive migration to the urban centres.

At first blush, the political contest between the ANC and Inkatha was mirrored in the peculiar interchange between town and country. For the most part, Congress-aligned mass movements dominated the metropolitan townships and their squatter-camp satellites. But the web of affiliations and loyalties that radiated outward from the urban areas thinned out as they approached the more conservative rural areas. It was here that Inkatha largely held sway. Its popular base, especially among village headmen and penetrating the ranks of landless migrants, made it a formidable force. Despite concerted efforts to transform its traditionalist image and broaden its popular appeal, the lifeblood of Inkatha remained the KwaZulu home-land. On a map, KwaZulu resembled, as one political commentator put it in another context, a 'colony of amoeba, amorphous blobs swimming in the land mass of South Africa'.[97] These fragmented pieces of land frequently abutted or even enveloped townships on the fringes of large cities. Since they were administered by KwaZulu authorities, they created fertile ground for nourishing and sustaining pockets of support for Inkatha. These were territorial strongholds where hereditary chiefs and tribal elders, umbilically linked to the Zulu monarchy and its patronage, ruled with an iron fist and a resolute will. The central KwaZulu state administration, bunkered down north of the Tugela river in Ulundi, was ready and willing to underwrite the covert use of officially sanctioned coercion and reprisal against those who dared challenge its undisputed rule.[98]

Partisan gang warfare

The 'Inkathagate' scandal dealt a serious blow to Buthelezi's credibility, from which Inkatha never really fully recovered. The spread of political violence into previously unaffected areas of the Natal countryside reflected an even further erosion of Inkatha's power-base. Along the south coast, politicized youth, who had accused traditional chiefs and *indunas* of corruption, nepotism and inefficient administration, undermined the power and influence of the existing tribal authorities. By 1990, the civil adminis-tration reached a state of virtual collapse, and the peri-urban settlements around Port Shepstone had plunged into 'total anarchy'. In order to regain lost ground, the traditional chiefs went on the offensive. Powerful Inkatha 'warlords', who ruled squatter settlements near Durban with an iron fist, 'loaned' them vigilante 'shock troops' who had been dragooned from the ranks of the unemployed and bussed to the battlefields. The KwaZulu government also supplied German-made G3 rifles, a deadly weapon with firepower superior to the AK–47 assault rifle favoured by the ANC 'comrades'. In 1990 and 1991, Inkatha 'warriors' time and again raided ANC redoubts along the south coast, leaving scores of people dead and causing thousands of terrified residents to flee from their homes during bouts of heavy fighting.[99] This deadly game was replayed elsewhere. Daily reports of skirmishes between Inkatha gunmen and ANC supporters filtered in from areas as far apart as the north coast near Richards Bay, the Table Mountain area east of Pietermaritzburg, Bruntville near Mooi River, and the devastated peri-urban settlements surrounding Richmond.[100] In the 'war zone' near Pietermaritzburg, the fighting took a dramatic turn as both sides brought automatic weapons and hand grenades into regular use and engaged in well-orchestrated military manoeuvres, including ambushes and planned assaults on 'enemy territory'.[101]

The years of politically motivated violence had set in motion a recurrent cycle of attack, revenge, retaliation and retribution which had become firmly embedded in the social fabric. Rival paramilitary bands carved out separate spheres of influence, and partitioned strife-torn areas into one-party fiefs. The unresolved antagonisms between combatants on both sides settled into a kind of protracted trench warfare that yielded neither clear victory nor workable peace inspired by compromise. On the one side, Inkatha strongmen, 'warlords' and tribal authorities came to rely on Mafia-style enforcers, hired gunmen and professional 'hit squads' to maintain order and discipline in areas under their control. On the other, MK guerrillas, with their specialized training in small-arms tactics, infiltrated the battle zones in order to assist embattled communities loyal to the ANC. More often than not, the security forces, especially the KwaZulu police, cooperated in the carnage by turning a blind eye to Inkatha attacks on ANC supporters. This tacit approval of Inkatha sorties prompted their Congress rivals to retaliate, thereby effectively institutionalizing organized, partisan violence as the principle means of resolving intra-communal conflicts.[102]

A new, more ominous pattern emerged. In contrast to the past, when the skirmishes were generally out in the open and the two sides struggled over territorial supremacy, the violence after the middle of 1990 became more sudden and cunning, largely unaccountable, and immune to the preventative tactics of well-meaning peace monitors and local dispute-resolution committees. The fighters used their intimate knowledge of the rugged terrain to keep out of sight of the SADF reinforcements, which had been sent to the strife-torn areas ostensibly as a deterrent to full-scale warfare. 'Hit-and-run' tactics and pre-emptive raids on 'enemy' strong-holds replaced set-piece battles, as both sides resorted to stealth and manoeuvre. As Brian Pottinger so eloquently put it, 'combatants carve their territory tree-line by tree-line, stream by stream, path by path'.[103]

In the violence that brought the region to the brink of open civil war, each side accomplished its share of wanton killing. Some of the violence appeared to be the work of partisan vigilantes operating outside the firm and direct control of their organizations, and of armed gangs masquer-ading as political guerrillas, but instead pursuing their own agenda of vengeance and intimidation. Even if political notables speaking on behalf of Inkatha and the ANC wanted discipline among their rank-and-file followers, local 'warlords' and power-brokers were largely unwilling to accept it.[104] From the mid 1980s, an estimated one-half of the politically motivated killings took place in Natal, home for a fifth of South Africa's population.[105] Inkatha claimed with a great deal of bitterness that ANC-led 'hit squads' assassinated over 200 IFP officials between 1990 and 1993 alone, and that MK guerrillas carried out a number of massacres of IFP loyalists that went virtually unnoticed in the media. The region was awash with lethal weapons, many of them assault rifles supplied long ago under a cloak of secrecy by the SADF to RENAMO in Mozambique, that began to flow back across the border. Other weapons spilled from the secret arms caches stowed by MK when the ANC leadership suspended its guerrilla war against white minority rule. With an arsenal this formi-dable at their disposal, the battle-scarred combatants settled down to a long war of attrition.[106]

6

The Political Spectrum

[Marginalized black youth] are, to judge from a day among them in Guguletu [Cape Town], spirits caloused by *apartheid* and resistance. They scorn deals made in their name at negotiating tables. They anticipate the nation's first free elections either with bottomless cynicism, or with fantastic expectations. Even their leaders wonder if they can be led.... The young have nothing to lose, not even prospects.[1]

Long before it was unbanned in 1990, the ANC had succeeded in moving out of the shadows of underground politics to take its place at the helm of the liberation movement. The release of Nelson Mandela and his subsequent 'globe-trotting' tour rekindled worldwide interest in South Africa and breathed new life into the international anti-apartheid movement, particularly the sanctions campaign. At home, the ANC basked in the glory of having survived decades of unrelenting, brutal repression, and, despite setbacks and organizational difficulties in adjusting to the quickening pace of political change in South Africa, had built a formidable presence on the ground, particularly in COSATU-affiliated trade unions, civic associations, and student and youth groups.[2]

For decades, the ANC leadership continually reminded its diverse constituencies that the primary task of political struggle was to remove apartheid and to establish genuine democracy, race-blind equality before the law, and full citizenship rights for all South Africans. The organization was able to tie together varied strands of anti-apartheid sentiment into a single national movement. In the context of the omnipresent potential for chauvinism and polarization along racial and ethnic lines in South Africa, this ability to attract diffuse social forces under an all-encompassing umbrella was indeed a remarkable achievement. The central tenet of the *Freedom Charter* – 'South Africa belongs to all who live in it, black and white' – has remained the touchstone of Charterist ideology since the

1955 Congress of the People. The ANC has long operated more as a clearing house for different points of view, a self-styled 'ecumenical church' without doctrinal discipline in which diverse currents jockeyed for influence, than as an ideologically coherent revolutionary organization. This amorphous ideology has been both a source of strength and a point of weakness. On the one side, the ANC has rarely suffered from the type of political splintering characteristic of so many left-wing parties. On the other, by operating as 'all-things-to-all-people', the ANC acquired a reputation for careening back and forth between seemingly contradictory positions, where considerable ad hoc decision-making power rested within its tight-knit leadership core.[3]

Between Compromise and Confrontation: The ANC and its Allies at the Crossroads

During the decades in which it was outlawed by Pretoria, the ANC constructed a close-knit bureaucracy shaped by the requirements for surviving both in exile and clandestinely inside the country. The external ANC maintained a guerrilla army, administered schools and vocational training centres, operated farms and workshops in Zambia and Tanzania, exercised judicial authority over its far-flung membership, supervised a vast publications network which kept its message alive, and received quasi-diplomatic recognition from many governments and international agencies. Outside South Africa, the ANC represented perhaps ten to fifteen thousand people scattered through as many as twenty-five countries, but concentrated mainly in Tanzania, Zambia and, until 1990, Angola. The largest single constituency consisted of members of its armed wing, Umkhonto weSizwe, who were stationed until late 1989 in military training camps in war-torn Angola.[4]

The ANC developed a complicated hierarchical structure to administer its internal affairs. The supreme governing body was the National Executive Committee (NEC). In theory, membership of the NEC was determined by regular elections. But in practice the leadership core changed very little over the years, and a large share of positions were held by veteran 'old-timers' like Oliver Tambo, Alfred Nzo, and Thomas Nkobi – president, secretary, and treasurer respectively. The ANC functioned as the centrepiece of a constellation of allied organizations that worked closely together in exile. Its partners included the remnants of the trade-union federation, the South African Congress of Trade Unions (SACTU), a skeletal entity which was almost invisible inside South Africa and which confined itself primarily to international solidarity work. The

ANC's most important alliance partner by far was the South African Communist Party (SACP). The SACP, all of whose members belonged as a matter of strict policy to the ANC, maintained a firm grip over MK and was disproportionately represented on the NEC. Beyond a shadow of doubt, the Party registered a profound impact on the ANC's intellectual development. SACP members did not monopolize the ANC's ideological discourse, but because they were the only organized political tendency within the organization, they were able to play a more dominant role than were social democrats, noncommunist Marxists, liberals and nationalists. The influence of SACP thinking was clearly visible in the tenets of the *Freedom Charter*, in the policy of nonracialism, and in the elevation of the working class to the 'leading role' in the national liberation movement.[5]

The exodus of at least six thousand politicized young people from the townships after the 1976–77 Soweto rebellion provided the ANC with a large reservoir of ready-and-willing recruits for MK. Between 1977 and 1984, guerrilla activities were largely restricted to acts of sabotage, where railway communications, power lines, electrical substations and other state-owned industrial installations, administrative buildings, courts and township municipal offices were favoured targets. The modest level of armed attacks in this period brought disproportionately large political rewards in terms of enhancing the popularity of guerrilla warfare and building the prestige of MK. On occasion, MK 'special operations' teams scored spectacular successes, of which the carefully planned bombardment of the Sasolburg synthetic fuel refinery in June 1980, the rocket attack on SADF headquarters at Voortrekkerhootge near Pretoria in August 1981, the assault on the Koeberg nuclear power station in December 1982, and the car-bomb explosion that severely damaged the airforce command centre in downtown Pretoria in May 1983, represent prime examples.

However, these high-profile actions – the phase of the military struggle called 'armed propaganda' – must be weighed against the multifaceted, calculated response of Pretoria to what was perceived as a 'total onslaught'. Military strategists intuitively understood that guerrilla armies in Angola, Mozambique, Zimbabwe and elsewhere swept to power only because they had secure sanctuaries in neighbouring countries. Mindful of the sympathies for the national liberation struggle in the frontline states, Pretoria unleashed a punishing programme of regional 'destabilization', and this brutal campaign proved effective in ruthlessly neutralizing its neighbours by economic and military disruption and depriving MK of relatively secure forward staging areas from which to launch cross-border attacks.[6] The security forces, who were given virtual carte blanche to destroy the guerrilla 'menace', proved adept at effectively penetrating MK command centres with police spies. As a result, a large percentage of guerrillas who managed to infiltrate across the borders were either captured or killed. The cumulative effect of these setbacks was to disrupt MK's offensive capabilities. The 'spy scare' poisoned the atmosphere in the military ranks, many planned operations came to a standstill, and thousands of guerrilla fighters were 'marooned in their Angolan camps, in poor condition and thoroughly demoralised'.[7]

Despite these problems, MK was still able clandestinely to infiltrate trained saboteurs into the country, who then fled back across the border once their missions were accomplished. But these 'commuter bombers', as military intelligence disparagingly called them, were dependent upon external lines of communications, command and supply. MK had made little headway in establishing permanent logistical support and supply bases inside South Africa that could sustain military operations.[8] The outbreak of the township rebellion in September 1984 offered the ANC a propitious opportunity to accelerate both the scale and the intensity of guerrilla warfare inside South Africa. Delegates who assembled for the June 1985 consultative conference at Kabwe, Zambia, vowed to implement a strategy of people's war, the immediate objective of which was 'to build an organized following in the townships and to convert emotional sentiment favouring the ANC into disciplined support'. Over the next several years, the number of armed actions climbed steeply from 136 in 1985 to 281 in 1989.[9] Estimates of the size of MK varied considerably. One knowledgeable observer suggested that Umkhonto forces numbered close to 10,000 in 1987, of which only around 500 were operating inside South Africa at any given time.[10]

However, the dismantling of MK military camps in Angola following the Namibia/South Africa peace accord brokered in late 1988 dealt a severe blow to the organization, requiring a major revision of the ANC's guerrilla strategy. The departure of the estimated 6,000 guerrillas from Angola extinguished the possibility of the ANC mounting significant armed incursions into South Africa of the sort required to initiate full-scale guerrilla warfare. In strictly military terms, MK never posed a serious threat to the state security forces. Although MK carried out close to 300 guerrilla attacks in both 1988 and 1989, the ANC's military wing was unable to transcend the limits of small-scale, hit-and-run 'armed propaganda' and to undertake 'people's war', a phase of armed struggle that depended upon the building of secure guerrilla bases inside the country. Yet, despite its limited military successes, the 'guerrilla ethos' captured the imagination of the impoverished masses and MK remained wildly popular among township youth.[11]

The ANC in the light of day

The decision in February 1990 by the National Party government to lift the ban on the ANC, to release its imprisoned leaders and to invite it to participate in open-ended negotiations over a democratic constitution placed the organization in an original situation. As a legal entity, the ANC leadership was called upon to respond to qualitatively new strains and stresses, most notably the 'growing pains' associated with transforming the organization 'from an exile-led, commandist revolutionary centre into an open, democratic, mass movement'.[12] The ANC – which proudly proclaimed itself to be the 'government in waiting' – faced the 'profound problem of establishing an identity suited to its new tasks'. For thirty years, the ANC had operated as a secretive bureaucracy, its 'organisational culture and administration moulded by the requirements of fighting a guerrilla war and conducting international diplomacy'.[13]

With the start of 'talks about talks', the ANC found itself in a novel situation where it was simultaneously involved in a dual role. On the one hand, its leadership was engaged in tense negotiations with de Klerk over delicate issues such as the return of exiles, the status of political prisoners, and the role of MK. On the other hand, its cadre were trying to build an above-ground, mass political organization virtually *ab initio*. In the first instance, its leadership was trying to steer the course of national political developments from above. In the second instance, its supporters were attempting to translate its newly acquired legal status into an organized and visible presence on the ground.[14]

From the outset, the government insisted that MK cadres should identify themselves and hand in their weapons, and that further recruiting for MK should cease.[15] The August 1990 Pretoria Minute broke the political logjam. The ANC agreed to suspend armed struggle and related military activities. In exchange, under an amnesty accord worked out between the government and the ANC, exiles who had undergone military training while members of MK were allowed to return to South Africa, and were to be granted indemnity from prosecution if they agreed to renounce violence.[16] In February 1991, the ANC went further by agreeing to end all violent and underground activities, including the in-filtration of armed cadres into South Africa, stockpiling of weapons, and conducting military training inside the country, in return for government pledges to widen indemnity provisions and accelerate the release of political prisoners and the return of exiles.[17]

On the eve of the July 1991 national conference, the ANC's first fully elective conference since 1958, rank-and-file supporters castigated the organization on a range of issues, including the lack of consultation with its 'alliance partner', COSATU, and in making unilateral policy decisions and expecting others to follow; lack of preparedness in the *Realpolitik* negotiations with de Klerk, with the result that the leadership conceded 'too much, too soon'; glaring organizational weaknesses in bringing about the transition from underground movement to political party; and the secretive, authoritarian style of the 'old-guard' exile leadership.[18] At the time of the national conference, ANC membership exceeded 500,000 people, a substantial achievement in the face of the continuing violence in the PWV townships and Natal.[19] The 2,244 conference delegates elected an NEC purged of nearly half its former members. The balance of power in the new NEC shifted decisively in favour of younger, internal activists, thereby successfully bridging the gap between the previously self-elected NEC and its somewhat disenchanted grassroots organizations.[20]

The euphoria accompanying the early days of legal existence quickly dissipated and, as it struggled to come to terms with the world of *Realpolitik*, the ANC fell to earth. The years of clandestine existence had fostered an unrealistic image of a confident exile leadership at the head of a powerful organization, bolstered by widespread international support and energized by a vast network inside South Africa, ready and willing to assume the reins of government at a moment's notice. During its years in exile, the ANC functioned as a military-run, authoritarian structure. The covert nature of operations meant that there was little room for dissent, and those who opposed the 'party line' were often accused of collaborating with the enemy. This leadership style created a tendency towards high-handedness among former exiles that did not sit well with younger, more militant middle-level leadership with roots in the township struggles of the 1980s. The 26-member National Working Committee – the ANC's 'cabinet' – was dominated by former exiles who tended to coalesce around a middle-of-the-road ideology. Pragmatists, like Jacob Zuma and Thabo Mbeki, advocated a piecemeal strategy of building upon tactical gains achieved at the conference table in order gradually to weaken the National Party's bargaining position. Because of the influence of regional 'power-brokers' and its stronger links with grassroots supporters, the 90-member National Executive Committee was more radical in its outlook.[21]

The shocking allegations that *Mbokhodo* ('the boulder which crushes'), the ANC's security section, engaged in gross human-rights violations of MK recruits on suspicion of spying for Pretoria in its military detention camps in Angola, Uganda, Zambia and Tanzania while the movement was in exile greatly tarnished the its image as holding the moral 'high ground' in the heroic battle against apartheid.[22] The ANC came under intense pressure to investigate these alleged wrongdoings and to make full disclosure. The ANC-appointed Motsuenyane Commission of Inquiry, the third attempt of the organization to put the sordid matter to rest, confirmed that the ANC security personnel were indeed responsible for detention without trial, beatings, solitary confinement, torture, humiliation, cruel and inhuman treatment, and execution by firing squads and prison guards. Human-rights and local civil organizations both at home and abroad expressed considerable dismay at the reluctance of the ANC leadership to take disciplinary action against prison-camp officials accused of gross misconduct against detainees and to offer compensation for victims.[23]

Following its unbanning, the ANC leadership oscillated somewhere between the polarizing extremes of obliging accommodation and hardline militancy. While this flexible approach appeased both its moderate and radical wings and averted serious political rifts, it did sow confusion within the ANC's rank-and-file supporters. The most volatile segment of the ANC's constituency were the 'legions of impoverished and illiterate, the restive demobilised guerrillas, the militant young unemployables'. It was widely believed that if these followers were not quickly assuaged by a future non-racial government, they could abandon their loyalty to the Congress in favour of rival political organizations with more radical agendas.[24] Former MK cadres harboured particular resentments and frustrations. The forcible seizure by MK dissidents of the ANC's Durban regional headquarters in August 1993 merely highlighted the plight of those ex-guerrillas who returned home not as conquering heroes but 'to a life of poverty and perceived rejection by the organization for which they were prepared to sacrifice their lives'. As these former MK soldiers drifted back to South Africa in small groups, they were welcomed with few employment opportunities and little prospect for resuscitating the career plans that had been abandoned when they abruptly left the country for military training years earlier. Some disgruntled MK cadres turned to freelancing, using weapons and skills acquired in exile for violent crime. Others joined self-defence units in the townships – often formations of dubious character.[25]

For many ANC loyalists, and especially those active in the middle ranks of the trade unions and civic associations, the leadership had lost its radical vocation and had capitulated to the familiar siren song of accommodation with the established white oligarchy. There was a growing sentiment that the ascendent coalition in the ANC leadership was composed of moderate nationalists, social democrats, and free-market liberals whose political programme consisted of selective state intervention in a predominantly *laissez faire* economic environment, long-term guarantees for the existing state bureaucracy ('sunset clauses'), and a moderate foreign policy.

The assassination of the charismatic Chris Hani – the most popular politician in the ANC besides Nelson Mandela – left a yawning gap on the ANC's populist, militant left wing that could not readily be filled. An assortment of key figures with radical credentials were called upon to occupy this political space, but none matched the stature of Hani. Well-known mavericks like Nelson Mandela's estranged wife Winnie, flamboyant ANC Youth League leader, Peter Mokaba, and Harry Gwala, ANC kingpin in the Natal Midlands, were poised to tap into the growing disenchantment with the slow pace of negotiations and the widespread perception that the ANC leadership had compromised too much.[26] Winnie Mandela, who made a remarkable comeback to the political stage when she regained her position as president of the ANC Women's League in December 1993, successfully built her own independent power base among dwellers of squatter camps, particularly in the strife-torn East Rand. The fiery Mokaba, whose militant oratorical volleys and erratic political demeanour caused great consternation and embarrassment within the inner circles of the ANC's moderate leadership, cultivated a large following among the militant youths of the townships.[27]

The SACP/ANC Alliance:
Autonomous Organizations or Siamese Twins?

At a time when the worldwide fortunes of communism seem to have reached their nadir, the SACP has entered a phase of rapid growth in popularity and membership. Amid great fanfare, the Party was relaunched in South Africa in July 1991, and since that time was able to establish headquarters, along with clusters of branches, in six regions: the PWV, the Western Cape, the Eastern Cape, the Border, and two sites in Natal.[28] Its ranks were bolstered with a 'growing roster' of young members who turned to the Party because of its long-standing reputation as a bitter enemy of white minority rule. Paradoxically, with socialism in retreat virtually everywhere in the world, the SACP grew in numbers, strength and influence. Since the late 1980s, partly in response to the SACP's pledge to accommodate and respect rival points of view, a large number of well-known intellectuals, trade unionists and community activists joined the Party. Although no accurate figure is available, it was estimated in 1991 that Party membership exceeded 20,000 activists, and it has more than doubled in size since then, with black workers comprising the overwhelming majority.[29]

Perhaps the SACP's strongest recruiting advantage was the conception – widely held in the townships – that the apartheid system was umbilically joined to capitalism. From its growing grassroots strength, through its cross-membership with the national executive committees of the ANC and COSATU, the SACP was able to exert considerable influence within the mass democratic movement.[30] The Party attached itself to the political fortunes of the ANC decades ago, and there have been few indications that this symbiotic relationship was about to come unglued in the immediate future, despite the efforts of the de Klerk administration to drive a wedge between the two organizations. The Party had worked with the ANC since the 1930s, but the relationship was considerably strengthened during the popular struggles of the 1950s. In the early 1960s, the ANC and SACP jointly established Umkhonto weSizwe, and the formal linkage between the two organizations was more or less cemented at the 1969 Morogoro Conference when the ANC adopted the 'Strategy and Tactics' document which endorsed the struggle for a national democratic revolution. Since that time, the SACP and the ANC have become so inextricably entwined that de Klerk, complaining about how the leadership of the Congress was so filled with Communists, suggested that 'it is not an alliance, it is a scrambled egg'.[31]

Considerable attention has been devoted to counting the number of SACP members holding executive positions in the ANC. Conventionally, moderate and right-wing critics have pointed to what they regard as the unwarranted dominance of known SACP members on the ANC's NEC elected in 1991. Somewhere between 24 and 30 of the 90 seats on the NEC were filled by known SACP members, and at least 10 of the 25 standing members of the National Working Committee which functioned to oversee the daily affairs of the ANC were presumed by reputation also to be members of the Party.[32] Yet what is often overlooked is the extent to which the SACP virtually dominated the ANC's youth and military wings, the movement's most numerous and mobilized constituency. In addition to the ANC's security apparatus, these were strongholds for SACP sympathies, 'whose voice matters in ANC political life, especially at [national] Congresses'.[33]

For years the Party unhesitatingly fought inside the ANC to retain the Freedom Charter as the basic ANC programme. The Charter, which was adopted in 1955 by ANC faithful at the famous Kliptown 'Congress of the People', espouses nationalization of the commanding heights of the economy (including the banks, mines and heavy industry), calls for land redistribution, and advocates an extensive social welfare agenda. Despite the strenuous objections of key ANC/SACP luminaries over the years, left-wing critics have long criticized the document on the grounds that it does not contain an unambiguous socialist vision for post-apartheid South Africa, and that its vaguely worded clauses leave open differing and even contradictory interpretations. For nearly forty years, the Freedom Charter was enshrined in ANC/SACP lore as the unifying lodestar of the liberation movement, and its programmatic outlook acted as the linchpin of the Party's strategy of 'national democratic revolution', the first of the steps in the 'two-stage' route to socialism.[34] In retrospect, it must seem bitterly ironic to those who eagerly subscribed to the principles contained in the document that these social-democratic objectives still appeared almost as elusive as ever, somewhere beyond the immediate grasp of the liberation movement. As the World Trade Centre negotiations inched forward, the ANC leadership gradually distanced themselves from a full-fledged endorsement of the basic tenets included in the Charter, and prominent SACP stalwarts acquiesced in the abandonment of what had long been proclaimed as inviolable principles. While the Reconstruction and Development Programme and the ANC election manifesto incorporated many of its specific features, the all-encompassing vision of comprehensive, sweeping reforms contained in the Freedom Charter was missing.

For the ANC, the overriding focus of struggle remained steadfast opposition to racial oppression, the apartheid system and exclusive white minority rule. The ANC has long adhered to the belief that the achievement of political equality in an undivided South Africa was anterior to addressing socio-economic grievances. This single-minded attachment to the political terrain and questions of the race-blind franchise, civic liberties and representative instititions symbolized both the enduring strength and the potential weakness of the ANC as an organizational vehicle that could secure genuine material benefits for South Africa's majority. The SACP, as an integral part of the Congress tradition for the past forty years, was fully aware that the attainment of political democracy did not necessarily guarantee the improvement of living and working conditions, the issues for which the popular masses fought and died. The Party long believed that breaking the back of exclusive white minority rule would unleash a torrent of demands which the private enterprise system would be unable to satisfy. Because of its unbending commitment to building the Congress tradition, the main problem for the SACP since its legalization was to find the resources to establish its own party structures and to develop political positions independent of the ANC.[35]

For years, critics accused the Party of unblinking adulation of the Soviet system and uncritical support for every twist and turn of Soviet doctrine and policy. The Party also acquired a reputation for stifling emergent debates on socialism within the progressive trade-union movement, for 'vicious and sectarian attacks on left-wing groups who challenged Party positions', and for 'purges of Party members who disagreed with leadership positions'.[36] In 1989, Party General Secretary Joe Slovo circulated a widely discussed pamphlet entitled *Has Socialism Failed?* This self-critical evaluation of the Party's past performance, along with a fresh look at the failures of 'actually existing' socialism, indicated the beginning of genuine democratic renewal within the SACP and a willingness to question the doctrinal truths that guided Party practice for decades.[37] Some political analysts suggested that Slovo's truncated definition of Stalinism as 'socialism without democracy' limited the terms of the debate.[38] According to one commentator, 'the pamphlet focused largely on political malpractices (bureaucratic, authoritarian, anti-democratic) and their remedy (political pluralism and civil liberties)'. But the central theoretical assumptions guiding Party practice for decades – 'Colonialism of a Special Type' and 'the National Democratic Revolution' – were not fully exposed to critical reassessment.[39] Critics on the left were not convinced that the 'leopard had changed its spots', expressing considerable doubts that the legacy of political dogmatism and sectarianism was so easily jettisoned.[40]

With the failure of the Communist Parties of Eastern Europe and the Soviet Union to hold their crumbling regimes in power, the SACP was cast adrift from its long-standing ideological moorings and cut off from its principal sources of funding. In the rapid rush to stay ahead of the collapse of Soviet-bloc communism, the SACP abandoned so much of its ideological canon that some political observers suggested that the Party had become indistinguishable from a European-style social-democratic party.[41] The Party scrapped the Marxist conception of the dictatorship of the proletariat and questioned Leninist tenets claiming an inherent vanguard role for the Party. The SACP endorsed multiparty democracy and regular elections; independence of the trade unions; freedom of speech, worship and the press; and a mixed economy with a place for private enterprise and foreign investment.[42] In early 1990, Slovo astounded some political observers by declaring that 'the narrow issue of nationalization is a bit of a red herring', thereby depriving the Party of one of its most sacrosanct rallying cries.[43] The SACP's Central Committee, elected in 1992, included many reborn democratic socialists, and consequently the hard-line holdovers from the halcyon days of strict Party orthodoxy no longer played the prominent role they once did.[44] Despite the obdurate response of some key officials to the fall of socialism in the Soviet Union, the public positions of the Party came increasingly to resemble those of Western European-style social democrats.[45]

Since its unbanning, the SACP had embarked on a 'twin-track' strategy vis-à-vis the ANC. One path involved the remaking of the Party's image as a 'high profile' organization with visibility in the townships and trade unions. The other was to leave a corps of some of its best cadres, especially its younger and ablest militants, entrenched in key ANC decision-making bodies. The primary objective of the SACP for the foreseeable future was to keep the ANC a left-leaning, radical organization whose reformist programme would remain consistent with the Party's long-term vision of a socialist South Africa. The Party defined its role as that of 'praetorian guard of ideological correctness within the ANC', or as SACP stalwart Jeremy Cronin put it, as acting to 'ensure that [the ANC] stays true to its historical vocation'. The Party hoped to achieve this aim by assisting the ANC to ascend to power, after which it truly expected the appreciative ANC-dominated government to reciprocate by enacting 'worker-friendly social and industrial legislation'. One seemingly paradoxical consequence of this course of action was that leading SACP cadres devoted all their time and energies to ANC projects and drifted away from Party networks.[46]

A visible gap persisted between the popular enthusiasm that the SACP inspired and its ability to translate this support into a distinctive political role. As one analyst noted, the main problem for the Party remained that 'its activists had no clear sense of what to do as party members, which they could not do as ANC, COSATU, or civic members'.[47] To a large extent, the Party's theoretical hesitation and immobility influenced its practice. The tripartite alliance with the ANC and COSATU, and especially the overlapping leaderships, continued to blur an independent role for the SACP. The Party leadership seemed unable 'to forge an identity for itself as a working class party with a programme, practice, and policy that assert[ed] such an identity'. The Party genuinely attracted scores of dedicated, capable and articulate cadres, but without developing an original programme or strategy of its own to meet the challenge of legality, the SACP took the chance of settling for a Zelig-like existence mirrored largely through its alliance partners.[48]

The death of Chris Hani deprived the SACP of its most inspirational and politically astute figure. Under his populist leadership, the SACP was poised to benefit greatly from the expected disenchantment almost certain to follow in the wake of the April 1994 elections. The SACP, buoyed by Hani's militant credentials, would have become 'the natural home' for the disgruntled, dispossessed and powerless. Unlike many in the Party leadership, Hani cultivated close links with scores of militant populists outside the ANC mainstream. These ties could have been transformed into a powerful militant nexus to the left of the ANC, 'catapulting the Party into a critical role as a key political power-broker' with which the first post-apartheid government 'would have been forced to make deals'. Charles Nqakula, the man who replaced Hani as SACP general secretary, was industrious, articulate and disciplined, but lacked the popular following that only Hani could muster.[49]

South Africa's 'Other Left'

For all sorts of reasons, the more powerful ANC dwarfed its rivals within the liberation movement. Nevertheless, South Africa's 'other left', primarily the Pan-African Congress (PAC) and the Azanian People's Organization (AZAPO), along with independent socialist organizations like Workers' Organization for Socialist Action (WOSA), took advantage of the post-1990 period of political openness to expand their influence and contend for political space to the left of the ANC/SACP alliance. 'For an organisation that was almost forgotten inside the country before its unbanning in February 1990', one commentator contended, the PAC – which split from the ANC in 1959 – 'has staged a remarkable political comeback'. The surprisingly strong revival of the PAC inside South Africa was more a testament to the enduring legacy of the Africanist sentiments than to the organizational acumen of its exiled leadership.[50]

'Africa for the Africans'

During its long years of exile, the PAC leadership suffered from such internal feuding and ideological about-turns that political observers had dismissed the organization on numerous occasions as moribund and rudderless. During the early 1980s, the small but militant Azanian National Youth Unity (AZANYU) functioned in the mass movement as a surrogate for PAC-oriented currents inside the country. Beginning in 1985, the PAC's armed wing, the Azanian People's Liberation Army (APLA) launched a number of 'hit and run' guerrilla attacks aimed primarily at members of the security forces. What also began to emerge during this period was 'a heightened expression of PAC traditions in the symbolic repertoire of legal political groups'. Besides AZANYU, a number of organizations openly 'used Africanist phraseology, PAC iconography, and the open-handed PAC salute'. In 1989, PAC supporters launched the Pan Africanist Movement (PAM), a legal front for Africanist activities that paralleled in some respects the functions of the UDF. Two groups were particularly well represented in the above-ground leadership: old-time veterans of the early days of the PAC, including PAM's president Clarence Mlamli Makwetu, a 62-year-old farmer from the Transkei who joined the ANC's Youth League in 1948 but left to assist in creating the PAC in the Western Cape, one of its original strongholds; and a much younger generation of trade unionists who had been instrumental in building the NACTU affiliates.[51]

Under the capable leadership of a number of ex-Robben Islanders and a core of younger militants drawn from student, youth, and trade-union politics, the PAC underwent a Phoenix-like rebirth. Since its unbanning in 1990, it has outflanked the ANC in terms of its radical posture and rhetoric on some issues, particularly the land question, but has never succeeded in presenting a coherent alternative programme of action. Makwetu was confirmed as president. Benny Alexander, who emerged through the ranks of the trade-union movement, Carter Seleka, a founder of AZANYU, and Barney Desai, the first PAC exile to return to South Africa under the general amnesty, were elected into the internal leadership.[52] Capable leaders, including national organizer Maxwell Nemadzivhenani, former APLA commander Johnson Mlambo, and World Trade Centre negotiator Patricia de Lille, assumed higher-profile roles in the organization. In a manoeuvre designed to tighten organizational discipline, the PAC incorporated AZANYU, its restive and often unpredictable youth wing with a hundred branches countrywide, into the component structures of the parent body instead of its remaining a semi-autonomous affiliate.[53] The Pan African Students' Organization (PASO) was affirmed as its student wing.[54] The rise of Islamic fundamentalism in the Western Cape also served to strengthen the political base of the Africanists. The PAC forged an alliance with Qibla, a Muslim youth organization centred in Cape Town, where, according to security force allegations, the later agreed to support APLA insurgents inside South Africa in return for PAC-sponsored military training abroad.[55]

PAC leaders hoped to capitalize on the mounting frustration of relatively politicized, restive township youth, whom they expected would grow weary of waiting for tedious negotiations to bear fruit and eventually switch their allegiance from the ANC in favour of the more militant Africanists. Because it was overshadowed in popular consciousness by the rival ANC, the PAC often seemed pulled between staking a claim to an independent course of action and adopting political positions defined in reaction to the Charterist tradition. The organization consistently criticized CODESA as an unwieldy body, undemocratic because of the presence of unelected homelands delegations and weighted in favour of the status quo because of the absence of a neutral convenor. The PAC strongly objected to what it regarded as self-appointed leaders negotiating 'over the heads of the masses', and demanded instead 'one-person, one-vote' elections to a constituent assembly. But by agreeing first to multiparty talks to finalize the passage to democracy, and to a transitional authority to oversee the preparatory stages prior to nationwide elections, the PAC greatly modified its decolonization model for an abrupt transfer of power.[56]

The burning question for the PAC remained whether it could produce a comprehensive political programme, gather mass support from those who at the moment maintained at least nominal support for the ANC, and adjust organizationally to the new circumstances of legality inside South Africa. For the Africanists, the enemy, as best as could be defined, was a marauding settler colonialism with its roots in early European conquest of the African continent and intent on maintaining an economic and political stranglehold despite concessions toward parliamentary democracy. To challenge the white oligarchy, the PAC called for socialist democracy and insisted that whatever post-apartheid regime came to power had to embark as a matter of principle on a comprehensive programme of redistribution in order to rectify past inequities of wealth and gross imbalances in political power. Despite the efforts of the liberal media to paint the Africanists as an extremist, racialist-inclined fringe group roughly equivalent to the neo-Nazi far right, the PAC established itself 'as a significant political force'. In fact, the PAC was able to make 'unmeasurable but unmistakable gains' with a coded message that in many respects was curiously conservative in outlook. The Africanists stood firm in their commitment to unity among the oppressed, suggesting that 'much of the harassment of township dwellers is carried out by hoodlums claiming allegiance to the ANC.' They steadfastly refused to participate in disruptive school boycotts because, they said, education was essential to black betterment; and, unlike militant ANC youth, they opposed attacks on Inkatha loyalists.[57]

Despite its organizational weaknesses, the PAC was able to galvanize political support, especially among recent migrants and unemployed township youth, behind a vast, rather ill-defined crusade for restoration of ownership and control of the land, including its natural resources and productive capacities.[58] This Africanist vision of taking back the land and its wealth from the 'settler colonialists' who stole it from the original inhabitants has deep roots in South Africa. Impoverished rural communities that suffered at the hands of the white usurpers who forcibly removed and uprooted them from their ancestral homes well before the apartheid era still cling to the belief that some day they will get the land back. The PAC rekindled such hopes for economic equality as birthright. Its slogan 'Africa for the Africans' evoked the powerful, emotive image of 'the world turned upside down'. Placed against the broad panorama of rising expectations and the groundswell of anger and impatience that gripped black South Africa, the uncompromising posture of the Africanists embodied the desire for absolute solutions and for a liberating catharsis that found expression in the imagery of the armed struggle.[59]

However, in the outpouring of popular support for the PAC, some of it no more than sentimental attachment to deeply ingrained radicalism, there was scant analysis of what precisely the PAC would do if it were to gain access to political power. Unless it was able to stand and deliver on some of its promises, the PAC ran the risk of falling prey to self-imposed sectarian isolation. Because of its intransigence, the PAC found it difficult to attract foreign donors willing to lend the financial support necessary to maintain offices and to prepare for the election campaign. The organization operated on a shoestring budget and was constantly plagued by a shortage of funds, which hampered its effectiveness.[60]

Black consciousness, socialism and Africanism

AZAPO inherited the mantle of the Black Consciousness ideology originally popularized by an impressive group of young black intellectuals, including Steve Biko, in the 1970s. AZAPO is a national organization, but its influence is unevenly distributed. For example, its organizational weakness in Natal is matched by its strength in the Northern Transvaal. AZAPO consistently maintained that unity amongst the oppressed is a non-negotiable 'first principle' that ought to precede all efforts to establish relations with parties or organizations linked with the ruling class.[61] AZAPO was opposed to the participation of homelands leaders in formal negotiations over a new constitution and rejected calls for an interim government, proclaiming that this arrangement would mean 'governing with the National Party regime, with its laws, security forces and its white oppressive structures'.[62] Over the course of the multiparty negotiations, AZAPO became increasingly marginalized as a political force. With its leadership positions largely in the hands of academics and intellectuals rather than grassroots and pragmatic politicians, the organization edged closer to 'the political wilderness by its ideological purity and no-compromise philosophy'. As 'foolhardy and self-defeating' as the AZAPO boycott of the elections may have appeared on the surface, 'a measure of political calculation' lay behind it. AZAPO reasoned that once the euphoria of a liberated South Africa faded and the shortcomings of parliamentary democracy became evident, its message would resonate with greater clarity among those whose interests were ignored in the negotiations and their aftermath. But AZAPO would only be able to capitalize on the growing disenchantment and disillusionment if it were able to improve its organizational capacities. AZAPO had scant financial resources, a highly inefficient national network, and a limited base in popular movements.[63]

WOSA is an explicitly socialist-oriented organization with a political following concentrated in the Western Cape, the traditional stronghold of left-wing opposition groups like the recently revived New Unity Movement. WOSA, which emerged out of the National Forum, took the lead in calling for a mass workers' party in South Africa as a way of bringing together socialist forces with political roots in the working class.[64] Its strength lies with its political influence within organizations of teachers and students, sports bodies and some trade unions, including SACCAWU and NUMSA in COSATU, along with several unaffiliated independents.[65]

While the ideological positions of AZAPO and PAC dovetailed in many important respects, the social bases of their political support differed considerably. Africanist ideas resonate most strongly among landless families, divided by decades of migrant labour, who have experienced, a first hand, the face-to-face racial oppression that forced them out of the countryside. The PAC has tapped into this seemingly bottomless reservoir of resentment, and has fashioned a following in rural areas in the Northern Transvaal, the Eastern Cape, Ciskei and northern Transkei. This support base prompted one commentator to suggest that 'the PAC can be seen as a "peasant movement" because of the strong and traditional emphasis on the redistribution of the land.'[66]

Whilst it is impossible to test the accuracy of the figures, the PAC claimed to have a signed-up membership of around half a million, excluding its large student, youth and women's wings, with twenty regional structures and somewhere between 250 and 850 branches nationwide.[67] Because of its strong appeal in rural areas and among recent migrants to the overcrowded townships, the social base of PAC more closely resembled that of Inkatha than that of the more urban-oriented ANC. While the ANC attracted the visible support of the emergent black middle class and the intelligentsia, the PAC 'speaks on behalf of some of the least privileged and less educated members of the subordinate majority'. In contrast, AZAPO has always comprised a better educated elite, with considerable following among university staff, clergy, journalists and other professionals. 'In short, and with crude oversimplification', one political analyst suggested, 'AZAPO constitutes a sophisticated intellectual elite in search of a constituency, while the PAC represents a potentially powerful army with disorganized and quarrelling generals.'[68]

'One settler, one bullet': APLA and armed struggle

The refusal of the PAC and AZAPO to follow the lead of the ANC in suspending armed struggle remained largely a symbolic gesture, despite alternating waves of attacks. APLA military commander Sabelo Phama and the 'internal' leadership insisted that the PAC's armed wing, headquartered in Dar es Salaam, maintained operational independence from the legal organization inside the country. After a recruiting drive in the wake of the PAC's unbanning, APLA expanded its numbers to perhaps one thousand fighters, some of whom received advanced military training in Libya, the Middle East and China. However, APLA did not even approach the numerical strength and military sophistication of the ANC's armed wing, which reached a peak of close to ten thousand trained guerrillas before its partial demobilization in 1991.[69]

Beginning in the early 1990s, APLA vowed to accelerate its campaign to target township police, and in the first six months of 1993 alone its armed attacks had claimed the lives of over a hundred police personnel. What evolved along the borderlands of the northeastern Cape and eastern Orange Free State was a low-intensity war where APLA guerrilla raids on outlying farms, allegedly carried out from safe havens in neighbouring Transkei and Lesotho, caused panicky white farmers to demand military protection.[70] However, it was the firestorm of controversy following armed attacks in late 1992 on a posh golf club in King William's Town and a family steak restaurant in Queenstown in which five innocent whites were killed and thirty-five injured that brought the PAC's secretive guerrilla brigade the public attention it had long been denied. With just a few terrorist attacks on 'soft targets', APLA managed to awaken white nightmares of a impending race war and to popularize their view that armed struggle should continue until an accord involving a 'mutual cessation of hostilities' was reached with the government. The PAC's observation – that it took white deaths to make the government take serious notice of political violence – struck a responsive chord with township dwellers who had grown cynical with the inability of the established authorities to put an end to wanton attacks on their communities. But the two armed attacks also highlighted internal tensions within the PAC camp between moderates reluctantly committed to negotiations and hardliners virulently opposed to compromises with the 'settler neo-apartheid regime'. There were strong indications that the armed operations launched by the unrepentant militant wing were aimed as much at undermining the intentions of pragmatists to join multiparty talks as they were against the white minority regime.[71]

These guerrilla attacks inspired many township youths disillusioned by the slow pace of negotiations, despite a steady stream of concessions from ANC negotiators. Within the restive ranks of the politically volatile unemployed and unemployable youth of the townships and squatter camps, unrestrained adulation for the real or imagined exploits of APLA replaced some of the sentimental attachment to MK. A portion of this bravado spills over into thinly veiled 'anti-white' sentiments.[72] 'The militant leaders who provide the vocabulary for the anger say they discourage racial hatred by delicately avoiding the word "white" and describing the enemy as "settlers" or "oppressors",' one political observer noted. 'But they concede that such distinctions are often lost on the streets.'[73]

Entrenched Forces of Reaction: The Kaleidoscopic Right Wing

Political upheaval and rapid social change always seem to breathe new life into seemingly moribund ideas, and South Africa's far right has been no exception to this rule. Right-wing organizations counted on a gradually shrinking base of political support from blue-collar workers in mining and industry, from the poorly-paid civil service including the police and the army, and from the white farming community.[74] English-speaking South Africans increasingly embraced conservative ideas, but Afrikaners, who numbered close to three million, remained the bedrock of right-wing politics. On balance, right-wing parties and organizations reacted to the changing times instead of being in the forefront of shaping them. At times, they seemed hopelessly trapped between a nostalgic yearning for a mythical past embodied in a whites-only *Boerestaad* (homeland) and the great fear of a coming apocalyptic 'race war'.[75]

After February 1990, Afrikaner unity – that illusory long-standing dream of holding the *volk* together – once again dissolved into myth as it had so many times in the past. The uncertainties and fears raised by the real prospect of losing power and privilege seriously unsettled Afrikaner nationalists, who consequently splintered into narrow interest groups which feuded among themselves. After having shared in the bitter fruits of apartheid for nearly five decades, they were cast adrift in a political world not of their own making. The political loyalties of these right-wing white nationalists were spread between a number of parties and movements, including the Herstigte Nasionale Party (HNP), the extremist hardline Verwoerdian party whose support has dwindled to a fraction; the 'respectable' ultra-right Conservative Party; and scores of small, squabbling extra-parliamentary splinter groups whose political alliances changed faster than the seasons.[76]

The HNP, which from its founding in 1969 offered a haven for disgruntled conservatives, never attracted a large following. Its shrill message was unequivocally racist, its appeal narrowly Afrikaner chauvinistic, and its phraseology crude and inflammatory. This extremism served as a rallying cry for fanatics, but was distasteful to many conservatives.[77] In contrast, the Conservative Party (CP), which was founded in 1982 by twenty-three MPs who abandoned the National Party over its early reformist initiatives, became the leading voice of 'respectable' right-wing parliamentary politics. By winning 31 per cent of the white vote in the 1989 general election, the party, under the leadership of Andries Treurnicht, otherwise known as 'Dr No', consolidated its place as official Opposition in the white chamber of parliament. Its political ideology appealed mainly to rural but also to urban lower-middle-class voters, particularly in the

Transvaal, Orange Free State and Northern Cape. The party insisted on maintaining legal barriers separating the races and opposed majority rule. Yet failing to obtain a return to old-fashioned apartheid, the CP called for ethnic 'self-determination' and raised the spectre of partitioning South Africa into two self-governing homelands, one for segregation-minded whites and the other for everyone else.[78]

The death knell to ultra-right-wing hopes of forestalling the inevitable collapse of white minority rule came with their disastrous showing in the March 1992 nationwide referendum, in which de Klerk and the National Party received a resounding vote of confidence from the white electorate to stay the reformist course. The thin cracks in the ideological patina of the Conservative Party steadily widened into deep fissures that polarized the organization into rival camps. Months before the national referendum, a secret internal policy document, entitled 'Strategy for a Changing Situation', conceded that South Africa had already experienced 'the sunset of apartheid'. The 'new right' pragmatists argued that unless the Conservatives made a policy U-turn and entered the negotiations process they ran the risk of becoming politically irrelevant. These more accommodating Conservatives, whose public disavowals of racist sentiments distinguished them from their former colleagues, broke away from the CP to form the ill-fated Afrikaner Volksunie (AVU) under the leadership of Andies Beyers, MP for Potchestroom. The opposing pro-apartheid diehards retreated behind the familiar siren song of Afrikaner 'self-determination' coupled with an all-embracing demonology of all who did not share their racist views.[79]

The material and social foundation for white reaction can be found in the harsh socio-economic realities of the 'new' South Africa. The protracted economic recession claimed its share of white victims, and the fearful prospect of downward mobility without the apartheid 'safety net' created a fertile environment for revanchist ideas. White wage earners (including civil servants and miners), farmers and those engaged in farm-related activities, and the petty bourgeoisie form the backbone of conservative politics. To cite a single example, white commercial farming is likely to remain one of the last bastions of racial conservatism in the country. A large proportion of white farmers have been economically hard pressed and politically insecure. The abolition of the 1913 and 1936 Land Acts, which prevented black people from owning land in 87 per cent of the country, unleashed white anxieties about land redistribution, and these feelings of vulnerability were ruthlessly exploited by the Conservative Party and other far-right groups. Transvaal farmers moved quickly to the forefront of uncompromising white opposition to the National Party reformist initiatives. The high point of their militant action was the

May 1991 'Siege of Pretoria' where farmers blockaded streets and 'brought
the city to a halt'. While the South African Agricultural Union remained
in the National Party fold, the regional Transvaal Agricultural Union broke
away from the parent body to become, as one political observer suggested,
'the right wing's equivalent of COSATU, doing for conservative politics
what COSATU did for the Left — using grassroots action rather than
words to pressure the politicians in [the] Union Buildings'.[80]

Witman, Waar is jou Tuisland?[81]

Within Afrikaner intellectual circles, the dread of an uncertain future
nourished a flurry of painstaking efforts, the main purpose of which was
to insist that 'their people' owned by right of occupation a separate part
of Africa. Theologians cited Holy Scripture to infuse the idea of racial
separation with moral backbone. Experts in international law combed the
statute books, looking for historical precedents to provide legal justification
to buttress their claims to 'self-determination'. Amateur cartographers
painstakingly constructed one imagined community after another out of
whole cloth, drawing and redrawing the existing political boundaries of
South Africa in order to find a place for the cherished *volkstaat*.[82] Yet for
all the nostalgia about the salad days of Verwoerdian-style white supremacy,
far-right thinkers were remarkably vague about how they would partition
the country. For the most part, right-wing organizations failed to provide
details of the proposed boundaries; nor did they say how partition was to
be achieved without black consent, or indicate the extent of forced
removals it would require, given that there was no part of South Africa
where whites formed a majority. Despite its rhetorical and emotive appeal
for many right-wing whites, the notion of a white Valhalla was as futile as
the effort to unscramble an egg.[83]

Yet the Afrikaner Volkswag (AVW) (Afrikaner People's Guard), founded
by former Broederbond chairman Carel Boshoff, grew impatient with
those Afrikaner intellectuals who merely dreamed of geographical separation. Married to the daughter of Hendrik Verwoerd, the architect of apartheid, Boshoff was a former professor of theology at the University of
Pretoria. The AVW spearheaded a drive by white supremacists to create
their own 'whites only' Utopia, a haven for hard-working Afrikaners
opposed to de Klerk's plans to integrate South Africa and extend the vote
to black people. In 1991, Boshoff declared Orania, a ghost town on the
banks of the Orange River midway between Cape Town and Johannesburg, the capital of a proposed Afrikaner republic, the last bastion of
white supremacy in Africa. He warned that black people were not allowed
to set foot in this privately owned village, where whites would cook,

clean and cultivate their gardens.[84] The place was meant to become a pilot project for a South African white homeland with white solidarity and self-sufficiency as watchwords. The idea of a whites-only homeland appealed to unrepentant diehards who lamented the loss of simpler times when race hierarchies seemed to remain transfixed in time and space. However, by early 1994, the movement had attracted fewer than 350 *Boere-Afrikaners* (real Afrikaners) from all parts of country to settle there permanently, and even this minuscule number of residents were hopelessly fractured into sundry religious and political factions. Many newcomers to this abandoned construction town, originally built in the arid Karoo scrubland twenty-five years earlier for people working on an irrigation scheme, seemed less the pioneering idealists that the AVW had championed, and more a motley residue of 'resentful misfits who have lost jobs or businesses in the sour economy and blame blacks for it'.[85]

Thunder on the extreme far right

It is difficult, if not impossible, to get a clear fix on the kaleidoscopic profusion of political organizations on the extreme far right. It was estimated that there were at one time 193 parties, paramilitary militias and minuscule groups to the right of the Conservative Party. The proto-fascist Afrikaner Weerstandsbeweging (AWB), with an estimated membership of 10,000, along with its separate 5,000-strong, khaki-clad military wing, the Wenkommando (Victory Commando), dominated the field. The uncontested leader of the AWB, Eugene Terre'Blanche, whose fiery oratorical skills and emotional appeal to the *Afrikanervolk* made him a virtual 'cult hero' with the faithful, transformed the organization from its inauspicious beginnings as a fanatical fringe group into a formidable force with more than 150,000 people who attend its meetings and with perhaps 500,000 silent sympathizers.[86]

To a large extent, the multitudinous array of ultra-conservative organizations that comprised the extreme far right were either deliberate creations of the AWB or else splinter groups that remained loosely tied to AWB activities. They existed for the dual purpose of maintaining a convenient cloak of secrecy over AWB terrorist operations and making the far right 'look like a spontaneous and dangerous uprising of the *Volk*'. For the most part, these extremist far-right organizations were deeply distrustful and suspicious of one another, and divided as much by personal rivalries among their leaders as by real political differences. What they lacked in numerical strength they compensated for in bombastic rhetoric, accusing their 'unfaithful' brethren of 'selling out' the 'white race' and promising Armageddon if the National Party went ahead with extending political equality to the black majority. Their threats of crippling work stoppages, sabotage, forcible removal of illegal squatters, and armed 'resistance' were overblown but not empty. The far right enjoyed considerable support in the security forces, estimated in 1991 as ranging between 80 and 90 per cent in the SAP, and 70 to 80 per cent in the SADF.[87]

Private armies linked to the far-right lunatic fringe sprouted everywhere. Police intelligence sources estimated that around thirteen paramilitary groups had provided rudimentary instruction for somewhere between 8,000 and 10,000 recruits in secret training camps in the bush. 'There is no doubt that things could become very nasty indeed should these bands of former policemen and soldiers run amok', one political analyst suggested. 'They are better organized, more mobile and skilled in their deadly craft than the MK, the ANC's military wing ever was.' These paramilitary groups operated in small-unit cells without a centralized command structure, and it was this self-conscious fragmentation that made them particularly worrisome to the established authorities.[88]

The number of right-wing terror attacks increased dramatically in the early 1990s, particularly bombings of public buildings and random shootings of innocent black people. One visible display of right-wing mob violence came in August 1991 at Ventersdorp – the home turf of Terre'Blanche – when the AWB tried in vain to disrupt a National Party gathering. In the ensuing fracas, the police fired on demonstrators, killing three people and injuring many more.[89] However, the genuine high point of right-wing bravado came in June 1993 with the armed invasion of the World Trade Centre while constitutional negotiations were in full session. Hundreds of unruly white commandos, dressed in battle fatigues and armed with an assortment of weapons, disrupted the staid proceedings, daubing slogans on the walls, urinating in the chambers, and generally causing havoc.[90]

As the ANC and the NP tightened their political embrace, rumours circulated that extremist right-wing groups were busy stockpiling arms and ammunition, medical supplies and fuel in remote parts of Northern and Eastern Transvaal, and in northern Natal, in advance of the scheduled April general election. The reports also claimed that in preparation for stubborn resistance, intransigent *bittereinders* were conducting training exercises in guerrilla warfare tactics. AWB members were arrested in connection with planned attacks on the Koeberg nuclear plant, the World Trade Centre, venue of multiparty talks, and the SADF's Lohatla Army Battle School.[91]

7

The Trade Unions and the Working Class

How many times has a labour movement supported a liberation movement, only to find itself betrayed on the day of liberation? There are many examples of this in Africa. If the ANC government does not deliver the goods you must do to it what you did to the *apartheid* regime.

Nelson Mandela, speaking at
COSATU Special Congress, September 1993.[1]

The unstable transition from the 'hot' turbulence of the mid 1980s to the 'cool' inauguration of formal constitutional negotiations marked more than just the pendular swing of a recurrent political cycle. It also signalled a qualitative shift in the balance of political forces. As old lines of demarcation broke down and long-standing political alliances came unglued, new ones evolved to take their place. The once-solid firmament of apartheid rule upon which the white oligarchy had depended for nearly fifty years began to weaken and fall apart. The general framework within which the interests of the propertied classes and their myriad dependants found political expression came under severe stress and strain. The employers of labour, whose ownership of capital left the decisive nucleus of economic activity squarely in their hands, suddenly found themselves thrust into the unsettled position of trying to find a new and precarious equilibrium, grounded not on the revival of outmoded 'racialist' prescriptions but upon new interest-group compromises and new forms of technocratic and neo-liberal legitimation. The historic burden of mounting the impassioned defence of the rights of private property, reconciling intra-capitalist competition, and locating new sources of socio-economic harmony fell largely to the corporate associations of capital, most notably the South African Chamber of Business (SACOB), the Afrikaanse Handelsinstituut (AHI), the Steel and Engineering Industries Federation (SEIFSA), and the South African

Consultative Committee on Labour Affairs (SACCOLA), the Chamber of Mines, and the Consultative Business Movement (CBM).

During the 1980s, the popular upsurge against white minority rule and the apartheid system spilled over into a genuine grassroots rebellion against the logic and the rules of the capitalist marketplace. For the liberation movement, the imagined remedies for the severe socio-economic deprivation of black people and their exclusion from full-scale political participation as rightful citizens in an undivided South Africa centred primarily on demands for fundamental economic restructuring and a wholesale transfer of political power into the hands of the disenfranchised majority. Yet, with the onset of multi-party negotiations in the post-1990 period, the profound political realignment through which political parties sought literally to reinvent themselves in the changing circumstances of pluralist electoral competition favoured a Thermidorian, or moderating, thaw in the locus of thinking about the future. With the political calculus shifting in the direction of creating a level playing field on the political terrain, the main actors sought to carve out a stake for themselves within the existing institutional frameworks, rather than remoulding them out of whole cloth. The new arithmetic of brokered compromises and concessions created an arena for economic cooperation and political stabilization of the social order that invariably undermined the radical aspirations that had previously defined the popular movement. These moderating outcomes had a profound impact on the democratic trade unions and the civic associations, both of which came under increasing pressure to focus less on transforming the social order as a whole than on consolidating a share of working-class power within existing parameters. In light of the unanticipated resilience of the capitalist economic order, the democratic trade unions and the civics modified their strategies to reflect a political approach more appropriate for pluralist competition than for radical restructuring.

The Nonracial Trade Union Movement

In most western European countries, the 'collective civil rights' of labour – as T.H. Marshall called the right to bargain collectively and to negotiate a common labour contract – were preceded by the attainment of individual civil rights.[2] For organized labour in South Africa, the reverse was largely true. This historically peculiar set of circumstances shaped the social identity and political consciousness of black workers. To a significant degree, the visible political strength of the working-class movement in South Africa can be observed along two distinct but interrelated dimensions: labour organizations and strikes. Labour organizations, especially the trade unions but also including all the mutual-aid, research and advice centres that served them, were the leading edge of the movement. The leadership consisted of a veteran core of individuals drawn from the radical intelligentsia, sometimes with white middle-class backgrounds but increasingly less so, and 'advanced workers' – shopfloor militants, generally semi-skilled or unskilled, whose experience had pulled them in radical directions and who had acquired basic familiarity with the ideas of socialism, class struggle and political organization. The social composition of the rank and file was largely composed of unskilled and semi-skilled wage earners, and the labour organizations welded this heterodox mixture of social groupings into a coherent whole.

The capacity, whether organized or spontaneous, to disrupt capitalist production was the other face of the working-class movement. Slowdowns and strikes constituted a distinctive form of working-class activity that epitomized the antagonistic relationships between the propertied and nonpropertied classes. These actions served as an important outlet for the accumulation of grievances. They were consciousness-raising experiences through which working people learned, in the most direct and dramatic manner, what class struggle and politics were all about. In particular, the form and structure of strikes, their timing and substance, offered valuable insights into working-class organizational capacities and political expectations. Social weight in the marketplace – especially the ability to paralyse economic activities – translated into political influence. As a result, the 'labour question' became one of the most crucial tests of political stability. Class-based socio-economic relations between capital and labour were significant in their own right, but they also signified political disputes with far-reaching implications. Working-class forces that experienced defeats in the marketplace almost always suffered setbacks in the political arena as well.

The balance sheet for labour

Despite the recession and retrenchments, South Africa lost more labour days due to work stoppages during the five-year period from 1986 to 1990 than during the previous seventy-five years. Trade unions experienced steady growth in numerical size beginning in the mid 1970s, and only levelled off in the early 1990s. By 1994, trade-union membership, including the estimated 450,000 workers in independent (that is, not affiliated to a particular federation) unions, approximated 3.2 million wage earners, or about 23 per cent of the economically active population. Membership in registered trade unions alone accounted for over 40 per cent of the labour force in sectors falling under the Labour Relations

Act, thereby making South Africa one of the most heavily unionized countries in the world.[3]

The two main federations, COSATU and NACTU, spearheaded the growth and development of the progressive trade-union movement, which achieved remarkable success in greatly expanding its membership, particularly among black semi-skilled and unskilled workers.[4] Despite temporary setbacks, these trade unions displayed all the signs that, barring some unforeseen turn of events, they would grow in numerical strength as long as they continued to provide workers with collective protection against autocratic management practices, to exert upward pressure on wages and social benefits, and to pursue successfully a nationwide social policy that served the broad interests of the working class as a whole. While trade unions made giant strides in organizing workers in the mining, metallurgical and the diverse manufacturing sectors, there was plenty of room for expansion. A few unions had only just begun to make organizational inroads into the state sector and had barely penetrated the domestic service and farm-labour sectors, where millions of workers languished in dire poverty, without any fixed conditions of employment, and with few legal remedies for redress of grievances.[5]

The Congress of South African Trade Unions (COSATU)

Membership in the fourteen COSATU affiliates climbed from 450,000 at the time of its formation in 1985 to more than 1.3 million in 1994, with over 1,000 full-time officials and more than 25,000 shop stewards. The NUM, with approximately 300,000, NUMSA with 273,000 and SACTWU with 185,000 paid-up members, were the three largest COSATU affiliates.[6] COSATU had originally set a quick deadline for consolidating its founding thirty-five affiliates into ten giant trade unions to match the main sectors of the South African economy. Over the years, a number of important mergers brought COSATU much closer to this goal. On balance, the process of amalgamation was relatively quick and painless; nevertheless, particular instances were accompanied by friction and conflict.[7]

COSATU affiliates adhered to the principles of internal democracy, worker control and accountability of leadership.[8] Yet even the medium-sized unions became complex bureaucracies, and constantly battled with problems of efficient administration, financial responsibility and the growing social distance between the 'head office' and the rank and file.[9] For example, NUMSA, which more than doubled its membership between 1987 and 1993, was divided into ten regions with sixty-five offices, representing workers in the engineering, iron, steel, metallurgical, auto assembly, motor, and tyre and rubber industries.[10]

It has long been a convenient shorthand to treat COSATU and NACTU as monolithic, idealized wholes separate from their constituent parts. Both federations were umbrella bodies composed of distinct trade unions, embracing numerous tensions and dynamics, cross-cutting strengths and weakness, and heterodox political points of view.[11] The launch of COSATU in 1985 brought together trade unions representing three different approaches to organizing.[12] The first approach, which was associated with FOSATU and a few powerful independent unions, primarily stressed shop-floor unionism and worker independence. These unions emphasized the creation of democratic, factory-based structures around the principles of worker control and accountability of leadership. To a certain extent, these unions exhibited syndicalist leanings; and, as a matter of principle, they assiduously avoided political entanglements outside the workplace which threatened to detract from their main vocation of serving the interests of their members. The second approach, embodied in the nineteen unions which had heeded the call to affiliate with the UDF, stressed the essential indivisibility of working-class struggles in the factories and in the townships. With strong ties to the communities from which they sprang, the UDF bloc traced their ideological roots to the 'national-democratic' tradition exemplified by the Congress-aligned South African Congress of Trade Unions (SACTU) in the 1950s. The third approach, which consisted of the 100,000-strong NUM, (A)FCWU, SFAWU, PPWAWU, and TGWU, bisected these extremes. While generally sympathetic to the UDF/ANC bloc, these centrist unions were not prepared to throw themselves wholeheartedly into community struggles at the expense of building a durable trade-union presence at the point of production.[13]

The passionate and often acrimonious wrangling which accompanied the formation of COSATU was called the 'workerist–populist' debate. Both terms have pejorative overtones, and those who used them did so in order to disparage their opponents. In the minds of their antagonists, 'workerists' were those unionists who focused so narrowly on economistic (wages and hours) issues that they failed to grasp the significance of wider political struggles for working-class advancement. Conversely, 'populists', or 'nationalists', were those unionists who concentrated on community struggles at the expense of ignoring day-to-day concerns of workers on the shop floor. The 'workerist–populist' debate revolved around alternative approaches to building the labour movement, but the controversy itself reflected much deeper and more long-standing political differences over strategy and tactics. At their heart lay one question: what political role should the trade unions play? Other questions followed logically: how should the unions relate to the country's political movements, and, correlatively, to the state administration? While the organizational terrain shifted over time and the main protagonists changed, the basic political questions remained.[14]

The 'workerist–populist' rivalry shaped the early debates in COSATU over the relationship of the labour movement to the ANC-led national liberation struggle. From the outset, the 'populist' tendency insisted that COSATU affiliates swear allegiance to the ANC's Freedom Charter and thereby declare their willingness to participate more fully in the national liberation struggle. The 'workerist' tendency countered with calls to endorse a Workers' Charter as a means of placing questions of workers' rights and socialism squarely on the political agenda. Those who proposed the Workers' Charter did so because they believed that the ANC's Freedom Charter, adopted in 1955, paid insufficient attention to the particular interests of workers and was open to competing class interpretations.[15]

This controversy came to a head at the third COSATU congress held in 1989. COSATU delegates adopted the Freedom Charter as 'a guiding document which reflects the views and aspirations of the majority of the oppressed and exploited in our struggle against national oppression and economic exploitation'. But they also took the position that combating national oppression and economic exploitation were 'complimentary to each other and part of an uninterrupted struggle for total liberation', thereby setting aside the classic 'two-stage' theory of revolution in favour of an alternative position that the struggle for national liberation was part and parcel of the struggle for socialism.[16] COSATU pledged its whole-hearted support for a Workers' Charter campaign. But in the end, apart from the staunchly workerist union SACTWU, few affiliates took the campaign seriously. What was lost in the charged atmosphere of state-sponsored repression and semi-clandestine trade-union organizing was the fact that the 'workerist' and 'populist' tendencies had gradually edged closer to a 'strategic compromise' that transcended political abstentionism, on the one side, and the neglect of shopfloor organizing, on the other. In pooling their resources, the COSATU leadership and the Congress-aligned UDF joined together to form the Mass Democratic Movement (MDM), a protean entity which operated as an all-purpose, above-ground surrogate for political organizations that found themselves in legal limbo. Bred of practical necessity, this convergence led to a cross-fertilization of membership and ideas across a broad organizational front. Over time, the growing ties between COSATU and the still-underground ANC and SACP evolved into a functioning tripartite alliance.[17]

In June 1990, at its first mass rally following its unbanning, the SACP unveiled its public leadership, including prominent trade unionists like NUMSA general secretary Moses Mayekiso, COSATU vice president John

Gomomo, FAWU president and COSATU vice president Chris Dlamini, and COSATU assistant general secretary Sydney Mafumadi. This surprise announcement brought to a head tensions that had been brewing beneath the surface for some time. What was clear was that not only had COSATU and the SACP forged an alliance between separate organizations, but these formally distinct entities had intertwined leadership.[18] This question of overlapping leadership triggered what came to be known as the 'two hats' debate. In the ensuing controversy, three positions emerged. One position encouraged trade-union leaders to hold administrative posts in government or political parties in order to strengthen working-class interests in these bodies. The second position offered a more cautious approach, accepting that it was necessary for union officials to hold these posts during a period of transition, but that in the long run they would not be able to take official positions without sacrificing the independence of the unions. The third position suggested that trade-union officials should not simultaneously hold office in government or in political parties since their sole responsibility as leaders was to represent their members.[19] John Copelyn, general secretary of SACTWU, for example, strenuously argued that dual leadership involved a conflict of interest and, as such, signalled a 'fundamental surrender' of trade-union independence. 'You cannot serve two masters', he proclaimed.[20]

In the actual debate, these three positions represented more 'ideal type' currents toward which the trade-union movement gravitated rather than hard-and-fast doctrinal stances. While COSATU did not officially endorse a ban on holding multiple leadership positions, the breadth of opposition indicated widespread wariness regarding the inherent dangers of spreading the leadership ranks too thin. Thousands of militants, who were radicalized as a consequence of their practical experience in building the labour movement *de novo* during the 1970s and 1980s, fiercely guarded trade-union independence. This commitment to trade-union autonomy, which perhaps not surprisingly cut across the political spectrum, marked a decisive departure from past practice where trade unions largely operated as a subservient mass base, or conveyor belt, for popular-nationalist organizations.[21]

The 'other federation': the National Council of Trade Unions (NACTU)

Two loosely affiliated groupings of trade unions, the Black Consciousness-oriented CUSA and the Africanist AZACTU, had decided not to join in the launch of COSATU, and in 1986 they merged to form NACTU. From the outset, NACTU was overshadowed by the stronger and better-organized COSATU.[22] In 1988, when a decidedly Africanist leadership was elected to replace outgoing Black Consciousness figures, many political analysts suspected that NACTU had moved much closer to the PAC camp, and that the federation would be unwilling to seek broader working-class unity with COSATU. Over the next several years, NACTU was plunged into a period of internal disarray. Many workers 'voted with their feet' by joining rival COSATU affiliates; and, as a result, NACTU membership plummeted to below 150,000 workers.[23] Yet NACTU made steady gains in recruitment, and claimed to have 327,000 paid-up members by late 1993, of whom more than 40 per cent were women. Several key mergers reduced the number of affiliates from twenty to fifteen, and this internal consolidation improved the effectiveness of the organization.[24]

In many respects, the basic operating principles and organizing strategies of NACTU affiliates were remarkably similar to those of COSATU. Like its larger and more formidable rival, NACTU's greatest organizational strength lay in the manufacturing sector, particularly the chemicals, metals, construction, furniture and food industries. Yet NACTU was strongest where COSATU had only medium-sized affiliates, particularly in chemicals and construction. Where NACTU affiliates confronted COSATU's giant unions (especially NUM and NUMSA), it had little hope of expanding beyond its relatively narrow base. If more COSATU affiliates merged to form huge 'mega-unions' with enhanced organizational capacities, NACTU's potential for future membership growth was likely to be greatly restricted. Unlike COSATU, few NACTU affiliates had a truly strong national presence, with the exception of the South African Chemical Workers' Union (SACWU) which rivalled the COSATU-affiliated CWIU.[25]

At its 1990 Congress, NACTU delegates re-elected the Africanist-oriented executive and adopted political positions which dovetailed neatly with those of the PAC. Key NACTU leaders, like its general secretary, Cunningham Ngcukana, and its president, James Mndaweni, openly declared their allegiance to the PAC, and there was reason to believe that NACTU and PAC membership overlapped to a significant degree. While some political commentators speculated that the PAC gained control of the federation, its leadership strongly professed its adherence to the principle of political non-alignment, insisting that NACTU would 'cooperate with all political organizations within the policies and principles of the federation'. The federation nurtured genuine contacts with a wider range of political forces than COSATU; and, in particular, 'its relationship with the ANC and SACP seem[ed] fairly healthy'.[26]

COSATU and NACTU worked together in a number of joint efforts, notably the Workers' Charter Campaign, to build broad-based working-class solidarity outside the parameters of existing union structures. However, the most successful joint COSATU/NACTU effort was the marathon three-year campaign to oppose amendments to the Labour Relations Act. The struggle ended in victory when the two federations and SACCOLA, South Africa's largest business association, reached an agreement between themselves and the government, called the 1990 Laboria Minute, that effectively annulled the 1988 Labour Relations Amendment Act (LRAA) which had permitted the Industrial Court to interdict lawful strikes and lockouts.[27] The 'unity-in-action' that evolved between COSATU and NACTU affiliates over the course of the anti-LRAA campaign gave a clear sign that the two main labour federations had drawn closer together in many important respects.[28] The NACTU leadership consistently preached trade-union unity, insisting that genuine cooperation had to be forged not merely at the leadership level but at the grassroots as well. The federation also advocated drawing in other sections of organized labour, including the nonracial Federation of Salaried Staff (FEDSAL) and the unaffiliated independent unions, into the process of closer cooperation. NACTU complained that divisions between the ANC, PAC and AZAPO on strategic and political questions were the main obstacles to forging trade-union alliances.[29]

Limits and possibilities of trade union expansion

During the 1980s, the main task facing the nonracial, progressive trade-union movement was to organize and unite black workers. In the 1990s, the situation became much more complex. The trade unions faced the challenge of building unity out of the increasing occupational differentiation and social diversification of the working class. In addition, political divisions within the black working class became more pronounced as the epoch-making 'struggle for liberation' was replaced by the single-minded pluralist competition at the heart of parliamentary democracy and electoral politics. It was not easy for COSATU organizers and shop stewards to maintain the rock-solid allegiance of union members who supported the IFP, NP or PAC, and at the same time campaign for ANC votes. The real challenge facing the organized labour movement was this: how could trade unions maintain their own internal unity in the absence of political homogeneity among their members? There was growing sentiment that the trade unions needed to respect the diversity of political beliefs within their own ranks if they were to grow and develop. At the same time, the combination of economic restructuring and the elimination of apartheid-era protections ushered in a period of political turmoil for the white trade unions. As their privileged marketplace and workplace bargaining positions disappeared, white workers responded with increased racism and increased militancy. For the nonracial trade-union movement, this original situation opened new opportunities to forge common action with white unions and to combat racism via class-wide solidarity.[30]

The divisions of colour, skill, gender and occupation were reflected in the heterogeneous and complex labour market. These cleavages were also mirrored in the growth and development of the labour movement. COSATU evolved as the dominant labour centre, but despite its profound diversity, its affiliates were still unable to claim to represent all layers of the working class. COSATU was organized as a mass movement of black workers, mostly African, and its membership consisted almost entirely of blue-collar wage earners below the level of artisan. In structure and organization, NACTU shared a similar profile. In most sectors of employment, the majority of artisans were white wage earners, and they were organized historically into predominantly white craft unions or into industrial craft unions dominated by white, coloured and Indian workers. The majority of white-collar workers in the private sector were either unorganized or were members of trade unions affiliated to FEDSAL. In the public sector, most white wage earners were members of conservative staff associations.[31]

Generally speaking, craft and industrial-craft unions enjoyed a privileged position in relation to state agencies and employers in industrial councils, and this arrangement reinforced their tendency to function as 'sweetheart unions'. Where COSATU affiliates tried to recruit members of these unions, they invariably encountered a number of problems. Many members of craft and industrial craft unions harboured racist and conservative attitudes, exhibiting fear of African-dominated unions and a reflexive aversion to militant mass struggle. Because they were set apart from other workers by their specialized training, by their strategic position in the production process, and by higher rates of pay, many artisans and skilled operatives exhibited the customary symptoms of 'craft consciousness'. Many of these wage earners held supervisory positions, and most identified more with management than with the rest of the workers.[32]

Trade union experts long predicted the merger of COSATU and NACTU and the realization of the goal of 'one union, one federation'. Yet for every two steps forward, there was always one step backward. 'The advantages of a merger would be far-reaching', Cunningham Ngcukana, NACTU general secretary, insisted. 'It will help to stop violence and ideological and political fights in the factories, and it will strengthen the hand of the workers.' However, the main stumbling block to trade-union unity was the question of political alliances. Whatever the reservations on the side of COSATU affiliates, NACTU was unwilling to contemplate seriously a merger as long as COSATU leadership maintained its formal alliance with the SACP and the ANC.[33]

There were organizational difficulties as well. For example, the NACTU-affiliated Metal and Electrical Workers Union of South Africa (MEWUSA) debated the possibility of merging with the COSATU-affiliated NUMSA. But the MEWUSA leadership decided to concentrate first on concluding the merger process among metal unions affiliated with NACTU before embarking on negotiations with its larger and more powerful COSATU counterpart.[34] Perhaps more importantly, several key affiliates in both federations continued to be plagued by long-standing organizational difficulties, some grounded in ideological differences and others in regional rivalries, thereby slowing down the merger process. For the most part, these difficulties were ironed out over time. The deep ideological divisions that eventually tore SACCAWU asunder was an exception to the general rule. Even before its formation in the late 1980s out of a merger of several COSATU affiliates, SACCAWU was split according to political sympathies: on the one side, the ANC; and on the other a loose coalition of 'workerists', the PAC, and a variety of socialist groupings.[35] From the outset, bitter infighting between its branches haunted SACCAWU, and these surfaced with a vengeance at its 1993 annual conference. Prior to the conference, conflicts had emerged around well-founded allegations of financial irregularities (including theft and fraud) at head office, and the unilateral decision of the union's national executive to suspend the Witwatersrand branch leadership. SACCAWU did not handle the strain, and the union fissioned into three warring camps.[36]

Moderate and Right-wing Voices of Labour

The 273,000-strong FEDSAL, an alliance of mainly white clerical workers in seventeen affiliates, principally located in the banking, mining, and state sectors, carved out the middle ground between the nonracial, progressive trade unions on the one side, and the all-white, right-wing trade unions on the other. FEDSAL, which lay dormant for quite some time, was resuscitated in 1985, and after that time experienced dramatic growth. The federation represented mainly white-collar workers, but around 20 per cent were blue-collar. The social composition of its membership was 70 per cent white and 30 per cent black. FEDSAL leaders set their sights on becoming a moderating force in the trade-union centre, rather than a white-collar federation per se. Although the federation had blue-collar affiliates, its growth was mainly in the white-collar fields of technically skilled and administrative employment. These areas were becoming of increasing strategic importance for the trade-union movement. While manufacturing employment remained stagnant, the financial sector has more than doubled in size over the past eleven years. FEDSAL and

COSATU shared a mutual concern about trade-union and worker rights, but parted company over the issue of political involvement. FEDSAL leaders insisted that their federation was a moderate, apolitical voice of labour that restricted itself to purely economic, labour and consumer issues. The federation declared that it was oriented toward improving the free-market economy rather than changing it.[37]

FEDSAL maintained cordial relations with two other middle-of-the-road trade-union federations, namely, the Confederation of Metal and Building Unions (CMBU) and the Federation of Independent Trade Unions (FITU). The launch of FITU in 1991 enabled a plethora of small, unaffiliated and anti-sanctions trade unions to speak with a common voice. FITU claimed to have twenty-two affiliates with a combined membership of around 217,000 workers. Of this number, 10 per cent were white, and the rest were split, more or less equally, between African workers and coloured and Indian workers. Labour analysts regarded the formation of FITU as a revival of the defunct Trade Union Council of South Africa (TUCSA); certainly three of its largest affiliates – the South African Typographical Union (SATU), the South African Boilermakers' Society (SABS), and the Amalgamated Union of Building Trade Workers (AUBTW) – once belonged to TUCSA.[38] The 100,000-strong CMBU was a federation formerly composed of eight craft unions, three of which had left the fold to join FITU. These two labour groups professed a commitment to nonracialism and to free market principles.[39]

'An endangered species': the whites-only trade unions

Throughout the modern history of industrial South Africa, the exclusivist white trade unions have long served as the main social base for right-wing political parties. Over the past decade, the steady erosion of 'job reservation' clauses in labour legislation meant the virtual extinction of the special privileges that white workers once regarded as their automatic birthright in 'white South Africa'. Despite dire threats of work stoppages and bombastic racist rhetoric, the whites-only Mynwerkersunie (MWU) – a bastion of reactionary white supremacist ideas – failed to stop the Chamber of Mines phasing out job colour bars in the mining industry during the 1980s. As one astute observer remarked, 'The "white worker" in the traditional South African sense of a person mollycoddled from birth to death by the National Party government, is an endangered species'.[40] White workers responded to the turbulent, troubled times with a heterodox mixture of racism and increased militancy.[41]

According to a 1990 National Manpower Commission report, 32 of South Africa's 212 registered trade unions had an exclusively white membership. Sizeable trade unions, like the 25,000-strong Amalgamated Engineering Union (AEU) and the 22,000-strong South African Electrical Workers' Association (SAEWA), did not have black workers in their ranks, but expressed no reservations about joint bargaining with trade unions which had black members. 'The AEU is a white union', its general secretary proclaimed, 'but it is not a rightist union. It is not politically orientated.' The South African Confederation of Labour (SACOL), formed in 1957 during the heyday of apartheid, remained the *bittereinder* stronghold of the conservative white trade-union movement. Once the pre-eminent force in the labour arena, SACOL gradually shrank to seven affiliates with a combined membership of around 100,000 workers. The two most powerful blue-collar affiliates were the 50,000-strong MWU and the South African Iron, Steel, and Allied Industries Union (Yster & Staal) with close to 41,000 members. The MWU experienced rapid growth in the early 1990s in the coal mines, steel plants and power stations of the eastern and northeastern Transvaal. The region accounted for some 6,000 of its national membership. The conservative white trade unions boycotted the lengthy deliberations over the LRAA and, as a result, were ignored in the final COSATU/NACTU/SACCOLA accord. The refusal of the National Party to obstruct the enactment of this joint accord into law caused deep resentment within the ranks of white labour, prompting the MWU General Secretary to conclude that 'this means that the old order, in which the white worker was the most important ally of successive governments, [is] obviously gone for good'.[42]

Taking their cue from the giant strides of both COSATU and NACTU in building powerful organizational structures, the conservative white trade unions recognized the need to forge greater unity amongst their splintered and shrinking constituencies. Yster & Staal envisaged the formation of a tightly organized federation where affiliates were obliged to abide by collective decisions. In contrast, the MWU advocated the creation of a single 'super white union' for white workers in all economic sectors as a way of providing white workers with more negotiating power and protection in the workplace. 'We have learnt from COSATU that you need to have power to make the company listen', a MWU official stated. 'We want all white workers in one union'.[43] Despite their shared outlook, personal animosities and the territorial anxieties of union leaders, some of whom managed to cling desperately to carefully nurtured fiefdoms, prevented the exclusivist white trade unions from realizing this cherished goal of building a workable united front.[44]

What was apparent was that the privileged 'glory days' for white workers were long gone and that the white trade unions were trapped in a race against time.[45] In several key instances, class outweighed race as threatened white workers, particularly the less skilled sectors, turned to militant black unions with the 'muscle to protect them'. Small numbers of white workers in the metal, mining, food and commercial sectors joined COSATU unions. But the most striking advances were made on the railways, once a privileged sanctuary for 'poor white' wage earners, where the COSATU-affiliated SARHWU claimed 1,500 white members.[46] On occasion, historical events seem to defy expected codes of conduct, and the temporary alliance between NUMSA and the all-white MWU during the successful 1993 wage strike at Anglo American's Highveld Steel in Witbank was a remarkable example. This joint work stoppage marked not only the 'first time that a predominantly black union and a white union downed tools together over the same demand', but also 'the first legal wage strike by a white union since the 1950s'.[47]

Organizational Strategies and Political Goals

The revival of the 'modern labour movement', to use von Holdt's phrase, can be traced to the 1973 Durban 'wildcat' strike wave and the upsurge of organizing activities that it engendered.[48] The evolution of the non-racial, democratic trade-union movement was a highly complex and uneven process. The successes and failures of trade-union organizing strategies varied significantly from plant to plant, from industry to industry, from region to region, and even over the course of time, all in accordance with historically specific constellations of circumstances. For these reasons alone, generalizations are difficult to make. Yet, at the risk of over-simplification, it is possible to distinguish three distinct arenas of conflict and accommodation – the workplace, the sectoral and national levels – where employers and the organized trade-union movement squared off against each other, and to offer a cautious assessment of the outcome of these confrontations.

Workplace bargaining power

At the enterprise (or plant) level, workers came face to face with the autocratic factory despotism that bore the distinct imprint of apartheid rule. This occurred on the shop floor, where labour and capital stood in opposition not as abstract, faceless forces, but as actual social collectivities divided between those who worked and those who ordered them to do so. It was in this harsh environment that the bitter conflicts between employers and workers appeared in their sharpest form, and it was here that the organized labour movement had its initial and, in a real sense, perhaps its most enduring impact.

Before the advent of the progressive trade-union movement, work rules governing methods of production were in theory entirely the prerogative of management. Almost without exception, white managers and black workers viewed each other with suspicion and hostility. Black workers had little control over hours of work, payment of wages and conditions of employment. They were exposed to physical hardships and dangers, and were subjected to often arbitrary and capricious discipline within a racially demarcated hierarchy that placed them at the bottom of the social order. From the standpoint of the individual worker, the prospect of losing one's job almost certainly loomed large as the most formidable weapon in the employer's arsenal of techniques to ensure a docile and dependable labour force.

During the early years of trade-union organizing, the de facto rights of workers to bargain collectively at their place of work emerged as the most fiercely contested area of contention. To a considerable extent, the workers themselves improvised their own leadership, organization and methods of collective action. One of the greatest achievements of the organized labour movement was the development of new forms of work-place organization and representation. The formation and growth of the shop stewards' movement enabled the nonracial trade unions to make considerable headway in securing and implanting a permanent working-class presence on the shop floor. As elected rank-and-file delegates, shop stewards symbolized the organized labour movement in microcosm, and they acted as the most elementary organs of workers' power. In the early stages of the movement, it was this dedicated nucleus of militant activists who led struggles, who negotiated informally with supervisors, and who established networks between their own and other groups on the factory floor. By aggressively seeking redress of day-to-day grievances, shop stewards presented a direct challenge to managerial prerogatives at the workplace.[49]

The trade unions effectively harnessed this rank-and-file militancy, transforming what in many important respects resembled a spontaneous mass movement into a more coherent organizational form embodied in an embryonic network of factory councils. By relentlessly pursuing demands that went beyond narrow economistic issues to include such concerns as racism and sexism, the organized labour movement under-mined the established management hierarchies and patterns of authority, and thereby altered the balance of power on the shop floor. The erosion of the exclusive domain of managerial prerogative was particularly evi-dent with regard to disciplinary matters, dismissals and retrenchments. In some cases, such as the Volkswagen plant at Uitenhage, the role of shop stewards went well beyond these issues. Shop stewards were centrally

involved, via consultations with senior management on a Joint Union/
Management Executive Committee, in implementing changes of work
practices to the extent that they held an effective veto right over managerial instructions.[50] For the trade unions, the growing consciousness of
collective empowerment that evolved out of the 'democratic character of
these shopfloor struggles' laid the groundwork for the 'longer term goal
of worker control of the production process' itself.[51]

Strictly speaking, the development of militant trade unions made it
impossible for management unilaterally to impose coercive methods to
increase productivity and ensure efficiency and quality of work. Employers
reacted to the successful challenge to their workplace authority by seeking new forms of collaboration and partnership with organized labour.
The strongest shop-floor unions were assiduously courted by employers
anxious to maintain labour peace and procure productivity agreements.
The most class-conscious companies introduced 'participative management'
schemes, like Quality Circles, Just-in-Time, and Green Areas, in the hope
of securing greater cooperation from their employees by creating a working environment that encouraged workers to use their skills and initiative.[52]

But for every two steps forward, there was one step back. While many
companies introduced various 'worker participation' and productivity
schemes, trade unions made very little progress towards reaching agreements on co-determination or democratizing the workplace. In large
measure, workers on the shop floor were confused and perplexed by the
hocus-pocus of 'flexible production' schemes, which they often saw as
merely cynical ploys designed to introduce the speed-up and the stretch-
out through the backdoor. In most instances, managers bypassed the trade
unions by implementing their up-to-date schemes without consultation
with shop stewards. While trade-union officials negotiated the principles
of team-work and co-determination with employers at the national level,
shop stewards on the factory floor complained that management aggressively pursued a strategy of 'lean production' by threatening wholesale
retrenchments if agreements could not be reached on flexibility, multi-
tasking and new work schedules.[53]

Collective bargaining at the sectoral level

From the mid 1980s onward, contestation between employers and organized labour at the sectoral level evolved naturally from the steady agglomeration of workplace struggles. The most powerful trade unions turned
with increasing regularity toward centralized collective bargaining and
participation in industrial councils to replace plant-level bargaining. There
were two main reasons why this shift of focus took place. First, agreements

secured at the factory level tended to be ad hoc and fragile affairs which required constant vigilance. Those trade unions that had reached agreements with particular firms sought to cement and consolidate these gains at the industry-wide level. Second, intransigent employers were often successful in placing all sorts of bureaucratic encumbrances in the way of negotiations at the factory level. Frustrated unions wishing to circumvent these blockages sought industry-wide standards in order to pressurize these employers into conformity.[54] As a general rule, as Morris has shown in his study of NUMSA, the varying attitudes of different trade unions toward participation in national collective bargaining and the industrial council system were motivated less by long-standing ideological positions than by changing material conditions and concrete organizational circumstances.[55]

Both employers and trade unions faced a severe test of organizational strength and political will at the sectoral level. The basic features of South Africa's industrial-relations system remained more or less intact since the enactment of the 1924 Industrial Conciliation Act. On balance, this cumbersome legislation was the main institutional mechanism for resolving industry-wide capital–labour disputes. The modifications that did take place over the years did little or nothing to alter its basic features. The most significant alteration came with the 1979 amendments (along with subsequent clarifying clauses) that extended registration privileges to African workers, allowing them to form and join trade unions.[56]

From the outset, the industrial-relations system was a bureaucratic maze, loaded with plenty of confusing loopholes, that established a largely passive framework which depended, strictly speaking, on voluntary participation. It provided a mechanism for resolving work-related disputes, but left the interpretation of 'unfair labour practices' to the discretion of the courts. It gave workers the freedom to strike, but conferred few protections against employers who engaged in vindictive practices like dismissals and lockouts. It allowed parties to bargain through industrial councils, but did not compel them to join or establish them.[57]

Those trade unions that engaged in sectoral-level collective bargaining experienced mixed results. The industrial council system never truly evolved into a coherent framework regulating industry-wide, national collective bargaining. Instead, a diverse patchwork developed where there were some national councils, but few were industry-wide. Most councils were regional or local, and in many instances covered only subsectors of industries for particular geographical areas.[58] The most powerful trade unions, which dwarfed rival craft unions on the industrial councils, achieved appreciable gains in protecting jobs from retrenchment, improving living standards, standardizing working conditions, and enhancing skills.

COSATU affiliates in the clothing and textile, metal and engineering, motor assembly and tyre, electronics, and mining industries were in the forefront of establishing industry-wide negotiating forums linking broader considerations of industrial restructuring, productivity and economic growth with profit-sharing schemes, tariffs and import policies, long-term employment security, and job training.[59] Agreements over a new framework for job grading and training laid the basis for production based on higher skills, flexibility, better quality and more complex technology. The long-term goal of the most powerful trade unions was to reach co-determination agreements in the spheres of business and industry-wide planning, product development and investment.[60]

On balance, however, this voluntaristic system tended to reward disproportionately the most strongly organized unions – in practice, those representing workers in a few key manufacturing sectors and in larger, more capital-intensive companies – to make real gains over an extended period. Nevertheless, there were cases which broke the general pattern: for example, TGWU negotiated an industrial council for cleaning workers in 1993; SARHWU established formal negotiating rights for railway and harbour workers; SAMWU dramatically extended its bargaining activities; and POTWA transformed informal bargaining structures into genuine trade unionism. These exceptions to the general rule notwithstanding, the unanticipated consequence of this largely *laissez faire* approach to industrial relations was to strengthen the relatively 'privileged' sections of organized labour by reinforcing the prevailing wage gaps between 'organized' and 'unorganized' workers, between 'strong' and 'weak' trade unions, and between workers in the same union but in different industrial sectors.[61]

It was perhaps bitterly ironic that the success of the trade unions in wresting higher wages, improved working conditions, and other concessions for organized workers from reluctant employers was accompanied by growing differentiation and fragmentation of the working class. Without the collective power of the organized labour movement, the unorganized, casualized and marginalized sections of the proletariat sunk ever closer to abject impoverishment.[62] Liberal commentators spoke in gloating terms of the emergence of a unionized labour aristocracy. This designation, with everything it implied about political orientation and class collaboration, was well off the mark. The recession caused the trade unions to temper their demands out of fear of triggering mass layoffs. Even trade unions powerful enough to conduct national collective-bargaining campaigns within specific industrial sectors often failed to match wage increases with spiralling inflation. The expanding segmentation of the working class into distinctive layers exacerbated sectoral, regional, gender and skill differences, thereby hampering the development of class-wide organizational and political unity.[63]

Organized labour at the national level

The democratic trade-union movement did not really enter into full-fledged tripartite agreements with state agencies and employer bodies until 1990. The *Laboria Minute*, signed by COSATU, NACTU, SACCOLA, the National Manpower Commission (NMC) and the Department of Manpower in September 1990, marked a breakthrough in multilateral bargaining at the national level. This agreement stipulated that no future amendments to the Labour Relations Act would be put before parliament until all the participating parties had been consulted. This decision paved the way for bilateral negotiations between COSATU/NACTU and SACCOLA on amendments to the 1988 Labour Relations Act, and eventually led to the passage of the 1991 Labour Relations Amendment Act (LRAA), the first act in parliament that was the result of trilateral negotiations between the state administration, large-scale employers, and the democratic trade-union movement.[64] The accord reached between COSATU and the minister of manpower in November 1992 represented a similar experiment at national-level negotiation with the state administration. According to this agreement, the minister and department of manpower consented to promulgate legislation extending basic working conditions and labour-relations rights to farmworkers and domestic servants. This agreement also cleared the path for legislation that would extend labour relations rights to certain categories of public-sector employees.[65]

After 1990, the trade-union movement actively sought to secure a voice for itself in shaping macro-economic policy. To this end, the organized labour movement sat on statutory bodies pertaining to labour matters, including the revamped NMC, the National Training Board (NTB), the National Housing Forum, the National Electricity Forum, and the National Economic Forum (NEF).[66] In particular, COSATU and NACTU actively campaigned to transform the NMC from a 'toothless advisory body of government appointees into a tripartite negotiating forum with powers to place legislation before Parliament'.[67] The two federations also sought to restructure the Labour Appeals Court by enlarging its powers, extending its focus beyond labour legislation, and ensuring trade-union representation in decision-making.[68]

At various times and places, the trade-union federations tested their collective powers of mobilization, coordination and unity in carrying out a number of countrywide work stoppages that resembled, in an embryonic way, Rosa Luxemburg's strategic conception of the 'mass strike'.

Building on the experience of the anti-LRAA campaign, the COSATU-led anti-VAT coalition culminated in the highly successful November 1991 general strike. This effort gathered so much momentum that COSATU shifted the emphasis of the campaign to the demand for a national economic negotiating forum to parallel the CODESA multi-party talks. Perhaps the high point of labour militancy was the 3–4 August 1992 general strike – following in the wake of the Boipatong massacre – that involved an estimated four million workers.[69]

The Political Outlook of the Organized Labour Movement

For the organized labour movement clustered around COSATU and NACTU, these strategic initiatives, which were aimed at taking advantage of whatever temporary weaknesses of big business could be found, formed part of an overall vision of replacing capitalism altogether. As a general rule, the leading trade unions did not shy away from expressing their ideological commitment to a socialist future. Both COSATU and NACTU jealously guarded their autonomy and vowed not to become 'transmission belts' feeding politically conscious workers into popular organizations. In 1991, COSATU unveiled its comprehensive constitutional proposals, including the right to strike and to organize, independent media and a separate labour court. These proposals clearly reflected deeply entrenched sentiments shared by most COSATU affiliates to ensure their independence from whatever political party, or coalition of parties, came to power in the 'new' South Africa. Over the long haul, COSATU called for a 'democratically planned' economy, 'worker control' of factories, mines and shops; equality between men and women; full employment with living benefits granted to the jobless; and collective ownership of the 'commanding heights' of the economy.[70]

The organized labour movement was confronted with the age-old dilemma of linking its long-term programme of collective ownership and worker control with the immediate day-to-day concerns of the workers to whom it appealed. Although the process was highly uneven and the results varied considerably, the leading trade unions pursued an incrementalist strategy involving a steady expansion of workplace control and increased participation in centralized collective bargaining at the sectoral level. This 'boring from within' approach achieved appreciable gains for organized workers and, on a broader front, bolstered the self-confidence of the labour movement and enhanced the credibility of trade unionism amongst the unorganized sections of the working class.[71] In the process, the leading trade unions gradually shifted from the old style 'militant abstentionism', where trade unions refused to accept co-responsibility for such issues as productivity, profitability and growth, to a new position which encouraged direct union involvement in these key economic problem areas. This approach, called 'flexible accommodation', entailed the abandonment of a strictly adversarial approach toward employers in favour of a pragmatic 'principled engagement'.[72] 'A recognition of the benefits of cooperation must surely take the place of the adversarialism characteristic of the relationship of labour and capital to date', two leading members of the influential, COSATU-affiliated Economic Trends research group argued. '[C]ollaborative relationships – between manufacturers, companies and unions, the company via employer federations and industrial policy makers – are an essential ingredient of any successful industrial policy.'[73]

The trade unions were inextricably drawn into complex multilateral bargaining positions, and even de facto partnerships, with the central state administration, political parties and powerful representatives of big business. The organized labour movement developed comprehensive guidelines for new labour legislation, constitutional rights, economic growth, job creation, industrial restructuring, job training and reorganization of the workplace. These proposals amounted to nothing less than a prefigurative vision of an entirely new industrial-relations system. Large-scale business enterprises realized that for South African industry to become internationally competitive, companies required new technologies, increased efficiency and productivity, higher quality of output, and greater skills. The choice of standing idly by or 'becoming centrally involved' in the inevitable process of industrial restructuring, as Marcel Golding, NUM assistant general secretary put it, lay at the heart of this emerging vision of a new kind of trade unionism.[74] This proactive participation, which trade-union analysts called 'strategic unionism', crystallized around a multi-faceted strategy of far-reaching reforms involving macro-economic planning, industry-wide reorganization, and workplace democracy.[75] The driving force behind this approach was 'a broad-based coalition of interest groups, at the centre of which is the labour movement'. The principal objective was to 'develop step-by-step programme of radical reforms – each of which extends the arena of democratic decision-making, and deepens the power of the working class'.[76]

'Strategic unionism' was premised on the understanding that this incrementalist strategy of radical, or structural, reforms was capable of effecting a gradual rupture with the existing capitalist order. Embedded in this line of reasoning were two key presumptions: first, in contrast to the pursuit of self-contained 'improvements' that merely strengthened the capitalist system, structural reforms contained an inbuilt dynamic which, once unleashed, carried a momentum all of their own, propelling the labour movement towards socialism; and second, structural reforms were rooted in popular initiatives in such a way that they left a permanent 'residue of empowerment' which automatically created a platform for further struggles.[77] Advocates of 'strategic unionism' claimed that this approach offered a way of mobilizing workers around a set of immediate and significant demands and, at the same time, of strengthening the institutional power of the labour movement. As von Holdt put it, 'a labour-led programme for economic and social renewal, democracy and development holds out the hope, if successful, of winning broad support for ongoing and more radical transformation and democratisation.' This strategy of structural reforms enabled the organized labour movement to link immediate bread-and-butter issues with the long-term goal of socialist transformation.[78]

The dangers of corporatism

COSATU and its affiliates floated a number of all-embracing proposals, variously called 'reconstruction accords', 'social contracts' and 'co-determination pacts', all of which plotted an immediate course of action for the organized labour movement. Whatever their real or imagined differences, these strategic initiatives all envisioned some sort of accommodating *modus vivendi* between organized labour, the central state administration and large-scale capital, involving long-term planning for economic growth and redistribution.[79] This emergent corporatism – as Johann Maree called this embryonic tripartite *entente cordiale* – triggered an intense debate with wide-ranging political implications.[80]

To provide a critical analysis of the many and varied political positions that emerged from this controversy would require the kind of careful examination of myriad details and nuanced meanings that is beyond the scope of the present work.[81] Yet, at the risk of oversimplifying what were indeed very complex issues, it is nevertheless possible to acquire a general understanding of what was at stake by highlighting the main currents of the debate. On the one side, those trade-union analysts who embraced the trend toward an ever-widening circle of tripartite cooperation defended 'social contracts', reconstruction accords' and 'co-determination pacts' on the grounds that they did not represent the tired old formulas of a reformist social democracy aimed at stabilizing capitalism, but instead signalled a progressive challenge to the logic of profit-making itself. Advocates of 'bargained corporatism' – to use Baskin's phrase – argued that these formalized agreements constituted a dynamic framework within which the trade-union movement protected jobs, achieved a higher standard of living, and provided higher quality goods and services, while at the same time bringing about a fundamental and irreversible shift in the balance of power and social wealth in favour of working people. They contended that it was possible to take advantage of the partial or immediate interests that labour and capital had in common, and that corporatist deal-making represented essentially tactical compromises that in no sense jeopardized the pursuit of system-transformative ends and socialist goals. Their political prescription called for active engagement, not passive abstentionism, and they contended that this option was the only viable route available for organized labour if it wished to achieve social progress during a period of acute political instability and economic distress.[82]

On the other hand, critics warned that by constructing a tripartite alliance with big business and key state agencies, where the immediate objective was to restore the competitiveness and profitability of stagnating industries, organized labour was tempting fate.[83] They pointed to the dangers of cooptation where trade unions could find themselves trapped in a seamless web of binding agreements with employers from which escape was virtually impossible. They stressed the inevitable capitalist reaction if organized labour became powerful enough to threaten the private-enterprise system itself. They warned that institutionalized class compromise conveniently downplayed the structural constraints on the exercise of working-class power within capitalism and overlooked the possibility of cooptive incorporation. They emphasized that the power of capital was grounded in proprietary ownership and juridical control of the means of production, whereas trade-union power rested solely on the effectiveness of the collective organization of workers. Under these conditions, private businesses made investment decisions solely on profitability criteria. These critics charged that partnerships between capital and labour usually meant that the workers sacrificed more than owners, with the inevitable result that these compromises often degenerated into old-fashioned corporatist-style, 'interest-group' politics where, in the name of marching toward a socialist future, the organized labour movement was enticed into guaranteeing labour peace, imposing wage restraints, accepting layoffs, and ensuring productivity increases in exchange for woefully inadequate material gains.[84] They argued further that it was not possible to implement a far-reaching programme of radical reforms while simultaneously assisting in the process of revitalizing rates of growth and the competitive advantage of economic sectors still predominantly in the hands of a white oligarchy hostile to socialist thinking.[85] An elite-bargained accommodationist approach risked laying the groundwork for the growth of a privileged labour aristocracy, and also came dangerously close to institutionalizing class collaboration that would succeed only in restoring capitalist profitability and competitiveness instead of paving the way for structural reforms of a radical nature.[86] By their very nature, 'social contracts' were 'state-structured, class collaboration' mechanisms that merely 'enforce[d] union bureaucratisation undermining democracy and accountability'.[87]

Even political analysts who were genuinely sympathetic to the co-operative course of action inspired by 'strategic unionism' urged caution and restraint. Von Holdt worried aloud about 'social partnerships' between employers and workers: 'Do such projects mean abandoning socialism for a "reformist" social democratic vision? Or are they steps on the long road of a democratic struggle for participatory socialism?'[88] By making strategic compromises, von Holdt suggested, organized labour took the chance of 'gaining influence but losing power'.[89] More specifically, Bird and Schreiner warned of the dangers of narrow corporatist models which excluded the poorest and most marginalized sections of the population. 'In our view,' they suggested, 'corporatist arrangements (70/30 solutions) driven by union members together with organized (big) business and endorsed by a weak state hungry for political support, are a real danger for the future.' Instead of these narrow tripartite bargains, they advocated a 'multi-partite model', involving as a matter of principle, 'civics, women's groups, associations of the unemployed and the aged, [and] consumer and rural organisations', to provide a counterweight to these exclusivist corporatist possibilities.[90]

Preparing for an uncertain future

As the date of South Africa's first nonracial democratic elections approached, COSATU was forced to evaluate its role in the tripartite alliance with the ANC and the SACP. At its Special Congress in September 1993, COSATU delegates reaffirmed their commitment to a strong version of union independence in relation to political parties and political action. The most visible sign of this sentiment was the unanimous adoption of the COSATU Platform on Worker Rights, a comprehensive set of guidelines that called for workplace democracy, human resources development, and an enforceable system of collective bargaining which gave workers an influential role in industry decision-making, and which ensured that unions were 'fully involved in designing and overseeing changes at workplace and industry levels'. The insistence that the ANC endorse this comprehensive manifesto prior to the April elections as part of a wider Reconstruction Accord became a litmus test by which to measure the sincerity of the Congress leadership in meeting the demands of its trade-union supporters. By reserving twenty places on its parliamentary election list for key COSATU officials, the ANC gave concrete expression to its working alliance with the trade-union federation. COSATU leaders figured that this electoral partnership offered an opportunity through which the organized labour movement could seek to shape the policies of the new government. The trade-union nominees for the National Assembly included COSATU general secretary Jay Naidoo, COSATU first vice president Chris Dlamini, NUM assistant general secretary Marcel Golding, NUMSA general secretary Moses Mayekiso, SACTWU general secretary John Copelyn, and NEHAWU general secretary Phillip Dexter. Numerous other trade-union candidates were nominated via ANC regional structures to stand for election for regional parliaments, thereby providing the trade-union movement with a visible and vocal presence at both national and regional levels of the new government.[91]

From the outset, key COSATU figures, especially Jay Naidoo and Alec Irwin, actively participated in the protracted process of formulating the Reconstruction and Development Programme (RDP), a jointly negotiated – and much revised – manifesto encompassing broad policy guidelines for ANC-elected officials once they assumed their places in government. The RDP represented a state-driven, social-democratic alternative to the neo-liberal agenda of the National Party and big business. The RDP called for the construction of a million homes over the next five years, electrification and telephones for 2.5 million homes, free infant health clinics, free and compulsory schooling for ten years, land redistribution (with compensation), and the creation of some 2.5 million jobs through extensive public-works programmes. This Keynesian-style programme was subject to considerable debate during the election campaign, with the discussion focusing primarily on projected costs and sources of funding.[92] Supporters of the RDP contended that because it 'expresse[d] the demands of the poor, women, youth and other sectors that bear the brunt of exploitation', it provided a concrete mechanism for mobilizing the ANC's mass base around a programme of socio-economic upliftment. Critics worried aloud that without proper means for ensuring its implementation the RDP might amount to no more than a 'well-meaning wish list'. Almost without exception, COSATU affiliates expressed reservations, ranging from mild to severe, about the comprehensiveness of the RDP. The final document evolved out of much negotiation and compromise, and critics charged that each successive version signalled a further erosion of the original ideas that COSATU had endorsed in earlier years as part and parcel of a post-apartheid programme of reconstruction and development.[93]

The extensive debate within and between COSATU affiliates over the RDP reflected much deeper political concerns regarding the future of the ANC/COSATU/SACP alliance in the post-election period. The inevitable denouement of white minority rule and the transition to parliamentary democracy shattered old political alliances and their economic programmes and set the stage for the creation of new historic blocs representing different class and popular forces under the limited terms of the new constitution. Whatever their permutations, two main positions emerged. On the one side, what could be loosely called the 'workerist' current in COSATU called for the formal dismantling of the tripartite alliance partnership once the ANC formed part of the government. In contrast, the 'national-democratic' current in COSATU advanced the idea of the 'national democratic revolution, thereby underscoring the continuing 'need for an enduring Tripartitie Alliance' grounded in a 'shared strategic perspective − precisely our common commitment to a far-reaching process of national democratic transformation'.[94]

The unstated premiss underpinning the 'workerist' argument was that the ANC was not, nor was it truly capable of becoming, a suitable organizational vehicle for the pursuit of socialism, and that the trade-union movement ought jealously to guard its autonomy during the difficult transitional period. COSATU's third largest affiliate, SACTWU, argued that 'unions should not descend to being the labour wing of government', and that 'democratic practices should be transparent not lobbyist'. Both SACTWU and NUMSA saw the perpetuation of formal alliances with the ANC once an interim government of national unity was formed as a potential 'barrier to the actual unity of the trade-union movement [within a single labour federation] both within the oppressed and across the race barriers'.[95]

While the 'workerist' trade unions spoke with one voice about the principle of worker independence and the need to remain at arm's length from political parties represented in parliament, they diverged significantly on the question of what mechanisms were required to realize this goal. The underlying issue concerned the size, character and function of the state sector. On the one side, NUMSA advocated the creation of a sizeable state apparatus with active and powerful agencies playing a vital role in socio-economic reconstruction. At its 1993 annual Congress, NUMSA reiterated its long-standing position calling for extensive nationalization, without compensation, of the 'leading heights' of the economy. SACTWU, by contrast, held the view that trade unions should fulfil their role as independent representatives of workers outside of the state structures. SACTWU developed a more pragmatic and moderate approach, becoming the first South African trade union to call explicitly for a social market economy.[96]

This discussion over the perplexing question of trade-union independence dovetailed with the controversial call for a mass workers' party, an idea which unexpectedly exploded like a bombshell at the July NUMSA conference.[97] In the ensuing debate, the political lines were drawn more sharply around a number of points of contention, including the future of the ANC, the place of trade unions, and the historical role of the SACP.[98] The underlying concern that framed this discussion was the growing fear within progressive, left-wing circles that the elite bargaining at the World Trade Centre negotiations had been at the expense of organized labour, the working poor and the permanently marginalized. Interpretations of what the proposed 'unity of the socialist Left' actually meant in practice varied from the position of the 'minimalists', who called for a strategy of united action on concrete issues that brought together socialists from existing organizations, and that of the 'maximalists', who advocated the creation of an independent organization of socialists 'that will advance the long- and short-term demands of working people'.[99]

In contrast, the strong 'national-democratic' current – with roots in the trade-union movement and the SACP – took the position that only through active participation in the internal ideological struggles of the broad ANC-led Congress movement could the cause of socialism be adequately advanced. The SACP's Jeremy Cronin, for example, argued that the place of the left and working-class movements was within the ANC. 'The most important strategic challenge of our time', he contended, '[is] the battle for the life and soul of the ANC.' Only by remaining firmly attached to ANC would it be possible to ensure that the Congress movement fulfilled 'its historical and strategic vocations'.[100] In this view, the ANC retained its distinctive identity as a left-leaning reformist movement with a fluid multi-class constituency that had not yet crystallized into a political party of the European social-democratic type. The 'national-democratic' current hoped to transform the ANC-led Congress movement into a sizeable lever of popular mobilization, seeking the broadest possible alliances, championing the cause of all sectors of the oppressed, supporting and leading their struggles, and infusing their demands with a socialist content.[101]

8

Civic Associations and
Popular Democracy

The dramatic changes that took place in South Africa in the wake of President de Klerk's historic February 1990 speech created both new opportunities and new pressures for altering the country's basic political and economic institutions. On balance, political attention focused on reform initiatives to dismantle the formal institutional framework of apartheid at the national level. Yet what was often overlooked were those efforts that emerged out of township and community struggles to foster operative, nonracial self-government at the local level. Government officials, city and regional planning experts, and political activists recognized that the transition to parliamentary democracy and the extension of formal citizenship rights at the national level required local roots, capacities and expressions in order to be effective and meaningful.[1]

Yet even before the conspicuous post-1990 political *apertura*, the process of nascent democratization 'from below' was already under way, germinating, as it were, in the pores of the crumbling apartheid system. The political opposition to white minority rule, which was largely embodied in the trade unions and civic movements, was characterized by an anti-authoritarian and 'anti-statist' orientation. An embryonic 'democratic ideology' evolved as a counterpoint to the exclusionary logic of what Angel Flisfisch – in another historical context – has called 'the Napoleonic conception' of politics, or one which routinely considers the state and government as holding the monopoly on political rationality.[2] By stressing the value of expressive and participatory forms of autonomous political action, this emergent democratic ideology found expression in the imagined construction of a vibrant and vital 'civil society' as a terrain separate from the state and the process of production.[3]

Throughout the 1980s, popular demands at the local level for the redress of socio-economic grievances led inexorably to a rapid politicization of conflicts over the distribution of scarce resources in the absence of legitimate institutional channels under the white minority regime. The task of forging these struggles into a coherent and focused assault on political power fell largely to the civic associations. In reorganizing and democratizing the social sphere, the civic movement transformed an aggregation of social actors, as Alain Touraine puts it, into new 'popular subjects', with a collective identity and oriented toward an 'alternative popular project'.[4]

The Origins of the Civic Movement

The origins of the civic movement can be traced to the post-1976 clampdown that eviscerated Black Consciousness organizations and closed off avenues for 'above-ground' political dialogue that had only tentatively emerged before the eruption of the Soweto rebellion. The emphasis of the Black Consciousness movement on inward-looking strategies of community development crystallized in a flowering of 'self-help' grassroots organizations at the township level. In 1979, the Soweto Civic Association, led by Dr Nthato Motlana, was established. It was quickly followed by the formation of neighbourhood associations like the Port Elizabeth Black Civic Organization (PEBCO), led by Thozamile Botha, and the Cape Housing Action Committee (CAHAC) in Cape Town. These local movements popularized the idea of non-partisan popular organizations representing the interests of ordinary people on matters that directly affected their daily lives.[5]

In a significant departure from earlier paternalistic practices, the 1982 Black Local Authorities Act transferred administrative authority and financial responsibility to black local authorities (BLAs). In the townships, however, there were few paved roads, there was limited access to potable water, an extensive reliance on the 'bucket system' for sewerage services, and limited or no access to electrical, drainage or waste collection and removal services. The virtual absence of a commercial and industrial tax base ensured that the BLAs were unable to become financially self-sufficient and meant, furthermore, that they were almost exclusively dependent upon rents and service charges levied on township residents to cover expenses.[6]

The outbreak of the 1984–86 popular rebellion drew the civic associations, or 'civics' as they were popularly known, into the very centre of the political maelstrom. By affiliating to the United Democratic Front (UDF), the civics acquired a national voice while retaining their local organizational base. The intolerable financial burden placed on township residents to 'pay for their own oppression' triggered scores of rent and consumer boycotts, beginning in 1984, to protest against escalating fees and the generally low level and quality of services. But the subsequent state-sponsored harassment and repression virtually paralysed 'above ground' popular protest.[7]

The revival, around 1989, of township organization and overt protest gave the civics a much-needed political boost. Older, established civic associations were reactivated, and many new ones were formed in hitherto unorganized metropolitan and homeland areas.[8] Although civics ostensibly organized township residents around immediate issues, their chief objective was to increase grassroots pressure on the state administration – less to gain concrete improvements in squalid urban conditions than to use these issues as a platform from which to attack the white minority regime on its weakest front and to create conditions for a transfer of power. By 1990, an estimated two thousand civics were in operation across the country. Rent and bond boycotts were under way in no fewer than forty-nine of the Transvaal's eighty-two townships.[9]

Strictly speaking, the civic associations were social movements in the true sense of the term. Although they differed in many respects, they tended to share several important characteristics. First, because their executives were elected by local members/supporters, they were directly accountable to their active constituencies, and not to higher bodies or external organizations. Second, their organizational structures were based on active grassroots participation by the membership, and they depended upon the voluntary effort of local leaders and on financial support from members and supporters. Third, they alone possessed the capacity to define local grievances and assume sole responsibility for deciding which strategies and actions were appropriate to the local context.[10]

The civic associations adopted political agendas at the risk of alienating local supporters. In particular, the magnitude of their political support was directly proportional to their capacity to articulate day-to-day grievances of ordinary township residents. Their success was dependent upon their ability to perform a dual role. On the one hand, they mobilized and organized around basic socio-economic demands such as rent and housing, transport and other services, and land allocation and use. On the other hand, they were forced to link the resolution of these demands to the wider national political struggle against apartheid and white minority rule.[11]

For the most part, civics functioned as 'single-issue' protest organizations except when they developed strong grassroots structures providing a range of administrative, representative, decision-making, policing and judicial functions. Their strength rested with their ability to mobilize local constituencies to lobby over 'community-based' issues and to link these to national concerns. Yet civics were handcuffed by their lack of control

over material resources. This weakness underlay their sometimes fragile
social base, uneven organization, restricted leadership, limited active participation, and periods of languid passivity.[12]

With the collapse of the BLAs, civic associations in many parts of the
country became the de facto local civil administration. In the most
exemplary instances, and notably in the Eastern Cape, civics assumed full
or partial responsibility for the development of school curricula, the
administration of justice through 'people's courts, community policing,
rubbish collection, the allocation of licenses for businesses, and the grant-
ing of permits for housing sites. With the eventual collapse of fifty-one
BLAs in the Eastern Cape, civic leaders effectively transferred power to
themselves by occupying the offices in the buildings once used by their
erstwhile enemies, the town councillors.[13] In the typical case, elected
civic leaders approached town administrators with a list of priorities and
suggestions for reallocation of budgetary resources. Civic associations used
tactics such as consumer boycotts, work stayaways, and rent and bond
boycotts to ensure that negotiating forums were established to address
these local grievances.[14]

Civic associations: local government in waiting?[15]

The sudden and unexpected thaw in the political climate after 2 February
1990 forced the civics to clarify their relationship with the unbanned
political organizations and to reassess their new role in 'civil society'.
Perhaps ironically, the start of multiparty negotiations, characterized by
the lure of 'elite pacting' and secretive quid pro quo brokerage, contributed to a division between the political and social spheres which in turn
translated into a growing chasm between parties and social movements.
After considerable debate, civic leaders reached a broad consensus that
they should not simply collapse their organizations into emergent local
ANC branches. The mobilization of mass action against the odious state
structures would be left to the unbanned political organizations, and this
division of political labour would free the civics to represent the immediate concerns of their constituencies. As the prospect of national elections and a new constitution neared, it became clear to the civic leadership
that a change of political power at the centre would not guarantee that
the needs of township residents would be addressed, let alone heard. To
some civic strategists, this set of circumstances meant that 'since civics
cannot rely on the state to achieve their goals for them, they cannot pin
their hopes on achieving control of the state by the movement they
favour.' Therefore, civics needed to maintain independence from particular
political movements to ensure that they were able to negotiate the interests

of their constituents with whatever party or coalition of parties formed the government of the day.[16]

One perspective that gained influence within the civic movement was the view that these community-based associations ought to represent the concerns of township residents in much the same way as trade unions represented the interests of workers. Yet the real dichotomy between workers at the point of production and residents at the point of consumption created problems for political organisers. Put conceptually, what defines the trade-union movement is the contradiction between labour and capital as manifested in the specific relations of production within particular firms. In contrast, the defining characteristic of social movements encompassing spatially demarcated neighbourhoods and communities is political struggle over access to collective consumption. Put in another way, social movements actively contest the prevailing forms of political representation and the legitimacy of political rule. In order to become genuine social movements, the civics were compelled to open their membership to persons of all political persuasions and party affiliations. They were voluntary associations defined by geographical boundaries where their constituencies comprised not just working-class people, but the unemployed and the emergent petty bourgeoisie, along with homeowners, squatters and hostel dwellers. The civics embraced an extremely complex pattern of diverse opinion reflecting all the myriad wage earners in different trades and occupations, socio-economic circumstances and generational cohorts. Their greatest challenge was how to reconcile these diverse interests under a single universalizing platform of reform.[17]

With the disbanding of the UDF, the National Interim Civic Committee embarked on an organizational strategy of bringing local civics together into regional federations. The federal structure enabled the civics to retain their jealously guarded autonomy, and provided local leaders with sufficient political flexibility to avoid becoming identified as 'spokespersons' solely for the ANC. In mid-1990, the formation of two regional federal bodies – the Civic Associations of the Southern Transvaal (CAST), representing somewhere between twenty-six and thirty-eight civics on the Witwatersrand; and the Eastern Cape Civics Organization (ECCO) – marked the tentative first step in a highly uneven process of consolidation and amalgamation of local civic associations.[18] At its inaugural meeting, CAST called for continued boycotts and 'mass action' until all BLAs were abolished, until genuine negotiations on a nonracial local government system got under way, and until 'all discriminatory laws' were rescinded.[19]

From the outset, regional civic bodies – and about fifteen were formed in 1990 – launched scores of local protest actions which centred on demands for the removal of the BLAs, the writing off of arrears, affordable tariffs, the transfer of rented houses to outright ownership, and the delivery of services. The long-term objective of these campaigns was to promote the idea of 'one city, one council', or the creation of nonracial local governments with a single budget and tax base.[20] CAST took the lead in launching a full-scale campaign to undermine the beleaguered town council system in all townships of the southern Transvaal.[21] The town councils, elected in polls where seldom more than 10 per cent of those eligible bothered to vote, had neither financial nor political power and were widely regarded as fawning puppets of the apartheid system. By November 1990, 45 per cent of BLA seats in the Orange Free State, 37 per cent in the Cape, 34 per cent in the Transvaal and 21 per cent in Natal were vacant as councillors resigned under pressure.[22] By early 1991, about half of the 1,867 town councillors who had assumed office after nationwide elections in 1988 had resigned. In the Transvaal, around thirty-one of the eighty-two black local authorities had completely collapsed and others barely operated. Some councillors had heeded the call by CAST to resign, while others simply quit in frustration.[23] Because the town councils were left without a quorum, the Transvaal Provincial Administration (TPA) was forced to appoint more than one hundred white administrators to manage the townships by proxy.[24]

Without much fanfare, informal discussions between white municipalities and civics in such disparate places as Klerksdorp, Port Elizabeth, Soweto, Benoni, Alexandra, Kimberley and Bloemfontein resulted in bilateral agreements that took the first tentative steps toward normalizing relations at the local level.[25] Negotiations strengthened the civics involved, and civics were recognized as a significant stakeholder in local government, and had earned the right to be a full-fledged partner in its transformation. Despite initial optimism that interim solutions could be found to manage local government until a comprehensive system of local government was created, the negotiations failed to move beyond agreements over service charges, the ending of rent boycotts, and, in a few instances, minor adjustments to administrative systems. Local-level negotiations encountered similar obstacles everywhere: despite promises, there was little improvement in the provision of services; the white municipalities generally refused to share their resources with surrounding black townships; and often agreements were distorted or not implemented. In some parts of the country, notably the eastern Transvaal, very few negotiations got off the ground, mainly as a result of the hardline attitudes of white town councils under the control of the Conservative Party. In Ermelo and Carolina, for example, town councils cut off services, including water, in an effort to crush rent and service boycotts.[26]

Stalled local negotiations exposed some of the organizational and structural weaknesses of the civic movement. Many civics were 'little more than collections of activists', and they sometimes lacked the capacity and the requisite skills to negotiate on complex matters of urban policy with the appointed white officials who had taken over the administration of many townships.[27] In a number of celebrated cases, interim agreements negotiated between civics and white authorities simply collapsed amid charges of duplicity and bad faith. Stronger, more powerful civics worried that weaker ones had caved in to pressure and had made 'quick deals' unfavourable to their own constituents and to the civic movement as a whole. Mindful of these problems, CAST suspended talks with intransigent BLAs and their arrogant white mouthpieces, arguing instead that the civic movement should negotiate directly with the TPA at a regional level in order to establish coherent, uniform guidelines for local negotiations. One key obstacle to negotiations at the local level was the demand of regional civic bodies that the BLAs dissolve and the government's insistence that they stay.[28]

The resignations of town councillors and the disintegration of the BLAs signalled a clear victory for the popular movement.[29] But the embattled forces of reaction retaliated. In 1991, the two leading black local government organizations, the United Municipalities of South Africa and the Urban Councils of South Africa, merged into a single organization to create a formidable counterweight against CAST.[30] Defiant town councillors in the Transvaal who resisted calls by CAST to resign soon found a welcome ally, and in a tangible display of solidarity in February 1991 they joined Inkatha en masse. By placing all functioning town councils in its hands, Inkatha scored an important organizational breakthrough in the urban townships of the Transvaal.[31]

In response to the spread of negotiations, the ruling National Party threw its administrative weight behind local-government bodies to counteract the growing influence of the civic movement. The enactment of the Interim Measures (for Local Government) Act (IMA) in June 1991 empowered state bodies to decide unilaterally on the course of negotiations, and reduced the status of local negotiating forums. This top-down effort to impose a restrictive framework on all local negotiating efforts was, as two political analysts put it, 'a crude and extremely cynical piece of legislation, where the central state acts as "big brother" for its local-level surrogates'. Its primary aim was to 'ensure that the state and its allies control the management of the urban transition'.[32]

The launch of the South African National Civic Organization (SANCO) in March 1992 marked a decisive step in the consolidation and amalgamation of the civic movement. The 'multi-hatted' Moses Mayekiso was elected president, and members of the executive committee were drawn mainly from the Eastern Cape and Border region. This transformation of the civic movement from a loosely federated body of autonomous affiliates into a unitary organization of branches sparked controversy. Critics charged that local civics surrendered their independence and accountability by joining centralized bodies. SANCO leaders responded that nationwide coordination was required to deal with the array of roadblocks preventing the elimination of the artificial barriers between 'white areas' and 'black areas'.[33]

The creation of the Local Government Negotiating Forum (LGNF) represented a clear victory for SANCO. The LGNF was launched in March 1993, and comprised two separate delegations. The statutory bodies included state local government employees and councillors. The non-statutory delegation was headed by SANCO and included representatives from the ANC, SACP and COSATU, particularly the South African Municipal Workers' Union (SAMWU).[34] On the surface, the influence and credibility of the civic movement appeared to grow: civics were represented on key national and regional policy forums; they acquired a significant voice in local-development initiatives; they played a partnership role in the LGNF; and they were engaged in striking deals with businesses and business groupings. But the transformation from protean, 'single-issue' protest organizations to 'multi-issue' participants in local development initiatives proved difficult. At a national level, civics in many parts of the country did not belong to SANCO. At a local level, most civics could not 'legitimately claim' to represent their communities, as their base of support was limited to particular social categories of residents like shackdwellers or homeowners.[35]

Local Government and White Separatism

In order for autonomous local governments to exist and function effectively, they required adequate revenues derived from reliable sources. However, South Africa's long-standing policy of formalized segregation ensured that South Africa's economically interdependent urban areas were divided into separate zones that were administered along racial lines. Within the 'apartheid city', a concatenation of laws, proclamations and regulations restricted black settlement and growth to segregated, confined townships that were located great distances away from city centres on the peripheries of the metropolitan areas. When all was said and done, economic revitalization of the financially starved townships, with their exceedingly narrow tax base, woefully inadequate infrastructure, and stunted commercial space, depended upon administrative fusion with nearby white municipalities, with their more secure tax base. It appeared self-evident that without a wholesale transfer of funds from the wealthier white areas to the poorer black areas, the disparities of the apartheid era would remain firmly entrenched. Despite some initial success in bringing together city officials from the white municipalities and civic leaders from adjoining townships to discuss consolidation, these efforts floundered on the shoals of mistrust and mutual recrimination.[36]

On balance, there were at least three formidable obstacles preventing the classical segregationist model of urban settlement, characterized by white cities surrounded by satellite black townships, from breaking down. First, the uneven distribution of the built environment ensured the on-going reproduction of spatial inequalities. The social relations embedded in the physical landscape, which appeared under class and racial guises, could not be overcome without massive reordering of urban space. Second, the strength of the *laissez faire* doctrines foreclosed on the possibility of massive state spending to rectify the imbalances. If left to private initiative, the prospects of a significant infusion of investment capital into the bleak townships were grim indeed. Third, the obstinacy of incumbent authorities in the white towns was legendary. The Conservative Party (CP) capitalized on growing white fears by capturing majorities on at least 104 small town councils. During the late 1980s and early 1990s, these CP-controlled city councils fought a strenuous rearguard action to preserve such odious apartheid-era regulations as the Separate Amenities Act.[37] In late 1993, twenty-one towns, all Conservative Party strongholds in the right-wing Western Transvaal, declared that they would defy the creation of the Transitional Executive Council (TEC), and vowed to keep their towns 'white'. In reality, these responses to changing circumstances were just the tip of a much deeper reactionary iceberg.[38]

Subterranean anxieties

In countless white municipalities, city officials adamantly dug in their heels, resisting preliminary discussions on the mechanics of incorporation, common voters' rolls and multiracial governing bodies. They took advantage of inflated layers of obscure regulations to construct invisible barriers preventing incorporation. They recited a lengthy litany of imaginary evils, including caricatured portrayals of declining community standards, increasing crime rates and falling property values. In several celebrated cases, white homeowners – in a classic NIMBY [Not in my back yard] response – resisted efforts by state authorities to provide low-cost housing for black homeless in nearby areas.[39] Right-wing groups pounced on the anxieties of white homeowners, menacingly conjuring up bleak images of communities swamped by the high tide of black impoverishment. By currying favour with white homeowners, these groups succeeded in stirring up fears of the *swart gevaar*, or the black peril.[40]

Taken as a whole, these baroque efforts to stifle the transcendent ideal of racial harmony struck a responsive chord buried deep in South Africa's fractious and divisive past. The insular identity of 'whiteness' was a synonym for the great racial divide, but it was also a way of expressing cultural and class differences. The protracted trench warfare over the structural configuration of post-apartheid local government marked a subtle shift in the language of domination. Words changed, but their original meanings lingered on in coded, nuanced phraseology. Neo-apartheid ideology and practice thrived in an atmosphere rife with political tensions and uncertainties. The new discourse of white separatism differed from its Verwoerdian roots in that the idiom of 'self-determination' replaced 'segregation of the races' as its central organizing principle. By camouflaging an ingrained racism behind the benign patina of vaguely democratic-sounding formulas, local government officials and neighbourhood associations laboriously tried to shift the terms of the local-government debate away from universalist principles and onto the terrain of nitty-gritty, interest-group politics. The rhetoric of self-governance and popular will put a nice face on white separatism.

Resolving the Identity Crisis: Civics at the Crossroads

Reshaping apartheid-era local administrations into nonracial, inclusive municipal bodies proved more difficult than participants in the negotiating process initially imagined. Local trends were highly uneven, but there was an appreciable movement toward de facto joint administration, where 'white' local authorities took greater responsibility for providing services to outlying townships. 'Power-sharing' in the LGNF complicated economic and development policy-making. ANC/COSATU/SANCO alliance negotiators acknowledged that the existing bureaucracies of white municipalities would form the 'core' of consolidated city administrations. The LGNF resolved that black and white local authorities were to be dissolved and replaced by appointed structures composed of half statutory and half non-statutory parties. In the end, the agreement brokered between the main negotiating parties ensured that post-apartheid 'power-sharing' at the local level would include weighted votes in favour of affluent neighbourhoods. This bargained compromise suggested that established interests would enjoy far greater local influence than was warranted by the numbers they represented.[41]

In a last-ditch effort to placate the right wing, the multiparty negotiators at Kempton Park included clauses in the Interim Constitution that reserved 30 per cent of local council seats for existing (white) local authorities. Along with their proportional vote, this arrangement thus guaranteed white *plattelanders* a disproportionate share of power in local authorities. As a 'sunset clause', this provision was meant to accommodate white fears during the transition. Without some form of weighting, many small towns in the rural Transvaal would not have any white representatives under a strictly proportional representation system.[42] This compromise to recast local government on a racially inclusive basis came as a rude shock to many progressives, who denounced these alleged conciliatory gestures as unjustifiable backsliding on the inviolable principle of nonracialism.[43]

'Civil society' and the transition to parliamentary democracy

The concept of 'civil society', together with accompanying ideas like democracy, interest groups and citizenship, experienced an intellectual renaissance in South African political discourse in the 1990s. Political analysts spoke reverentially of creating a vibrant 'civil society', by which they meant a 'sector outside of government which would provide a forum for people to express themselves'. They warned against the rise of authoritarian statism in which 'a concentration of power' invariably 'emasculated democracy'.[44] 'Civil society', or that 'autonomous sphere composed of myriad associations which contribute to democratic public life',[45] it was claimed, 'has been both a base for overthrowing oppression and an embryo for a new nation'.[46]

The debate on 'civil society' in South Africa evolved out of an effort to identify a radical political alternative to one-party government along with the accompanying '*étatist* theories which focus on the political kingdom as the centre of all power and source of all development'. As the theoretical orientation of the left, the perspective of 'civil society' declared that the 'new' South Africa would be constructed out of a combination of 'good government' on the one side, and dynamic community, trade union, women's, youth, and other grassroots, voluntary associations in the public sphere on the other. 'In opposition to the grim prospect of a "new class" of officials, intellectuals, and politicians running post-apartheid South Africa from above', Robert Fine contended, 'civil society' theory sought to specify the logistical space for a 'radical populism committed to participatory democracy, workers' control, political self-education, and the autonomy of particular communities'. The aim of this perspective was 'to define an alternative realm of the "public" that is beyond the private concerns of individuals but not identical with the political realm of the state'.[47] The twin hallmarks were the autonomy of voluntary associations and the dispersal of political power.[48]

One of the chief accomplishments of this new emphasis on 'civil society' was to validate diverse experiences, popular initiatives, and novel organizational forms that had been previously subsumed under 'the highly centralized, *étatist* visions of emancipation from apartheid which characterized the dominant communist and African nationalist currents of opposition'.[49] However, the idea of 'civil society' is a vague notion that is open to competing interpretations.[50] Its primary focus on the public realm of free association constitutes a valid line of reasoning within the framework of liberal theories of democratic rights. Yet how this approach could be reconciled not only with the deeply entrenched realities of class and institutional power but also with the challenge of forging diverse and sometimes rival interest groups into a common socialist project remains an open question. Its central weakness, as Fine argued, is above all to reinforce 'the illusion that the "big" questions of society can be resolved by particular, local struggles in the context of existing political organizations'. Put more forcefully, 'civil society' is a sphere of association, but it is also 'the realm of force, self-interest, inequality, and exploitation'.[51]

The deficiencies of 'civil society' theorizing were mirrored in the civic movement. The civics seemed trapped on the horns of a classic dilemma: on one side, they focused on carving out a separate space in the townships that energized grassroots initiative, nurtured self-directed activities, and fostered participation in localized campaigns; and on the other side, they sought to institutionalize their local power by assuming control over state functions; that is, by transforming themselves into a 'state within the state'. With the onset of parliamentary democracy, civics were faced with an identity crisis where the way forward was far from self-evident. On balance, there were three available options: (1) to consolidate on a non-partisan basis, but with a coherent programme for development and democracy, where 'they would remain outside local government, acting as a watchdog over working class interests'; (2) to enter into an strategic alliance with 'the political grouping that is closest to the positions and demands' of their constituencies; and (3) to remain unaffiliated to any political party, but to enter candidates for local government elections. All these scenarios were premised on a notion of a vigilant citizenry seeking to empower itself in the public sphere. Yet without a distinctive political programme of its own that would enable it to chart a course of action largely independent from political parties and state institutions, the civic movement risked marginalization and eventual disappearance as a viable social force.[52]

9

The Brokered Eclipse of
White Minority Rule

On the eve of F.W. de Klerk's surprise speech of 2 February 1990, South Africa's main political antagonists had reached a political deadlock. Neither the dominant bloc of class forces whose socio-economic interests were primarily embodied in the ruling National Party, nor the liberation movement, were sufficiently powerful to impose their own singular vision upon the future. On the one side, that powerful cabal of propertied classes which had benefited from the apartheid system was unable to rule in the old ways. The National Party, the organizational vehicle responsible for modernizing white domination, was no longer capable of holding the established political order in place through a promiscuous blend of wholesale repression and piecemeal, graduated reforms sponsored 'from above'. On the other side, the liberation movement, politically divided along interest-group, class and ideological lines, did not possess the organizational capacity, political power or military leverage to dislodge the white oligarchy from its entrenched positions of power and privilege. Yet with the capability of disrupting the everyday operations of the 'system', the popular organizations, particularly those within the ambit of the Congress tradition, held effective veto power over the ability of the National Party to impose its own unilateral solution to the intractable crisis of legitimacy.

What should be made clear, however, is that to characterize the balance of political forces in this way is not to suggest that South Africa approached a post-1990 historical situation resembling 'dual power'. To define the relations between contending political forces as a stalemate leaves the false impression of stasis. Instead, changing circumstances created a highly fluid situation where the ruling National Party clung to the levers of administrative power and the broad-based opposition steadfastly refused to accept anything other than full citizenship rights in an undivided

South Africa. Like all crisis-prone transitional periods, the evolving 'fields of force' offered both opportunities and pitfalls for the antagonists.[1]

Sworn adversaries do not easily bury their differences, and South Africa was no exception to this rule. Negotiating an end to white minority rule and creating in its place a widely acceptable constitutional framework for a new, nonracial South Africa is not an easy process to explain, above all because of the multiple levels at which it was played out. From the outset, the negotiations process became, as one political analyst put it, 'a political equivalent of protracted warfare', where 'the ANC hope[d] to force the [National Party] government to abandon one defensive position after another', and conversely, the National Party fortified 'its trenches in preparation for a long siege'.[2] What made this post-1990 'reluctant reconciliation' possible was that both the ANC and the National Party, the two main contenders for political power, had come to the sobering conclusion that they were unable to defeat the other militarily.[3]

The Tangled Web of Negotiations

The launch of the Conference for a Democratic South Africa (CODESA) – as the session convened in December 1991, comprising nineteen political parties and organizations headed by the National Party and the ANC, was called – marked a turning point in the discussions laying the groundwork for a new constitution that would extend equality to the nation's disenfranchised black majority. In the interim, between the early, tentative 'talks about talks' and the opening of formal negotiations, both sides came a long way. The ANC retreated from its original demand for a simple transfer of power and, despite considerable internal dissent, agreed to suspend armed struggle and rein in its military wing, Umkhonto weSizwe, under the terms of the May 1990 Pretoria Minute. The National Party accepted the formula of a universal franchise, or 'one person, one vote', and conceded that there should be no distinction according to race, colour, creed or gender in the new constitution.

Over the course of these preliminary discussions, the National Party and the ANC reached agreement in principle on a proposed constitutional framework, but they differed in many important respects on not only the exact mechanisms for bringing about the political transition but also what kind of state machinery would emerge in the future.[4] Under pressure from its own diverse constituencies, as well as from political organizations to its left, the ANC held fast to its original demands for the establishment of an interim government with sovereign powers to replace the existing administration, and for a popularly elected constituent assembly mandated to draft the new constitution which would eventually be endorsed in a referendum.[5] While both sides pledged to stay the course, mutual trust remained fragile, with each party suspicious that the other nurtured a hidden agenda. Congress officials accused the National Party of seeking to perpetuate white privilege under another guise and of tolerating if not conniving with covert elements within the security forces to foment unrest in the townships. On the other side, the National Party charged the ANC with wanting to grab uncontested power and of seeking to impose unworkable socialistic panaceas on South Africa.[6]

At the risk of oversimplifying the highly nuanced and complex issues involved, it can be said that both sides clung tenaciously to particular goals in the deliberations over the terms of the new constitution. What the de Klerk negotiating team wanted to achieve from protracted discussions were guarantees, *beforehand*, which would ensure for its mainly white constituency a political outcome which would leave the National Party with a share of political power that amounted to an effective veto on any effort by a hypothetical 'tyrannical majority' wishing to deprive white people of economic or personal rights. For years, National Party think-tanks floated various proposals, including vague ideas about 'consociationalism', enforced 'power-sharing', and a radically decentralized federal system where political power was dispersed between regions. These suggested remedies all had a single purpose in mind, namely, to establish limits to blanket majority rule enshrined in a Westminster-type, 'winner-take-all' political arrangement. National Party leaders, for obvious historical reasons, sought a political formula which enabled them to protect the group rights and privileges of white people. The ANC, for equally obvious reasons, was steadfastly opposed to formulas that suggested the entrenchment of white power and advantage.[7]

The Nationalist mantra of 'no domination', 'consensus' and 'power-sharing' was simply a coded way of assuring themselves a decisive voice in South Africa's political future. What National Party leaders wanted were constitutional guarantees ensuring what Willem de Klerk, the president's brother and the quintessential Afrikaner *verligte* (enlightened one), called a 'compulsory coalition' of all significant political parties, involving consensual decision-making with built-in veto power for minority parties. They wished to parcel power among different levels and branches of government, and to mandate the sharing of power by multiple parties within these proposed decentralized institutions. For its part, the ANC derisively dismissed this formula as a 'loser-take-all' system. During these early stages of the negotiations process, the Nationalists adamantly refused to surrender on the principles of power-sharing, effective vetoes and federalism, all designed to dilute the feared 'tyranny of the majority' and safeguard the interest of minorities. The National Party endorsed these principles, and sought to enshrine them in the new constitution, not simply because they provided essential checks to protect minority interests, but also because 'they would endow it with *offensive* capabilities, establishing a springboard for fragmenting the unity of the "majority" by encouraging (ethnic) particularism and multiple parties'.[8]

Things Fall Apart; The Centre Cannot Hold

From the outset, CODESA I was an unwieldy forum. In almost no time, its nineteen separate participating delegations became hopelessly bogged down in internecine squabbling. Despite the initial optimism forecasting a swift transition to nonracial democracy, the negotiations process proceeded in fits and starts, with the two main interlocutors viewing each other suspiciously and searching for ulterior motives lurking behind every proposal. The ANC insisted that the National Party government was unfairly trying to operate as both a 'player and a referee' in the delicately poised transition process, and accused de Klerk of harbouring a 'double agenda' or 'twin-track' approach, embracing negotiations while secretly conniving with efforts to destabilize the opposition. On the other side, the National Party accused the ANC of failure to control its armed wing and of using disruptive 'mass action' tactics to further its own narrow partisan objectives. By agreeing to revamp the format for multiparty talks, the main players were able to jump-start CODESA II. But in May 1992, negotiations deadlocked on what size majority of an elected national assembly would be required to ratify a new constitution, with the National Party insisting on 75 per cent and the ANC demanding 70 per cent.[9]

The stalemate led to bitter recriminations, accompanied by escalating political violence, which reached a peak with the Boipatong massacre on 17 June in which more than forty people in an ANC stronghold south of Johannesburg were randomly slaughtered by a marauding band from a nearby IFP-controlled hostel, assisted by elements in the security forces. Mandela's decision to withdraw indefinitely from multiparty talks after this senseless atrocity was a carefully crafted compromise to prevent a mutinous rift between moderates who favoured negotiations and radicals who advocated an escalating campaign of 'mass action' to force the National Party to resign. The suspension of negotiations averted a certain crisis within the ANC that had been brewing for quite some time. Rankand-file members, especially in those regions like the strife-torn Vaal triangle south of Johannesburg and Natal where the ongoing unrest had the most grievous effects, were angered that negotiations had accomplished little toward curbing the violence in their communities. The pause in negotiations reinvigorated the ANC's radical wing. Key figures like SACP stalwart Ronnie Kasrils, ANC Youth League president Peter Mokaba, SACP general secretary Chris Hani, Natal Midlands chief Harry Gwala, and powerful PWV regional leader Tokyo Sexwale had been pushed into the background with the start of multiparty talks. They placed the blame for the lack of political progress on all fronts squarely on what they regarded as a consistent pattern of National Party intransigence. Under this highly charged atmosphere, these ANC/SACP militants were able to win approval for the 'Leipzig option', an escalating campaign of popular protest and defiance which drew its intellectual inspiration from the public demonstrations in the German Democratic Republic, culminating in the breaching of the Berlin Wall. The launch of this 'mass action' programme, codenamed Operation Exit Gate, was aimed at wresting immediate concessions from the National Party government and, ultimately, securing its removal from power, or at least from a position of monopoly power.[10]

As the wave of strikes and street demonstrations gathered momentum, the tripartite ANC/SACP/COSATU alliance assumed a considerably higher profile, with the troika of Cyril Ramaphosa, Chris Hani and Jay Naidoo, general secretaries of the ANC, the SACP and COSATU respectively, emerging as the main power-brokers. On balance, the 'mass action' campaign was a modest success. The high point came with the COSATU-sponsored two-day 'general strike' on 3-4 August involving more than four million workers, and the massive display of strength and discipline on the following day where over 100,000 ANC supporters marched on the seat of government – the Union Buildings in Pretoria. The tripartite alliance demonstrated, once again, its ability to paralyse South African economic life. This programme of action significantly boosted ANC morale and empowered its grassroots members. The successful general strike reinforced the independence and political clout of COSATU. By singlehandedly bringing industrial production to a virtual standstill in the largest work stoppage in South African history, COSATU gave clear warning to key business associations of what was in store for them in the future if the two sides were unable to reach broad consensus on macroeconomic policy matters.[11]

The ANC also made plans to carry its 'mass action' campaign to the 'self-governing' and the nominally 'independent' homelands. The chief targets were the autocratic regimes in Bophuthatswana, QwaQwa and Ciskei, along with Buthelezi's KwaZulu. But the ANC militants underestimated the reckless determination of homeland strongmen to resist intrusions into their fiefdoms, with brutal measures if necessary. This grave miscalculation was tragically demonstrated at Bisho in Ciskei on 7 September, when troops loyal to Brigadier Oupa Gqozo opened fire without warning on thousands of unarmed ANC demonstrators, killing at least twenty-eight and wounding hundreds more.[12] Paradoxically, the Bisho massacre seemed to have a sobering effect on the minds of the principal negotiating partners. By bringing South Africa once again face to face with an escalating spiral of political violence, the wanton killings instilled a 'new realism' which led the ANC abruptly to suspend planned marches in Mmabatho and Ulundi, the capital cities of Bophuthatswana and KwaZulu respectively, for fear of provoking the forces of reaction there as well.[13]

The lurking threat of secession and the spectre of 'tribalism'

For those who favoured the negotiations option, the collapse of the CODESA II forum marked a low point of mutual cooperation between the ANC and the National Party. The cumulative effect of de Klerk's landslide victory in the March 1992 referendum, the breakdown of multiparty talks, the 'mass action' campaign, and the escalating cycle of politically motivated violence was the restoration of the pre-February 1990 stalemate. Yet despite the formal deadlock at CODESA, both the ANC and the National Party intuitively understood that they would be unable to continue their abstentionist positions indefinitely without conceding the initiative to their rivals.[14] While the ANC and the National Party traded accusations of 'bad faith' and blamed the other side for the stalled talks, their chief negotiators, Cyril Ramaphosa and Roelf Meyer, quietly opened what became known as 'the Channel', or a series of unpublicized meetings that paved the way for the September 1992 summit between de Klerk and Mandela. This high-profile conclave produced the historic 'Record of Understanding' in which the ANC and National Party reached agreement on a number of sensitive issues, including the fencing of hostels and the outlawing of 'cultural weapons'. But what clearly overshadowed this mutual understanding on substantive matters was the symbolic importance attached to strictly bilateral consultations. By their actions, the ANC and the National Party had laid the groundwork for two-way talks on a political settlement before seeking multiparty approval. By sidestepping Inkatha as a major player in the negotiations process, the 'Record of Understanding' gave a clear signal that the once-cosy relationship between Buthelezi and the National Party government was no longer secure.[15]

Buthelezi reacted strongly to this affront by withdrawing the IFP delegation from the multiparty negotiating forum, alleging that the ANC and National Party were making secret deals behind the backs of the other participants. The IFP leader also sought to cement stronger ties with right-of-centre political forces, including homelands leaders, the Conservative Party, and the right-wing breakaway Afrikaner Volksunie (AVU). This improbable alliance of Zulu nationalists, Afrikaner separatists, white supremacists, fervent anti-Communists and autocratic homelands leaders were united primarily by their belief that a unitary state with strong centralizing powers would loosen their grip on political power. The inherent weakness of this opposition front – which crystallized in the Concerned South Africans Group (COSAG) – was that it was built on decaying apartheid foundations. This 'anti-election' front shared a common distrust of the ANC, but a loose alliance cobbled together around the ephemeral notion that 'the enemy of my enemy is my friend' was a fragile one indeed.[16]

This dramatic realignment of political forces introduced a dangerous game that contained a great deal of risk. In December, Buthelezi unveiled an ambitious constitutional proposals calling for a federal KwaZulu/Natal state with built-in guarantees securing its regional autonomy. The deliberate ambiguity of the proposal led to frenzied speculation about possible secessionary intentions. Many political observers dismissed this well-timed manoeuvre as a carefully staged smokescreen – or, more precisely, a stalking horse – seeming to promote the National Party's cause of federalism. But others feared that intransigence of this sort could degenerate into a Yugoslavia-style civil war. By raising the spectre of secession, Buthelezi's 'UDA' (Unilateral Declaration of Autonomy), along with Brigadier Oupa Gqozo's declaration of an 'autonomous Kei Republic', came frighteningly close to activating latent but potentially powerful centrifugal forces in South Africa. Many of the ANC's political adversaries, from Mangope in Bophuthatswana, to ultra-right-wing Afrikaners who dreamed of establishing a separate whites-only *Volkstaat*, 'put secession on the agenda as a last desperate option'.[17]

Buthelezi, a tough and resilient politician, was willing to do whatever he could to sabotage any constitutional deal for South Africa that left him out in the cold. Ironically, by courting favour with non-elected strongmen in the homelands, the ANC fell into the trap of allowing Buthelezi to dismiss its demand for the dismantling of KwaZulu as a sinister Xhosa-led plot.[18] Once again, he played what political analysts describe as the 'tribal card', accusing his political foes of 'anti-Zulu racism' and proclaiming that KwaZulu, far from being a 'construct of apartheid', had its own 'historically established sovereignty'. Buthelezi masterfully intervened in a chaotic situation, and by manipulating cultural symbols he mobilized Zulu ethnicity in the service of Inkatha's political project. This 'politicized ethnicity', to use Gerhard Maré's phrase, enabled Buthelezi to present himself as the defender of the 'Zulu nation' against external threats from the 'Xhosa-led' ANC and its 'Marxist-inspired' SACP and COSATU allies.[19]

The growing prospect of severing political ties with Buthelezi widened the already existing divisions in the NP Cabinet, parliamentary caucus and party congresses. Liberal Cabinet members, like chief negotiator Roelf Meyer, Cape leader Dawie de Villiers, Leon Wessels, and foreign minister Roelof 'Pik' Botha, believed Buthelezi's flirtations with the right wing made him a costly liability. They feared that catering to the IFP's erratic political course would only jeopardize their carefully nurtured but still delicate relations with the ANC. But a large portion of the party rank and file and a significant faction in the Cabinet were instinctively sympathetic to the IFP, insisting that Buthelezi remained the NP's most reliable black electoral ally and that nothing should be done to alienate him. The hardline pro-Inkatha supporters who saw the NP as the leader of an anti-ANC coalition had some powerful allies, including Cabinet ministers, senior NP caucus members, and the military intelligence axis of the security establishment.[20]

Power-Sharing and the ANC/National Party Axis

Artful diplomacy conducted by silver-tongued dignitaries urging caution and compromise was the flip-side of the orchestrated campaign of political violence carried out by 'unknown assailants' in the townships and ghettos, aimed at bludgeoning residents into silent submission. While career diplomats and political notables were engaged in a war of words over highly nuanced negotiating platforms, township residents were locked in a war of bullets with civilian-clothed gunmen who killed and maimed with impunity. The chameleon-like character of the negotiations process, with an ever-changing pace and rhythm all its own, stood in stark contrast to the grim, seemingly endless monotony of routinized township violence. These manifestly different images lent an almost surreal, schizophrenic air to the 'moment' of political transition.

After nearly three years of constant bickering, repeated breakdowns in formal negotiations, and periods of bitter recrimination punctuated with fresh outbreaks of political violence, the National Party and the ANC narrowed their differences to the point where they arrived on the threshold of a far-reaching historic compromise on the future of South Africa. Barring some unforeseen catastrophic turn of events, South Africa's two main political rivals inextricably locked themselves into a course of action, the outcome of which was a power-sharing agreement between them extending almost to the next century. In November 1992, de Klerk and Mandela reached agreement in principle on the goal of forming a 'government of national unity' through which a governing alliance, or coalition, would be established between the National Party and the ANC for an indefinite period of time in order to bring stability and facilitate a smooth transition to nonracial democracy.[21] In contrast to majority rule in a strict sense, this deal was designed to guarantee an enforced, not just voluntary, power-sharing arrangement. De Klerk had long advocated an open-ended *entente cordiale* that would not set a deadline for the power-sharing period. But even ANC moderates insisted that eventually there had to be a fixed time limit, and that there could be no question of a National Party veto. Pragmatists in the ANC camp, including SACP chair Joe Slovo, maintained that power-sharing with the National Party offered the most viable option to break the stalemate at CODESA. This compromise, which included the olive branch of 'sunset clauses' aimed at placating the mainly white civil service and the security establishment by guaranteeing jobs and pensions, spelled out the ground rules for ANC/NP cooperation during the three phases of the transition envisaged by the CODESA II agreements: an administrative transitional executive council, an elected constitution-making body/interim government, and a transitional government of national unity to emerge after the adoption of a new constitution.[22]

For Congress moderates, the major stumbling block to a power-sharing agreement was the strident opposition of ANC/SACP hardliners to any compromise that would provide the National Party with an effective veto over majority rule and that would leave the security establishment intact. Winnie Mandela's denunciation of power-sharing as a devil's pact between the 'elite of the oppressed and the oppressors' struck a resonant chord within large sections of the militant rank and file.[23] On the other side, the NP leadership encountered its own difficulties in promoting the power-sharing option. Within the NP rank and file, there was a strong, visceral, and sentimental attachment to the IFP, particularly because its unfettered advocacy of 'free market' economics offered an effective counterweight to the 'anti-capitalist' impulses of the SACP. In addition, the security establishment, which remained a powerful force dictating policy in Ciskei, KwaZulu and Bophuthatswana, was determined to prevent de Klerk from relinquishing power to the ANC in a way that would undermine its power base and expose operatives to retribution by an ANC-dominated judiciary.[24]

With mounting pressure to get meaningful negotiations back on track, the political battle lines, which at the start of talks had appeared quite heterodox and fluid, gradually assumed a distinctive shape. The ANC pieced together an unsteady alliance which included, besides its own delegation, the SACP, the Transvaal/Natal Indian Congresses, two tricameral parliamentary parties – the (Coloured) Labour Party and the (white) Democratic Party – and five homeland governments (Transkei, Venda, Lebowa, KwaNdebele and KaNgwane). In contrast, the government and National Party delegations marshalled the support of the two Indian parties in the tricameral parliament (Solidarity and the National People's Party), along with the remaining five homelands administrations (Ciskei, Gazankulu, QwaQua, Bophuthatswana and KwaZulu). From the outset, the powerful ANC and National Party delegations determined the pace and direction of negotiations. The galaxy of fringe parties played only a minor role in the eventual outcome, and their mercurial allegiances generated nothing more than an intriguing sideshow. None of the parties constituted a dominant force in its own right. But by acting in coalition with one or the other of the two main players, each hoped to acquire sufficient credibility to ensure its own survival.[25]

One remaining bone of contention between the National Party and the ANC concerned the proper balance of powers between the central government and regional authorities. The NP government, backed by Buthelezi and other allies in several of the homelands, favoured strong regions where minority parties would stand a reasonable chance of at least partially holding on to the levers of political power. In contrast, the ANC and its core allies regarded this scenario as a recipe for frustration of the national government. In bilateral talks in December and again in January 1993, the National Party government and the ANC inched closer to a mutual understanding on power-sharing and regionalism. Even before multiparty talks resumed in March, the government agreed to forfeit its insistence on entrenched power-sharing at the executive level, embodied in its idea of a rotating presidency and an executive council. In turn, the ANC accepted the principle of a high degree of local autonomy.[26]

The intense jockeying for power and position at the top was reflected in increased volatility at the bottom. For the months January to March 1993, the average daily death toll was 4.5, well below the daily average of 8 for 1992 and 10 for 1990. Beginning in July, when the IFP and the right-wing Conservative Party withdrew from the multiparty negotiating forum when it became clear that a bilateral power-sharing deal between the ANC and the National Party was imminent, the situation on the ground took an ominous turn for the worse. Over the next three months, nearly two thousand people died in politically related violence, or an average of around 18 per day.[27]

The politics of fission

As the negotiations process inched along, the National Party faced a host of disturbing organizational and ideological problems, especially growing discontent and demoralization within its own ranks and declining popularity among the wider electorate. With the prospect of securing winnable seats in the forthcoming election next to nil, many lame-duck MPs expended their energies on making 'other arrangements' to cope with their anticipated departure from parliamentary politics. A few long-time NP stalwarts retired from active politics, citing 'mental exhaustion' but fuelling suspicion that they were gravely disillusioned with de Klerk's willingness to put relations with the ANC ahead of what many party veterans recognized as a natural alliance with the IFP. Two NP Members of Parliament, Jurie Mentz and Hennie Becker, defected amid great fanfare to the IFP. The spectacle of a divided, feuding Cabinet and a dispirited party damaged de Klerk's standing among the white electorate. While political pundits had once cheerily forecast that the NP might be capable of garnering at least one-third of the vote in a nonracial election, the electoral appeal of the Nationalists plummeted alarmingly. An opinion poll conducted in September 1993 by the independent Integrated Marketing Research indicated that overall political support for the NP had slipped to an all-time low of 13 per cent. Disgruntled party insiders openly accused de Klerk of appeasement, and denounced his key negotiators – Roelf Meyer, the minister of constitutional affairs, Leon Wessels, the minister of manpower, and Dawie de Villiers, the Cape NP leader – for offering too many concessions to the ANC without making tangible gains in return. Rumours that they were promised Cabinet posts under an ANC-dominated government of national unity led to angry charges that the 'Kempton Park 3' – as de Klerk's trio of negotiators came to be known – had cynically traded compliance with the ANC for personal advancement.[28]

The National Party, which had restricted its membership to whites until 1990 and even barred Jews in the 1940s, experienced a radical transformation in its ethnic hue. 'The Nats', as one correspondent put it, were 'becoming browner by the day'. The most visible sign of this dramatic conversion to nonracialism was its growing support among Coloured and Indian voters and the number of black candidates on its electoral ticket.[29] However, the growing collusion between de Klerk and Mandela was accompanied by a haemorrhaging of the once-bedrock white support for the National Party. The IFP, which opened its ranks to all races in mid 1990, sought to cash in on the NP's failure to maintain a firm grip over its traditional constituencies. In the first eight months of 1993, the IFP opened more than 30 regional offices across the country in white areas once thought to be secure bastions of NP electoral strength, with many more at the planning stages. A Human Sciences Research Council survey showed that voters whose first choice was the NP overwhelmingly gave the IFP as their second preference. Opinion polls found that a surprising 27 per cent of the white electorate in the densely populated Witwatersrand intended to vote for the IFP, against 40 per cent for the Nationalists. A further indication of the 'whitening of the IFP' was that in its stronghold of Natal where key industrialists, especially the powerful coastal sugar barons, had thrown their muscle behind Buthelezi, Inkatha meetings drew large audiences of curious whites. Surveys suggested that white voters switched allegiance to the IPF largely because of Buthelezi's stand on federalism and Inkatha's support for market-driven free enterprise as opposed to the vaguely socialist formulas of the ANC.[30]

The End of the Beginning: Slouching towards 'Free and Fair' Elections

Blatantly provocative acts like the assassination of the immensely popular ANC/SACP stalwart Chris Hani in April 1993 failed to derail the multi-party talks. The momentum behind the negotiations process was simply too great. South Africa's tortuous search for a political settlement took a major step forward with the agreement at the negotiating council in September to establish a multiparty Transitional Executive Council (TEC). This 'super Cabinet', as some called it, was intended to function as a parallel Cabinet operating alongside existing structures that remained temporarily in place. The formal accord on the TEC, which acquired effective veto powers over the lame-duck de Klerk Cabinet, was part of a larger package hammered out at the negotiating forum and subsequently endorsed by the already irrelevant parliament. The TEC was designed for three key purposes: to provide the parties at the negotiating council with a share in the governance of South Africa; to enable the parties to monitor the various armed formations, from the existing security forces to the underground armies of the ANC and the PAC; and to facilitate the formation of a 'national peace-keeping force', drawn from the miscellany of armed units. Besides the TEC, the negotiators at the World Trade Centre venue at Kempton Park concurred on the need to establish an independent electoral commission, an autonomous media commission, and an impartial broadcasting authority. The objective behind this quartet of agreements was to prepare the way for free and fair elections of a 400-member transitional parliament to serve two roles: as a legislature for the interim government of national unity and as a constituent assembly mandated to draft a permanent constitution to replace the transitional one.[31]

The greatest threat to the negotiations process and the preparation of 'free and fair' elections was the inability, or unwillingness, of the security establishment to curb the ongoing political violence. In this swirling atmosphere of fear and intimidation, the most daunting challenge for the TEC was to ensure that all political parties were able to campaign freely in advance of the scheduled April elections. One of the seven subcouncils established under the TEC covered defence and public order. The objective behind the creation of the 'National Peacekeeping Force' (NPKF) was to bring together South Africa's diverse collection of police agencies and rival armies into a single body that would be truly national, multiracial and politically neutral. The long-term objective was to establish the nucleus of an eventual integrated defence force. Yet, from the outset, the entire project was clouded in controversy. Military analysts were grievously divided over its composition, mandate, leadership and orientation. Its very legitimacy was disputed by those political forces that refused to recognize the TEC. Some experts doubted the viability and wisdom of hastily cobbling together heterogeneous military and police units, many with a long history of animosity, after just four weeks of training.[32]

On the eve of a negotiated constitutional settlement, South Africa had five official armed forces: the SADF, with a standing force of 110,000, more than half of them black, and another 440,000, nearly all white, drawn from the Citizen Force and commandos; and the defence forces of the four nominally independent states, Bophuthatswana (35,000), Transkei (5,000), Ciskei (2,000), and Venda (1,800). In addition, Umkhonto we-Sizwe claimed over 10,000 guerrillas, thousands of whom remained in Uganda and Tanzania in anticipation of a political settlement at home. The paramilitary forces of the AWB were estimated at between 4,000 and 10,000 irregulars. Besides these, there were no fewer than eleven separate police forces. The most important was the SAP, whose overall numerical strength, including administrative staff and the controversial special constables, was put at 114,000. Its trained policemen numbered 86,000, more than half of them black. The total strength of the police agencies of the ten homelands was around 20,000.[33]

The severe storms and stresses that battered the wider political landscape rocked the security establishment as well. For years, South Africa's black police were ridiculed for their collaborating role in propping up white minority rule and crushing township resistance. However, growing numbers of them switched their allegiance to the ANC and, in a few cases, to the more radical PAC. The catalyst for the early radicalization of black policemen was the Police and Prison Civil Rights Union (POPCRU), which was founded in late 1989 by a dissident prison officer, Gregory Rockman. After three years of apparent quiescence, POPCRU experienced a resurgence of popularity, especially among poorly paid and badly trained categories of police. Official threats of disciplinary action failed to stem the flow of recruits to POPCRU. The Ministry of Law and Order accused the ANC, which developed strong contacts with the POPCRU leadership, of trying to hijack the 20,000-member union for its own purposes. The greatest fear in the upper echelons of the SAP was that the leftward drift of black policemen towards the ANC–POPCRU axis might trigger an equally dramatic reaction on the part of white policemen whose political loyalties were already largely right of centre. Political observers were agreed that political polarization along racial lines threatened to undermine the fragile unity of the police force, and that increased racial tension on the job could lead to internecine violence.[34]

Awaiting the new dawn: countdown to the elections

On 17 November 1993, after nine months of intensive and often bitter debate, the 21-party negotiating council adopted an interim constitution, 'classically liberal' in form, containing a Bill of Rights along with other guarantees of citizenship. This agreement, which effectively ended white minority rule after 341 years, marked a watershed in South African political history. The participants endorsed provisions creating a Transitional Government of National Unity (TGNU), which was to come into existence with the nationwide elections scheduled for 27 April 1994 and was authorized to rule for five years until 1999 unless the Cabinet lost the confidence of parliament. The installation of an elaborate electoral system called for voters to cast a single ballot for the party they wished to represent them in the new national parliament and in provincial legislatures. The parliament was mandated to craft a permanent constitution to replace the interim one, and act simultaneously as the country's first nonracial legislature. There would be two houses: a 400-member national assembly elected by proportional representation from prearranged party lists, with half the representatives from a national list and half from regional lists. In addition, there would be a senate composed of ten members from each of the nine provinces, elected by members of the provincial legislatures. The assembly was also to elect a president. There would be at least two deputy presidents, with the one selected from the largest party acting as prime minister. The 27-member Cabinet was to include ministers from all parties winning more than 5 per cent of the popular vote; seats would be allocated proportionately. Cabinet decisions were to be arrived at by consensus, but where impossible the view of the president would prevail.[35]

When acting as a constituent assembly, parliament would take decisions by two-thirds majority and would be constrained by constitutional principles set out in the interim constitution. If the constituent assembly could not agree by two-thirds majority within two years, there would be a referendum requiring a 60 per cent vote. If this mandate was not achieved, the constituent assembly would continue seeking agreement for a further three years with a 60 per cent majority required. When acting as a legislature, a simple majority would suffice, though constitutional amendments and bills affecting the powers of provincial governments must pass by a two-thirds majority of both houses.[36]

The interim constitution, which the negotiating council agreed would serve as South Africa's supreme law until an elected assembly could write a permanent version, 'fairly bristle[d] with checks and balances and was laden with assurances to guard against the feared 'tyranny of the majority'. It protected the jobs and pensions of white soldiers and civil servants, delegated important powers to provincial governments, and buttressed a long list of 'fundamental rights' with an all-powerful constitutional court. The list of fundamental rights included not only such democratic basics as free speech and fair trials, but also guarantees that reflected the abuses of the recent past: a specific prohibition against torture; a promise that people could live where they chose; an assurance that no one may be stripped of their citizenship; and limitations on the president's powers to declare a state of emergency, a favourite apartheid-era tool for crushing dissent. The constitution also prohibited discrimination not only by race, but by gender, sexual orientation, physical disability, or age. The president was also to appoint an eleven-member constitutional court, drawing from a list of candidates approved by a nonpartisan judicial panel.[37]

One of the provisions that alarmed many white property-holders gave the estimated 3.5 million people forcibly displaced under apartheid the right to claim restitution of their land or lost property. Many white farmers feared that this provision could lead to the expropriation of their land. Disputes would be settled by the courts, taking into account the market value of property, its use and the history of its acquisition, with built-in guarantees of 'just and equitable' compensation in the event of expropriation of property. The state would be obliged to buy the land or, if a claims court decided that the current landholder also had a legitimate claim, to give the former occupant a cash settlement.[38]

The interim constitution called for the creation of nine new provinces and provided for significant devolution of power to provincial legislatures in areas such as education, health, welfare, policing, and other services. However, the central government reserved the right to intervene to impose uniform national standards, to regulate provincial activities where national economic policy or security was involved. In the end, the question of a precise division of powers between the central government and the regions was left deliberately vague. Provincial legislatures would be entitled to adopt constitutions for their provinces, with the proviso that these must be consistent with the constitutional principles contained in the national constitution. The Constitutional Court was empowered to certify that the provincial constitutions were in compliance with these guidelines, thereby giving this body considerable leeway to interpret the kind of federal system that would eventually prevail.[39]

Multilateral negotiations over the form and substance of local-government structures took place via the Local Government Forum which was largely separate from the World Trade Centre multiparty talks. What emerged here was that the administration of local affairs would be transformed more slowly than the structure of national government. Local negotiating forums, or 'councils of local unity', would oversee the two-year transition to local government elections, with the rights of property owners protected, even after elections, by a formula which ensured that white residents would have disproportionate representation.[40]

At the last moment, National Party negotiators capitulated on their previous demands for minority vetoes on strictly enforced power-sharing. To this end, they agreed that the first democratic government should consist of all parties on a proportional basis, and that it should not require special majorities to make policy. They hoped that the stark realities of South Africa's power equilibrium – the fact that an entrenched white oligarchy faced no visible threat to its dominance of the private enterprise system, and that the civil service, security establishment, and judiciary remained more or less intact – would serve as a more effective protection for minority interests than any numerical formula.[41]

The package failed to deliver several of the checks and balances which the National Party had earlier insisted were essential to protect minority rights and hence were non-negotiable. When de Klerk first began negotiations, he held out for mechanisms such as a rotating presidency to guarantee a minority veto. The government miscalculated, believing that the longer talks dragged on, the weaker the ANC alliance would become. In fact, the reverse proved to be true, and the position of the NP was undermined by a sharp decline in its visible popularity among the electorate.[42] Amid charges from the right wing that they compromised too much, NP negotiators countered that the agreed-upon weakened form of power-sharing was part of a larger, more comprehensive package which provided other safeguards against the abuse of power: a Bill of Rights, a second change in the legislature which provided for regional representation, a guarantee that the government of national unity would remain in force for five years, and agreement that a final constitution must be passed by at least a 60 per cent majority.[43] However, overall, the NP did settle well below its bottom line on checks and balances. The Party's 1991 constitutional proposals called for political power to be divided between three tiers of government – central, regional and local – with each tier to have 'original and entrenched authority with which other tiers of government may not interfere'. Under the terms of the interim constitution, the central government retained wide powers to 'interfere' with regional governments: though the regions (divided into nine provinces) are to be granted principle responsibility for such areas as primary and secondary eduction, housing, health and policing, the central government reserved the right to intervene in these areas to impose uniform national norms and standards, to ensure proper regulation, to protect the national economy or national security, and where implications exist for national economic policy. In short, the constitution authorized the central government to intervene in terms so vague as seriously to undermine regional autonomy.[44] For all the built-in checks and balances, the party that won the election acquired most of the power. In effect, although it was called a government of national unity, the power-sharing arrangement depended on the good will and pragmatism of the majority party.[45]

On the other side, the ANC retreated from its earlier insistence on the wide-ranging powers of an elected constituent assembly. The administrative body selected to draft a permanent constitution will not have a free hand, but instead will be bound by prearranged 'constitutional principles' guaranteeing 'strong regional government' with considerable local authority. Final adoption of the permanent constitution will require 'special majorities' rather than a simple majority. Local authorities will reserve 30 per cent of their seats for whites – a share that far exceeds their presence in most local areas.[46]

The 'Unholy Alliance': White Separatists and Zulu Nationalists

The far-reaching 'power-sharing' agreement reached between Mandela and de Klerk in February 1993 sealed the fate of the once-fond hope of a centrist multiracial alliance comprised of the National Party, the Conservative Party and the IFP to challenge the ANC in the country's first democratic elections. Within months of the power-sharing deal, former chief of the SADF, General Constand Viljoen, emerged from retirement to build a bridge between the fragmenting right wing of Afrikanerdom and dissenting 'anti-de Klerk' factions in the NP. Along with several other retired generals, Viljoen sought to recast right-wing Afrikaner nationalism under the umbrella of the Afrikaner Volksfront (AVF) (Afrikaner People's Front) into a powerful political force. At one stage, it was estimated that there were more than sixty right-wing parties, organizations and groups, all proclaiming broad 'Afrikaner aspirations' but seriously weakened by wide-ranging differences over detail. The arrival of the 'committee of generals' infused a new sense of purpose into the right wing, in part by introducing a degree of moderation into the often reckless demagogy characteristic of right-wing political discourse. This 'enlightened' leadership, with strong roots in the Afrikaner *nouveau riche* establishment, added some respectability to a protean right-wing movement whose public standing was seriously soiled by the thuggery directed at black people by CP supporters in public places and the neo-Nazi posturing of the racist AWB.[47]

With the tacit support of the still influential Broederbond and the full knowledge of senior officers in military intelligence, the 'committee of generals' set out to weld disparate right-wing groups into a single confederation, with the major aim of creating an Afrikaner *volkstaat* in one of the proposed nine regions. The AVF proposed a *volkstaat* with Pretoria as the hub supporting segmented spokes radiating out from it. This scheme offered a sort of promised land to which Afrikaners in the rest of the country could look as the symbol of their nationhood and culture, and to which they could gravitate as personal circumstances permitted. While its geographical pretensions were genuinely outlandish, what made this idea of an 'Afrikaner Israel' attractive for Afrikaner nationalists was that most recognized the practical impossibility of living in the *volkstaat*, but they continued to cherish the dream of their own 'homeland'. The AVF plan had much more appeal than the unrealistic and impractical aspirations of the CP, which at one stage defined its 'Afrikaner homeland' as the whole of South Africa excluding the ten homelands. While the CP subsequently narrowed its proposed boundaries to incorporate a vaguely defined area of uncertain dimensions stretching over large parts of the Transvaal, Orange Free State, and Northern Cape provinces, this imagined *volkstaat* never amounted to anything more than wishful thinking.[48]

The 'committee of generals' also intended to ensure that the right wing remained in 'responsible' hands and was not hijacked by unpredictable mavericks, such as AWB firebrand Eugene Terre'Blanche and CP leader Ferdinand Hartzenberg, whose supporters had access to military intelligence and sophisticated weaponry which, in the event of a selective but highly disruptive 'terror' campaign, had the potential of igniting uncontrollable violence. Viljoen was confident he could deliver the right wing to a solution that defined Afrikaner 'self-determination' within the context of a federal state. He was the prime mover behind the effort to forge an electoral alliance between conservatives in COSAG and Afrikaner nationalists in favour of federalism.[49]

In October 1993, the AVF, the CP, the IFP, and the homeland leaders of Ciskei, KwaZulu and Bophuthatswana announced the formation of the Freedom Alliance (FA) to press their demands for a federal system of government. Buthelezi and Viljoen insisted that the boundaries and powers of federal states, including an Afrikaner *volkstaat* and a KwaZulu state, had to be secured and finalized before an election. Critics charged that a prearranged pact of this sort amounted to an endorsement of ethnic cleansing. The ruling NP was caught in the middle, divided from top to bottom. Its dilemma was that it needed the support of the ANC to legitimize the transition to democracy, but many members were sympathetic to the idea of regional autonomy and favoured stronger ties with the IFP.[50]

By themselves, the AVF and the IFP did not have sufficient political weight to impose a political settlement. But if the AVF was able to join hands with the IFP in an alliance marshalled in defence of the right of self-determination, their combined capacity for disruption of agreements forged so laboriously at the negotiating council was formidable. Viljoen made a dramatic show of calling upon Afrikaners to join the Commandos and Police Reserve, and thousands of armed volunteers responded, creating what was amounted to the backbone of an embryonic 'Boer army'.[51] In fact, the AVF maintained important links with the security forces, particularly the part-time commando units. Ex-intelligence chief and a principal strategist for the AVF, General Tienie Groenewald, boasted that the Afrikaner Volksfront could mobilize 500,000 men with military training to defend the right of Afrikaners to self-determination. This claim was undoubtedly an exaggerated boast, but there was an ominous ring of truth to it.[52]

Despite the desperation that drew the AVF and the CP into closer association with the AWB, there remained a great deal of abhorrence among upper-class conservatives toward the vigilante 'terror' of the AWB. Viljoen and other AVF leaders carefully distanced themselves from the AWB ruffians who assaulted black delegates and urinated on the walls of the conference chamber during the raid on the World Trade Centre negotiations forum in June. Formidable divisions over tactics and public image suggested that efforts to forge disaffected right-wingers into a strong rebellious army would prove difficult if not impossible.[53]

The Eleventh Hour: A Curious Mixture of Disruption and Compromise

The steady barrage of veiled threats of civil war from FA leaders brought pressure on the ANC and NP government to accommodate their demands for 'self-determination' and a federal structure. The complex network of bilateral and trilateral negotiation between the government, ANC and FA severely strained existing tensions inside the main parties and brought several close to the breaking point.[54] In an eleventh-hour effort to salvage full participation in the elections, the multiparty negotiating forum incorporated a number of last-minute changes into the transitional constitution that were designed to win favour with the Freedom Alliance and break the deadlock. The negotiating forum replaced the single ballot with a system of separate ballots for national and provincial elections. The ANC also made notable concessions which shifted the interim constitution substantially towards federalism. The overriding 'concurrent' powers that the central government was supposed to have acquired were significantly diluted, and the federal aspects of the new constitution were strengthened by transferring extensive powers to the new provinces, including powers of taxation, exclusive powers in all areas of competence, and a guarantee that provincial powers would not be substantially inferior to those of the new national assembly.[55]

Nowhere was the prospect of 'free and fair' elections more fragile on such a grand scale than in the battle-scarred province of Natal. Despite last-minute efforts to reach a *modus vivendi*, Buthelezi pledged that Kwa-Zulu would never capitulate to 'foreign rule', and continued to issue thinly veiled threats sanctioning the brutal partition of South Africa if constitutional guarantees for an acceptable regional autonomy for KwaZulu/Natal were not granted. In a manoeuvre designed to assuage King Goodwill Zwelithini, Mandela and de Klerk promised that the post-election status of the Zulu monarch would be secure and his salary would be paid by the government of the day, regardless of what happened to the self-governing homeland of KwaZulu.[56] Yet in a significant hardening of his position, King Zwelithini – with Buthelezi's blessing – accused de Klerk of trying 'to completely obliterate us as a people from the face of South Africa', and demanded complete restoration of the old Zulu Kingdom in accordance with pre-1836 territorial boundaries.[57]

In its public pronouncements, the IFP refused to endorse the elections and vowed not to participate, but left the door slightly ajar in case of a last-minute change of heart. In the months preceding the voting, Mandela and Buthelezi crisscrossed the province, raising funds, offering their competing visions of the future, urging their followers to register, and mobilizing logistical backing on the ground. But the rival parties were largely restricted to campaigning within their own secure bastions of support. For Inkatha loyalists, the ANC was 'an undisciplined army of young upstarts indoctrinated with revolutionary ideas and scornful of traditional tribal authority'. For ANC supporters, the tradition-encrusted socio-political habits of Inkatha were hopelessly backward and out of touch with modern realities. Nonpartisan election experts believed that rising fear and intimidation greatly reduced the likelihood of genuinely democratic elections, and they worried that an electoral majority would not translate into an unambiguous mandate to govern. On the ground, where political calculations were considerably more mundane and immediate, lofty principles like federalism and 'self-determination' carried little weight. In those divided communities comprising a patchwork of loyalties, rival camps feared that the eventual winners would exact a heavy price in the form of massive retribution.[58]

The 'fool's errand': the last trek of the lunatic fringe?

There were strong indications that the Conservative Party had come to rely on the roughneck neo-Nazi AWB movement to act as 'storm-troopers' in breaking up ANC-sponsored political meetings in small towns in the rural Transvaal, Orange Free State, and Northern Cape, the heart-lands of right-wing support. These actions formed part of a wider right-wing strategy of civil disobedience and selective violence in pursuit of a *volkstaat*. Beginning in late 1993, there was a dramatic escalation of bomb attacks, directed mainly at railway lines, electricity pylons, ANC and trade-union offices, and gas supply lines. The blasts, more than thirty in all, carved out a map in the western Transvaal and northern Orange Free State which partly delineated the proposed Afrikaner homeland. Some AWB members were arrested in connection with planned attacks on the Koeberg nuclear plant, on the World Trade Centre venue of multiparty talks, and on the SADF's Lohatla Army Battle School, but the bombings continued. They were carried out by small cells of highly trained saboteurs with military experience operating under the AVF umbrella. Unconfirmed rumours suggesting that extremist right-wing groups were busy stock-piling arms and ammunition, medical supplies and fuel in remote parts of Northern and Eastern Transvaal, and in northern Natal, in advance of the scheduled April elections raised serious doubts about political stability both before and after the scheduled elections. There were also reports that right-wingers were involved in conducting regular training exercises in guerrilla warfare tactics in preparation for last-ditch resistance to the alleged 'communist-inspired takeover'.[59] The AVF/CP alliance claimed to control civil councils in 283 towns stretching from Richards Bay in Natal, through the Transvaal and Free State to the Cape Province and as far north as Namaqualand.[60] Political observers expected that the next phase of the right-wing plan to seize territory for a *volkstaat* involved symbolic takeovers of some of these CP-controlled towns and municipalities where the modern-day Boer rebels would declare themselves part of a homeland 'in-the-making'.[61]

The high point to feverish right-wing 'war preparations' came in March with the bizarre armed incursion by white separatists of Bophuthatswana. The origins of simmering tensions in Bophuthatswana can be traced to the short-lived military coup led by Rocky Malebane-Metsing, who eventually emerged as an ANC regional candidate for the northwest province. While the South African security forces intervened to crush the revolt and restore Lucas Mangope to power, the political crisis exposed the lack of popular support for the regime. What proved to be the penultimate crisis for the Mangope regime originated with a strike by civil servants in March for a 50 per cent pay increase, the repayment of their pension contributions, and the reincorporation of Bophuthatswana into South Africa. The strike spread and was accompanied by open rebellion in the streets of Mmabatho and the adjoining town of Mafeking, especially outside the University of Bophuthatswana. Two political demands lay behind the rebellion and, to a lesser extent, the wildcat strike: the reincorporation of Bophuthatswana into South Africa and the right to free and uninhibited political activity in the territory. The defection of a large contingent of Mmabatho police to 'the people' precipitated the onset of large-scale looting and joyous celebrations. Faced with his pending demise, Mangope played his final card: he enlisted the support of General Viljoen's AVF to assist the remnants of his army and police in suppressing what he believed – with some justification – was a campaign orchestrated by the 'communist-inspired ANC' along with PAC supporters to overthrow his regime. By extending an invitation to the AVF, Mangope inadvertently opened the door to the neo-fascist AWB. Viljoen responded to Mangope's plea for help by issuing a dramatic call for 'volunteers'; and, by some estimates, around 5,000 white irregulars arrived in the capital of Mmabatho, including a sizeable 'uninvited' detachment of AWB paramilitaries.[62]

At first, the white extremists had the run of the city, careening through the streets in long convoys of pick-up trucks and Mercedes limousines, and shooting randomly at black passers-by. The ignominious *coup de grâce* to this tawdry affair came when Bophuthatswana soldiers who had broken ranks with the tattered Mangope regime turned on their would-be rescuers. While the withdrawal of AWB commandos from Mmabtaho was initiated by orders from the AVF for them to pull out, the exodus was accelerated by Bophuthatswana police and soldiers who 'shepherded [the white right-wingers] like goats' to the border. There were exchanges of gunfire between the retreating AWB commandos, who fired indiscriminately into civilian crowds, and the Bophuthatswana soldiers and police. In the most serious incident, Bophuthatswana security forces disabled the last vehicle in an AWB convoy, killing one khaki-clad AWB vigilante in the fusillade of bullets, and killing his two companions by summary execution as they lay wounded beside their car.[63]

The sudden collapse of the Mangope dictatorship signalled the end of the Bophuthatswana homeland and a turning point in the halting march toward elections. At the cost of an estimated forty lives and uncounted destruction of property, the 'Battle of Bophuthatswana' produced at least three critical gains for the ANC/NP political forces struggling to hold the centre. First, the blundering intervention of white separatists badly discredited those who favoured violent resistance. The Bophuthatswana debacle activated bitter recriminations between Viljoen and Terre'Blanche, where each blamed the other for the fiasco. The heightened tensions within the AVF led to further splintering and realignment of the far right. Humiliated by his own grave miscalculation and wishing to minimize the damage done to his cherished goal of creating an Afrikaner Homeland, Viljoen resigned as co-leader of the AVF, abandoned the FA, and decided at the last minute to contest the elections under the hastily constructed banner of the Freedom Front. Second, despite their campaign rivalry, Mandela and de Klerk demonstrated by their joint resolve to use the SADF to depose the despotic Mangope regime and install hand-picked interim administrators that they were de facto partners in running the country. Third, the upheaval in Bophuthatswana, coupled with the capitulation of the dictatorial Oupa Gqozo regime in Ciskei less than a week later, stripped Buthelezi and KwaZulu of their last serious allies in the pro-federalist alliance and left the IFP isolated as the last major party (with the exception of AZAPO) to hold out against participation in the scheduled elections.[64]

The last gasp of successionism: Buthelezi's kamikaze strategy

On the eve of the April elections, the alliance of election 'refusniks' had dwindled to two loosely affiliated camps: the white separatists, particularly the CP under the uninspiring leadership of Ferdie Hartzenberg, and paramilitary groups like the AWB, the Boereweerstandsbeweging (BWB), the Eastern Transvaal Boerekommando (ETB), and the Pretoria Boerekommandogroep (PBKG); and the 'Zulu nationalists', bringing together Buthelezi's IFP along with unswerving followers of the KwaZulu monarch, King Goodwill Zwelithini. What set Buthelezi apart from other homeland rulers was that he was able to attach his fortunes to the clientelist politics of an erstwhile monarchy frozen in time. He was able to gain the support of the Zulu king on three critical issues: his rejection of the transitional constitution, his refusal to participate in elections, and his demand – in view of the failure of the multiparty negotiating forum to offer a genuinely federal constitution – for the restoration of the pre-colonial Zulu kingdom. The rise to prominence of Zulu royalists – men and women who were fanatically loyal to Zwelithini and the cause of the Zulu monarchy – altered the political equation in Natal/KwaZulu decidedly in favour of the IFP. By opposing Buthelezi and the IFP, the ANC found itself in the unenviable position of fostering conflict with the king.[65]

Despite quiet entreaties from key ANC and NP luminaries, including the offer of a senior position in the post-election government, Buthelezi kept shifting the bottom line, expanding his list of demands to embrace the postponement of the April voting and broader concessions on regional autonomy. In spite of Buthelezi's assurances to the Independent Electoral Commission that all political parties would be permitted to campaign freely in KwaZulu/Natal, IFP 'warlords' stepped up their feverish prepa-rations to disrupt the elections. Immediately following the mid-March appeal of King Zwelethini and Buthelezi to their followers to boycott the voting and defend the sovereignty of KwaZulu, 'one settlement after another erupted in fresh outbreaks of killing and house-burning'. Attacks by Inkatha partisans became 'more audacious, more concerted, and more coordinated'. IFP loyalists twice occupied township stadiums scheduled for ANC rallies, sparking raging gunfights. In townships from northern KwaZulu to the south coast on the Indian Ocean, election monitors reported that large groups of armed IFP followers invaded communities where Congress supporters predominated.[66] In March, at least 290 people died in political violence in Natal, the highest monthly total in three years.[67]

In several well-monitored cases, the assailants arrived by bus wearing khaki outfits – the uniforms of a new 5,000-man Inkatha 'self-defence' force trained by ex-SADF intelligence operatives at the Umfolozi military camp outside Ulundi. The raw recruits came in small batches, selected by tribal leaders 'who [were] still the supreme authority in the rural hills of KwaZulu'. The graduates of the training course, who were issued illegal weapons from Inkatha caches – either black-market AK-47 assault rifles or weapons procured by the IFP from suppliers in the SAP – formed the nucleus of a growing 'Zulu paramilitary legion' aimed at serving intransigent tribal leaders who rejected the prospect of an ANC-led government.[68]

Details about these secret 'guerrilla warfare' training camps in KwaZulu raised grave doubts concerning the probability of supervising the elections in Natal and ratifying the outcome. But it was the Goldstone Commis-sion that delivered the most shocking pre-election bombshell. Justice Goldstone submitted a hundred-page report to President de Klerk offer-

ing *prima facie* evidence implicating three top SAP generals in a range of
clandestine 'destabilizing' activities, including complicity in an illicit gun-
running network supplying key Inkatha lieutenants with illegal weapons.
The three senior-level police officers – deputy police commissioner
General Basie Smith, the second highest ranking SAP officer in the country; counter-intelligence chief Major-General Krappies Engelbrecht; and
Criminal Investigation Department chief Lieutenant-General Johan le
Roux – were linked with the notorious SAP 'hit squad' base at Vlakplaas
police barracks near Pretoria. According to this judicial report, the plot
was hatched in 1989, after which time the secret police cabal began to
funnel automatic weapons (with their original serial numbers erased) and
hand grenades to Inkatha loyalists, to train its 'hit squads', and even to
assist in the planning of attacks. The Goldstone brief offered few specifics,
but alleged that police officials, using black policemen and Inkatha members, launched assaults from hostels, terrorized black commuters on local
trains, and organized assassinations. In the KwaZulu homeland, SAP
saboteurs worked closely with KZP units that were already in effect a
partisan army for Inkatha. These discoveries were based on testimony
from an informant, codenamed 'Q' to protect his identity, who claimed
that this secret police network acquired weapons destined for Inkatha
largely from secret *Koevoet* stockpiles in Namibia, and that many landed
in the hands of well-known IFP Witwatersrand leaders Thema Khoza and
Victor Ndlovu.[69] For progressive forces in South Africa, these disclosures
provided a long-awaited confirmation of an officially sanctioned 'destabilization' campaign and signified the 'tip of the iceberg' of a 'third force'
intent on destabilizing not only the April elections but also the new
ANC government after it took office.[70]

On 28 March, perhaps as many as 40,000 royalist supporters of King
Zwelethini staged a massive rally in the heart of downtown Johannesburg
that erupted in running gun battles in which at least 56 persons were
killed and more than 400 injured. Successive waves of IFP marchers carrying spears, axes, clubs, pistols and, in some instances, AK-47 assault
rifles, converged on the central business district from Soweto in the south-
east, Alexandra in the north, and from IFP-controlled hostel strongholds
in outlying townships in the eastern suburbs of the city. At Library Gardens, snipers perched on nearby rooftops shot randomly into crowds assembled below. Armed marchers, police officers and mysterious
sharpshooters hidden in surrounding office buildings 'blazed away at each
other along several blocks of banks and offices'. Less than a mile away, at
Shell House, the 21-storey skyscraper housing ANC headquarters, ANC
'security guards' opened fire on well-armed IFP bands who menacingly
encircled the building, probing for weaknesses in its defences. This grue-

some spectacle marked the first time that the 'factional carnage so familiar to black settlements had reached so dramatically into the country's commercial center'. There was widespread suspicion that the still-elusive 'third force' had exploited the volatile situation, possibly planting *agents provocateurs* in the vicinity, to cause destabilization in an attempt to prevent the April elections from taking place. This shocking 'street war' was a grim reminder of the fragility of a peaceful settlement in South Africa.[71]

In a bid to curb the violence which threatened to disrupt the elections in KwaZulu/Natal, de Klerk, acting in concert with the TEC, declared a state of emergency in the province on 31 March. SADF reinforcements, along with special police units, were deployed to patrol known 'unrest' flashpoints, and stringent regulations were promulgated providing the security forces with increased powers, including the right to detain suspects for as long as thirty days and to search premises without a warrant. The SADF took command of KwaZulu's police force, which with its 3,500 members was widely believed to have collaborated in the murder of Congress-aligned rivals, but stopped short of officially occupying the homeland and forcing the recalcitrant administration to resign.[72]

With less than a month to go before the elections, the multiparty TEC busily prepared for a possible bloody showdown in KwaZulu/Natal. The Zulu nationalists pursued a high-risk strategy of brinkmanship to achieve their immediate goal of postponement of the 26–28 April elections. Inkatha wielded tribalism and ethnicity as watchwords to whip up popular support. Buthelezi reacted indignantly, denouncing the clampdown as 'humiliating' and 'another chapter of oppression'. A hastily arranged summit meeting between de Klerk, Mandela, Zwelithini and Buthelezi on 8 April ended in stalemate. Zwelethini rejected ANC guarantees of a special status for the Zulu monarchy in post-election South Africa, including the creation of a ceremonial kingdom, a budget to maintain his tribal patronage networks, and a royal constabulary, in exchange for a promise to restrain armed Inkatha partisans during the voting. The ANC refused to capitulate to Zwelethini's demands to keep control of the vast tribal landholdings and to preserve the tribal court system. The King renewed his demand for the resuscitation of a sovereign monarchy, or what amounted to an independent Zulu kingdom, across the territory controlled by Shaka before the British conquest. A high-powered mediation team, headed by former US secretary of state Henry Kissinger and a former British foreign secretary, Lord Carrington, attempted to bridge the seemingly unbreachable chasm between the two sides, but made no appreciable headway in the face of Buthelezi's intransigent stance.[73]

The Zulu royalists were unwelcome envoys of a fragmented and dangerous age in which the politics of ethnic/racial identity dwarfed the universalist principles of welding together a single nation. Ethnicity and tribal identity provided ruthless and ambitious leaders with a window of opportunity to manipulate prevailing tensions and uncertainties about the future of South Africa to their own political advantage. The fiery rhetoric of secession, coupled with the ominous threat of protracted armed resistance, were the first steps down a slippery slope that risked plunging KwaZulu/Natal into full-fledged civil war. The rising crescendo of partisan violence transformed large stretches of the rural areas and scores of townships and shantytowns of the province into a fluid free-for-all where the virtual collapse of law and order enabled various armed militias, operating largely without central command, to adopt quasi-political agendas to suit their own narrow, sectarian ends.[74]

The grim prospect that the post-apartheid order would face implacable opposition from two unlikely allies – diehard Afrikaner nationalists and resolute Zulu royalists – evaporated a week before the election with Buthelezi's surprise agreement on 19 April to call off his election boycott and allow his IFP to be included on the ballots for a new national assembly and for provincial legislatures. With this abrupt *coup de théâtre*, the only organizations opposing the elections ending white minority rule were white extremist fringe groups and the Black Consciousness-inclined AZAPO. In exchange for ending their boycott and encouraging their supporters to participate in the voting, Buthelezi and Zwelethini received assurances from both Mandela and de Klerk that the Zulu king would retain his status as largely ceremonial monarch with a limited role in a tribal chamber of the provincial parliament, and that after the election foreign mediators would consider Inkatha's demands for greater autonomy in the KwaZulu/Natal region.

Buthelezi had painted himself into a corner, and finding a face-saving way out of the cul-de-sac was not easy. On 27 April, when the new interim constitution was scheduled to take effect, the KwaZulu homeland ceased to exist, leaving the lame-duck chief minister without a civil service, a police force and the budget 'that support[ed] his network of tribal satraps'. Political pundits speculated that, after nine months of cat-and-mouse brinkmanship, Buthelezi staged this last-minute turnabout for two principal reasons. First, unable to budge an implacable opposition with their unsuccessful bid to secure postponement of the election and to gain exclusive entrenched powers for provincial governments, Buthelezi and the IFP failed to achieve their aims. Isolated from the political mainstream and faced with the prospect of dwindling popular support from rank-and-file Inkatha supporters who wanted to participate in the electoral process, Buthelezi suddenly found himself 'staring into the abyss of political irrelevance'. Second, while Buthelezi remained adamant in his refusal to participate in the elections, Zwelethini was not. By all indications, the Zulu king had been lured into accepting the ANC's offer of an elevated status afforded by a constitutionally guaranteed monarchy. Faced with the imminent defection of the king and Inkatha moderates who strongly objected to the thought of being sidelined with the political pariahs of the far-right lunatic fringe, Buthelezi abruptly changed course.[75]

Postscript: Entering the Political Kingdom

As South Africans vote in this first multiracial elections, the question is not who will win but what it will mean.[1]

Prelude to the Elections

Seen in retrospect, the thunderous car-bomb blast in downtown Johannesburg near ANC headquarters on 24 April, which killed nine people and injured at least ninety-two more, signalled the beginning of the end of a frantic *blitzkrieg* mounted by frenzied white separatists bent on disrupting the electoral process. More than a dozen bombs were reported on 26 April alone, in a horrific crescendo intended to demoralize and frighten the new South African electorate on the eve of its first vote. In the worst attack, a bomb left by a white male in a van at a taxi rank in downtown Germiston, near the offices of the ANC and COSATU, claimed the lives of ten innocent black bystanders. Other bomb blasts took place at a Pretoria shebeen, in which two people were killed, at a taxi rank in Randfontein, and at the international departures section of Johannesburg's Jan Smuts Airport. These were only the tip of the iceberg: for example, from the beginning of April, there were around forty bomb blasts in the Transvaal alone.

On the eve of elections, bombs were detonated at six polling stations and Independent Election Commission offices, including Potgietersrus (Northern Transvaal), Steynsburg (Northern Cape), and Bloemhof (Western Transvaal). These wanton acts of indiscriminate terror carried out by small cells of white racist fanatics prompted the security forces to bolster the largest peace-time mobilization in South African history, with 100,000 police officers and thousands of army reservists called up to guard polling stations. Despite vociferous denials of involvement from the far-right AWB, the security forces raided a paramilitary hide-out near Rustenburg in the Western Transvaal, arresting thirty-two white suspects, mainly members of the AWB's elite *Ystergarde* armed wing, and charging them with an assortment of crimes linked to the bombing campaign. Informants helped police capture the far-right militants and uncover large caches of deadly explosives and firearms. These arrests dealt a crushing blow to the leadership of the white terrorist movement. Notwitstanding the possible damage that could be done to life, property and the national mood by unrepentant saboteurs, the far right was thrown into near-complete disarray as a viable social force. But the several tens of thousands of committed, virulently racist, militarily trained white right-wingers, many belonging to terrorist cells that were mainly clones of the neo-fascist AWB, were positioned to continue selective assassinations and sporadic bombing campaigns.[2]

All in all, the 'anti-election' bomb blitz failed to deter the 22.7 million eligible voters who flocked to an estimated 9,000 far-flung polling stations to chose a predetermined slate of candidates from one of nineteen parties listed on the ballot. Three out of four voters were newly enfranchised and were intent on casting their ballots in the country's first nonracial elections. Voters were amazingly calm, with some impatient voters beginning to queue in Soweto as early as 1 a.m. on the first day of the general elections. There were numerous reports of white farmers intimidating farmworkers and confiscating identification books. But the sporadic racial attacks directed at black voters at several polling stations in outlying Conservative-dominated towns occurred against the backdrop of a vote in which intimidation and violence were largely absent.

Despite calls from the Transitional Executive Council for a moratorium on public-sector strikes, South Africa was hit in the days immediately preceding the elections with a tidal wave of walkouts by nurses, ambulance workers, teachers and police in Natal, Venda, Lebowa and Transkei. The mining industry was gripped by several 'wildcat' strikes, including the action of 10,000 mine workers who walked off the job at Gold Fields platinum near Rustenburg, and an illegal work stoppage of 8,000 Rusplats miners.

On the eve of the elections, the TEC declared huge stretches of the country, particularly rural and peri-urban towns where the right-wing whites parties held sway, as 'unrest areas'. In the East Rand townships of Katlehong, Vosloorus and Thokoza, the long-standing 'turf war' pitting ANC 'comrades' against Inkatha loyalists, who were holed up in places like the Mshayezafe ('beat him until he dies') hostel, erupted once again. The hastily formed National Peacekeeping Force, which was created as a prototype of the integrated forces that would to serve an ANC-led government, replaced the SADF on the East Rand, but were incapable of putting a stop to the carnage.[3] The military crackdown in Natal, including a state of emergency and the deployment of 3,000 troops, did little to stem the tide of sectarian violence. For example, residents of Umlazi, eleven miles from Durban and South Africa's second largest township after Soweto, complained that overstretched SADF patrols were ineffective in curbing 'a tide of death, arson, and disappearances' that swept the sprawling satellite city.[4]

On the whole, the election, as one commentator put it, 'was a clumsy improvisation, so riddled with irregularities that the electoral commission threw away the rule book in order to validate the outcome'.[5] The process itself was plagued by frustrating logistical problems, including ballot shortages at many voting stations. The last-minute decision of Inkatha to contest the elections created the need to distribute special IFP stickers to affix to the ballot papers, and these were often unavailable. As a result of the late entry of Inkatha into the electoral process, the Independent Electoral Commission was unable to establish sufficient voting stations in KwaZulu to handle the rush of voters. Across the country, some polling stations opened later than announced, and several failed to open at all. Widespread and incontrovertible complaints that ballots and polling machinery were not available at hundreds of voting stations prompted the Independent Electoral Commission to announce an extra day of voting in parts of three provinces. There were numerous reports of voter fraud and tampering. For example, government-seconded officials almost certainly engaged in acts of deliberate sabotage as large quantities of unused ballot materials were discovered in warehouses after the final tallies were completed. However, in the opinion of most election experts, these irregularities did little to alter the final outcome at the national level in any appreciable way.[6]

The Election Results

Beyond a shadow of a doubt, what is certain is that South Africa's first nonracial general elections marked a political watershed of enormous historical significance from which there was no turning back. Under circumstances where millions of voters mixed the grim determination to cast their ballots with the unrestrained joy of making a choice for the first time in their lives, the ANC scored a landslide victory in South Africa's first nonracial elections held 26–29 April 1994. Buoyed by early returns that put the ANC in the lead by a comfortable margin over the National Party, an exuberant Nelson Mandela wasted little time in proclaiming on 2 May in a nationally broadcast speech that South Africa was 'free at last'.[7] Voting results trickled in with agonizing slowness, amid swirling controversy over widespread logistical difficulties and allegations of fraud, particularly in the hotly contested Natal/KwaZulu province. Six days after the official counting started and ten days after voting began, the Independent Electoral Commission, chaired by Judge Johann Kriegler, pronounced the election substantially 'free and fair' and announced the final results everyone had more or less expected. The ANC garnered the lion's share of the final tally, winning nearly 63 per cent of the nearly twenty million votes cast, which translated into 252 National Assembly seats. The results gave the ANC less than the two-thirds majority it needed to write the new constitution with few concessions to other parties, although Mandela swore beforehand that he would seek consensus rather than unilaterally imposing the will of his organization on other parties.

The runner-up in the election was the National Party, which despite its apartheid heritage, scored 20.4 per cent (with 82 National Assembly seats), mainly on the strength of somewhat surprisingly strong support from so-called Coloured and Indian voters in some areas, who apparently viewed the prospect of a huge ANC majority with a great deal of suspicion. The second-place result for the National Party guaranteed de Klerk a junior partnership in the government of national unity as second vice president, behind the ANC's first vice president, Thabo Mbeki. Any party polling 5 per cent of the votes was automatically entitled to a seat in the coalition Cabinet. The only other party to reach this agreed threshold was the IFP, which ended with 10.5 per cent and 43 national assembly seats.

The strength of ideas cannot be judged solely on electoral performance, and hence considerable caution must be used in attaching wider socio-cultural meaning than is warranted to voting tallies abstracted from their time and place settings. But the polling results do provide a social barometer by which to assess political sentiments at a particular moment, and these ought not be ignored. The Freedom Front, organized by retired general Constand Viljoen as a vehicle for recalcitrant whites devoted to a separate Afrikaner homeland, polled around 2.2 per cent. But the Front's unexpected visibility in several provinces was a palpable sign that, despite a boycott by the extreme right wing, most conservative white voters chose to pursue their perceived interests within the electoral system. Two parties with prominent histories suffered significant electoral defeats. The PAC, which many commentators had expected to do well in some areas, polled around 1.2 per cent of the vote, a failure attributed, among other things, to bland leadership, lack of financing, grave misgivings among its rank-and-file supporters about participating in the elections, and a fateful decision to campaign mainly on the issue of land redistribution. The other big loser was the Democratic Party, the long-

standing, plaintive voice of middle-class liberalism, which was able to win
only around 1.7 per cent of the vote.[8]

The flush of victory for the Congress movement at the national level
was tempered by mixed results in the provincial elections. The ANC held
insurmountable leads in the balloting for seven of nine new provincial
legislatures. But the organization faced certain defeat in the Western Cape,
where the Coloured electorate, which accounted for more than 50 per
cent of eligible voters, sided in large numbers with the Nationalists. In
the campaign, the National Party cynically played on the anxieties of
stable working-class 'mixed race' voters fearful of losing whatever modest
advantages they possessed to a surge of black affirmative action. The
Nationalists resorted to 'anti-African' demagoguery on such an unbending
scale that it reached both racially distasteful and politically dangerous levels.
The 'Nat' victory in the Western Cape ensured the installation of Hernus
Kriel, the current minister of law and order in the NP government and
one of the least penitent veteran 'hawks' of the ruling 'old guard', as the
new prime minister of the province. Nevertheless, the inability of the
ANC to offset the 'Nat' scare tactics in the Western Cape must be
measured against the electoral results in the Northern Cape and Eastern
Cape, where the ANC made a strong showing with Coloured voters.[9]

In KwaZulu/Natal, to the great surprise of 'pundits who had written
Mr Buthelezi's political obituary', the IFP won control over the provincial legislature with slightly more than 50 per cent of the vote. In the
minds of virtually all political commentators, Buthelezi's petulant theatrics
on the eve of the elections had undermined the IFP's chances of surpass-
ing the ANC in the voting. The KwaZulu/Natal results were tainted by
widespread allegations of 'gross irregularities' and outright fraud. The
murder of three ANC campaign workers in Ulundi on the eve of the
election symbolized the charged atmosphere of fear and tension. Internal
reports sent by official poll-watchers to the Independent Electoral Commission detailed scores of ballot boxes materializing from mysterious
origins, thousands of unaccounted-for ballot papers, along with numerous other reports of surreptitious cheating. Both ANC and independent
observers submitted affidavits to the Independent Electoral Commission
alleging widespread intimidation during the voting. The late entry of the
IFP meant that Inkatha loyalists and KwaZulu civil servants played a key
role in election organization, particularly in the more remote areas of
northern Natal, to the detriment of other political parties. However, in
the end, amid allegations that backroom deals had been cut, and over the
angry objections of ANC stalwarts in the province, the Commission certi-
fied the election outcome in the province and declared the IFP the victor.
The chairman of the Independent Electoral Commission, Johann Kriegler,

expressed the view that if the political parties wanted to 'horse-trade' over disputed ballot results, it was their own affair. The mandate of the Independent Electoral Commission was not to attest to the unassailable accuracy of the outcome, but to ensure that the process was free and fair.[10]

The historic compromise that propelled the ANC and National Party into a coalition government is both fragile and unstable. Under the 'power-sharing' arrangement, Mandela named eighteen of the twenty-seven ministers who will serve in the unity Cabinet. In a move designed to reassure the business class and overseas investors, he asked Derek Keys, the minister of finance, to retain his portfolio in the new government. Yet, without quick results to reverse the long-term economic malaise and to provide a 'fair share' of material rewards for its deprived supporters, the ANC's honeymoon could possibly be shortlived. If there is a lesson in history, it is that the momentary epiphanies accompanying political emancipation often yield to the more mundane problems of poverty and deprivation. While a comparison between the mid 1980s Corazon Aquino regime in the Philippines and the post-apartheid political order in South Africa may be well off the mark, the dashed hopes that eventually followed in the wake of the 'people power' euphoria offers only one recent historical example of 'failed revolution', where a wildly popular political movement symbolizing an open-ended promise of structural reform and social progress ran aground.

Facing an Uncertain Future

The dramatic entry of the ANC onto the centre-stage of politics prompted analysts to search for historical analogies and ideal-types by which to situate the organization and its key figures within a wider comparative and socio-historical context. For all of Mandela's charisma, many key players in the South African political drama contend that they are unsure what lies at the heart of his political vision. For sure, political labels cannot substitute for critical analysis and, because they sometimes obscure more than they illuminate, they ought to be employed with considerable care. Nevertheless, it can be said that Mandela is often regarded as a chameleon-like figure. At key points in his career, political observers have identified him as a 'militant and a moderate, an autocrat and a democrat, an economic populist and a friend of big business'.[11] The surge of popular support for the ANC engendered by its electoral victory has provided Mandela with a propitious opportunity to construct a political platform that will enable him temporarily to reconcile through his own person the conflicting social demands placed on the new regime. Because of its deep roots in the popular classes, its legitimate claims to mass loyalty, and its doctrinal commitment faithfully to serve a multiclass constituency, the ANC-in-government has acquired some of the main features that characterize populist regimes. Populism is simply a concrete expression of Marx's concept of Bonapartism, an unstable political situation which entails a temporary equilibrium of all social and class forces, the exact character and form of which differs in accordance with its peculiar historical circumstances. 'A key element of all populist regimes', Tariq Ali suggests in another context, is '"the man on horseback" who for a time reflects the hopes of both the oppressor and oppressed classes, but who ultimately destroys the illusions of the latter and is then struck down by the former'.[12] These historical limits of populism loom large for reformist-minded political regimes that put blind faith in their long-term ability to 'stand above' the nitty-gritty of class and social antagonisms. The ANC leadership is aware of the inherent dangers and pitfalls of populism, and has taken giant strides toward avoiding this fate.

· The elections are only the springboard for renewed struggles over the shape and pace of socio-economic policies. The most perplexing dilemma facing the new economic managers of post-apartheid South Africa is how to offset the debilitating effects of self-sustaining capital flight, while meeting repayments on the US$17 billion debt and managing a R45 billion rand financial liability. The fierce conflicts between those organized interest groups promoting private enterprise and *laissez faire* doctrines and those committed to strongly interventionist (in some cases avowedly socialist) economic-recovery programmes are still in their infancy. For the ANC, the centrepiece of its alternative economic strategy is the Reconstruction and Development Programme (RDP). The RDP acts as the guiding framework for a comprehensive policy agenda and a philosophy of governance for the ANC and its major allies – Communists, trade unionists, civics, small businessmen, progressive professional associations, and others. The main objective of the RDP is to unlock existing resources to meet housing, electricity, education and health needs of the vast majority of the population. The ANC leadership is banking so much of its future on the success of the RDP that it appointed the highly respected former general secretary of COSATU, Jay Naidoo, minister without portfolio, with the principal task of coordinating the programme's implementation across various ministries and administrative departments.[13]

On balance, the observed tendency of the ANC leadership to gravitate to the political centre has caused concern within left-wing circles about the metamorphosis of the ANC into an 'electoral machine' resembling something akin to a traditional social-democratic party. Manoeuvring to forestall any tendencies toward post-election backsliding on prior commitments, the militant left wing of the ANC has adopted the RDP as its watchword. Socialist and radical forces inside the ANC promote implementation of the RDP as the linchpin of an ongoing political strategy to uplift and energize the popular masses.[14] The RDP housing programme, which was borrowed almost verbatim from SANCO policy statements, is premissed on the inviolable principle that decent shelter is a 'human right'. The ANC has set a target of providing one million low-cost homes over the first five years, with 300,000 houses a year thereafter. These houses, complete with a full set of internal services, will carry sufficient state subsidies to be affordable to even the poorest residents of the townships.[15]

There is no doubt that this first post-apartheid government of national unity faces problems of such magnitude and scope that they defy solution within the framework of the existing social system. The root causes of economic malaise and political instability are structural in nature, and can be traced to gross inequalities in wealth, power, skills and opportunities. Without a massive shift in state expenditures for housing and welfare, coupled with job creation on a significant scale, the feared 'insider/ outsider', or '30–70 per cent solution', will certainly become a permanent feature of the post-apartheid socio-economic landscape. Burgeoning shack settlements that rival the Brazilian *favelas* are the result of at least a decade of uncontrolled mass migration of impoverished work-seekers from small towns and rural areas. These teeming slums are only sporadically organized, and neither the ANC, Inkatha, PAC, nor the civics can claim to have broken the back of autocratic 'warlordism' and the accompanying degraded clientelism which it spawned, and to have steered the survivalist-oriented politics in a progressive direction.

From a broader standpoint, South Africa is currently in the midst of a complex historical process involving the wholesale dismantling of an economic-growth model and an accompanying political system that took shape during the post-1948 apartheid era. Free-market liberalization, deregulation, privatization, restructuring of industrial relations, and embryonic corporatism are not just ad hoc, momentary responses to international and local pressures, but the opening move in a wide-ranging effort on the part of large-scale capital and its allies to initiate a new accumulation strategy inextricably linked to the competitiveness of South African business enterprises in the world marketplace. In the minds of the propertied classes, restoring the vitality of capital requires the recasting of the hegemonic bloc of class forces under a new and enlightened leadership where rights of citizenship and political participation can no longer be grounded in the restrictive codes of formalized racial discrimination. The transition to formal democratic rule signals a wider acceptance of liberal-democratic norms, but does not indicate an endorsement of programmes designed to distribute social resources more equitably or a willingness to transfer accumulated wealth from the 'haves' to the 'have-nots'. For left-wing critics, the installation of an ANC-dominated government of national unity merely modifies and reconfigures the physiognomy of the dominant bloc of class forces, and marks a displacement of direct oligarchic control into a wider hegemony that is neither stable nor permanent.

At the centre of the struggle over democracy, as Evelyne Stephens contends, 'lies the question of power – of access to state power and the consequences of access to state power for control over economic resources'.[16] The ANC pins its hopes on the capacity of purposive state action to alter present-day realities and to chart a more equitable and productive future. Yet from the outset, the ANC is handicapped in several ways. The paradigm of liberal-democratic politics rests on a narrow range of issues (notably, economic growth, distribution of state-accumulated resources, and national security) and modes of conflict resolution (particularly, pluralist party competition, representative government and collective bargaining).[17] By its very nature, 'power-sharing' is a prescription for accommodation that often entails a subtle 'feudalization' of the state administration, where, in accordance with the disaggregating logic of 'parcellized sovereignty', the branches, agencies, boards and commissions are divided into 'mini-fiefdoms' shared out amongst rival interest groups. A weakened state administration, divided along party and institutional lines, is an undisguised recipe for stasis and inaction. Without the infra-structural power of the state machinery to implement and enforce its policy innovations, the ANC may find its reformist efforts frustrated at every turn and its economic recovery and upliftment proposals derailed by fractious infighting. With the paralysis of the state–party nexus, the theatre of struggle would shift to the popular classes, and their efforts to break the deadlock would hinge largely on their capacity to exert sufficient pressure from below and to envision a historically viable alternative.

Notes

Introduction

1. Percy Qoboza, editor, *City Press*, 20 April 1986, cited in Colin Bundy, 'Introduction', in David Everatt and Elinor Sisulu, eds., *Black Youth in Crisis*, Johannesburg 1992, p. 1. This quotation is perhaps an overly gloomy way to begin. I do not want to convey the utterly false message that children *en masse* constitute a wayward, rootless 'lost generation', somehow beyond the pale of respectability. But I do want to lay stress on the 'dehumanizing' consequences of apartheid rule.

2. Seymour Martin Lipset, 'Compromise Needed in Pretoria', *Times Literary Supplement*, 20 September 1991, p. 9.

3. Tom Lodge, 'Review', *African Studies Review*, vol. 34, no. 2, 1991, pp. 134–5.

4. Nicos Poulantzas, *Classes in Contemporary Capitalism*, London 1975, p. 97.

5. Charles Maier, *Recasting Bourgeois Europe: Stabilization in France, Germany, and Italy in the Decade after World War I*, Princeton 1975, pp. 3–10.

6. 'Degreening the Land', *Africa Events*, May 1990, p. 29.

7. Interview with Dennis Brutus, cited in Kole Omotoso, 'Exile', *Southern African Review of Books*, vol. 5, no. 1, 1993, p. 7.

8. 'South Africa: The End of the Beginning', *Africa Confidential*, vol. 35, no. 1, 1994, pp. 3–4.

1. Shifting Political Alignments in the Twilight of Apartheid Rule

1. *The Economist*, 3 August 1991.

2. James Selfe, 'South Africa's National Management System', in Jacklyn Cock and Laurie Nathan, eds., *Society at War: The Militarisation of South Africa*, London 1989, p. 149; and R.W. Johnson, *How Long Will South Africa Survive?*, London 1977.

3. Robert Rotberg, 'South Africa's Nixon', *New York Times*, 14 March and 9 July 1989.

4. It must be noted that Nelson Mandela had consulted with key National Party figures long before the ANC was unbanned. So the surprise lay not in the fact that legal restrictions on outlawed political organizations were lifted and political prisoners were released, but in the precise timing and circumstances.

5. 'South Africa: Reforms Yes, Contrition … Certainly Not', *Africa Report*,

May/June 1991, p. 5.

6. These themes are covered in more detail in Robert Price, *The Apartheid State in Crisis: Political Transformation in South Africa, 1975–1990*, New York 1991, esp. pp. 99–152, 249–84.

7. Alexis de Tocqueville, *The Old Regime and the French Revolution*, trans. Stuart Gilbert, New York 1955, pp. 176–7; and Seymour Martin Lipset, 'Compromise Needed in Pretoria', *Times Literary Supplement*, 20 September 1991, pp. 9–10.

8. Ronald Aronson, 'Is Socialism on the Agenda? An Open Letter to the South African Left', *Transformation* 14, 1991, pp. 5–8; 'South Africa I: Two Kings, One Crown', *Africa Confidential*, vol. 31, no. 4, 1991, pp. 1–2.

9. David Everatt, 'Death Squads', *Southern African Review of Books*, vol. 5, no. 1, 1993, p.4.

10. *Observer*, 18 September 1992.

11. In the initial rounds of discussions, the ANC insisted on a president who would be head of state and chief executive, along with a prime minister and Cabinet, both appointed by the president and subordinate to him. The National Party deviated from conventional arrangements in this regard, basing its alternative proposal of a multi-party executive college on the Swiss example. The college would consist of three to five members of each of the strongest parties in the first house of parliament, and it would decide matters by consensus and its chairmanship would rotate. A multi-party Cabinet would be appointed by, and be subordinate to, this executive college. Both the ANC and the National Party agreed on the creation of two houses of parliament. Whereas the ANC wanted the second house to have delaying powers, the National Party wanted it effectively to have a veto, which would mean that legislation could only be passed if both houses agreed. In the end, the ANC position triumphed. At one point the National Party proposed that at the local level property owners, tenants and rate-payers should have greater representation than other voters. For the ANC, this qualified franchise represented nothing more than a thinly veiled mechanism for using class privilege in order to maintain racial imbalances (Harold Pakendorf, 'Coming to Grips with Power', *Africa Report*, November/December 1991, pp. 49–51; 'Slowly Taking Shape', *Financial Mail*, 6 September 1991).

12. 'Optimism as *Apartheid* Dies', *Tribune*, 21 June 1991.

13. 'South Africa: New Reality', *New York Times*, 23 December 1991; 'The Struggle Continues', *The Economist*, 2 November 1991; 'Fewer Options for South Africa's Rightists', *New York Times*, 1 March 1992.

14. Mike Morris, 'State, Capital, and Growth: The Political Economy of the National Question', in Stephen Gelb, ed., *South Africa's Economic Crisis*, London 1991, pp. 54–5.

15. 'Keeping the Promise', *Financial Mail*, 21 June 1991; *Argus*, 7 September 1991; Patrick Laurence, 'The Browning of FW's Nats', *Star*, 31 May 1991; *New York Times*, 9 February 1992; Michael Morris and Shaun Johnson, 'Sensation as "House of Hendrickse" is Toppled', *Star*, 1 February 1992; and 'Poaching Guns in the Rumour Factory', *Weekly Mail*, 5–11 February 1993.

16. 'South Africa: Back on Speaking Terms', *Africa Confidential*, vol. 33, no. 17, 1992, p. 4.

17. 'Optimism as *Apartheid* Dies'; and *New York Times*, 4 April 1992.

18. Morris, 'State, Capital, and Growth', pp. 57–67.

19. Morris, 'State, Capital, and Growth', pp. 33–58; and Stephen Gelb, 'Over-

view', in Gelb, ed., *South Africa's Economic Crisis*, pp. 1–32.

20. Mark Swilling, 'Introduction: The Politics of Stalemate', in Philip Frankel, Noam Pines and Mark Swilling, eds., *State, Resistance and Change in South Africa*, London 1988, p. 11.

21. 'Falling on Deaf Ears', *Financial Mail*, 1 November 1991; and 'South Africa I: The Economic Battlefield', *Africa Confidential*, vol. 32, no. 23, 1991, pp. 1–2. While the state administration succeeded in breaking up some of these state-owned monopolies into smaller economic units, neo-liberal state managers, largely due to the counter-campaign organized by COSATU, were unable to carry out their desired goal of selling the accumulated assets of these companies to private investors.

22. Sampie Terreblanche, 'Equity and Growth', in Robert Schrire, ed., *Wealth or Poverty? Critical Choices for South Africa*, Cape Town 1992, p. 559.

23. Gelb, 'Overview', p. 29.

24. Colin McCarthy, 'Industrial Development and Distribution', in Schrire, ed., *Wealth or Poverty?*, pp. 458–9; Ronald Bethlehem, 'Issues of Economic Restructuring', in ibid., pp. 540–42; and Terreblanche, 'Equity and Growth', pp. 559–60.

25. Mike Morris appropriately called this process the 'Great Lockout' where 'a 50% solution will allow some South Africans to embrace opportunity and privilege, but banish the rest to the margins.', Mike Morris, 'Who's In and Who's Out?', *Work in Progress* 87, 1993, p. 6. See Mike Morris and Vishnu Padayachee, 'State Reform Policy in South Africa', *Transformation* 7, 1988, pp. 1–27; Morris, 'State, Capital, and Growth', pp. 33–58.

26. Patrick Laurence, 'Freedom Charter is ANC Beacon', *Star*, 22 October 1991.

27. Nicoli Nattrass, 'The ANC's Economic Policy: A Critical Perspective', in Schrire, ed., *Wealth or Poverty?*, pp. 623–4. The quotation from Nelson Mandela is taken from the *Sowetan*, 5 March 1990.

28. Nattrass, 'The ANC's Economic Policy', pp. 624–5.

29. For a detailed summary, see the extract from the ANC Macroeconomic Research Group Report entitled 'Making Democracy Work: A Framework for Macroeconomic Policy in South Africa (December 1993)', in *IDS Bulletin*, vol. 25, no. 1, 1994, University of Sussex, pp. 3–9.

30. See ibid., p. 3; and Avril Joffe, David Kaplan, Raphael Kaplinsky and David Lewis, 'An Industrial Strategy for a Post-*Apartheid* South Africa', *IDS Bulletin*, vol. 25, no. 1, 1994, University of Sussex, pp. 17–23.

31. See 'Recommendations on Post-*Apartheid* Economic Policy', *Transformation* 12, 1990, pp. 2–15; Stephen Gelb, "Democratising Economic Growth: Alternative Growth Models for the Future', ibid., pp. 25–41; and Raphael Kaplinsky, 'A Growth Path for a Post-*Apartheid* South Africa', *Transformation* 16, 1991, pp. 49–55.

32. Nattrass, 'The ANC's Economic Policy', pp. 623–4. See also Dave Lewis, 'Markets, Ownership, and Industrial Competitiveness', Industrial Strategy Project, background paper for June and July presentations, unpublished, June 1993.

33. Glenda Daniels, 'Growth through Redistribution', *Work in Progress* 78, 1991, pp. 37–8.

34. Terreblanche, 'Equity and Growth', pp. 559–60.

35. See, for example, Terence Moll, 'Macroeconomic Redistributive Packages in Developing Countries', in Peter Moll, Nicoli Nattrass and Lieb Loots, eds., *Redistribution: How Can it Work in South Africa?*, Cape Town 1991, pp. 22ff. See also

Albert Hirschman, *The Rhetoric of Reaction: Perversity, Futility, and Jeopardy*, Cambridge, Mass. 1991.

36. For a summary, see John Saul, 'South Africa: Between "Barbarism" and "Structural Reform"', *New Left Review* 188, July–August 1991, pp. 3–44.

37. 'South Africa I: The Economic Battlefield', pp. 1–2; and Barry Streek, 'Big Four Control 80.7% of Shares of JSE', *Business Day*, 20 April 1990.

38. 'South Africa II: Dividends from Democracy', *Africa Confidential* vol. 35, no. 9, 1994, pp. 3–4.

39. Patrick Bond, 'Scenario Plundering', *Southern African Review of Books* 26, July/August 1993, p. 3.

40. 'Falling on Deaf Ears', *Financial Mail*, 1 November 1991.

41. See, for example, Bobby Godsell and Jim Buys, 'Growth and Poverty: Towards some Shared Goals', in Schrire, ed., *Wealth or Poverty?*, pp. 635–56.

42. Peter Moll, ed., *The Great Economic Debate*, Johannesburg 1991. See also Bill Freund, 'Reviews', *South African Labour Bulletin*, vol. 16, no. 5, 1992, p. 79.

43. Robert Davies, 'Rethinking Socialist Economics for South Africa', *African Communist*, 2nd quarter 1991, p. 39.

44. 'Struggling with the New Orthodoxy', *Africa Confidential*, vol. 35, no. 9, 1994, p. 4.

45. These issues are spelled out in Nattrass, 'The ANC's Economic Policy', pp. 623–4.

46. Colin Bundy, 'Theory of a Special Type', *Work in Progress* 89, 1993, p. 18.

47. Bill Keller, 'Can South Africa Do It?', *New York Times*, 24 April 1994. 'Another brake on economic radicalism is the rapid growth of the black middle class which is a key constituency for the ANC and vitally important to policy input. Recent research from the University of Natal indicates that the income gap between rich and poor blacks is almost as wide as that between whites and blacks. Of the wealthiest 20 per cent of households, about a quarter are black; their incomes are rising faster than any others in society. However, the incomes of the 40 per cent of the poorest blacks have been declining in relative terms for 20 years. A white underclass is now growing' ('South Africa II: Dividends from Democracy', p. 3).

48. 'Mandela Actively Courts Foreign Investors', *African Business*, November 1993, p. 5.

49. 'ANC Woos Foreign Investors', *African Business*, October 1993; and Anne Shepard, 'Waiting for Investment', *Africa Report*, November/December 1993, pp. 17–19.

50. Leslie Wayne, 'A New Day Dawns for South African Investment', *New York Times*, 7 June 1994.

51. 'Mandela Actively Courts Foreign Investors', p. 5; NAFCOC Promotes Black Businesses Abroad', *African Business*, June 1994, pp. 28–9.

52. *Southern Africa Report*, 29 October 1993 and 28 January 1994.

53. 'What Happens Now to Investor Confidence?', *African Business*, May 1994, pp. 12–13; and 'U.S. Mounts a Major Thrust', *Southern Africa Report*, 3 December 1993.

54. Leslie Wayne, 'A New Day Dawns for South African Investment', *New York Times*, 7 June 1994.

55. Shepard, 'Waiting for Investment', pp. 17–19; 'Honeywell's Route Back to South Africa Market', *New York Times*, 31 January 1994; and 'What Happens Now

to Investor Confidence?', pp. 12–13.

56. 'South Africa II: Dividends from Democracy', p. 5.

57. Joseph Hanlon, 'Can COSATU Ride the IMF Tiger?', *Work in Progress* 89, 1993, pp. 26–7. In the desire to offset the potentially deleterious effects of overseas investments, both COSATU and the ANC developed investor codes emphasizing socially useful investments as well as basic trade-union rights.

2. The Fateful Bounty of Apartheid

1. 'Starry-eyed Optimism', *Financial Times*, 18 November 1993.

2. Patrick Bond, 'South Africa: Towards Grassroots Socialism', *Against the Current*, vol. 7, no. 2, 1992, pp. 21–7; Alan Hirsch, 'The Origins and Implications of South Africa's Continuing Financial Crisis', *Transformation* 9, 1989, pp. 31–50; and Zavareth Rustomjee, 'Capital Flight Under *Apartheid*', *Transformation* 15, 1991, pp. 89–103.

3. 'South Africa I: The Economic Battlefield', *Africa Confidential*, vol. 32, no. 23, November 1991, p. 1.

4. For various estimates, see Dot Keet, 'Unemployment', *South African Labour Bulletin*, vol. 16, no. 2, 1991, pp. 37–41; 'Business Sitting on its Hands and Waiting', *Financial Times*, 18 November 1993.

5. *Sunday Tribune*, 26 January 1992; 'South Africa I: The Economic Battlefield', pp. 1–2; *Sowetan*, 25 April 1991; 'Business Sitting on its Hands and Waiting'; *Business Day*, 10 January 1991; 'Pay One, Pay All', *Financial Mail*, 29 March 1991, p. 22.

6. *Africa News*, 17–30 August 1992; *Financial Mail*, 7 December 1990; James Henry, 'Growing Nowhere', *The New Republic*, 20 and 27 August 1990, pp. 21–2; Samir Amin, SA in the Global Economic System', *Work in Progress* 87, 1993, p. 10; Keet, 'Unemployment', pp. 37–8; 'South Africa Faces Lingering Wounds to its Economy', *New York Times*, 14 July 1991; 'Time to Move On', *New York Times*, 21 July 1991; 'South Africa I: The Economic Battlefield', p. 3.

7. Douglas Anglin, 'Ripe, Ripening, or Overripe? Sanctions as an Inducement to Negotiations: The South African Case', *International Journal* 45, Spring 1990, pp. 360–85; Robert Edgar, ed., *Sanctioning South Africa*, Trenton, NJ 1989; Heribert Adam and Kogila Moodley, *The Opening of the Apartheid Mind: Options for the New South Africa*, Berkeley, Los Angeles and London 1993, pp. 54–8.

8. Brian Kahn, 'The Crisis and South Africa's Balance of Payments', in Stephen Gelb, ed., *South Africa's Economic Crisis*, Cape Town 1991, pp. 59–87; Kahn, 'Capital Flight and Exchange Controls in South Africa', Research Paper No. 4, Centre for the Study of the South African Economy and International Finance, London School of Economics; B.W. Smit and B.A. Mocke, 'Capital Flight from South Africa: Magnitude and Causes', *South African Journal of Economics*, vol. 59, no. 2, 1991, pp. 101–17; and 'South Africa I: The Economic Battlefield', p. 3.

9. See Stephen Gelb, 'South Africa's Economic Crisis: An Overview', in Gelb, ed., *South Africa's Economic Crisis*, pp. 1–32; Fuad Cassim, 'Growth, Crisis and Change in the South African Economy', in John Suckling and Landeg White, eds., *After Apartheid: Renewal of the South African Economy*, London and Trenton, NJ 1988, pp. 1–18; and Patrick Bond, *Commanding Heights and Economic Control: New Economics for a New South Africa*, Johannesburg 1991. For a more conventional liberal view,

see Nicoli Nattrass and Elisabeth Ardington, eds., *The Political Economy of South Africa*, Cape Town 1990; and Iraj Abedian and Barry Standish, eds., *Economic Growth in South Africa: Selected Policy Issues*, Oxford 1992.

10. The term 'racial Fordism' is closely linked with the French-inspired 'regulation' approach. See Gelb, 'South Africa's Economic Crisis: An Overview', pp. 1–32. This perspective is not without controversy. See Bond, *Commanding Heights and Economic Control*, pp. 29–36.

11. Servaas van der Berg, 'Long Term Economic Trends and Development Prospects in South Africa', *African Affairs*, vol. 88, no. 351, 1989, pp. 187–204.

12. Cassim, 'Growth, Crisis, and Change in the South African Economy', pp. 1–2.

13. Jean Leger and Martin Nicol, 'South Africa's Gold Mining Crisis: Changes for Restructuring', *Transformation* 20, 1992, p. 17.

14. 'Gone are the Golden Days', *Weekly Mail*, 28 March–4 April 1991; Bill Freund, 'South African Gold Mining in Transformation', in Gelb, ed., *South Africa's Economic Crisis*, pp. 110–28.

15. 'More Gold Mines under Threat', *Weekly Mail*, 4–11 April 1991; 'A Sad Stope Opera', *Financial Mail*, 5 April 1991, pp. 20–21; 'Mining Wage Settlement: Another Step Sideways', *South African Labour Bulletin*, vol. 16, no. 1, 1991, pp. 41–5; 'South Africa I: The Economic Battlefield', pp. 1–2; 'Hard Thinking', *Financial Times*, 5 June 1992; 'Gold Price Drop', *Africa News*, 8–21 February 1993.

16. Leger and Nicol, 'South Africa's Gold Mining Crisis', pp. 23–4.

17. Many of the ideas for this paragraph were derived from Avril Joffee, Judy Maller, and Eddie Webster, 'South Africa's Industrialization: The Challenge Facing Labour', unpublished MS, Sociology of Work Unit, University of the Witwatersrand, Johannesburg.

18. Cassim, 'Growth, Crisis, and Change in the South African Economy', p. 4; David Lewis, 'The Character and Consequences of Conglomeration in the South African Economy', *Transformation* 16, 1991, pp. 29–48. For a lengthy discussion, see Robert Davies et al., 'The Capitalist Ruling Class: Major Forces and Social Organisations', *The Struggle for South Africa*, Volume One, London 1984, pp. 51–130.

19. Anthony Black, 'Manufacturing Development and the Economic Crisis', in Gelb, ed., *South Africa's Economic Crisis*, pp. 156–74; and Avril Joffe and Moses Ngoasheng, 'Industrial Restructuring in the De Klerk Era', in Glenn Moss and Ingrid Obery, eds., *South African Review 6: From 'Red Friday' to CODESA*, Johannesburg 1992, pp. 478–9.

20. Joffe and Ngoasheng, 'Industrial Restructuring', pp. 479–80; and Black, 'Manufacturing Development and the Economic Crisis', pp. 161–3.

21. 'South Africa I: The Economic Battlefield', pp. 2–3; and *Business Day*, 22 January 1992.

22. David Cooper, 'Ownership and Control of Agriculture in South Africa', in Suckling and White, eds., *After Apartheid*, pp. 48–9; and Eckart Kassier and Jan Groenewald, 'Agriculture: An Overview', in Robert Schrire, ed., *Wealth or Poverty? Critical Choices for South Africa*, Cape Town 1992, pp. 330–52.

23. Simon Brand et al., 'Agriculture and Redistribution: Growth with Equity', in Schrire, ed., *Wealth or Poverty?*, pp. 353–75; and Karl Magyar, 'South Africa's Political Economy: Perspectives on the Country as a Fragile Economic Arrangement', in Albert Venter, ed., *South African Government and Politics*, Johannesburg 1989, pp. 222–3.

24. Cooper, 'Ownership and Control', pp. 49–50.

25. 'Crisis Year for Farmers', *Financial Times*, 5 June 1992; Magyar, 'South Africa's Political Economy', pp. 222–3; and Mike De Klerk, 'The Accumulation Crisis in Agriculture', in Gelb, ed., *South Africa's Economic Crisis*, pp. 198–227.

26. Doug Hindson and Owen Crankshaw, 'New Jobs, New Skills, New Divisions – The Changing Structure of SA's Workforce', *South African Labour Bulletin*, vol. 15, no. 1, 1990, pp. 23–31; and Doug Hindson, 'The Restructuring of Labour Markets in South Africa: 1970s and 1980s', in Gelb, ed., *South Africa's Economic Crisis*, pp. 228–32.

27. Adrienne Bird and Geoff Schreiner, 'COSATU at the Crossroads', *South African Labour Bulletin*, vol. 16, no. 6, 1982, pp. 26–7.

28. One visible sign of the growing socio-economic polarization is the fact that one-third of Soweto's households employ domestic servants, recruited from the impoverished homelands and paid only R90 per month (*Natal Witness*, 25 March 1992).

29. David Lewis, 'Unemployment and the Current Crisis', in Gelb, ed., *South Africa's Economic Crisis*, pp. 244–66.

30. The NUM estimates that unless gold prices rise dramatically, 100,000 jobs will be lost in the mining industry over the next decade ('Mass Retrenchments', *South African Labour Bulletin*, vol. 16, no. 6, 1991, p. 11).

31. Christian Rogerson, 'Deregulation, Subcontracting, and the "(In)formalization" of Small-scale Manufacturing', in Eleanor Preston-Whyte and Christian Rogerson, eds., *South Africa's Informal Economy*, Cape Town 1991, pp. 365–85; and C.M. Rogerson, 'Industrial Subcontracting and Home-Work in South Africa: Policy Issues from the International Experience', *Africa Insight*, vol. 23, no. 1, 1993, pp. 47–54.

32. Gilton Klerck et al., 'Casualisation and Sub-Contracting: Employer Weapons Against Unions', *South African Labour Bulletin*, vol. 15, no. 7, 1991, p. 47.

33. Adam and Moodley, *The Opening of the Apartheid Mind*, p. 93.

34. 'Business Sitting on its Hands and Waiting'; and Claudia Manning, 'Dynamo or Safety Net', *Work in Progress* 87, 1993, pp. 12–13. The Development Bank of South Africa (DBSA) arrived at considerably higher figures, estimating the informal sector labour-force at around 3.5 million and its economic impact at about R30 billion, where hawking alone accounted for R44 million a month. See Gwen Amell (with Patrick Bond), 'The Crazy Pavement War Goes On', *Africa South & East*, November 1992, p. 27.

35. See Wolfgang Thomas, 'Supporting Job Creation: Small Business and Informal Sector Development', in Schrire, ed., *Wealth or Poverty?*, pp. 481–94.

36. 'Business Sitting on its Hands and Waiting'; Manning, 'Dynamo or Safety Net', pp. 12–13; Marie Kirsten, 'A Quantitative Assessment of the Informal Sector'; and Leslie Bank, 'A Culture of Violence: The Migrant Taxi Trade in Qwa-Qwa, 1980–90', both in Preston-Whyte and Rogerson, eds., *South Africa's Informal Economy*, pp. 148–60, and 124–5, respectively.

37. Belinda Bozzoli, 'The Meaning of Informal Work: Some Women's Stories', in Preston-Whyte and Rogerson, eds, *South Africa's Informal Economy*, pp. 15–16; L. Peattie, 'An Idea in Good Currency and How it Grew: The Informal Sector', *World Development* 15, 1987, pp. 851–60. '[The informal sector] is neither informal nor a sector, but its designation as such represents the urgent desire of social engineers to separate an economic arena where legal regulations and official categories pre-

vail and an arena where they do not', Frederick Cooper cogently argued. 'The so-called informal sector represents a negation of the kind of well-ordered, hard-working city that capital and the state [would prefer].' See Frederick Cooper, *On the African Waterfront: Urban Disorder and the Transformation of Work in Colonial Mombasa*, New Haven 1987, pp. 181–2.

38. Eleanor Preston-Whyte and Christian Rogerson, 'South Africa's Informal Economy: Past, Present and Future', in Preston-Whyte and Rogerson, eds., *South Africa's Informal Economy*, pp. 2–3.

·39. Ibid., p. 2; and Kirsten, 'A Quantitative Assessment of the Informal Sector', pp. 148–9.

40. C.M. Rogerson, 'Late *Apartheid* and the Urban Informal Sector', in Suckling and White, eds., *After Apartheid*, pp. 135–6; Christian Rogerson, 'Tracking the Informal Economy', *South African Review* 6, pp. 378–87; Christian Rogerson 'The Absorptive Capacity of the Informal Sector in the South African City', in David Smith, ed., *The Apartheid City and Beyond: Urbanisation and Social Change in South Africa*, London 1992, pp. 161–71; and W.H. Thomas, 'South Africa's Growing Informal Sector', *Sash*, vol. 31, no. 3, 1988, pp. 31–5.

41. Rogerson, 'Late *Apartheid* and the Urban Informal Sector', pp. 132–3; and Paulus Zulu, 'Legitimating the Culture of Survival', in Preston-Whyte and Rogerson, eds, *South Africa's Informal Economy* pp. 115–23.

42. Manuel Castells and Alejandro Portes, 'World Underneath: The Origins, Dynamics, and Effects of the Informal Economy', in A. Portes, M. Castells, and L.A. Benton, eds., *The Informal Economy: Studies in Advanced and Less Developed Countries*, Baltimore 1989, p. 11.

43. See Trudi Hartzenburg and A. Leiman, 'The Informal Economy and its Growth Potential', in Abedian and Standish, eds., *Economic Growth in South Africa*, pp. 187–214; and Iraj Abedian, and M. de Smidt, 'The Informal Economy of South Africa', *South African Journal of Economics*, vol. 58, no. 4, 1990, pp. 404–24.

44. See Deborah Hart, 'The Informal Sector in South African Literature'; Rolf Dauskardt, '"Urban Herbalism": The Restructuring of Informal Survival in Johannesburg'; Mary de Haas, 'Of Joints and Jollers: Culture and Class in Natal Shebeens'; all in Preston-Whyte and Rogerson, eds., *South Africa's Informal Economy*, pp. 68–86, 87–100, 101–114, respectively.

45. Preston-Whyte and Rogerson, 'South Africa's Informal Economy: Past, Present and Future', p. 1.

46. Claudia Manning, 'Rand a Bag!', *Work in Progress* 87, 1993, p. 13.

47. Meshack Khosa, 'Routes, Ranks and Rebels: Feuding in the Taxi Revolution', *Journal of Southern African Studies*, vol. 18, no. 1, 1992, pp. 232–51; M. Khosa, 'The Black Taxi Revolution', in Nattrass and Ardington, eds., *The Political Economy of South Africa*, pp. 207–16; and J.B. Barolsky, 'Follow that Taxi: Success Story in Informal Sector', *Indicator South Africa*, vol. 7, no. 2, 1990, pp. 59–63.

48. Meshack Khosa, 'Capital Accumulation in the Black Taxi Industry', in Preston-Whyte and Rogerson, eds., *South Africa's Informal Economy*, pp. 310–25; and Leslie Bank, 'A Culture of Violence', pp. 124–141.

49. Bill Keller, 'Deadly Free Market: South Africa's Warrior Taxis', *New York Times*, 17 August 1994.

50. Meshack Khosa, 'Changing State Policy and the Black Taxi Industry in Soweto', in Smith, ed., *The Apartheid City and Beyond*, pp. 182–92.

51. C. McCaul, *No Easy Ride: The Rise and Future of the Black Taxi Industry*,

Johannesburg 1990; 'Bloody War as Industry Implodes on Itself' and 'Sabta Fat Cats Should Take the Blame', *Weekly Mail*, 5–11 February 1993; and Bill Keller, 'Deadly Free Market: South Africa's Warrior Taxis', *New York Times*, 17 August 1994.

52. Bank, 'A Culture of Violence', pp. 131–6; and Leslie Bank, 'The Making of the QwaQua "Mafia"? Patronage and Protection in the Migrant Taxi Business', *African Studies* 49, 1990, pp. 71–93.

53. Colin Murray, 'Displaced Urbanization: South Africa's Rural Slums', *African Affairs*, vol. 86, no. 344, 1987, p. 311.

54. John Pickles, 'Industrial Restructuring, Peripheral Industrialization, and Rural Development in South Africa', *Antipode*, vol. 23, no. 1, 1991, pp. 68–91; and Murray, 'Displaced Urbanisation', pp. 313–14.

55. Paul Maylam, 'The Rise and Decline of Urban *Apartheid* in South Africa', *African Affairs*, vol. 89, no. 354, 1990, pp. 57–84; and Doug Hindson, *Pass Controls and the Urban African Proletariat*, Johannesburg 1987, pp. 1–15, 52–96.

56. William Cobbett with Brian Nakedi, 'Behind the "Curtain" at Botshabelo: Redefining the Urban Labour Market in South Africa', *Review of African Political Economy* 40, 1987, pp. 32–46; Jeremy Grest, 'The Crisis of Local Government in South Africa', in Philip Frankel, Noam Pines and Mark Swilling, eds., *State, Resistance, and Change in South Africa*, London 1988, pp. 90–93; and Alan Mabin, 'The Dynamics of Urbanization since 1960', in Mark Swilling, Richard Humphries and Khehla Shubane, eds., *Apartheid City in Transition*, Cape Town 1991, pp. 33–47.

57. See J. McCarthy and P. Wellings, 'The Regional Restructuring of Politics in Contemporary South Africa', *Social Dynamics*, vol. 15, no. 1, 1989, pp. 15–35; Richard Tomlinson, *Urbanization in Post-Apartheid South Africa*, London 1990; and Mike Kenyon and Barry du Toit, 'From Forced Removal to Upgrade: State Strategy in the Border Corridor', in Glenn Moss and Ingrid Obery, eds., *South African Review* 5, Johannesburg 1989, pp. 446–56.

58. William Cobbett, '"Orderly Urbanization": Continuity and Change in Influx Control', *South African Labour Bulletin*, vol. 11, no. 8, 1986, pp. 106–21; Vanessa Watson, 'South African Urbanisation Policy: Past and Future', *South African Labour Bulletin*, vol. 11, no. 8, 1986, pp. 77–90.

59. Cecil Seethal, 'Restructuring the Local State in South Africa: Regional Services Councils and Crisis Resolution', *Political Geography Quarterly*, vol. 10, no. 1, 1991, pp. 8–25; Richard Humphries, 'Whither Regional Services Councils?' in Swilling et al., eds., *Apartheid City in Transition*, pp. 78–90; and V. Watson and A. Todes, 'Local Government Reform, Urban Crisis, and Development in South Africa', *Geoforum* 17, 1986, pp. 251–66.

60. See Dhiru Soni and Brij Maharaj, 'Emerging Urban Forms in Rural South Africa', *Antipode*, vol. 23, no. 1, 1991, pp. 47–67.

61. See Cobbett with Nakedi, 'Behind the "Curtain" at Botshabelo', p. 45; William Cobbett, 'A Test Case for Planned Urbanization', *Work in Progress* 42, 1986, pp. 15–19; William Cobbett, 'Industrial Decentralisation and Exploitation: The Case of Botshabelo', *South African Labour Bulletin*, vol. 12, no. 3, 1987, pp. 95–109.

62. Cobbett with Nakedi, 'Behind the "Curtain" at Botshabelo', p. 44.

63. 'South Africa: What Future for the Homelands?', *Africa Confidential*, vol. 29, no. 2, January 1988, pp. 1–2.

64. Andrew Boraine, 'Managing the Urban Crisis, 1986–1989', in *South African Review* 5, pp. 109–10.

65. Ibid., pp. 108–9; and Humphries, 'Whither Regional Services Councils?', pp. 78–90.

66. *Business Day*, 19 February 1991.

67. Rogerson, 'Industrial sub-Contracting and Home-Work in South Africa', pp. 47–9; Rogerson, 'Deregulation, Sub-Contracting and the "(In)formalization" of Small-scale Manufacturing', pp. 374–6; and D. Simon and S. Birch, '"Formalizing" the Informal Sector in a Changing South Africa: Small-scale Manufacturing on the Witwatersrand', *World Development* 20, 1992, pp. 1029–45.

68. 'Shifts in the Heartbeat of our Future', *Weekly Mail*, 11–17 April 1991; 'Guess Who's Here?', *Financial Mail*, 19 April 1991. For a discussion of 'global cities', see Saskia Sassen, *The Global City: New York, London, Tokyo*, Princeton, NJ 1991.

69. Jonathan Steinberg, Paul Van Zyl and Patrick Bond, 'Contradictions in the Transition from Urban *Apartheid*: Barriers to Gentrification in Johannesburg', in Smith, ed., *The Apartheid City and Beyond*, pp. 266–78; and Swilling et al., eds., *Apartheid City in Transition*.

70. One particularly distinctive, circular highrise housing complex situated on the edge of Yeoville near Hillbrow is often referred to as 'little Zaire' because of the large numbers of French-speaking African refugees who live there.

71. Steinberg et al., 'Contradictions in the Transition from Urban *Apartheid*', pp. 266–78.

3. On the Edge of Extinction

1. Mzwanele Mayekiso, 'The "Civics", Hope of the Townships', *Times Literary Supplement*, 1 April 1994.

2. Philip Harrison, 'The Policies and Politics of Informal Settlement in South Africa: A Historical Perspective', *Africa Insight*, vol. 22, no. 1, 1992, pp. 18–22.

3. W. Garces, 'Slum Improvement', in R. Pama et al., eds., *Low Income Housing, Technology, and Policy*, New York 1977, cited in Harrison, 'The Policies and Politics of Informal Settlement', p. 2.

4. *Cape Times*, 2 May 1991; and A. Bernstein, 'Informal Settlers: South Africa's New City Builders', *Optima*, vol. 37, no. 1, 1989, pp. 18–23.

5. Urban Foundation, *Informal Housing: The Current Situation*, Johannesburg 1991, p. 24; and Owen Crankshaw, 'Squatting, *Apartheid*, and Urbanisation on the Southern Witwatersrand', *African Affairs* 92, 1993, pp. 31–51.

6. This paragraph is based on Harrison, 'The Policies and Politics of Informal Settlement', p. 18.

7. Urban Foundation, *Informal Housing*, p. 7, Table 1. Some analysts estimated that around three million people lived in informal housing in the greater Durban area. However, the Witwatersrand and Durban areas exhibit quite dissimilar patterns when the type of informal housing is taken into account. In spite of the high media profile afforded to free-standing (illegal) squatter settlements, an estimated 85 per cent of shacks on the Witwatersrand were located in the backyards of the formal African townships. Peri-urban squatter settlements comprised less than a quarter of the total population of free-standing settlements on the Witwatersrand. At the other extreme of the national pattern, informal housing in the Durban metropolitan region occurs mainly as free-standing, peri-urban squatter settlements spread over a relatively wide geographical area (Crankshaw, 'Squatting, *Apartheid*,

and Urbanisation on the Southern Witwatersrand', pp. 34–5). For a historical overview of Durban, see Gavin Maasdorp, 'Informal Housing and Informal Employment: Case Studies in the Durban Metropolitan Region', in David Smith, ed., *Living Under Apartheid*, London 1982, pp. 143–63.

8. 'Dealing with Squatter Lords', *Reconstruct* 11, July 1993, p. 11.

9. *Cape Times*, 25 February 1991; *Sowetan*, 25 April 1991.

10. Harrison, 'The Policies and Politics of Informal Settlement', p. 18. Overall figures are considerably higher. By 1991, the estimated demand for housing, including the needs of the self-governing homelands, had climbed to 2.2 million units (*Cape Times*, 20 March 1991; and *Eastern Province Herald*, 25 April 1991).

11. *Cape Times*, 2 May 1991.

12. *New York Times*, 31 March 1991.

13. Urban Foundation, *Informal Housing*, Part 1, p. 7.

14. *Cape Times*, 20 March 1991; and *Eastern Province Herald*, 25 April 1991.

15. *New York Times*, 31 March 1991; and Crankshaw, 'Squatting, *Apartheid*, and Urbanisation', pp. 34–5.

16. Mosito Raphela, 'Alex Violence', *Work in Progress* 83, 1992, pp. 16–17.

17. *Business Day*, 19 February 1991.

18. For an excellent critique of the simplistic understanding of the strategy of 'ungovernability', including the work of Karen Jochelson referred to below, see Mzwanele Mayekiso, 'The Legacy of "Ungovernability"', *Southern African Review of Books*, vol. 5, no. 6, 1993, pp. 24–7.

19. Eddie Koch and Sarah Blecher, 'Youth "Comstotsis": Can the ANC Ride the Tiger?', *Weekly Mail*, 8–14 February 1991.

20. Karen Jochelson, 'Reform, Repression and Resistance in South Africa: A Case Study of Alexandra Township, 1979–1989', *Journal of Southern African Studies*, vol. 16, no. 1, 1990, p. 6.

21. It is not suggested here that the white minority regime was able successfully to crush the popular opposition in its entirety, but rather that the state-sponsored repression enabled the forces of law and order to prevent the insurrectionary current from developing beyond a certain point. See Pippa Green, 'Trade Unions and the State of Emergency', *South African Labour Bulletin*, vol. 11, no. 7, 1986, pp. 47–50; and Pippa Green, 'Northern Natal: Meeting UWUSA's Challenge', *South African Labour Bulletin*, vol. 12, no. 1, 1986, pp. 73–95.

22. Jenny Cargill, 'Creating a Culture of Debate', *Work in Progress* 73, 1991, p. 6.

23. Jo-Anne Collinge, 'The Struggle for Power', *Weekly Mail*, 15–21 February 1991.

24. 'More Townships Hit by Power Cuts', *Weekly Mail*, 18–24 January 1991; and *Star*, 26 January 1991.

25. *Citizen*, 28 February 1991; *Sowetan*, 6 February 1991; *Sowetan*, 8 February 1991; *Business Day*, 30 January 1991; and *Sowetan*, 17 January 1991.

26. Properly understood, the conjoined ideas of a 'lost generation' and 'marginalized youth' must be located within a wider analytic framework, and seen as a symptom of a deeper malaise caused by the social disintegration of black communities in South Africa. See Steve Mokwena, 'Living on the Wrong Side of the Law: Youth, Marginalisation, and Violence'; and Mamphela Ramphele, 'Social Disintegration in the Black Community'; both in David Everatt and Elinor Sisulu, eds., *Black Youth in Crisis: Facing the Future*, Johannesburg 1992, pp. 30–51, and pp. 10–29, respectively.

27. *Citizen*, 7 February 1991; *Citizen*, 8 February 1991; and Jeremy Seekings, *Heroes or Villians: Youth Politics in the 1980s*, Johannesburg 1993.

28. 'Acid Test for the ANC', *New Era*, vol. 6, no. 1, 1991, pp. 29–31; Paul Trewhela, 'The Trial of Winnie Mandela', *Searchlight South Africa*, vol. 2, no. 3, 1991, pp. 33–47.

29. *Sunday Times*, 31 March 1991.

30. *Sunday Tribune*, 7 April 1991; and 'ANC/PAC Battle Splits Border Township', *Weekly Mail*, 25–31 January 1991.

31. *Sunday Times*, 13 January 1991; and *Business Day*, 15 January 1991.

32. See Keith Breckenridge, 'Migrancy, Crime and Faction Fighting: The Role of the Isitshozi in the Development of Ethnic Organisations in the Compounds', *Journal of Southern African Studies*, vol. 16, no. 1, 1990, pp. 55–78; and Paul la Hausse, '"The Cows of Nongoloza": Youth, Crime and Amalaita Gangs in Durban, 1900–1936', *Journal of Southern African Studies*, vol. 16, no. 1, 1990, pp. 79–111.

33. Don Pinnock, 'Stone's Boys and the Making of a Cape Flats Mafia', in Belinda Bozzoli, ed., *Class, Community and Conflict: South African Perspectives*, Johannesburg 1987, pp. 418–35.

34. *Argus*, 5 January 1991; 'Gangs Thrive in Miasma of Mistrust', *Weekly Mail*, 11–17 January 1991. For an analytic treatment, see Wilfried Schärf, 'The Resurgence of Urban Street Gangs and Community Responses in Cape Town during the Late Eighties', in Desirée Hansson and Dirk van Zyl Smit, eds., *Towards Justice? Crime and State Control in South Africa*, Cape Town 1990, pp. 232–64.

35. Mokwena, 'Living on the Wrong Side of the Law', pp. 40–41; Shärf, 'The Resurgence of Urban Street Gangs'; and Dullah Omar, 'An Overview of State Lawlessness in South Africa', in Hansson and Smit, eds., *Towards Justice?*, pp. 17–27.

36. *Echo*, 24 January 1991; *Sowetan*, 4 January 1991. In April 1991, more than ten thousand people took to the streets in an unauthorized march to protest against police indifference to the 'Three Million Gang' terrorism and to the ongoing victimization of township residents (*Cape Times*, 26 April 1991). *Citizen*, 21 June 1991.

37. *Financial Mail*, 15 February 1991; *Pretoria News*, 28 January 1991.

38. *Cape Times*, 21 March 1991.

39. *Citizen*, 20 November 1990.

40. Mokwena, 'Living on the Wrong Side of the Law', p. 30.

41. *Cape Times*, 4 February 1991.

42. In investigating illegal trafficking in weapons, the *Weekly Mail* uncovered a well-organized smuggling network supplying heavy weaponry to Inkatha supporters on the East Rand. For R1,500 (US$600), a person could buy a used AK-47 rifle, carrying case, magazine of ammunition, and basic training in how to use it (see 'We Buy an Ak–47', *Weekly Mail*, 25 April 1991; and *Daily Dispatch*, 19 April 1991).

43. *Southern Africa Report*, 3 September 1993.

44. *Cape Times*, 3 January 1991; *Business Day*, 4 January 1991; and Allister Sparks, 'Terror in the Townships', *Washington Post*, 26 June 1992.

45. *South African Report*, 12 February 1993; 'SAP "Executions": Evidence Mounts', *Weekly Mail*, 23–29 July 1993.

46. In South Africa, private security guards outnumbered police officers by a ratio of four to one ('Crime Overwhelms Pretoria's Police', *New York Times*, 6 January 1991).

47. The 1990 Christmas Day abduction and rape of ten girls from the Bethanie

Salvation home sheltering teenagers epitomized in microcosm the anti-social nature of gangsterism in the townships. Like few other incidents of mindless violence, this event touched a raw nerve. Residents of Soweto's Mopholo and Phomolong districts, where the attacks took place, had such little confidence in the police that they assembled a posse of men who tracked down nineteen Soweto youths belonging to the notorious 'Zebra Force' gang and delivered them to the police station (*Sowetan*, 23 January 1991).

48. Mokwena, 'Living on the Wrong Side of the Law', pp. 41–3. In Diepkloof (Soweto), youths captured and killed at least fifteen suspected members of the notorious Jackroller gang of rapists between June and November 1990. In January 1991, enraged residents of Mdantsane near East London beat to death two members of a gang called 'The Beasts' following an incident in which the gangsters went on a rampage, indiscriminately attacking people on the streets and breaking into homes (*Sowetan*, 23 January 1991; *Eastern Province Herald*, 22 January 1991).

49. 'Dealing with Squatter Lords', p. 11; and 'Violence in Informal Settlements', *Reconstruct* 5, August 1992, p. 5. Two of the quotations in this paragraph can be attributed to Mike Morris.

50. Pierre du Toit and Jannie Gagiano, 'Strongman on the Cape Flats', *Africa Insight*, vol. 23, no. 2, 1993, pp. 102–11.

51. Ibid., pp. 106–7; and Rene Lemarchand, 'Comparative Political Clientelism: Structure, Process and Optic', in S.N. Eisenstadt, ed., *Political Clientelism, Patronage, and Development*, London 1981, pp. 7–32.

52. S. Sole, 'Shabalala: I won't change', *Sunday Tribune*, 28 January 1990.

53. A. de V. Minnaar, *Mafia Warlords or Political Entrepreneurs? Warlordism in Natal*, Pretoria 1991.

54. *Argus*, 9 April 1991.

55. Thanks to Jane Barrett for some of these insights. Shaun Johnson, 'Crossroads War not a Faction Fight', *Weekly Mail*, 17–23 May 1986; L. Venter, 'Crossroads', *Frontline*, August 1986, pp: 18–22; and Josette Cole, *Crossroads: The Politics of Reform and Repression*, Johannesburg 1987.

56. Du Toit and Gagiano, 'Strongman on the Cape Flats', pp. 102–11.

57. '"Witdoek" Leaders on NP Lists', *Weekly Mail & Guardian*, 4–10 February 1994; and *Weekly Mail & Guardian*, 18–24 February 1994.

58. Deborah Posel, *The Making of Apartheid, 1948–1961: Conflict and Compromise*, Oxford 1991; and Alan Mabin, 'The Dynamics of Urbanisation since 1960', in Mark Swilling, Richard Humphries and Khehla Shubane, eds., *Apartheid City in Transition*, Cape Town 1991, pp. 33–47.

59. Deborah Newton, 'Forced Removals in South Africa', in Glenn Moss and Ingrid Obery, eds., *South African Review* 5, Johannesburg 1989, pp. 403–14.

60. See Christina Murray and Catherine O'Regan, eds., *No Place to Rest: Forced Removals and the Law in South Africa*, Cape Town 1990. Thanks to Jane Barrett for pointing out some of these ideas to me. See Vanessa Watson, 'South African Urbanisation Policy: Past and Future', *South African Labour Bulletin*, vol. 11, no. 8, 1988, p. 90.

61. The story of Cato Manor is derived from Bill Keller, 'Squatters Test Limits as *Apartheid* Crumbles', *New York Times*, 14 November 1993.

62. 'South Africa: What Future for the Homelands?', *Africa Confidential*, vol. 29, no. 2, 1988, pp. 1–3.

63. John Pickles and Jeff Woods, 'Taiwanese Investment in South Africa', *African*

Affairs, vol. 88, no. 353, 1989, pp. 507–10.

64. John Pickles and Jeff Woods, 'Reorienting South Africa's International Links', *Capital & Class* 38, 1988, pp. 49–55.

65. Pickles and Woods, 'Taiwanese Investment', p. 527.

66. For example, companies in South Africa, Germany, Italy, Israel and the Far East collectively invested more than R400 million (US$100 million) into the Ekandustria industrial area of KwaNdebele homeland. Ekandustria began in 1985, since which time over 100 companies have been established there. In 1990, about 28 new factories were established (*Business Day*, 18 January 1991).

67. 'South Africa: The Homelands Fall Apart', *Africa Confidential*, vol. 31, no. 6, 1990, pp. 1–2.

68. Peter Tygesen, 'The Homelands Rebellion', *Africa Report*, May/June 1990, p. 40; 'South Africa: The Homelands Fall Apart', pp. 1–2.

69. J.B. Peires, 'The Implosion of Transkei and Ciskei', *African Affairs* 91, 1991, pp. 365–87.

70. Robert Rotberg, 'Homelands' Demise', *The Christian Science Monitor*, 19 March 1991; and Paul Daphne and Francine de Clercq, 'Bophuthatswana: From "Independence" to Regionalism', in Glenn Moss and Ingrid Obrey, eds., *South Africa Review 6: From 'Red Friday' to CODESA*, Johannesburg 1992, pp. 128–40.

71. 'South Africa: The Homelands Fall Apart', pp. 1–2.

72. See Peires, 'The Implosion of Transkei and Ciskei', pp. 365–87. For a response, see Leslie Bank, 'Between Traders and Tribalists: Implosion and the Politics of Disjuncture in a South African Homeland', *African Affairs* 93, 1994, pp. 75–98. See also Edwin Richken, 'The KwaNdebele Struggle Against Independence', in *South African Review* 5, pp. 426–45; and Leslie Bank, 'The Making of the QwaQua "Mafia"? Patronage and Protection in the Migrant Taxi Business', *African Studies* 49, 1990, pp. 71–93.

73. *New York Times*, 11 December 1990; and 'South Africa: What Future for the Homelands?, pp. 2–3.

74. *Southern Africa Report*, 3 September 1993; and *Southern Africa Report*, 1 October 1993.

75. Peires, 'The Implosion of Transkei and Ciskei', p. 382.

76. 'South Africa: The Homelands Fall Apart', pp. 1–3; and Francine de Clercq, 'Bophuthatswana: At the Edge of Time', *Work in Progress* 74, 1991, pp. 17–19.

77. For a historical overview, see T.R.H. Davenport, *South Africa: A Modern History*, 4th edn, Toronto and Buffalo 1991, pp. 155–7, 182–7, 250–53. See also Anne Shephard, 'Problem Child', *Africa Report*, May/June 1993, pp. 28–31; and 'South Africa III: Platinum-plated Bophuthatswana', *Africa Confidential*, vol. 31, no. 4, 1990, p. 3.

78. Richard Stengel, 'Dinosaurland', *The New Republic*, 4–11 January 1993, pp. 11–12.

79. 'South Africa III: Platinum-plated Bophuthatswana', p. 3; *New York Times*, 11 December 1990; *Argus*, 2 May 1991; *Evening Post*, 3 May 1991; and *New York Times*, 28 November 1993.

80. See Eckart Kassier and Jan Groenewald, 'Agriculture: An Overview'; and Simon Brand et al., 'Agriculture and Redistribution: Growth with Equity'; in Robert Schrire, ed., *Wealth or Poverty? Critical Choices for South Africa*, Cape Town 1992, pp. 330–52, and 353–75, respectively.

81. Pieter Gous, President of the Free State Agricultural Union, and MP for

Parys, gave substance to this attitude in a public speech at a Farmers' Day held at Uitenhage. 'Our point of view on labour legislation in the Free State is well-known', he said. 'We are willing to support one or two labour laws for agriculture, and we will implement them if they are written in conjunction with farmers and have been submitted to them beforehand for approval. Such a law will not be able to support the right to strike. No intelligent supporter of a market economy and capitalism can speak up in favour of a Wage Act which enforces minimum wages in a country with millions of unemployed.... The main problem in South Africa is the high unit costs of products combined with a low productivity level. Agriculture suffers the least from this malady. Why is this? Because minimum wages and other distortions are not affecting agriculture' (*Farmer's Weekly*, 24 September 1993).

82. Lauren Segal, *A Brutal Harvest: The Roots and Legitimation of Violence on Farms in South Africa*, Johannesburg 1991, pp. 2, 15, 20–21.

83. Hennie Kotzé and Francois Basson, 'Land Reform: An Overview', *Africa Insight*, vol. 23, no. 4, 1993, pp. 190–97; Mike de Klerk, ed., *A Harvest of Discontent: The Land Question in South Africa*, Cape Town 1991; and Francis Wilson and M. Ramphele, *Uprooting Poverty: The South African Challenge*, Cape Town 1989.

84. Anne Shepard, 'The Land Inequity', *Africa Report*, January/February 1994, pp. 65–7.

85. See Daniel Weiner and Richard Levin, 'Land and Agrarian Transition in South Africa', *Antipode*, vol. 23, no. 1, 1991, pp. 92–120; Michael de Klerk, 'Addressing Land Hunger'; and David Cooper, 'Re-forming the Land Question', in Schrire, ed., *Wealth or Poverty?*, pp. 376–404 and 405–19 respectively.

86. Makhosazane Gcabashe and Alan Mabin, 'Preparing to Negotiate the Land Question', *Transformation* 11, 1990, pp. 58–74.

87. *Financial Mail*, 1 March 1991; and 'Food Production in a Major Crisis', *Work in Progress* 78, 1991, p. 4.

88. Many of the ideas and some of the references for the following paragraphs are borrowed from Richard Levin and Daniel Weiner, 'The Agrarian Question and Politics in the "New" South Africa', *Review of African Political Economy* 57, 1993, pp. 29–45.

89. Simon Brand, N.T. Christodoulou, C.J. Van Rooyen, and N. Vink, *Agriculture and Redistribution: A Growth with Equity Approach*, Johannesburg 1991, pp. 1–2, 28.

90. African National Congress, *Ready to Govern: ANC Policy for a Democratic South Africa*, adopted at National Conference 28–31 May 1992, p. 28.

91. 'Back to the Land', *Work in Progress* 94, December 1993, pp. 39–40; and 'Ramaphosa on Redistribution', *Farmer's Weekly*, 22 October 1993.

92. Levin and Weiner, 'The Agrarian Question and Politics in the "New" South Africa', pp. 31–5.

93. Robert Fine, '"Civil Society" Theory and the Politics of Transition in South Africa', *Review of African Political Economy* 55, 1992, p. 74.

94. 'Barricades in the Bush', *Weekly Mail*, 28 August–3 September 1992.

95. 'Direct Action to Restore the Land', *Work in Progress* 81, April 1992, pp. 26–7.

96. 'They're Refusing to Succumb to APLA', *Star*, 5 June 1993.

97. '10,000 Farmers Ready to Quit', *The Citizen*, 9 June 1993; and 'ANC Condemns Farm Violence', *The Farmer's Weekly*, 25 June 1993.

98. 'Angry Farmers Dig In', *Star*, 5 June 1993; Phillip van Niekerk, 'Engaging in a Little Bit of Redistribution', *Weekly Mail*, 9–15 October 1993.

99. 'ANC Condemns Farm Violence'. As Jane Barrett pointed out to me, the 'Kill the Boer, Kill the Farmer' slogan predated the spate of armed attacks. It was a chant used during the 1980s. The media 'discovered' the slogan and linked it to the armed attacks, thereby giving it new meaning in the context of growing white insecurity.

100. 'Security Special', *The Farmer's Weekly*, 25 June 1993.

101. 'Rural Security', *The Farmer's Weekly*, 8 August 1993.

4. Destabilization and Counter-Revolutionary Warfare

1. See Martin Murray, *South Africa: Time of Agony, Time of Destiny*, London 1987, for a full account of how and why the rebellion took place. For a summarized version, see Martin Murray, 'The Popular Upsurge in South Africa, 1984–1986', *Critical Sociology*, vol. 16, no. 1, 1989, pp. 55–76.

2. See Ivor Sarankinsky, 'The State of the State and State of Resistance', *Work in Progress* 52, 1988, p. 51.

3. See J. Richert, 'The Silent Scream: Detention without Trial, Solitary Confinement and Evidence in South Africa's "Security Law" Trials', *South African Journal on Human Rights*, vol. 1, no. 3, 1985, pp. 245–50.

4. In effect, many of these persons, especially a core group of around a thousand held for over two years, became the forgotten people of South Africa, victims of a Gulag syndrome where key figures were subjected to prolonged incarceration without prospect for release, until prison hunger strikes in February and March 1989, which generated a glare of negative publicity, led to their eventual release. See David Webster and Maggie Friedman, *Suppressing Apartheid's Opponents: Repression and the State of Emergency, June 1987 to March 1989*, Johannesburg 1989; and David Webster and Maggie Friedman, 'Repression and the State of Emergency: June 1987–March 1989', in Glenn Moss and Ingrid Obery, eds., *South African Review 5*, Johannesburg 1989, pp. 16–41. Around 40 per cent of the 1986–88 Emergency detainees were children under eighteen years of age, and some as young as ten; and about 75 per cent belonged to UDF affiliates. Politicized youth, followed closely by trade unionists, community activists, teachers, and clergy, became the main targets of state repression. See David Webster, 'Repression and the State of Emergency', in Glenn Moss and Ingrid Obery, eds., *South African Review 4*, Johannesburg 1988, pp. 141–72; and D. Foster, D. Davis, and D. Sandler, *Detention and Torture in South Africa: Psychological, Legal, and Historical Studies*, Cape Town 1987.

5. Richard Merrett and Roger Gravil, 'Comparing Human Rights: South Africa and Argentina, 1976–1989', *Comparative Studies in Society and History*, vol. 33, no. 2, 1991, pp. 256–7; and 'South Africa: Security Tensions under the Emergency', *Africa Confidential* 29, 12, 1988, pp. 1–5.

6. Laurie Nathan, 'Troops in the Townships, 1984–1987', in Jacklyn Cock and Laurie Nathan, eds., *Society at War: The Militarisation of South Africa*, New York 1989, p. 67; 'South Africa: What Next for the ANC?' *Africa Confidential*, vol. 29, no. 5, 1988, pp. 1–3.

7. See Cock and Nathan, eds., *Society at War*; Philip Frankel, *Pretoria's Praetorians: Civil–Military Relations in South Africa*, Cambridge 1986; Kenneth Grundy, *The Militarisation of South African Politics*, London 1986; and Deon Geldenhuys and Hennie Kotzé, 'Aspects of Political Decision-making in South Africa', *Politikon*, vol. 10, no. 1, 1983, pp. 33–45.

8. Robert Griffiths, 'The South African Military: The Dilemmas of Expanded Influence in Decision-Making', *Journal of Asian and African Studies*, vol. 26, nos. 1–2, 1991, pp. 82–3; Robert Rotberg, 'The Process of Decision-making in Contemporary South Africa', in Helen Kitchen, ed., *South Africa: Transition to What?*, New York 1988, pp. 16–17.

9. Many political analysts believed that 'beneath the facade of civilian rule the generals run the country, sharing power only with their peers in the police and intelligence services' (*Weekly Mail*, 27 June–3 July 1987). See 'South Africa: The Government in the Shadows', *Africa Confidential*, vol. 28, no. 4, 1988, pp. 1–4; and *Washington Post*, 29 November 1989.

10. Annette Seegers, 'Extending the Security Network at the Local Level', in Chris Heymans and Gerhard Totemeyer, eds., *Government by the People?*, Cape Town 1988, pp. 119–39; and Annette Seegers, 'Extending the Security Network to the Local Level: A Clarification and Some Further Comments', *Politeia*, vol. 7, no. 2, 1988, pp. 50–67.

11. For an excellent survey of these issues, see Desirée Hansson, 'Changes in Counter-Revolutionary State Strategy in the Decade 1978–1989', in Desirée Hansson and Dirk van Zyl Smit, eds., *Towards Justice? Crime and State Control in South Africa*, Cape Town 1990, pp. 28–64. See also Mark Swilling and Mark Phillips, 'The Emergency State: Its Structure, Power and Limits', in *South African Review 5*, pp. 68–90; Craig Charney, 'From Resistance to Reconstruction: Towards a New Research Agenda in South African Politics', *Journal of Southern African Studies*, vol. 16, no. 4, 1990, pp. 761–70; and Rupert Taylor, 'Books Reviewed', *Journal of Southern African Studies*, vol. 16, no. 1, 1990, pp. 190–93.

12. 'South Africa: The Government in the Shadows', pp. 1–4; 'The Uniformed Web that Sprawls Across the Country', *Weekly Mail*, 2–8 October 1986, pp. 12–13; Annette Seegers, '*Apartheid*'s Military: Its Origins and Development', in Wilmot James, ed., *The State of Apartheid*, Boulder, Colo., 1987, p. 156; James Selfe, 'South Africa's National Management System', in Cock and Nathan, eds., *Society at War*, pp. 152–3; and Jack Spence, 'The Military in South African Politics', in Shaun Johnson, ed., *South Africa: No Turning Back*, London 1988, p. 250.

13. Selfe, 'South Africa's National Management System', p. 152.

14. This term, borrowed from US military strategists in Vietnam, referred to the establishment of 'strategic bases' from which the security forces believed that they could regain control over areas that had become 'ungovernable' during the unrest.

15. Mark Swilling, 'Whamming the Radicals', *Weekly Mail*, 14–20 May 1988; and Ivor Sarakinsky, 'State Strategy and the Extra-Parliamentary Opposition in South Africa, 1983–1989', *Politikon*, vol. 16, no. 1, 1989, pp. 69–82.

16. Counter-insurgency doctrines were borrowed directly from the British experiences in Malaya and Northern Ireland, the French in Algeria, and the US in Vietnam and El Salvador (Andrew Boraine, 'Managing the Urban Crisis, 1986–1989', *South Africa Review 5*, p. 112).

17. Mark Swilling and Mark Phillips, 'State Power in the 1980s: From "Total Strategy" to "Counter-revolutionary Warfare"', in Cock and Nathan, eds., *Society at War*, p. 144.

18. Selfe, 'South Africa's National Management System', p. 155.

19. 'I want to see', minister of defence, General Magnus Malan proclaimed, 'to what extent I can better the living conditions of the people, to what extent I can

get the people to accept the government so that they don't break with the authorities and drift into the hands of terrorists' (*Cape Times*, 30 March 1987).

20. 'South Africa: the Government in the Shadows', *Africa Confidential*, vol. 28, no. 14, 1987, p. 1.

21. 'Along with the Club Comes the Carrot', *Azania Frontline* 19, 1987, p. 12.

22. Stoffel van der Merwe, *Leadership SA*, April 1988, quoted in Swilling and Phillips, 'State Power in the 1980s', p. 147.

23. Helen Suzman, a leading liberal MP, for example, described the NSMS as functionally equivalent to a 'creeping *coup d'état* by consent in which accountable politicians have abrogated their power to non-accountable members of the security forces' (*Star*, 5 June 1987). See Mark Mitchell and Dave Russell, 'Political Impasse in South Africa: State Capacities and Crisis Management', in John Brewer, ed., *Can South Africa Survive? Five Minutes to Midnight*, London 1989, 312–35; Spence, 'The Military in South African Politics', pp. 240–57; and Simon Baynham, 'Security Strategies for a Future South Africa', *The Journal of Modern African Studies*, vol. 28, no. 3, 1990, pp. 401–30. See also 'Part II: Militarisation and Political Power' in Cock and Nathan, eds., *Society at War*, pp. 134–201.

24. Mike Morris, 'State, Capital, and Growth: the Political Economy of the National Question', in Stephen Gelb, ed., *South Africa's Economic Crisis*, Cape Town 1991, p. 55.

25. Charney, 'From Resistance to Reconstruction', pp. 764–5.

26. The distinction between a 'grand design' or a general strategy or broad outline for perserving the power of the white oligarchy, and a 'blueprint', a detailed construction plan for operationalizing a general conception, is a useful one in this context. See Robert Price, *The Apartheid State in Crisis: Political Transformation in South Africa, 1975–1990*, New York and Oxford 1991, pp. 99–101.

27. The creation of thirteen separate Departments of Education, for example, illustrates the extent of this seemingly absurd fragmentation.

28. See Murray, *South Africa*, ch. 2; and Price, *The Apartheid State in Crisis*, chs. 3 and 4.

29. Annette Seegers, 'South Africa's National Security Management System', *The Journal of Modern African Studies*, vol. 29, no. 2, 1991, pp. 271–3; Paul Botes, 'Die Sentrale Administrasie', in Charles Nieuwoudt, et al., eds., *Die Politieke Stelsel van Suid-Afrika*, Pretoria 1981.

30. Craig Charney, 'Vigilantes, Clientelism, and the South African State', *Transformation* 16, 1991, pp. 15–16; Charney, 'From Resistance to Reconstruction', pp. 764–5; Morris, 'State, Capital, and Growth', pp. 55–6.

31. This term is borrowed from Nicholas Haysom. See 'Vigilantism and the Policing of South African Townships: Manufacturing Violent Stability', in Hansson and van Zyl Smit, eds., *Towards Justice?*, pp. 63–84.

32. See Murray, 'The Popular Upsurge in South Africa', pp. 56–7.

33. Webster and Friedman, 'Repression and the State of Emergency', pp. 32–6; J.D. Van der Vyver, 'State-Sponsored Terror Violence', *South African Journal on Human Rights*, vol. 4, no. 1, 1988, pp. 70–71; Nicholas Haysom, 'Vigilantes and Militarisation of South Africa', in Cock and Nathan, *Society at War*, pp. 188–201; Nathan, 'Troops in the Townships', pp. 76–8; and Derrick Fine and Desirée Hansson, 'Community Responses to Police Abuse of Power: Coping with the *Kitskonstabels*', in Hansson and van Zyl Smit, eds., *Towards Justice?*, pp. 209–31.

34. Jacklyn Cock, 'Introduction', *Society At War*, p. 8; Catholic Institute of

International Relations, *Now Everyone is Afraid: The Changing Face of Policing in South Africa*, London 1988; Haysom, 'Vigilantes and Militarisation of South Africa', pp. 188–201.

35. Webster and Friedman, 'Repression and the State of Emergency', *South African Review 5*, pp. 16–41.

36. Charney, 'Vigilantes, Clientelism, and the South African State', pp. 1–4.

37. Haysom, 'Vigilantes and Militarisation of South Africa', pp. 188–201.

38. P. Harris, 'The Role of Right-Wing Vigilantes in South Africa', in Catholic Institute for International Relations, *States of Terror*, London 1989, pp. 1–13. F. Kruger, '"Wild Rats" of the Township', *Weekly Mail*, 8–15 April 1988; Webster and Friedman, *Suppressing Apartheid's Opponents*, pp. 20–26; Webster and Friedman, 'Repression and the State of Emergency', pp. 169–70; and *New Nation*, 8 December 1989.

39. Charney, 'Vigilantes, Clientelism, and the South African State', pp. 8–11.

40. Price, *The Apartheid State in Crisis*, pp. 262–3.

41. In particular, see Haysom 'Vigilantes and Militarisation of South Africa'; Charney 'Vigilantes, Clientelism, and the South African State'; and Harris, 'The Role of Right-Wing Vigilantes in South Africa'.

42. Charney, 'Vigilantes, Clientelism, and the South African State', pp. 2–3; and *Evening Post*, 6 January 1992.

43. I use this subtitle hesitatingly, because of its sexism, even though the phrase was used with regularity in the popular literature.

44. According to the South African Human Rights Commission, there were 113 attacks – bombings, arson and robberies – directed at anti-apartheid organizations or the buildings within which they had their offices, between 1984 and the beginning of 1989. See Karen Evans and Edyth Bulbring, 'Another Break-in. Another Wrecked Car. Another Fire-bomb. Another Co-incidence?', *Weekly Mail*, 20–26 May 1988, p. 9.

45. Webster and Friedman, 'Repression and the State of Emergency', p. 37.

46. Webster, whose funeral procession through downtown Johannesburg attracted over twenty thousand mourners, was a well-known academic and anti-apartheid activist. Between 1978, when Richard Turner was shot dead, and May 1989, when trade-unionist Jabu Ndlovu died in Pietermaritzburg, at least sixty-two political activists were selectively assassinated under mysterious circumstances. The numbers have steadily increased since then. See Rich Mkhondo, *Reporting South Africa*, London 1993, pp. 72–93; and Nico Steytler, 'Policing Political Opponents: Death Squads and Cop Culture', in Hansson and van Zyl Smit, eds., *Towards Justice?*, pp. 106–34.

47. Webster and Friedman, *Suppressing Apartheid's Opponents*, pp. 31–3.

48. 'Hit Squads: Can They be Tamed?', *Work in Progress 64*, 1990, pp. 14–17.

49. *Argus*, 31 January 1991.

50. See Jacques Pauw, *In the Heart of the Whore: The Story of South Africa's Death Squads*, Johannesburg 1990.

51. Patrick Laurence, 'Marked for Murder', *Africa Report*, March/April 1990, pp. 22–5.

52. Ibid.; 'Harms Commission: Sidestepping the Issue', *Sechaba*, May 1990, pp. 21–2.

53. According to self-confessed killer and former CCB agent Donald Acheson, the CCB had established more than forty-two cells across the country, CCB

operatives embezzled millions of rands and salted the funds away in secret overseas bank accounts, and formed a covert unit called the Dog Squad, consisting of professional assassins (*Sunday Times*, 13 January 1991).

54. *Evening Post*, 8 March 1991; *Sunday Times*, 28 April 1991; Patrick Laurence, *Death Squads: Apartheid's Secret Weapon*, Johannesburg 1991.

55. Andrew Meldrum, 'Apartheid's Long Arm', *Africa Report*, July/August 1990, pp. 25–7. During the 1980s, 87 activists were killed inside South Africa, and 138 killed outside the country (Pauw, *In the Heart of the Whore*, pp. 1–4).

56. *Argus*, 16 February 1991; *Sowetan*, 25 February 1991; and Catharine Payze, 'The Elimination of Political Opponents: The Maphumulo Assassination', in Anthony Minnaar, ed., *Patterns of Violence: Case Studies of Conflict*, Pretoria 1992, pp. 247–58. A self-proclaimed member of South African military intelligence stated in a sworn affidavit that he was involved in the assassination of Maphumulo, and that army intelligence officers and police in Natal province organized the 'hit' ('Hit-Team Killing', *Washington Post*, 4 May 1991).

57. Philippa Garson, 'The Third Force', *Africa Report*, May/June 1992, p. 68; 'Landmark Verdict Links Police to Killings', *Weekly Mail*, 24–29 April 1992; 'The Final Resort: Train Boycotts', *Weekly Mail*, 30 April–7 May 1992; and 'Cape Civics Unite Despite Assassination', *Weekly Mail*, 6–12 March 1992.

58. Patrick Laurence, 'Marked for Murder', pp. 22–5; Andrew Meldrum, 'The Assassination Bureau', *Africa Report*, May/June 1990, pp. 42–4; Philippa Garson, 'Libel or Liability?', *Africa Report*, January/February 1991, pp. 54–6; 'Harms Commission: Sidestepping the Issue', *Sechaba*, May 1990, pp. 21–2; *Sunday Times*, 28 April 1991.

59. 'Who's Behind the Violence?', *Weekly Mail*, 5–11 April 1991.

60. Nico Basson, 'De Klerk's Double Agenda', *Work in Progress* 79, 1991, pp. 9–14; 'Thunderstorm and Springbok – Twin Strategies to Bring the ANC to Heel', *Southscan* 25, June 1992; and Jo-Anne Collinge, 'Launched on a Bloody Tide', *South African Review 6*, Johannesburg 1992, pp. 18–24.

61. Mkhondo, *Reporting South Africa*, pp. 73–92.

62. 'Hidden Hand', *Africa Events*, December 1992, p. 11; *New York Times*, 8 March 1993; 'New Chief, Old Habits', *Africa Events*, November 1993, p. 12; and *Southern Africa Report*, 20 November 1992.

63. 'South Africa's Armor is Showing Signs of Tarnish', *New York Times*, 23 December 1992.

64. Patrick Laurence, 'Temperatures Rising', *Africa Report*, March/April 1993, pp. 30–31.

65. 'South Africa's Armor is Showing Signs of Tarnish; and 'South Africa: Looking Through the Mirrors', *Africa Confidential*, vol. 33, no. 15, 1992, pp. 4–6.

66. A renegade soldier, Felix Ndimene, a member of Five Recce who was originally abducted from Mozambique, testified that the September 1990 train massacres, in which black commuters living around Johannesburg were shot and hacked to death, were carried out by fellow mercenaries recruited from Namibia and Mozambique and disguised for the occasion as Inkatha vigilantes. Ndimene's sworn testimony reinforced a rising tide of allegations of the involvement of Special Forces units, particularly Five Recce which was based at Phalaborwa (a garrison town located on the edge of Kruger National Park in the Eastern Transvaal, and composed of a large number of abducted foreign nationals from Mozambique), in a series of unexplained violent acts that took place in 1990 and 1991 ('Speaking

with Forked Tongue', *Economist*, 27 July 1991; and *New Nation*, 23 August 1991).

67. 'We're Just a Bit Heavyhanded, Says Captain', *Weekly Mail*, 30 April–7 May 1992.

68. 'Mozambique/South Africa: The Special Forces behind RENAMO', *Africa Confidential*, vol. 28, no. 24, 1987, pp. 1–3.

69. 'South Africa: Genesis of the Third Force', *Africa Confidential*, vol. 32, no. 19, 1992, pp. 1–3.

70. It is important to note the the 'low level civil war' was not generalized equally throughout the black residential areas. It was largely confined to specific places: for example, around Pietermaritzburg, Durban, and Empangeni in Natal; the East Rand townships of Katlehong, Thokoza, and Vosloorus; Sebokeng near Vereeniging; and Alexandra on the northeastern fringe of Johannesburg.

71. See 'South Africa: Genesis of the Third Force', pp. 1–2; Selfe, 'South Africa's National Management System', pp. 149–52; Mark Swilling and Mark Phillips, 'State Power in the 1980s', pp. 134–148; and Charney, 'Vigilantes, Clientelism, and the South African State', pp. 1–4.

72. 'South Africa: Violent Reactions', *Africa Confidential*, vol. 33, no. 4, 1992, pp. 1–3.

73. 'South Africa: Looking through the Mirrors', p. 5.

74. Ibid., pp. 5–6; Denis Herbstein, 'Missing Presumed Dead', *Africa Report*, November/December 1992; and 'South Africa: Violence in Transition', *Africa Confidential*, vol. 33, no. 8, 1992, pp. 1–2.

75. Adam and Moodley strongly emphasize this point (see 'Political Violence', p. 493).

76. 'South Africa: Looking through the Mirrors', pp. 5–6.

77. Adam and Moodley, 'Political Violence', pp. 488–9.

78. 'South Africa: Partners in Policing', *Africa Confidential*, vol. 35, no. 2, 1994, pp. 1–2.

79. Adam and Moodley, 'Political Violence', pp. 493–4; and Mark Phillips and Laurie Nathan, 'The Changing of the Guard: The Security Forces in Transition', *Social Justice*, vol. 18, nos. 1–2, 1992, p. 114.

80. *Southern Africa Report*, 31 July 1992; 'Police are Still Using Torture', *Weekly Mail*, 16–22 July 1993; and 'New Chief, Old Habits', *Africa Events*, November 1993, p. 12.

5. The Roots of Political Violence

1. Heribert Adam and Kogila Moodley, 'Political Violence, "Tribalism," and Inkatha', *Journal of Modern African Studies*, vol. 30, no. 3, 1992, p. 485.

2. For helpful discussion of this literature, see Hein Marais, 'The Sweeping Inferno', *Work in Progress* 83, 1992, pp. 14–17; Brian McKendrick and Wilma Hoffman, eds., *People and Violence in South Africa*, Cape Town 1990; and N. Chabani Manganyi and Andre du Toit, eds., *Political Violence and the Struggle in South Africa*, Johannesburg 1990.

3. Mike Morris and Doug Hinson, 'The Disintegration of *Apartheid*: From Violence to Reconstruction', in Glenn Moss and Ingrid Obery, eds., *South African Review 6: From 'Red Friday' to CODESA*, Johannesburg 1992, pp. 152–4; and M. Morris and O. Hinson, 'South Africa: Political Violence, Reform, and Reconstruction', *Review of African Political Economy* 53, 1992, pp. 43–59.

4. Lawrence Schlemmer, 'Negotiations Dilemmas after the Sound and Fury', *Indicator SA*, vol. 8, no. 3, 1991, pp. 7–10.

5. Heribert Adam and Kogila Moodley, *The Opening of the Apartheid Mind: Options for the New South Africa*, Berkeley, Los Angeles and London 1993, pp. 121–3.

6. *Washington Post*, 18 November 1993.

7. Patrick Laurence, 'The Diehards and the Dealmakers', *Africa Report*, November/December 1993, pp. 15–16.

8. *Evening Post*, 6 January 1992; *New York Times*, 27 September 1992; *New York Times*, 3 March 1993.

9. Marais, 'The Sweeping Inferno', p. 14.

10. See William Beinart, 'Political and Collective Violence in Southern African Historiography', *Journal of South African Studies*, vol. 18, no. 3, 1992, pp. 455–86.

11. Patrick Laurence, 'Buthelezi's Gamble', *Africa Report*, November/December 1992, p. 17.

12. David Everatt, *Consolidated CASE Reports on the Reef Violence*, Johannesburg 1992; and Human Rights Commission (HRC), *A New Total Strategy: HRC Special Report SR-11*, Johannesburg 1991.

13. 'Baptism of Fire', *Africa Events*, August 1992, p. 13.

14. Gerhard Maré and Georgina Hamilton, *An Appetite for Power: Buthelezi's Inkatha and South Africa*, Johannesburg 1987; and Mzala, *Gatsha Buthelezi: Chief with a Double Agenda*, London 1988. For Inkatha's position, see Mangosuthu Gatsha Buthelezi, *South Africa: My Vision of the Future*, New York 1990.

15. Christopher Wren, 'The Chief Steps Forward', *New York Times Magazine*, 17 February 1991, p. 52.

16. See Doug Tilton, 'Creating an "Educated Workforce": Inkatha, Big Business, and Educational Reform in KwaZulu', *Journal of Southern African Studies*, vol. 18, no. 1, 1992, pp. 166–89.

17. His overseas supporters 'applauded Buthelezi for denouncing the ANC's alliance with the SACP and find his endorsement of free-market economics more palatable than the ANC's talk about nationalization and redistribution of wealth'. Buthelezi's admirers held him in high esteem, in short, 'for the very reason his enemies, at home and overseas, hate him: his ideology sounds neither revolutionary nor romantic but pragmatically middle-of-the-road' (Wren, 'The Chief Steps Forward', pp. 24, 52).

18. Peter Tygesen, 'The Man You Can't Ignore', *Africa Report*, January/February 1991, pp. 50–53.

19. *Financial Mail*, 10 January 1992; and *The Economist*, 15 February 1992.

20. Morris Szeftel, 'Manoeuvres of War in South Africa', *Review of African Political Economy* 51, 1991, pp. 72–3; and Gerhard Maré and Muntu Ncube, 'Inkatha: Marching from Natal to Pretoria', in Glenn Moss and Ingrid Obery, eds., *South African Review 5*, Jonannesburg 1989, pp. 474–90.

21. Gerhard Maré, 'Inkatha and Regional Control: Policing Liberation Politics', *Review of African Political Economy* 45/46, 1989, pp. 179–89.

22. Special thanks to Jane Barrett for this information. See 'Bus Drivers under Attack by Vigilantes', *South African Labour Bulletin*, vol. 13, no. 2, 1988, pp. 45–52.

23. For a general survey of the vast literature, see Anthony Minnaar, '"Patterns of Violence": An Overview of Conflict in Natal during the 1980s and 1990s', in

A. Minnaar, ed., *Patterns of Violence: Case Studies of Conflict*, Pretoria 1992, pp. 1–26. See also Heather Hughes, 'Violence in Inanda, August 1985', *Journal of Southern African Studies*, vol. 13, no. 3, 1987, pp. 331–54; Ari Sitas, 'Inanda, August 1985', *South African Labour Bulletin*, vol. 11, no. 4, 1986, pp. 85–121; Ari Sitas, 'The Making of the "Comrades" Movement in Natal, 1985–1991', *Journal of Southern African Studies*, vol. 18, no. 3, 1992, pp. 629–41; Shamim Meer, 'Conflict: in the Community and in the Factories', *South African Labour Bulletin*, vol. 13, nos. 4–5, 1988, pp. 66–86; and 'In Natal's "Year of Peace", More and More Devastation', *Weekly Mail*, 21 December–18 January 1990.

24. *The Times*, 31 March 1990; Wren, 'The Chief Steps Forward', p. 52; Nkosinathi Gwala, 'Political Violence and the Struggle for the Control of Pietermaritzburg', *Journal of Southern African Studies*, vol. 15, no. 3, 1989, pp. 506–24; Maritzburg Collective, 'Negotiations and the Violence in Pietermaritzburg', *South African Labour Bulletin*, vol. 13, no. 2, 1988, pp. 53–62; and Karl von Holdt, 'Vigilantes versus Defence Committees: The Maritzburg War, a Turning Point for Inkatha?', *South African Labour Bulletin*, vol. 13, no. 2, 1988, pp. 16–27.

25. Morris and Hindson, 'South Africa: Political Violence, Reform, and Reconstruction', pp. 50–51.

26. 'A Greatly Feared Zulu Watches over the Political Machine', *New York Times*, 26 April 1994.

27. John Aitchison, *Numbering the Dead: Patterns in the Midlands Violence*, Pietermaritzburg 1988; and Matthew Kentridge, *An Unofficial War: Inside the Conflict in Pietermaritzburg*, Cape Town and Johannesburg 1990.

28. Philippa Garson, 'South Africa: The Killing Fields', *Africa Report*, November/December 1990, pp. 46–9; and Nicholas Haysom, *Natal's Killing Fields*, London 1990.

29. One commentator described the conflict as 'fighting over a meatless bone' (Christopher Wren, 'Into the Valley of Death, Good Will Brings Peace', *New York Times*, 12 November 1990). See Aitchison, *Numbering the Dead*; and James Henry, 'Natal's Valley of Death', *Washington Post*, 22 July 1990. Young 'comrades' formed 'self-protection units' which resembled a ragtag army composed of around 300 young men and boys divided into four regiments armed with homemade rifles called *qwasha* to defend their strife-torn settlements from Inkatha *impis* who mounted frequent invasions ('Meeting with a Young General, Commander of 300 Soldiers', *Weekly Mail*, 5–11 May 1989).

30. Kentridge, *An Unofficial War*; John Jeffreys, 'Rocky Path to Peace in Natal', *South African Labour Bulletin*, vol. 14, no. 5, 1989, pp. 62–71; S. Stavrou and L. Shongwe, 'Violence on the Periphery. Part Two: The Greater Edendale Complex', *Indicator SA*, vol. 7, no. 1, 1989, pp. 53–7; and Gerhard Maré, 'History and Dimension of the Violence in Natal: Inkatha's Role in Negotiating Political Peace', *Social Justice*, vol. 18, nos. 1–2, 1992, pp. 186–8.

31. For a review of the extensive literature, see Harold Tessendorf, 'The Natal Violence and its Causes', *Africa Insight*, vol. 21, no. 1, 1991, pp. 57–61. See also Gavin Woods, 'Natal Violence: A Contemporary Analysis of Underlying Dynamics', in Minnaar, ed., *Patterns of Violence*, pp. 37–48.

32. See Anthony Minnaar, *Conflict and Violence in Natal/KwaZulu*, Pretoria 1990.

33. Aitchison, *Numbering the Dead*; Jeremy Irish and Howard Varney, 'The KwaZulu Police: Obstacle to Peace?; and Tim Smith, 'The Warlord and the Police': in Minnar, ed., *Patterns of Violence*, pp. 49–55 and pp. 57–60 respectively.

34. 'A Judge Links Police to Murder', *Weekly Mail*, 24–29 April 1992; Deneys Coombe, '"Of Murder and Deceit": The Trust Feed Killings', and Tim Smith, 'Trust Feed Wasn't a One-Off Massacre', in Minnaar, ed., *Patterns of Violence*, pp. 227–42 and pp. 243–6 respectively.

35. *Christian Science Monitor*, 1 March 1991; *New York Times*, 13 April 1990. In KwaZulu, 40 per cent of the people did not have proper homes, 48 per cent had no jobs, and 73 per cent of the employable youth had no work or the prospect of any (*Star*, 30 April 1990).

36. *Washington Post*, 30 March 1990; Allister Sparks, 'Natal's "Valley of Death" Goes to War', *Washington Post*, 8 April 1990; *New Nation*, 30 March 1990; and 'Into the Valley of Death', *Weekly Mail*, 5–11 April 1990. Eyewitnesses reported that policemen incited Inkatha *impis* to violence, and that police weapons and ammunition were used in the fighting (*The Times*, 4 April 1990).

37. *Washington Post*, 29 March 1990; and Wren, 'The Chief Steps Forward', p. 56.

38. *Observer*, 8 April 1990; Sparks, 'Natal's "Valley of Death" Goes to War'; *New York Times*, 4 April 1991; and *Washington Post*, 5 April 1991.

39. Jerelyn Eddings, 'Fierce Dispute', *The Sun*, 16 August 1990; and 'South Africa: Gatsha's Last Stand', *Africa Confidential*, vol. 33, no. 22, 1992, p. 3.

40. *New African*, 16 June 1990; *Star*, 15 May 1990.

41. *Cape Times*, 20 March 1991; *Star*, 30 April 1990.

42. Scott Kraft, 'Whites See Cost in Easing Apartheid', *Los Angeles Times*, 21 August 1990.

43. *New York Times*, 3 July 1990.

44. John Battersby, 'Zulus Form New Multiracial Party to Broaden South African Debate', *Christian Science Monitor*, 17 July 1990; *New York Times*, 25 July 1991.

45. Peter Tygeson, 'Pitfalls to Peace', *Africa Report*, November/December 1990, p. 50.

46. Garson, 'South Africa: The Killing Fields', pp. 48–9. See also Rupert Taylor, 'The Myth of Ethnic Divison: Township Conflict on the Reef', *Race & Class*, vol. 33, no. 2, 1991, pp. 3–14.

47. Ibid., p. 9.

48. Rich Mkhondo, *Reporting South Africa*, London 1993, p. 56.

49. For a sophisticated investigation of the hydra-headed consciousness of hostel-dwellers, see Lauren Segal, 'The Human Face of Violence: Hostel-Dwellers Speak', *Journal of Southern African Studies*, vol. 18, no. 1, 1992, pp. 190–231.

50. Garson, 'South Africa: The Killing Fields', p. 48.

51. Jane Barrett suggested these ideas to me.

52. Greg Ruiters and Rupert Taylor, 'Organise – or Die', *Work in Progress* 70/71, 1990, pp. 20–22,

53. *Los Angeles Times*, 21 August 1990; *Business Day*, 16 August 1990; *Financial Mail*, 31 May 1991; and Taylor, 'The Myth of Ethnic Divisions', pp. 8–10.

54. Alan Cowell, 'Township Violence: Separatist Legacy', *New York Times*, 20 August 1990; *New York Times*, 24 August 1990; *New York Times*, 25 August 1990; Christopher Wren, 'Around Squalid South African Hostel, a Battleground in Factional Fighting', *New York Times*, 9 September 1990; and Phillip van Niekerk, 'Toll Climbs', *Boston Globe*, 16 August 1990.

55. Allistar Sparks, 'Bloodshed Spreads', *Washington Post*, 21 August 1990.

56. Garson, 'South Africa: The Killing Fields', p. 47; *Star*, 17 September 1990.

57. Roger Thurow, 'Deepening Despair', *Wall Street Journal*, 14 September 1990; *Star*, 1 February 1991.

58. *Sunday Times*, 16 September 1990.

59. Christopher Wren, 'Days of Murder Dim the Hopes of South Africa', *New York Times*, 16 September 1990; *Washington Post*, 14 September 1990; 'To Stop the Killing', *Newsweek*, 1 October 1990; and 'A Stranger comes Calling...', *Weekly Mail*, 14–20 September 1990.

60. 'Terror Comes Home to Roost', *Star Review*, 16 September 1990.

61. Wren, 'Days of Murder', *New York Times*, 16 September 1990; *New York Times*, 14 September 1990; Gavin Evans and Paul Stober, 'The Renamo-style Massacres', *Weekly Mail*, 28 June–4 July 1991.

62. Garson, 'South Africa: The Killing Fields', pp. 48–9.

63. *New York Times*, 22 September 1990; Andrew Mapheto, 'The Violence: A View from the Ground', *Work in Progress* 69, 1990, p. 8; Chris McGreal, 'Violence Tears at Fabric of the ANC', *Independent*, 23 September 1990.

64. Wren, 'The Chief Steps Foward', p. 24.

65. *Los Angeles Times*, 15 February 1991; *The Sun*, 4 December 1991; Wren, 'The Chief Steps Forward', p. 56.

66. Charles Carter, 'Community and Conflict: The Alexandra Rebellion of 1986', *Journal of Southern African Studies*, vol. 18, no. 1, 1992, pp. 115–42. For an excellent critique of Carter's political understanding of Alexandra, see Mzwanele Mayekiso, 'The Legacy of "Ungovernability"', *Southern African Review of Books*, vol. 5, no. 6, 1993, pp. 24–7.

67. *Star*, 10 March 1991; 'Why Alex Exploded' and 'Killing Fields', *Weekly Mail*, 15–21 March 1991; *New York Times*, 10 March 1991; 'Fighting to Stay at the Bottom', *Weekly Mail*, 22–27 March 1991; and Mosito Raphela, 'Alex Violence', *Work in Progress* 83, 1992, p. 16.

68. *Argus*, 2 April 1991.

69. *New York Times*, 9 April 1991; and *Weekly Mail*, 19–25 April 1991.

70. Mathew Phosa, 'Apartheid, By Other Means', *New York Times*, 13 May 1991.

71. *Weekly Mail*, 14–20 September 1990, 21–27 September 1990; and *New York Times*, 12 June 1991.

72. 'On the Trail of the "Third Force"', *Weekly Mail*, 10–16 May 1991.

73. 'Police Paid Inkatha to Block ANC', *Weekly Mail*, 19–25 July 1991; 'The Funding Scandal', *Weekly Mail*, 26 July-1 August 1991; 'A Random List of 23 Claims About "Blind-Eyed" Police', *Weekly Mail*, 2–8 August 1991; 'The Inkatha Hit Squad', *Weekly Mail*, 9–15 August 1991; 'Inside Inkatha', *Weekly Mail*, 10–16 January 1992; and 'Goldstone Hears of Secret Account', *Weekly Mail*, 7–13 February 1992.

74. *City Press* 28 August 1991; *Natal Mercury*, 9 August 1991, 10 August 1991, and 13 August 1991; Eddie Koch and Philippa Garson, 'How a Small Group of Hitmen Held a Township to Ransom', *Weekly Mail*, 17–23 January 1992; and Mkhondo, *Reporting South Africa*, pp. 68–70.

75. *New Nation*, 2 February 1990.

76. 'Scandal Raging', *African Concord*, 5 August 1991; and *New York Times*, 31 July 1991.

77. 'Who Paid the Jackal?', *Weekly Mail*, 2–8 August 1991; 'This Deserted Base', *Weekly Mail*, 9–15 August 1991.

78. *Sowetan*, 17 January 1991.

79. *Sowetan*, 29 April 1991, 3 May 1991; 'ANC vs. Inkatha: Anatomy of a

Slaughter', *Washington Post*, 2 May 1991; Gavin Evans and Paul Stober, 'The Renamo-style Massacres', *Weekly Mail*, 28 June–4 July 1991.

80. 'Disarm Them!', *Weekly Mail*, 5–11 April 1991.

81. *New York Times*, 7 May 1991.

82. Phillip van Niekerk, 'The Post-*Apartheid* War is already Underway', *Weekly Mail*, 5–11 April 1991.

83. 'Peace in the Balance', *Weekly Mail*, 28 March-4 April 1991; *Sowetan*, 4 April 1991; *Business Day*, 26 March 1991, 29 March 1991; *Star*, 14 April 1991.

84. *Star*, 17 April 1991, 25 April 1991; 'ANC to set up Self-Defence Units', *Christian Science Monitor*, 15 April 1991.

85. *Business Day*, 3 May 1991; *The Sun*, 6 May 1991.

86. *Weekly Mail*, 27 March–2 April 1992.

87. Philippa Garson, 'The Gun Culture', *Africa Report*, July/August 1992, pp. 58–61.

88. Garson, 'The Gun Culture', pp. 58–61; and *Sunday Times*, 2 August 1992.

89. Nhlanhla Maake, 'Multi-Cultural Relations in a Post-*Apartheid* South Africa', *African Affairs* 91, 1992, p. 583. See also Jeremy Seekings, *Heroes or Villains: Youth Politics in the 1980s*, Johannesburg 1993.

90. Tom Carver, 'The Other Frontline', *New Statesman & Society*, 27 November 1992, p. 22.

91. Taylor claimed that at the time of the conflict there were around 243,000 migrants in 130 hostels in the broad Pretoria–Witwatersrand–Vereeniging triangle. Most of the hostels were constructed in the 1950s; and some were huge complexes, such as Diepmeadow hostel in Soweto which housed 29,000 migrants (Taylor, 'The Myth of Ethnic Division', p. 9).

92. *Los Angeles Times*, 28 June 1992; *Financial Mail*, 31 May 1992; and Patrick Laurence, 'Buthelezi's Gamble', *Africa Report*, November/December 1992, pp. 14–18.

93. Philippa Garson, 'The Third Force', *Africa Report*, May/June 1992, pp. 68–71.

94. Ibid., p. 68; *Weekly Mail*, 30 April–7 May 1992.

95. *Evening Post*, 6 January 1992.

96. Jeremy Seekings, 'The Revival of "People's Courts"', *South African Review* 6, pp. 186–200.

97. 'Homeland, *Apartheid*'s Child, is Defying Change', *New York Times*, 28 November 1993.

98. *New York Times*, 26 November 1993.

99. *Sunday Times*, 13 January 1991; and Anthony Minnaar, '"Patterns of Violence": An Overview', in Minnaar, ed., *Patterns of Violence*, pp. 16–18.

100. See Roy Ainslie, 'The North Coast: Natal's Silent Rural War'; Hadyn Osborn, 'The Richmond War: "A Struggle for Supremacy"'; and Minnaar, '"Patterns of Violence": An Overview'; in Minnaar, ed., *Patterns of Violence*, pp. 107–28; 187–202 and 18–21 respectively.

101. *Natal Witness*, 16 January 1991, 15 January 1991, 23 January 1991; *Daily Dispatch*, 16 February 1991; *Natal Witness*, 12 February 1991; *Echo*, 28 February 1991; *Zululand Observer*, 18 January 1991; *Star*, 6 March 1991; and *Sunday Times*, 24 March 1991.

102. The SDUs received an added boost by incorporating former MK guerrillas onto their rosters. Purportedly under the command of Harry Gwala, the hardline

ANC 'warlord' in the Natal midlands, these units were involved in offensive actions against Inkatha. See 'Banditry versus Politics', *The Economist*, 8 August 1992; and Antoinette Louw, 'Conflict Trends in Natal, 1989–April 1992', in Minnaar, ed., *Patterns of Violence*, pp. 27–36.

103. *Sunday Times*, 9 June 1991.

104. Shula Marks, 'Patriotism, Patriarchy, and Purity: Natal and the Politics of Zulu Ethnic Consciousness', in Leroy Vail, ed., *The Creation of Tribalism in Southern Africa*, London and Berkeley 1988, pp. 215–40; Gerhard Maré, *Ethnicity and Politics in South Africa*, London 1993; and Rama Melkote, '"Blacks against Blacks" Violence in South Africa', *Economic and Political Weekly*, 5 June 1993.

105. *New York Times*, 19 December 1993 and 2 March 1994.

106. *The Economist*, 3 October 1992; and *New York Times*, 18 November 1992.

6. The Political Spectrum

1. Bill Keller, 'A Brutalized Generation Turns Its Rage on Whites', *New York Times*, 7 December 1993.

2. John Saul has admirably outlined the problems and dilemmas confronting the ANC leadership at this historic juncture, and the details need not detain us here. See his 'South Africa: Between "Barbarism" and "Structural Reform"', *New Left Review* 188, July–August 1991, pp. 3–44. For earlier views, see John Saul, 'The Southern African Revolution', in Ralph Miliband et al., *The Socialist Register 1989*, London 1989, pp. 47–73.

3. Tom Lodge, 'The African National Congress in the 1990s', in Glenn Moss and Ingrid Obery, eds., *South Africa Review 6: From 'Red Friday' to CODESA*, Johannesburg 1992, pp. 44–78.

4. Tom Lodge, 'Rebellion: The Turning of the Tide', in Tom Lodge and Bill Nasson, eds., *All, Here, and Now: Black Politics in South Africa in the 1980s*, London 1991, p. 173.

5. Ibid., pp. 175–6.

6. 'South Africa: Hani's Rise', *Africa Confidential*, vol. 29, no. 16, 1988, p. 2; and Stephen Davis, *Apartheid's Rebels: Inside South Africa's Hidden War*, New Haven and London 1987, pp. 36–157.

7. Stephen Ellis and Tsapo Sechaba, *Comrades Against Apartheid: The ANC and the South African Communist Party in Exile*, London and Bloomington 1992, p. 120.

8. Tom Lodge, 'State of Exile: The African National Congress of South Africa, 1976–1986', in Philip Frankel, Noam Pines, and Mark Swilling, eds., *State, Resistance and Change in South Africa*, London 1988, pp. 229–58; Ellis and Sechaba, *Comrades Against Apartheid*, pp. 103–40; and Howard Barrell, *MK: The ANC's Armed Struggle*, Johannesburg 1990.

9. Lodge, 'Rebellion: The Turning of the Tide', pp. 178–81.

10. Howard Barrell, 'The Outlawed South African Liberation Movements', in Shaun Johnson, ed., *South Africa: No Turning Back*, Bloomington, Ind. 1989, pp. 61–3.

11. 'South Africa: Hani's Rise', p. 2; and Lodge, 'Rebellion: The Turning of the Tide', pp. 178–81.

12. 'South Africa I: De Klerk Faces the Big Heat', *Africa Confidential*, vol. 30, no. 19, 1989, pp. 1–2.

13. Lodge, 'Rebellion: The Turning of the Tide', p. 191.

14. Tom Lodge, 'The African National Congress in the 1990s,' *South African Review* 6, pp. 45–78.

15. 'South Africa: Umkhonto Packs its Bags', *Africa Confidential* vol. 30, no. 2, 1989, pp. 6–7; 'South Africa: Earthquake!', *Africa Confidential*, vol. 30, no. 7, 1989, pp. 1–2; 'South Africa: Crackdown Hits Hani's Men', *Africa Confidential*, vol. 30, no. 18, 1989, p. 3.

16. *Argus*, 6 February 1991.

17. *Cape Times*, 16 February 1991; *Cape Argus*, 18 February 1991.

18. 'The Search for Political Direction', *Work in Progress* 70/71, 1990, pp. 4–7; Saths Cooper, 'An Affair of the Nation', *Weekly Mail*, 28 June–4 July 1991; Oupa Lehulere, 'Power from Below?', *Work in Progress* 75, 1991, pp. 8–10; and Devan Pillay, 'The Politics of Specificity', *Work in Progress* 75, 1991, pp. 10–11.

19. David Niddrie, 'Using the Carrot or the Stick?', *Work in Progress* 75, 1991, p. 6. Surprisingly, ANC membership expanded in the areas most affected by the violence, but in quieter areas like the Eastern and Western Cape membership remained almost static. See 'The ANC Struggles to gain the Initiative', *Africa Confidential*, vol. 32, no. 13, 1991, p. 1.

20. 'South Africa: New Opportunities for the ANC', *Africa Confidential*, vol. 32, no. 15, 1991; 'South Africa Watchdog', *African Business*, August 1991, p. 9; Lodge, 'The African National Congress in the 1990s', pp. 44–78.

21. 'Icons of Liberation', *New Statesmen & Society*, 21 August 1992.

22. The London-based journal *Searchlight South Africa* was largely responsible for bringing these allegations to light. See Bandile Ketalo et al., 'A Miscarriage of Democracy', *Searchlight South Africa* 5, 1990, pp. 35–65; and Stephen Ellis and Tsepo Sechaba, *Comrades Against Apartheid*, pp. 124–59.

23. *Southern Africa Report*, 27 August 1993, 3 September 1993; 'The Two who Got Away', *Work in Progress* 92, 1993, p. 3.

24. *New York Times*, 28 January 1993.

25. 'Integrate the Military while We Still Can', *Weekly Mail & Guardian*, 20–26 August 1993.

26. 'South Africa: The Party's Reluctant Revisionists', *Africa Confidential*, vol. 34, no. 16, 1993, p. 1; 'South Africa: Rewriting Party Politics', *Africa Confidential*, vol. 34, no. 14, 1993, pp. 3–4.

27. *New York Times*, 9 December 1993.

28. *Natal Post*, 6 March 1991.

29. After years of repression, the Party is understandably reluctant to divulge names and numbers. *Pretoria News*, 21 February 1991; *Star*, 13 July 1991; *New Nation*, 12 April 1991; *Sunday Times*, 1 December 1991.

30. For example, in 1993 three of the six top positions in COSATU were held by SACP members. See Patrick Laurence, 'South African Communist Party Strategy since February 1990', *South African Review* 6, pp. 79–94. A word of caution is in order here. COSATU conducted extensive discussions regarding its leadership joining the SACP in order to influence the political direction of the Party.

31. *New York Times*, 30 August 1991.

32. 'South Africa: New Opportunities for the ANC', pp. 1–2; 'Few Reds in the ANC's Bed', *Weekly Mail*, 26 July–1 August 1991.

33. At the ANC's December 1991 congress, SACP members were elected to nearly half of the fifty positions on the National Executive, and filled at least half of the elected seats on the twenty-member ANC National Working Committee,

or 'inner cabinet'. See Laurence, 'South African Communist Party Strategy since February 1990', pp. 84–5; *Sunday Times*, 1 December 1991; R.W. Johnson, 'The Past and Future of the South African Communist Party', *London Review of Books*, 24 October 1991, pp. 10–12; and 'South Africa: the SACP Soldiers On', *Africa Confidential*, vol. 33, no. 3, 1992, p. 3.

34. For a historical discussion, see T.R.H. Davenport, *South Africa: A Modern History*, 4th edn, Toronto and Buffalo 1991, pp. 350–51; and Raymond Suttner and Jeremy Cronin, *Thirty Years of the Freedom Charter*, Johannesburg 1985.

35. 'Waiting to Govern', *New Statesmen & Society*, 4 December 1992.

36. See discussion in NUMSA Bulletin, 'The SACP: A Basis for Socialist Unity', *South African Labour Bulletin*, vol. 15, no. 3, 1990, pp. 28–29.

37. See Joe Slovo, 'Has Socialism Failed?' *South African Labour Bulletin*, vol. 14, no. 6, 1990, pp. 11–28.

38. See also Michael Burawoy, 'Painting Socialism in Hungary', *South African Labour Bulletin*, vol. 15, no. 3, 1990, pp. 75–85; Adam Habib and Mercia Andrews, 'Disinheriting the Heritage of Stalinism', *South African Labour Bulletin*, vol. 15, no. 3, 1990, pp. 86–93.

39. Colin Bundy, 'Theory of a Special Type', *Work in Progress* 89, 1993, p. 17.

40. Pallo Jordan, 'Crisis of Conscience in the SACP', *South African Labour Bulletin*, vol. 15, no. 3, 1990, pp. 66–74; and Mike Morris, 'Dangerous Liaisons?' *New Era*, vol. 6, no. 1, 1991, pp. 16–17.

41. David Kitson, 'Is the SACP Really Communist?' *Work in Progress* 73, 1990, pp. 27–30.

42. Jeremy Cronin, 'Building the Legal Mass Party', *South African Labour Bulletin*, vol. 15, no. 3, 1990, pp. 5–11; 'Interview with Joe Slovo', *South African Labour Bulletin*, vol. 14, no. 8, 1990, pp. 35–46.

43. Slovo coupled this retreat from one of the main pillars of the ANC's *Freedom Charter* with assurances to representatives of large-scale capital that only a mixed economy would be able to guarantee future economic growth in South Africa. Instead of bureaucratic state control along Eastern European lines, he advocated public control through effective democratic participation by 'producers at all levels'. Trade-union critics charged that this formula resembled a classic social-democratic programme of co-determination where large firms are held publicly accountable and union representatives sit on corporate boards (*Argus*, 28 February 1990).

44. Devan Pillay, 'Having its Cake and Eating It', *Work in Progress* 80, 1992, pp. 20–22.

45. 'The Party's Reluctant Revisionists', pp. 1–2.

46. 'South Africa: the SACP Soldiers On', p. 3; 'South Africa: Rewriting Party Politics', pp. 3–5; 'The Party's Reluctant Revisionists', pp. 1–2. For an occasionally insightful but thoroughly scathing attack on the ANC/SACP alliance, see R.W. Johnson, 'Beloved Country', *London Review of Books*, 8 July 1993, pp. 3, 6; 'When that Great Day Comes', *London Review of Books*, 22 July 1993, pp. 8–10; and 'Magical Socialism', *London Review of Books*, 5 August 1993, pp. 22–23.

47. Pillay, 'Having Its Cake and Eating It', p. 20.

48. Bundy, 'Theory of a Special Type', p. 18.

49. 'The Party's Reluctant Revisionists', pp. 1–2.

50. John Battersby, 'Running with the PAC', *Work in Progress* 92, 1993, pp. 13–15.

51. Lodge, 'Rebellion: The Turning of the Tide', pp. 196–7.

52. Joe Thloloe, 'No Negotiators', *Work in Progress* 72, 1991, pp. 14–15.

53. 'PAC's Tough Horse Trader', *Weekly Mail*, 9–15 July 1993; and *Citizen*, 30 January 1991.

54. PASO called for a united front of student organizations, but was opposed to the participation of NUSAS, the former white university student organization, because its members 'are drawn from the ranks of the oppressor' (*New Nation*, 18 January 1991).

55. *Cape Times*, 23 February 1991; and Lodge, 'Rebellion: The Turning of the Tide', pp. 196–7.

56. Thloloe, 'No Negotiators', pp. 14–15; and 'Can "No-Talks" PAC Put the Squeeze on the ANC?', *Weekly Mail*, 5–11 April 1990. The PAC popularized twin slogans: 'One Settler, One Bullet' and 'Africa for the Africans'. While the first proved somewhat embarrassing, the second sowed confusion. The PAC leadership has gone to great pains to define settlers as those who have stolen the land and exploit the people, and to describe Africans as those who, regardless of skin colour, express their loyalty exclusively to Africa. Rank-and-file supporters of the PAC sometimes fail to make these fine-tuned distinctions and, as a consequence, sometimes regard all whites as settlers.

57. 'The Voice that Defies De Klerk and Mandela', *New York Times*, 4 April 1993.

58. Pan Africanist Congress of Azania, *Towards a Democratic Economic Order*, Johannesburg n.d.

59. Evangelos Mantzaris, 'Trying to Keep Out by Being Too Far In', *Work in Progress* 92, 1993, pp. 16–18; and Marina Ottoway, *South Africa: The Struggle for a New Order*, Washington DC 1993, pp. 72–4.

60. 'PAC on the Rack over Elections', *Weekly Mail & Guardian*, 17–22 December 1993.

61. *Star*, 26 March 1991; *Natal Witness*, 5 March 1991; David Hirschmann, 'The Black Consciousness Movement in South Africa', *Journal of Modern African Studies*, vol. 28, no. 1, 1990, pp. 22ff; *Evening Post*, 8 January 1991; *Cape Times*, 10 January 1991; and *The Leader*, 1 February 1991.

62. *Citizen*, 11 March 1991; *Sowetan*, 11 March 1991. AZAPO deputy president Dr Nchaupe Mokoape argued that the 'Government has surrendered literally nothing to our people while the ANC has surrendered almost everything'. 'The armed struggle has gone out the window; so has socialism, so have sanctions and the sports and cultural boycott; so, too, have the unconditional return of exiles and release of prisoners'. He declared that AZAPO was not fighting for a constituent assembly but for 'the takeover of power by black people, the repossession of their land and the institution of a socialist order in a unitary, democratic Azania' (*Star*, 11 March 1991).

63. Mondi Makhanya, 'AZAPO: Will Out of Sight Mean Out of Mind?' *Weekly Mail & Guardian*, 27 August–2 September 1993.

64. B. Rramadiro and Salim Vally, 'Now is the Time', *Work in Progress* 94, 1993, pp. 29–31.

65. Pippa Green, 'Who's Left? Who's Right?' *Work in Progress* 72, 1991, pp. 16–17.

66. 'Trying to Keep Out by Being Too Far In', p. 18.

67. *Financial Mail*, 24 April 1992; Philippa Garson, 'The PAC Enters the Fray',

Africa Report, November/December 1992, pp. 19–22; and 'Trying to Keep Out by Being Too Far In', p. 18.

68. Kogila Moodley, 'The Continued Impact of Black Consciousness in South Africa', *Journal of Modern African Studies*, vol. 29, no. 2, 1991, pp. 249–50.

69. The exiled Black Consciousness Movement of Azania maintains an armed wing called the Azanian National Liberation Army (AZANLA). Both APLA and AZANLA have followed a proto-Guevarist 'foco' approach to guerrilla warfare where tiny bands of lightly armed guerrillas have carried out surprise 'hit and run' attacks inside South Africa. Despite their self-proclaimed successes, these isolated actions have amounted to really nothing more than 'armed propaganda'. See *Eastern Province Herald*, 1 January 1991, 4 January 1991; *City Press*, 10 February 1991; *Sowetan*, 8 April 1991; *Star*, 4 February 1991; and *Citizen*, 25 March 1991.

70. 'Trying to Keep Out by Being Too Far In', p. 18.

71. 'PAC Militants Win Battle Against Negotiations',*Weekly Mail*, 11–17 December 1992; 'Kei Raid Fear after Attack on Whites', *Weekly Mail*, 23–29 December 1992; and 'Inside APLA', *Weekly Mail*, 26 March–1 April 1993.

72. 'Running with the PAC', pp. 14–15. In the eyes of some observers, the elated response of PASO members to the suspension of charges against township youths suspected of murdering US Fulbright exchange student Amy Biehl – killed for being 'a white in the wrong place' – in Gugulethu near Cape Town in August 1993 gave substance to these suspicions (*New York Times*, 27 August 1993 and 12 December 1993).

73. Bill Keller, 'A Brutalized Generation Turns its Rage on Whites', *New York Times*, 7 December 1993.

74. *Evening Post*, 22 February 1991; and Janis Grobbelaar, '*Bittereinders*: Dilemmas and Dynamics on the far Right', *South African Review 6*, pp. 102–11.

75. Peter Tygesen, 'The Right's Show of Might', *Africa Report*, July/August 1990, pp. 21–24; 'Agriculture: Growing Pains', *Financial Mail*, 1 March 1991; and Brian Du Toit, 'The Far Right in Current South African Politics', *Journal of Modern African Studies*, vol. 29, no. 4, 1991, pp. 627–67.

76. *Southern Africa Report*, 24 September 1993.

77. Du Toit, 'The Far Right in South Africa', pp. 638–9.

78. Annette Strauss, 'The 1992 Referendum in South Africa', *Journal of Modern African Studies*, vol. 31, no. 2, 1993, pp. 339–60.

79. This document also contended that 'We have to accept that the days of *apartheid* are numbered – that *apartheid* that determines where people can live or work or go to school, or relax, who they may marry and whether they may have the vote in the country of their birth' (*Sunday Tribune*, 14 April 1991; and *New York Times*, 1 March 1992).

80. *Argus*, 7 September 1991.

81. This phrases translates as 'White man, where is your homeland?' and is borrowed from W.J.G. Lubbe, ed., *Witman, Waar is jou Tuisland?*, Pretoria 1983.

82. Du Toit, 'The Far Right in South Africa', pp. 648–52.

83. *Africa Events*, April 1992.

84. Participants in the inaugural ceremonies sold T-shirts with the African continent painted black, apart from a white spot representing Orania, emblazoned with the slogan (in Afrikaans): 'Our nation-state is not for every baboon' (*Citizen*, 15 April 1991).

85. *Southern Africa Report*, 22 October 1993; *New York Times*, 26 February 1994.

86. Terre'Blanche accused de Klerk of treachery, branding him 'the greatest traitor' in South African history because 'he favoured the communists, trusted the ANC, and sold out the Boer'. The AWB called for a 'mighty, united white action front to fight the anti-Christ in the name of God' (*Sowetan*, 15 February 1991). See *South*, 28 March 1991; Helen Zille, 'The Right Wing in South African Politics', in Peter Berger and Bobby Goodsell, eds., *A Future South Africa: Visions, Strategies, and Realities*, Boulder, Colo. 1988, pp. 55–94; and 'The Major Organisations', *Weekly Mail & Guardian*, 31 March–7 April 1994.

87. *Argus*, 2 September 1991; *New York Times*, 12 August 1991; and 'Bitterenders Prepare for the Last Stand', *Africa Confidential*, vol. 33, no. 6, 1992, pp. 5–6.

88. *Financial Mail*, 10 January 1992; *Natal Witness*, 20 January 1992. For example, see the discussion of the 'armies of the right' in 'The Major Organisations', *Weekly Mail & Guardian*, 31 March–7 April 1994; and Johan Van Rooyen, *Hard Right: The New White Power in South Africa*, Johannesburg 1993.

89. Du Toit, 'The Far Right in South Africa', p. 666.

90. 'Rightists Unleash "the Ten Plagues"', *Weekly Mail*, 2–8 July 1993.

91. *Southern Africa Report*, 12 November 1993.

7. The Trade Unions and the Working Class

1. Quotation taken from Karl von Holdt, 'COSATU Special Congress: The Uncertain New Era', *South African Labour Bulletin*, vol. 17, no. 5, 1993, p. 19.

2. T.H. Marshall, *Class, Citizenship, and Social Development*, New York 1965, pp. 103–4, 122.

3. Karl Von Holdt, '1993: Make or Break for Labour', *South African Labour Bulletin*, vol. 17, no. 1, 1993, pp. 38–9; John Copelyn, 'Collective Bargaining: A Base for Transforming Industry', *South African Labour Bulletin*, vol. 15, no. 6, 1991, p. 26; Ferial Haffajee, 'A Year of Gains and New Ground', *Weekly Mail*, 18–22 December 1992; *Business Day*, 1 February 1991; *Business Day*, 26 March 1991; and Ian Macun, 'South African Unions: Still Growing?', *South African Labour Bulletin*, vol. 17, no. 4, 1993, pp. 48–53.

4. A number of left-wing trade unions, mainly smaller and regionally based, remained unaligned to either COSATU or NACTU. One primary example is that of the 7,000–strong Health Workers Union (HWU). Linked with WOSA, the HWU conducted a highly successful strike in Cape Town hospitals, where it secured the right to strike, to have representatives on the shop floor, and to negotiate on behalf of workers ('Cape Health Workers Win Major Demands', *South African Labour Bulletin*, vol. 14, no. 8, 1990, pp. 18–22).

5. Simon Norfolk, 'Farmers Block Agricultural Workers' Unions', *Work in Progress* 78, 1991, pp. 28–30.

6. Karl von Holdt, 'Cosatu Congress', *South African Labour Bulletin*, vol. 16, no. 1, 1991, p. 16; 'NUM President', *South African Labour Bulletin*, vol. 13, no. 4, 1992, p. 13; Von Holdt, '1993: Make or Break for Labour,' pp. 38–39; and Zwelinzima Vavi, 'The Name of the Game is Membership', *South African Labour Bulletin*, vol. 16, no. 8, 1992, p. 42. The anticipated merger of SAMWU, POTWA, and NEHAWU to form a giant public-sector union with some 200,000 members will be an additional boost to the organizational strength of COSATU. See Karl

von Holdt, 'Impressive Gains, Organisational Crisis', *South African Labour Bulletin*, vol. 17, no. 6, 1993, pp. 1–20.

7. Rob Lambert and Eddie Webster, 'The Re-emergence of Political Union- ism in Contemporary South Africa?', in William Cobbett and Robin Cohen, eds., *Popular Struggles in South Africa*, Trenton, NJ 1987, pp. 33–4; John Ernstzen, 'SAMWU: Three Years on the March', *South African Labour Bulletin*, vol. 15, no. 8, 1991, pp. 30–35.

8. 'It is a tradition in NUMSA that full-time paid officials do not participate in the congress debate. This approach arises from our view that the value of a policy lies in its support, understanding, and participation by worker leaders. Carefully managed congresses may please the media but they don't reflect workers' views' (Moses Mayekiso, 'Nationalism, Socialism, and the Alliance', *South African Labour Bulletin*, vol. 17, no. 4, 1993, p. 15).

9. Bobby Mare, 'COSATU Faces Crisis', *South African Labour Bulletin*, vol. 16, no. 5, 1992, pp. 20–26.

10. *Sowetan*, 27 February 1991; and Drew Forrest, 'Numsa Delegates Meet to Discuss Strikes', *Weekly Mail*, 21–27 June 1991.

11. Pat Horn, 'Review of *Striking Back*', *South African Labour Bulletin*, vol. 16, no. 4, 1992, pp. 67–8.

12. Alan Fine and Eddie Webster, 'Transcending Traditions: Trade Unions and Political Unity', *South African Review 5*, Johannesburg 1989, pp. 256–7.

13. Martin Plaut, 'Debates in a Shark Tank – The Politics of South Africa's Non-racial Trade Unions', *African Affairs* 91, 1992, pp. 396–7; and Jeremy Baskin, *Striking Back: A History of COSATU*, London 1991, pp. 34ff, 102–4.

14. Plaut, 'Debates in a Shark Tank', p. 389.

15. 'South Africa: The Cracks in COSATU', *Africa Confidential*, vol. 29, no. 11, 1988, p. 3.

16. Duncan Innes, 'The Freedom Charter and Workers' Control', *South African Labour Bulletin*, vol. 11, no. 2, 1985, pp. 38–9; Renee Roux, 'Workers' Charter Campaign', *South African Labour Bulletin*, vol. 14, no. 7, 1990, p. 29.

17. Fine and Webster, 'Transcending Traditions', pp. 262–3; Yunis Carrim, 'COSATU: Towards Disciplined Alliances', *Work in Progress* 49, 1987, pp. 9–12; Robyn Rafel, 'Workers' Charter: Taking it to the Streets', *Work in Progress* 69, 1990, p. 27; and Devan Pillay, 'The Workers' Charter Campaign', *South African Labour Bulletin*, vol. 15, no. 5, 1991, pp. 37–44.

18. Devan Pillay, 'The Communist Party and the Trade Unions', *South African Labour Bulletin*, vol. 15, no. 3, 1990, pp. 19–27.

19. Plaut, 'Debates in a Shark Tank', pp. 399–400; and Ferial Haffajee, '"Two Hats" Debate Rages in Cosatu', *Weekly Mail*, 21–27 June 1991.

20. John Copelyn, 'Collective Bargaining', pp. 26–33; Jeremy Cronin, 'Prepar- ing Ourselves for Permanent Opposition', *South African Labour Bulletin*, vol. 15, no. 7, 1991, p. 56; and John Copelyn, 'Preparing Ourselves for Permanent Independ- ence', *South African Labour Bulletin*, vol. 15, no. 8, 1991, pp. 55–6.

21. Karl von Holdt, 'The COSATU/ANC Alliance: What Does COSATU Think?', *South African Labour Bulletin*, vol. 15, no. 8, 1991, pp. 17–29.

22. Robyn Rafel, 'NACTU: A Little Bit of This and a Little Bit of That', *Work in Progress* 68, 1990, p. 20.

23. 'Interview with NACTU', *South African Labour Bulletin*, vol. 14, no. 1, 1989, pp. 20–23; and 'Broadly Speaking', *South African Labour Bulletin*, vol. 14, no. 6, 1990, p. 8.

24. *Business Day*, 1 February 1991; *Sunday Times*, 1 December 1991; *Business Day*, 26 March 1991; 'NACTU Women Speak Out', *South African Labour Bulletin*, vol. 17, no. 1, 1993, p. 72; 'NACTU is Restructuring', *Work in Progress* 81, April 1992, p. 22; and Von Holdt, 'Impressive Gains, Organisational Crisis', pp. 19–20.

25. Von Holdt, 'Impressive Gains, Organisational Crisis', pp. 19–20.

26. Devan Pillay, 'NACTU's Third Congress', *South African Labour Bulletin*, vol. 15, no. 4, 1990, pp. 54–61; David Niddrie, 'Using the Carrot or the Stick?' *Work in Progress* 75, 1991, p. 6; Eddie Koch, 'NACTU Congress: Change of Direction?' *South African Labour Bulletin*, vol. 13, no. 7, 1988, pp. 16–19; *Finance Week*, 11 October 1990; and *Sunday Times*, 1 December 1991.

27. *Argus*, 10 April 1991.

28. Cunningham Ngcukana, 'Worker Rights and Trade Union Unity in South Africa', *South African Labour Bulletin*, vol. 16, no. 1, 1991, pp. 23–6.

29. 'NACTU: Pulling No Punches', *South African Labour Bulletin*, vol. 16, no. 4, 1992, pp. 16–19.

30. Karl von Holdt, 'Editorial', *South African Labour Bulletin*, vol. 17, no. 5, 1993, p. 3.

31. Karl von Holdt, 'COSATU and the Craft Unions', *South African Labour Bulletin*, vol. 17, no. 2, 1993, pp. 29–34.

32. Ibid.; and von Holdt, 'Editorial', p. 3.

33. Glenda Daniels, '"One Union, One Federation" is no Longer a Dream', *Work in Progress* 82, June 1992, pp. 26–7; 'Interview with Manene Samela', *South African Labour Bulletin*, vol. 16, no. 8, 1992, pp. 53–6.

34. 'Congress Season', *South African Labour Bulletin*, vol. 17, no. 4, 1993, p. 11.

35. See 'CCAWUSA Settlement the Beginning', *South African Labour Bulletin*, vol. 13, no. 2, 1988, pp. 84–100.

36. 'Congress Season', *South African Labour Bulletin*, vol. 17, no. 4, 1993, pp. 9–10; Ferial Haffajee, 'Officials Defraud Union of R60,000', *Weekly Mail*, 2–8 July 1993; and 'SACCAWU in Turmoil', *Weekly Mail & Guardian*, 25 February–3 March 1994.

37. 'FEDSAL: The Moderate Voice of Labour', *South African Labour Bulletin*, vol. 17, no. 3, 1993, pp. 56–60; '"In the Number Two Spot": FEDSAL Conference', *South African Labour Bulletin*, vol. 17, no. 3, 1993, pp. 61–3; and FEDSAL: Economic Policy', *South African Labour Bulletin*, vol. 17, no. 6, 1993, pp. 32–3.

38. The common feature unifying these workers was that most were either highly skilled or operated in supervisory positions. However, the 'United Front' unions which joined FITU, including the State, Muncipal, Farm and Allied Workers' Union (formerly the Orange Vaal General Workers' Union), the Black Allied Trade Union (railway workers), the Brickmaker's Union, and the Black Allied Workers Union consist mainly of unskilled workers. FITU promised to focus primarily on job security, economic growth and political stability ('Labour Action', *South African Labour Bulletin*, vol. 15, no. 8, 1991, pp. 10–11; *Eastern Province Herald*, 23 March 1991; and Drew Forrest, 'New Federation Sets "Moderate" Course', *Weekly Mail*, 22–27 March 1991).

39. *Sunday Times*, 27 January 1991.

40. Robyn Rafel, 'White Workers of the World Unite', *Work in Progress* 72, 1991, p. 36; and *Business Day*, 22 February 1991.

41. 'Editorial', *South African Labour Bulletin*, vol. 17, no. 5, 1993, p. 3.

42. William Matlala, 'Black and White at Highveld Steel', *South African Labour*

Bulletin, vol. 17, no. 5, 1993, pp. 7–10; and Rafel, 'White Workers', p. 37.

43. Matlala, 'Black and White at Highveld Steel', pp. 7–10.

44. *Citizen*, 30 January 1991. The MWU transformed itself into a prototype all-purpose general union, with around two-thirds of its membership falling outside the mining industry, particularly in such sensitive sectors as transport, communications, power stations, iron and steel, and chemicals. The MWU maintained a long association with right-wing political parties (Rafel, 'White Workers', p. 39).

45. Rafel, 'White Workers', p. 39.

46. 'Right-wing Super-Union falters in its Stride', *Weekly Mail*, 7–13 February 1991; and 'Recruiting White Members is Uphill Struggle for COSATU', *South African Labour Bulletin*, vol. 17, no. 2, 1993, pp. 48–52.

47. Matlala, 'Black and White at Highveld Steel', pp. 7–10.

48. Karl von Holdt, 'Editorial', *South African Labour Bulletin*, vol. 17, no. 3, 1993, p. 3.

49. For a survey of these issues, see S. Pityana and M. Orkin, eds., *Beyond the Factory Floor: A Survey of COSATU Shop-stewards*, Johannesburg 1992.

50. Johann Maree, 'The Economic Case for Worker Participation: Co-Determination', in Robert Schrire, ed., *Wealth or Poverty? Critical Choices for South Africa*, Cape Town 1992, pp. 244–5; and B. Smith, 'Volkswagen's Holistic Approach to Worker Participation,' in M. Anstey, ed., *Worker Participation: South African Opinions and Experiences*, Cape Town 1990, pp. 236–9. For a wider view, see Judy Maller, *Conflict and Co-operation: Case Studies in Worker Participation*, Johannesburg 1992.

51. Eddie Webster, 'The Two Faces of the Black Trade Union Movement in South Africa', *Review of African Political Economy* 39, 1987, pp. 35–40.

52. Andre Kraak, 'Human Resources Development and Organised Labour', in Glenn Moss and Ingrid Obery, eds., *South African Review 6: From 'Red Friday' to CODESA*, Johannesburg 1992, pp. 416–18; and Welcome Ntshangase and Apollis Solomons, 'Adversarial Participation: A Union Response to Participatory Management', *South African Labour Bulletin*, vol. 17, no. 4, 1993, pp. 31–5.

53. Von Holdt, 'Impressive Gains, Organisational Crisis', pp. 16–17.

54. 'We bargain at plant level, which is a nightmare. We have to go from one negotiations to another. It overstretches our resources,' said Muzi Buthelezi, acting general sectretary of CWIU. From these reasons alone, CWIU made centralized bargaining the main campaign of the union for 1992. 'CWIU: Organisation and Worker Control', *South African Labour Bulletin*, vol. 16, no. 4, 1992, p. 45.

55. Shane Godfrey and Ian Macun, 'The Politics of Centralised Bargaining', *South African Review 6*, pp. 388–402; and Mike Morris, 'Unions and Industrial Councils – Why Do Unions' Policies Change?', in Nicoli Nattrass and Elisabeth Ardington, eds., *The Political Economy of South Africa*, Cape Town 1990, pp. 148–62.

56. See Martin Murray, *South Africa: Time of Agony, Time of Destiny*, London 1987, pp. 147–50, 173–6; and Baskin, *Striking Back*.

57. Jeremy Baskin, 'Time to Bury the Wiehahn Model?', *South African Labour Bulletin*, vol. 17, no. 4, 1993, pp. 54–63; and Godfrey and Macun, 'The Politics of Centralised Bargaining', pp. 388–402.

58. Godfrey and Macun, 'The Politics of Centralised Bargaining', p. 393.

59. 'Textile Industry Sews Up New Restructuring Deal', *Weekly Mail*, 17–23 January 1992; Karl von Holdt, 'What Future for Labour?', *South African Labour Bulletin*, vol. 16, no. 8, 1992, pp. 31–2; Shane Godfrey and Ian Macun, 'The Politics of Centralised Bargaining', *South African Review 6*, pp. 388–402; and Martin

Nicol, 'Profit-sharing Schemes: A Look at the Gold Mines', *South African Labour Bulletin*, vol. 17, no. 4, 1993, pp. 37–45.

60. Von Holdt, 'Impressive Gains, Organisational Crisis', pp. 17–18.

61. I would like to thank Jane Barrett for pointing out these examples to me. See Baskin, 'Time to Bury the Wiehahn Model?', pp. 54–63.

62. See Jane Barrett, 'Difficult Sectors: A Challenge for Labour', *South African Labour Bulletin*, vol. 17, no. 6, 1993, pp. 44–50.

63. Rene Roux, 'National Strike Wave for Wages', *South African Labour Bulletin*, vol. 15, no. 2, 1990, pp. 4–10.

64. Johann Maree, 'Trade Unions and Corporatism in South Africa', *Transformation* 21, 1993, pp. 30–31; and Geoff Schreiner, 'Fossils from the Past: Resurrecting and Restructuring the National Manpower Commission', *South African Labour Bulletin*, vol. 16, no. 1, 1991, pp. 32–40.

65. Maree, 'Trade Unions and Corporatism in South Africa', p. 31.

66. Jeremy Baskin, 'The Trend towards Bargained Corporatism', *South African Labour Bulletin*, vol. 17, no. 3, 1993, pp. 64–69; and 'COSATU Platform on Worker Rights', *South African Labour Bulletin*, vol. 17, no. 5, 1993, pp. 32–3.

67. Schreiner, 'Fossils from the Past', pp. 32–40; and 'What is the Future of Labour?', p, 30.

68. *Business Day*, 7 February 1991, 15 February 1991; and *Daily Dispatch*, 21 February 1991.

69. 'What is the Future of Labour?', pp. 30–31; and 'National General Strike', *South African Labour Bulletin*, vol. 16, no. 2, 1991, pp. 13–17.

70. *Daily Dispatch*, 4 April 1991; and 'COSATU Congress', *South African Labour Bulletin*, vol. 16, no. 1, 1991, p. 12.

71. For a useful debate, see 'Debate: Social Democracy or Democratic Socialism', *South African Labour Bulletin*, vol. 17, no. 6, 1993, pp. 72–101.

72. Karl von Holdt, 'From Resistance to Reconstruction', *South African Labour Bulletin*, vol. 15, no. 6, 1991, p. 14; Kraak, 'Human Resources Development and Organised Labour', pp. 416–18; and Schreiner, 'Fossils from the Past', p. 35.

73. Avril Joffe and Dave Lewis, 'A Strategy for South African Manufacturing', *South African Labour Bulletin*, vol. 16, no. 4, 1992, pp. 30–31.

74. 'Productivity: Participating to Achieve Control', *South African Labour Bulletin*, vol. 16, no. 2, 1991, p. 19.

75. Karl von Holdt, 'The Dangers of Corporatism,' *South African Labour Bulletin*, vol. 17, no. 1, 1993, pp. 46–51.

76. Karl von Holdt, 'What is the Future of Labour?', p. 33.

77. See John Saul, 'South Africa: Between "Barbarism" and "Structural Reform"', *New Left Review* 188, 1991, pp. 3–44; and 'Structural Reform: A Model for the Revolutionary Transformation of South Africa?', in J. Saul, ed., *Recolonization and Resistance in Southern Africa*, Trenton, NJ, 1993, pp. 143–69. For a critical assessment of these ideas, see Lawrence Harris, 'One Step Forward', *Work in Progress* 89, 1993, pp. 20–22.

78. Karl von Holdt, 'What is the Future of Labour?', pp. 33, 37.

79. Karl von Holdt, 'Towards Transforming South African Industry: a "Reconstruction Accord" between Unions and the ANC?', *South African Labour Bulletin*, vol. 15, no. 6, 1991, pp. 17–25; John Copelyn, 'Collective Bargaining', pp. 26–33; Enoch Godongwana, 'Industrial Restructuring and the Social Contract', *South African Labour Bulletin*, vol. 16, no. 4, 1992, pp. 20–23; Geoff Schreiner and Adrienne

Bird, 'COSATU at the Crossroads: Towards Tripartite Corporatism or Democratic Socialism?', *South African Labour Bulletin*, vol. 16, no. 6, 1992, pp. 22–32; and Kraak, 'Human Resources Development and Organised Labour', pp. 417–420.

80. For excellent summaries, see Johann Maree, 'Trade Unions and Corporatism in South Africa', *Transformation* 21, 1993, pp. 24–54; and Geoff Schreiner, 'Beyond Corporatism: Towards New Forms of Public Policy Formulation in South Africa', *Transformation* 23, 1994, pp. 1–22.

81. The most eloquent critique is Lawrence Harris, 'South Africa's Economic and Social Transformation: From "No Middle Road" to "No Alternative"', *Review of African Political Economy* 57, 1993, pp. 91–102. 'The principle [of structural reforms] suffers from the weakness of all forms of determinism, for we know there is no such thing as a set of changes that necessarily flow from changes already achieved and we also know that while mass struggles can increase empowerment in the sense of heightened consciousness and the space in which to act, it is a "residue" which is easily erased by the high powered cleaning fluid (or dark paint) of reaction' (p. 94).

82. Baskin, 'The Trend towards Bargained Corporatism', pp. 64–8; Johann Maree, 'The Economic Case for Worker Participation: Co-determination', in Robert Schrire, ed., *Wealth or Poverty?*, pp. 237–59; Maree, 'Trade Unions and Corporatism', pp. 24–54; and Godongwana, 'Industrial Restructuring and the Social Contract', pp. 20–23.

83. Roger Etkind and Suzanna Harvey, 'The Workers Cease Fire', *South African Labour Bulletin*, vol. 17, no. 4, 1993, pp. 84–7.

84. For a broader discussion, see Leo Panich, 'Trade Unions and the State', *New Left Review* 125, January–February 1981, pp. 21–44.

85. Alex Callinicos, 'Reform and Revolution in South Africa: A Reply to John Saul', *New Left Review* 195, September–October 1992, pp. 111–15.

86. Callinicos, 'Reform and Revolution in South Africa', pp. 111–15.

87. These were the views of Salim Vally, education officer of SACCAWU (Glenda Daniels, 'Will Labour Agree to a Social Contract?', *Work in Progress* 81, 1992, pp. 25).

88. Karl von Holdt, '"Worker Control": New Meanings?', *South African Labour Bulletin*, vol. 16, no. 3, 1992, pp. 64–5.

89. 'Editorial', *South African Labour Bulletin*, vol. 16, no. 5, 1992, p. 1.

90. Schreiner and Bird, 'COSATU at the Crossroads', pp. 28–29.

91. Von Holdt, 'COSATU Special Congress', pp. 22–3; 'COSATU Platform on Worker Rights', *South African Labour Bulletin* vol. 17, no. 5, 1993, pp. 32–35; and Zolile Mtshelwane, 'First it was Two Hats', *Work in Progress* 92, 1993, pp. 29–31. For a biographical sketch of key trade-union officials slated to take their place in the National Assembly and in the Cabinet, see 'South Africa: the Fruits of Labour', *Africa Confidential* vol. 35, no. 8, 1994, pp. 1–3.

92. 'South Africa: The Mandate for Mandela', *Africa Confidential* vol. 35, no. 9, 1994, pp. 1–2.

93. The first quotation is from an avid supporter of the RDP (Phillip Dexter, 'Make the RDP Make the Left', *Work in Progress* 95, 1994, p. 30). The second is from Karl von Holdt ('COSATU Special Congress', p. 23).

94. 'Discussion Paper', *South African Labour Bulletin*, vol. 17, no. 4, 1993, p. 22.

95. 'Political Report to SACTWU Congress, 1993', *South African Labour Bulletin*, vol. 17, no. 4, 1993, p. 23; and Moses Mayekiso, 'Nationalisation, Socialism,

and the Alliance', *South African Labour Bulletin*, vol. 17, no. 4, 1993, p. 24.

96. Mayekiso, 'Nationalisation, Socialism, and the Alliance', pp. 14–24; and 'A Social Market Economy Offers the Best Hope', *South African Labour Bulletin*, vol. 17, no. 4, 1993, pp, 25–30.

97. The actual wording of the proposal was as follows: '[NUMSA's congress resolved to:] look at new forms of organisation that will unify the working-class organisations and parties, that will take forward a programme to implement socialism. This could take the form of a Working Class Party' (see Mayekiso, 'Nationalisation, Socialism and the Alliance', p. 19).

98. For various positions on the debate, see Jeremy Cronin, 'Back to the Future? A Brazilian Workers' Party in SA?', *Work in Progress* 91, 1993, pp. 30–32; Neville Alexander, 'Don't Dismiss a Workers' Party', *Weekly Mail & Guardian*, 30 July–5 August 1993; Mzwanele Mayekiso, 'Reinventing the Hammer and Sickle' *Work in Progress* 92, 1993, pp. 37–9; Fareed Abdullah, 'Let a Conference of the Left Decide', *Work in Progress* 92, 1993, pp. 40–41; and B. Ramadiro and Salim Vally, 'Now is the Time', *Work in Progress* 94, 1993, pp. 29–31.

99. For these two contrasting positions, see Mayekiso, 'Nationalisation, Socialism, and the Alliance', pp. 20–21; and Ramadiro and Vally, 'Now is the Time', pp. 29–31, respectively.

100. 'An independent, trade-union based workers' party ... is premised on the belief that the ANC will soon be "the government," and nothing but the government. Once in power the ANC will do exactly what certain other liberation movements have done – wave goodbye to popular aspirations. Could this happen? It certainly could. But to simply assume it will, is to walk away from the most important challenge of our time: the battle for the life and soul of the ANC.... The ANC must remain a broad, mass-based national liberation movement. The place of socialist, left and working-class formations is within this broad, ANC-led movement – not out on the margins.... The workers' party idea prepares workers for permanent opposition, permanent defence, permanent marginalisation' (Jeremy Cronin, '"Workers" Party Plays into Nat Hands', *Weekly Mail*, 23–29 July 1993). For the second quotation, see 'Discussion Paper', *South African Labour Bulletin*, vol. 17, no. 4, 1993, p. 22.

101. Dexter, 'Make the RDP Make the Left', pp. 30–32.

8. Civic Associations and Popular Democracy

1. Michael Bell, Philip Dearborn and Roland Hunter, 'Financing the Post-Apartheid City in South Africa', *Urban Studies*, vol. 30, no. 3, 1993, pp. 581–2; and Mark Swilling and Khehla Shubane, 'Negotiating Urban Transition: the Soweto Experience', in R. Lee and L. Schlemmer, eds., *Transition to Democracy: Policy Perspective in 1991*, Cape Town 1991, pp. 223–58.

2. Angel Flisfisch, *La Politica como Compromiso Democratico*, Santiago 1987, pp. 1–12.

3. Monty Narsoo, 'Civil Society: a Contested Terrain', *Work in Progress* 76, 1991, pp. 24–7.

4. Alain Touraine, *The Return of the Actor*, Minneapolis 1988.

5. Khehla Shubane, 'Black Local Authorities: A Contraption of Control', in Mark Swilling, Richard Humphries, and Khehla Shubane, eds., *The Apartheid City in Transition*, Cape Town 1991, pp. 72–5; and Jeremy Seekings, *Quiescence and the*

Transition to Confrontation: South African Townships, 1978–1984, unpublished Ph.D. thesis, Oxford 1990.

6. Shubane, 'Black Local Authorities' pp. 65–7.

7. M. Chaskalson, Karen Jochelson, and Jeremy Seekings, 'Rent Boycotts, the State, and the Transformation of the Urban Political Economy', *Review of African Political Economy* 40, 1988, pp. 47–66; and Jeremy Seekings, 'Township Resistance in the 1980s', in Swilling et al., *The Apartheid City in Transition*, pp. 290–308.

8. Jeremy Seekings, 'Civic Organisations in South African Townships', in Glenn Moss and Ingrid Obrey, eds., *South African Review 6: From 'Red Friday' to CODESA*, Johannesburg 1992, pp. 223–5.

9. Steven Friedman, 'Beyond Symbols? The Politics of Economic Compromise', in Robert Schrire, ed., *Wealth or Poverty? Critical Choices for South Africa*, Cape Town 1992, pp. 616–17; Jo-Anne Collinge, 'Defiance: A Measure of Expectations', *Work in Progress* 61, 1989, pp. 5–8; and Shubane, 'Black Local Authorities', pp. 65–7.

10. Ben Jacobs, 'Heading for Disaster?', *Work in Progress* 86, December 1992, pp. 23–24.

11. Cas Coovadia, 'The Role of the Civic Movement', in *The Apartheid City in Transition*, pp. 336–7.

12. Seekings, 'Civic Organisations in South African Townships', pp. 232–3.

13. 'Civics Move in as Councillors Move Out', *Weekly Mail*, 23–29 July 1993.

14. Jacobs, 'Heading for Disaster?', pp. 23–4; and Xolela Mangcu, 'Social Movements and City Planning: The Case of South Africa', *Working Papers in Planning*, *138*, Department of City and Regional Planning, Cornell University, October 1993, pp. 13–20.

15. Mangcu, 'Social Movements and City Planning', p. 18.

16. Friedman, 'Beyond Symbols?', pp. 616–17. Political activists in Natal fought to link the civics to the ANC. For a critique, see Mzwanele Mayekiso, 'Hands Off the Civics and Civil Society', *Work in Progress* 81, 1992, p. 21.

17. See Allan Horwitz, 'Civics at the Crossroads', *Reconstruct* 13, 1993, pp. 10–11.

18. Seekings, 'Civic Organisation in South African Townships', pp. 232–3.

19. 'Boycott: Settlement Hopes Recede', *Urban Focus*, vol. 1, no. 8, October 1990, p. 5.

20. *Business Day*, 13 February 1991; 'Struggle at the Local Level', *Mayibuye* 1, 1990, p. 1; and Leila McKenna and Pascal Moloi, 'Little Headway with Local Negotiations', *Reconstruct* 8, June 1993, pp. 12–13.

21. *Business Day*, 27 January 1991; This effort included the staging of mass marches demanding the resignation of town councillors, ostracizing their families, the dumping of litter and nightsoil outside their homes, and boycotts of their businesses (*Daily Dispatch*, 29 January 1991).

22. *Urban Focus*, vol. 1, no. 9, 1990, p. 4; and Rehana Rossouw, 'Civics Start Learning to Govern', *South*, 15–21 August 1991.

23. 'In Office, Under Fire in S. Africa', *Los Angeles Times*, 30 December 1990; *Christian Science Monitor*, 30 December 1990.

24. *Citizen*, 20 March 1991; *Financial Mail*, 7 December 1990.

25. *Business Day*, 18 January 1991; *Evening Post*, 5 April 1991; and *Business Day*, 19 February 1991.

26. See McKenna and Moloi, 'Little Headway with Local Negotiations', pp. 12–13.

27. Friedman, 'Beyond Symbols?', p. 617.

28. *Star*, 11 March 1991; and 'Local Interim Agreements in Trouble', *Urban Focus*, vol. 1, no. 9, November 1990, p. 7.

29. *Sowetan*, 4 January 1991; and Jo-Anne Collinge, 'Soul-Searching for Strategy to Define "New" Local Government', *Star*, 4 April 1991.

30. *Business Day*, 19 February 1991.

31. In Soweto, a steadfast groups of councillors banded together under the slogan 'Enough is Enough – An Injury to One Councillor is an Injury to All', and vowed to remain in their council seats until a new form of local government was introduced (*Sowetan*, 25 February 1991; *Business Day*, 15 February 1991; and 'All Transvaal Councillors now Members of Inkatha', *Weekly Mail*, 28 March–4 April 1991).

32. Graeme Reid and William Cobbett, 'Negotiating in Bad Faith', *South African Review 6*, pp. 239–40.

33. 'Civics go National', *Reconstruct* 2, April 1992, p. 1; Jacobs, 'Heading for Disaster?', pp. 23–5; and Mzwanele Mayekiso, 'Organising Civics: We Need a Tight Federation', *Work in Progress* 88, 1993, pp. 28–9.

34. 'In a Nutshell', *Reconstruct* 8, June 1993, p. 10.

35. 'Trends in Urban Organisation', *Reconstruct* 15, December 1992, p. 4; and 'Training for Transformation', *Reconstruct* 8, June 1993, p. 1.

36. 'Financing the Post-*Apartheid* City in South Africa', pp. 585–6; and Swilling and Shubane, 'Negotiating Urban Transition', pp. 224, 233–4.

37. Louwrens Pretorius and Richard Humphries, 'The Conservative Party and Local Government', in Swilling et al., *The Apartheid City in Transition*, pp. 309–20.

38. *Southern Africa Report*, 29 October 1993.

39. Kerry Cullinan, 'Zevenfontein – TBA meets Massive Resistance', *Reconstruct* 4, July 1992, pp. 4–5.

40. For an interesting description, see Bill Keller, 'Boksburg's Goofy White Smiles', *New York Times Magazine*, 19 September 1993.

41. Steve Friedman, 'Settlement Unlikely to Favour Urban Poor', *Reconstruct* 15, December 1993, pp. 1–3.

42. Mzwanele Mayekiso, 'From the Trench to the Table', *Work in Progress* 95, 1994, pp. 19–21; and Mzwanele Mayekiso, 'The "Civics", Home of the Townships', *Times Literary Supplement*, 1 April 1994, p. 8.

43. Hein Marais, 'Split Votes', *Work in Progress* 95, 1994, p. 21.

44. Shubane, 'Black Local Authorities', p. 75.

45. M.J. van Wyk, 'Civil Society and Democracy in South Africa', *Africa Insight*, vol. 23, no. 3, 1993, pp. 136–40.

46. Steve Mufson, 'Toward a Civil Society', *New Republic*, July 1990, pp. 20–25.

47. Robert Fine, 'Civil Society Theory and the Politics of Transition in South Africa', *Review of African Political Economy* 55, 1992, pp. 71–3.

48. M. Walzer, 'The Idea of Civil Society: A Path to Social Reconstruction', *Dissent*, Spring 1991, pp. 293–304.

49. Fine, 'Civil Society Theory', pp. 72–3.

50. Graeme Bloch, 'Let's Have Some Action!', *Work in Progress* 89, 1993, pp. 24–5.

51. Fine, 'Civil Society Theory', p. 82; and Steve Friedman, 'An Unlikely Utopia:

State and Civil Society in South Africa', *Politikon*, vol. 19, no. 1, 1991, pp. 5–19.
    52. Allan Horwitz, 'Civics at the Crossroads', *Reconstruct* 13, September 1993, pp. 10–11.

9. The Brokered Eclipse of White Minority Rule

    1. Mark Swilling, 'Introduction: The Politics of Stalemate', in Philip Frankel, Noam Pines and Mark Swilling, eds., *State, Resistance and Change in South Africa*, London 1988, p. 11.
    2. James Hamill, 'South Africa: from Codesa to Leipzig?', *World Today*, vol. 49, no. 1, 1993, p. 16.
    3. Heribert Adam and Kogila Moodley suggest that 'It [was] their mutual weakness rather than their equal strength, that [made] both long-time adversaries embrace nogotiations for power-sharing.' While this assessment contains a kernel of truth, it is an exaggerated position. See Heribert Adam and Kogilia Moodley, *The Opening of the Apartheid Mind: Options for the New South Africa*, London and Berkeley 1993, p. 1.
    4. Harold Pakendorf, 'Coming to Grips with Power', *Africa Report*, November/December 1991, pp. 49–51.
    5. Martin Plaut, 'Optimism as *Apartheid* Dies', *London Tribune*, 21 June 1991.
    6. 'South Africa: New Reality', *New York Times*, 23 December 1991.
    7. Seymour Martin Lipset, 'Compromise Needed in Pretoria', *Times Literary Supplement*, 20 September 1991, p. 10. For an elaboration of these positions, see Richard Humphries, 'Confusion of Options', *Democracy in Action*, vol. 6, no. 6, October 1992, pp. 14–15.
    8. Michael MacDonald, 'The Siren's Song: The Political Logic of Power-Sharing in South Africa', *Journal of Southern African Studies*, vol. 18, no. 4, 1992, pp. 715–18.
    9. Patrick Laurence, 'Deadlocked', *Africa Report*, July/August 1992, pp. 55–7.
    10. 'South Africa: After Boipatong', *Africa Confidential*, vol. 33, no. 14, 1992, pp. 1–3; Jeremy Cronin, 'The Boat, the Tap, and the Leipzig Way', *African Communist*, 3rd Quarter 1992; and Hamill, 'South Africa: from Codesa to Leipzig?, pp. 12–13.
    11. 'South Africa: After Boipatong', pp. 1–3; and 'South Africa: Back on Speaking Terms', *Africa Confidential*, vol. 33, no. 17, 1992, pp. 3–4.
    12. Hamill, 'South Africa', p. 14.
    13. See Patrick Laurence, 'Buthelezi's Gamble', *Africa Report*, November/December 1992, pp. 13–18.
    14. Vincent Maphai, 'Prospects for a Democratic South Africa', *International Affairs*, vol. 69, no. 2, 1993, pp. 223–37.
    15. Laurence, 'Buthelezi's Gamble', pp. 16–17.
    16. 'Zulu Chief Leads Unlikely Alliance', *New York Times*, 26 November 1993; and 'South Africa: The Generals are Nervous', *Africa Confidential*, vol. 35, no. 4, 1994, p. 3.
    17. *Southern Africa Report*, 4 December 1992; *The Economist*, 3 October 1992; Laurence, 'Buthelezi's Gamble', pp. 16–17; Philippa Garson, 'Raising the Stakes', *Africa Report*, March/April 1993, pp. 33–5.
    18. Heribert Adam and Kogila Moodley, 'Political Violence, "Tribalism" and Inkatha', *Journal of Modern African Studies*, vol. 30, no. 3, 1992, pp. 498–9. For

Venda, see also Mbulelo Mdledle, 'The Paradoxical Agenda of the "People's Brigadier"', *Work in Progress* 79, 1991, pp. 14–15.

19. Gerhard Maré, *Ethnicity and Politics in South Africa*, London 1992; Tom Robbins, 'The Real and Would-Be Zulu King', *Weekly Mail*, 20–26 November 1992; *The Economist*, 3 October 1992; and Mike Morris and Doug Hindson, 'The Disintegration of *Apartheid*: From Violence to Reconstruction', in Glenn Moss and Ingrid Obrey, eds., *South African Review 6: From 'Red Friday' to CODESA*, Johannesburg 1992, pp. 153–4.

20. 'South Africa: Gatsha's Last Stand', *Africa Confidential*, vol. 33, no. 21, 1992, p. 2; 'South Africa: Negotiations as Beirut Beckons', *Africa Confidential*, vol. 33, no. 23, 1992, pp. 2–3; 'Inkatha Prises Open Cracks in NP', *Weekly Mail*, 23–29 July 1993.

21. *Southern Africa Report*, 18 December 1992; 'South Africa: Negotiations as Beirut Beckons', pp. 2–3; *Southern Africa Report* 8 January 1993; and *New York Times*, 18 January 1993.

22. 'South Africa: Negotiations as Beirut Beckons', pp. 1–2; Paul Stober, 'Slovo's "Sunset" Debate is Red-hot', *Weekly Mail*, 30 October–5 November 1992; and Joe Slovo, 'Negotiations: What Room for Compromise?', *African Communist*, 3rd Quarter 1992.

23. 'South Africa: Sharing the Silken Sheets', *Africa Confidential*, vol. 34, no. 3, 1993, pp. 5–6.

24. 'South Africa: Gatsha's Last Stand', pp. 1–3; and 'South Africa: After Boipatong', pp. 1–3.

25. *Southern Africa Report*, 18 December 1992.

26. 'South Africa: Sharing the Silken Sheets', p. 5; and 'South Africa: All on Board', *Africa Confidential*, vol. 34, no. 6, 1993, pp. 3–4.

27. Patrick Laurence, 'The Diehards and the Dealmakers', *Africa Report*, November/December 1993, pp. 15–16; and 'South Africa: Biting the Ballot', *Africa Confidential*, vol. 34, no. 18, 1993, p. 1.

28. Laurence, 'The Diehards and the Dealmakers', pp. 15–16; J.E. Spence, 'South Africa: Countdown to Election', *World Today*, vol. 49, nos. 8–9, 1993, pp. 148–9; and *Southern Africa Report*, 12 November 1993.

29. *The Economist*, 14 August 1993; and *New York Times*, 3 January 1994.

30. *Southern Africa Report*, 29 October 1993; 'South Africa: Elections Under Threat', *Africa Confidential*, vol. 34, no. 17, 1993, pp. 3–4; and *The Economist*, 14 August 1993.

31. Laurence, 'The Diehards and Dealmakers', pp. 13–14.

32. *The Economist*, 11 September 1993; 'The Police from Paris', *Africa Confidential*, vol. 35, no. 2, 1994, p. 2; and *The Economist*, 15 January 1994.

33. *The Economist*, 11 September 1993.

34. *The Economist*, 6 November 1993.

35. Stanley Uys, 'The Retreating Right', *Times Literary Supplement*, 1 April 1994, p. 6; *Southern Africa Report*, 1 October 1993; *Southern Africa Report* 19 November 1993; 'Pact Ushers in Government of National Unity', *Financial Times*, 18 November 1993; and 'Constitution Provides a Framework for the New South Africa', *African Business*, February 1994, pp. 11–12.

36. 'Pact Ushers in Government of National Unity'.

37. *New York Times*, 18 November 1993.

38. Ibid.

39. *Southern Africa Report*, 19 November 1993; and Paul Taylor, 'South African Black, White Leaders Agree on New Charter', *Washington Post*, 18 November 1993.

40. 'Pact Ushers in Government of National Unity'.

41. Taylor, 'South African Black, White Leaders Agree on New Charter'; and 'South Africa: The End of the Beginning', *Africa Confidential*, vol. 35, no. 1, 1994, p. 3.

42. *Washington Post*, 18 November 1993.

43. Patti Waldmeir, 'Dawn of the New South Africa', *Financial Times*, 18 November 1993.

44. Patti Waldmeir, 'De Klerk Settles below Bottom Line on Safeguards', *Financial Times*, 18 November 1993.

45. *New York Times*, 18 November 1993.

46. *The Economist*, 10 July 1993, and 20 November 1993.

47. *Southern Africa Report*, 27 August 1993; 'The Right Bites Back', *Africa Confidential*, vol. 34, no. 11, 1993, p. 3; and 'Viljoen Unites the Volk', *Africa Confidential*, vol. 34, no. 18, 1993, p. 2.

48. *Southern Africa Report*, 27 August 1993.

49. 'Viljoen Unites the Volk', p. 2; and 'South Africa: Waiting for KwaZulu', *Africa Confidential*, vol. 35, no. 6, 1994, p. 1.

50. *Southern Africa Report*, 22 October 1993; and 'South Africa: Elections Under Threat', *Africa Confidential*, vol. 34, no. 17, 1993, pp. 3–4.

51. 'South Africa: Elections Under Threat', pp. 3–4.

52. Laurence, 'The Diehards and the Dealmakers', pp. 15–16.

53. *Southern Africa Report*, 15 October 1993.

54. 'South Africa: The End of the Beginning', pp. 1–2.

55. 'NP the Only Winner with New Concessions', *Weekly Mail & Guardian*, 25 February–3 March 1994.

56. 'South Africa: Partners in Policing', *Africa Confidential*, vol. 35, no. 2, 1994, p. 1; and Patrick Laurence, 'The 11th Hour', *Africa Report*, March/April 1994, pp. 35–9.

57. 'Zulu King Demands Sovereign State', *Weekly Mail & Guardian*, 11–17 February 1994; and *African Concord*, 7 February 1994.

58. 'Zulu Vendetta Clouds the South African Election', *New York Times*, 6 November 1993.

59. *Southern Africa Report*, 12 November 1993; and 'Document Reveals Right's War Plan', *Weekly Mail & Guardian*, 4–10 March 1994.

60. *Southern Africa Report*, 12 November 1993; and 'Fight for 283 Towns', *Weekly Mail & Guardian*, 4–10 March 1994.

61. 'South Africa: The Generals are Nervous', *Africa Confidential*, vol. 35, no. 4, 1994, p. 4.

62. 'South African White Separatists on Fool's Errand', *New York Times*, 12 March 1994; and Patrick Laurence, 'Civil Servants Bring Down Last "Homeland"', *Southern Africa Report*, 18 March 1994.

63. 'South African White Separatists on Fool's Errand'; Laurence, 'Civil Servants Bring Down last "Homeland"'; and Patrick Laurence, 'Aceeding to the Inevitable', *Africa Report*, May/June 1994, pp. 68–70.

64. 'A Homeland's Agony', *New York Times*, 13 March 1994; 'South Africa: Waiting for KwaZulu', p. 1; and 'South Africa: All Right for the Right', *Africa Confidential*, vol. 35, no. 7, 1994, pp. 1–2.

65. 'South Africa: Waiting for KwaZulu', p. 1; and Laurence, 'Acceeding to the Inevitable', p. 70.

66. 'The Major Organisations', *Weekly Mail & Guardian*, 31 March–7 April 1994; 'A Tide of Violence Swells in Zulu Area as Vote Nears', *New York Times*, 28 March 1994; and 'Zulu Leader', *New York Times*, 29 March 1994.

67. '9 in South African Family are Slain', *New York Times*, 4 April 1994; and Laurence, 'Acceding to the Inevitable', pp. 69–70.

68. 'Zulu Men Train for a Battle South Africa Hopes to Avoid', *New York Times*, 1 April 1994; and 'KwaZulu Gears up for Guerrilla War', *Weekly Mail & Guardian*, 25–30 March 1994.

69. *Southern Africa Report*, 25 March 1994; Drew Forrest, 'Peacemaker? The Records Tell Otherwise' and 'The Bloody Web of the "Third Force" Violence', *Weekly Mail & Guardian*, 25–30 March 1994; Oblie Chukwumba, 'Tension and Bloody Violence', *African Accord*, 11 April 1994; and 'War to Keep *Apartheid* Spawned Terror Network', *New York Times*, 20 March 1994.

70. Stanley Uys, 'The Retreating Right', p. 6.

71. 'Who Lost the Battle of Johannesburg?', *Weekly Mail & Guardian*, 31 March–7 April 1994; 'Breaking Point in Zululand', *Time*, 11 April 1994; 'At Least 31 Killed in Gun Battles in Johannesburg', *New York Times*, 29 March 1994; and *Southern Africa Report*, 31 March 1994.

72. *New York Times*, 1 April 1994; and Laurence, 'Acceding to the Inevitable', p. 70.

73. 'Zulu King', *New York Times*, 9 April 1994; and Laurence, 'Acceding to the Inevitable', p. 70.

74. 'South African Panel Urges Crackdown on Zulu Region', *New York Times*, 25 March 1994.

75. 'Zulu Party Ends Boycott of Vote', *New York Times*, 20 April 1994; 'Why Buthelezi Backed Down', *Weekly Mail & Guardian*, 22–28 April 1994; and Patrick Laurence, 'Buthelezi's Eleventh-Hour Entry into the Elections', *Southern Africa Report*, 22 April 1994.

Postscript

1. Craig Charney, 'Democracy Won', *New York Times*, 27 April 1994.

2. 'South Africa: Sharing Power', *Africa Confidential*, vol. 35, no. 10, 1994, pp. 2–3; and '31 White Rightists', *New York Times*, 28 April 1994.

3. Sarah Baxter, 'A Better Life for All?', *New Statesman & Society*, 22 April 1994, pp. 24–6.

4. 'Crackdown by Pretoria Barely Felt in Zulu Area', *New York Times*, 12 April 1994.

5. 'Mandela's Honeymoon', *New York Times*, 4 May 1994.

6. 'South Africa: the Mandate for Mandela', *Africa Confidential*, vol. 35, no. 9, 1994, pp. 1–3.

7. The estimated number of eligible voters were geographically distributed in the following way: PWV, 4.9 million; Natal, 4.6 million; Eastern Cape, 3.2 million; Western Cape, 2.4 million; Northern Transvaal, 2.3 million; North West, 1.7 million; Eastern Transvaal, 1.6 million; Free State, 1.6 million; and Northern Cape, 440,000 – a total of 22.7 million.

8. 'Mandela's Party Grasps Firm Lead', *New York Times*, 2 May 1994; 'Mandela

Proclaims a Victory', *New York Times*, 3 May 1994; 'The Ballot's Been the Bullet for the PAC', *Weekly Mail & Guardian*, 6–12 May 1994; and 'Defections and Debacles Hit Bruised DP', *Weekly Mail & Guardian*, 10–16 June 1994.

9. 'The Big Hole in the Northern Cape', *Weekly Mail & Guardian*, 13–19 May 1994.

10. 'De Klerk's Party is Dividing Nonwhite Vote in Cape Area', *New York Times*, 18 April 1994; 'Buthelezi Seems to Beat Mandela in Zulu Province', *New York Times*, 6 May 1994; 'A Liberating Election', *Africa Confidential*, vol. 35, no. 9, 1994, p. 2; 'South Africa: Sharing Power', *Africa Confidential*, vol. 35, no. 10, 1994, pp. 1–5; and 'ANC's Choice: Bloodshed or Buthelezi', *Weekly Mail & Guardian*, 6–12 May 1994.

11. 'The Man for South Africa's Future', *New York Times*, 1 May 1994.

12. Tariq Ali, *Can Pakistan Survive? The Death of a State*, London 1983, p. 131.

13. 'The Government of National Unity', *Africa Confidential*, vol. 35, no. 10, 1994, pp. 2–3.

14. 'The RDP must become a rallying programme for all left, democratic and progressive forces in our country', 'Editorial', *African Communist*, 1st Quarter 1994, p. 1.

15. Some of the ideas expressed here and in following paragraphs come from Patrick Bond.

16. Evelyne Stephens, 'Democracy in Latin America: Recent Developments in Comparative Historical Perspective', *Latin American Research Review*, vol. 25, no. 2, 1990, p. 168.

17. Frank Longstreth, 'Historical Political Economy and Liberal Democratic Capitalism', *Economy & Society*, vol. 19, no. 1, 1990, p. 111.

Index